Land Policies for Resilient and Equitable Growth in Africa

Land Policies for Resilient and Equitable Growth in Africa

Klaus Deininger and Aparajita Goyal

 **WORLD BANK GROUP**

Contents

Figures

Maps

Tables

Acknowledgments

This report was prepared as a collaborative effort with multiple units across the World Bank: the Development Economics Research Group (DECRG), the Independent Evaluation Group, and the Urban, Disaster Risk Management, Resilience and Land Global Practice (GPURL), as well as academic and policy experts from the African Economic Research Consortium, the African Tax Institute, Duke University, Hunter College, the London School of Economics, the Regional Centre for Mapping of Resources for Development, the University of Pretoria, the University of Richmond, and the University of Toronto, under the overall guidance of the World Bank's Office of the Chief Economist in the Africa Region (AFRCE).

The team was led by Klaus Deininger and Aparajita Goyal. Core team members included Daniel Ayalew Ali, Frank Byamugisha, Thea Hilhorst, Jon Mills Lindsay, Jorge Munoz, and Victoria Stanley. The team is grateful for the management, guidance, and support provided by Andrew Dabalen and Albert Zeufack (AFRCE), Bernice van Bronkhorst and Sameh Wahba (GPURL), and Deon Filmer and Carolyn Fischer (DECRG).

Invaluable technical inputs were provided by Rajul Awasthi, Richard Baldwin, Jonathan Conning, Renée Giovarelli, John Vernon Henderson, Matthew Hunter, Heather Huntington, Sandra Joireman, Ebru Karamete, Jennifer Beth Lisher, Vivian Liu, William James McCluskey, Pouirketa Rita Nikiema, Diego Restuccia, and Bekele Shiferaw, who authored background papers.

Our thanks go especially to Katherine Baldwin, Karol Boudreaux, Mark Cackler, Doug Gollin, Remi Camille Jedwab, Adnan Qayam Khan, Emmanuel Nkurunziza, and James Alan Robinson for their discussant inputs at the authors' workshop and to Issa Faye, Riel Franzsen, Ed Glaeser, Njuguna Ndung'u, Ed Parsons, and Iain G. Shuker who, in their role as peer reviewers, provided constructive feedback throughout the process of report preparation.

We are also grateful to Janet Edeme from the African Union Commission, Joan Kagwanja from the United Nations Economic Commission for Africa, David Laborde and Maximo Torero from the Food and Agriculture Organization of the United Nations, Jo Puri and Sara Savastano from the International Fund for Agricultural Development, members of the Governing Council of the Regional Centre for Mapping of Resources for Development, and attendees at the 2023 Conference on Land Policy in Africa for providing valuable feedback on earlier drafts. Funding from the Multi-Donor Trust Fund for Land Policies for Growth and Poverty Reduction is gratefully acknowledged.

Our thanks also go to the World Bank's Publishing Program, including Amy Lynn Grossman and Jewel McFadden. Kenneth Omondi and Rose-Claire Pakabomba provided able administrative support to the report team. The report cover was designed by Bill Pragluski, Critical Stages, LLC. The report was edited by Sherrie Brown, Sandra Gain, and Gwenda Larsen.

Main messages

Global evidence suggests that land institutions and policies will be critical to help African countries respond to the challenges of climate change, urban expansion, structural transformation, and gender equality. They will do so by (a) affecting urban dwellers' ability to create and access productive jobs, live in decent housing, and breathe clean air; (b) allowing farmers and women entrepreneurs to ensure against shocks, increase productivity, and diversify their income sources; and (c) providing the informational basis enabling governments to plan land use, urban expansion, and infrastructure construction; to tax property to provide services; and to transparently manage public land to provide sustained local benefits and encourage adaptation to increase local and global resilience to climate-induced risk.

Evidence from many African countries suggests that, because of institutional shortcomings that are often rooted in outdated laws and regulations, many African countries are unable to realize these benefits:

- Limited coverage with registered land rights even in cities impedes the development of long-term financial markets that rely on land as a durable form of collateral. In African countries for which data are available, less than 1 percent of agricultural land and at most 25 percent of urban land have an updated title. Moreover, at least 70 percent of those titles are solely in the name of a man, reducing women's entrepreneurship by limiting their ability to hold on to assets in case of widowhood or divorce.
- Land documents are unaffordable for all but the richest individuals: registering a parcel costs hundreds of dollars and involves a huge bureaucratic process. Transferring a parcel that is already registered costs on average 7 percent of the property value. Instead of an indispensable foundation for access to opportunities, secure land rights thus become a privilege for the rich, impeding economic activity. This issue in turn corrodes trust in institutions: almost two-thirds of Africans believe that for the right money, the rich will be able to have land ownership records manipulated in their favor.
- Limitations on the use of urban land as collateral for credit imposed by informality are often exacerbated by zoning regulations that further limit the supply of urban floorspace and drive individuals into informal arrangements for housing. Informality and lack of data also limit the scope for

own-source revenue generation by local bodies, forcing households to substitute more expensive private alternatives. Less than 0.3 percent of gross domestic product is collected in property taxes to finance local services, compared to 2–3 percent in several OECD (Organisation for Economic Co-operation and Development) countries.

• Growth of agricultural output has been driven largely by expanding cultivation into more marginal and often risky and fragile areas that may provide important climate benefits. Since 2003, 47 million hectares of uncultivated land have been brought into agricultural use. Unclear local rights and centralized, noncompetitive ways of transferring land with little local participation implied that a large push to attract investors following the 2007–08 food price shock often fostered speculative land acquisition or dispossession instead of generating opportunities for local development. Agricultural intensification and more frequent droughts have led to land-related conflict almost quadrupling since 2007, especially at the frontier between sedentary and pastoral agriculture.

A combination of digital interoperability, remote sensing, and connectivity has enormously expanded the technological opportunities available for low-cost land rights documentation and management:

• Digital interoperability allows countries to (a) reduce the cost and increase the transparency of land rights documentation and registration by adopting fully digital records and workflows via e-signature; (b) enhance the quality and currency of associated records by linking to other digital registries (for example, personal ID, legal entities, mortgages, court decisions, or building permits); and (c) improve public access to land registries by landowners, public entities, and the private sector, as well as disseminate information (for example, on prices) more widely to increase transparency.

• Availability of free satellite imagery allows observing current and past land use, as well as indicators of yield or carbon stock, among others, at high levels of spatial resolution and in near real time, thus allowing countries to (a) enforce land-use restrictions quickly and effectively as soon as violations occur; (b) contract on conservation outcomes, for example, for climate finance, in a way that can be objectively verified; and (c) link land-use rights to past cultivation, thus allowing users to establish a reputation for credit access and possibly better targeting of parametric insurance.

• Digital connectivity allows (a) improving documentation and enforcement of land rights by groups and secondary users, including spouses, who in the past were often ignored, as it allows the electronic gathering of consent and near-costless transfer of resources directly to rights holders without a need for intermediaries; (b) increasing the competitiveness of land markets by making information more widely available; and (c) providing easier access to output and other rural factor markets, including those for insurance.

While digitization can provide the technical tools to improve the functioning of land institutions to harness the associated benefits, translating this potential into action will require action on the regulatory side to allow the potential from broad-based digital land service delivery to be realized and on policy. Four areas are particularly relevant:

Operation of urban land and mortgage markets. To reduce urban informality and improve the functioning of land and mortgage markets, there is need for legal, regulatory, and institutional changes that enable (a) improving the quality and reducing the cost of land service delivery through the adoption of fully digital workflows and integration of spatial and textual data, (b) reducing or eliminating transfer taxes that drive transactions into informality, (c) ensuring full digital interoperability of the land registry with other key registries, (d) putting in place low-cost mechanisms for registration and enforcement of mortgages, and (e) revising planning regulations to be in line with ground realities and contribute to public goods.

Land taxation. Recurrent taxation of urban property (and large commercial farms) can improve own-source revenue, reduce speculation, and strengthen the social contract via (a) a complete digital tax roll based on satellite imagery, (b) computerized mass valuation of properties based on market prices, (c) public availability of valuations for each parcel, (d) minimal use of exemptions, (e) effective enforcement of payment (for example, by not registering any subsequent transaction without a tax clearance certificate), and (f) use of valuations to levy a capital gains tax and betterment levies to capture revenue from public infrastructure investment.

Public land management. To preserve public land and ensure that it continues to provide services to future generations, there is a need to (a) demarcate, document, and register all public land and clarify ownership and management responsibilities, including the assignment of use rights; (b) eliminate conflicts of interest that arise if the same institution owns, regulates, and disposes of public land; (c) put in place transparent and competitive mechanisms (such as electronic auctions) to transfer rights to public land; (d) ensure that contracts are public to facilitate third-party monitoring; and (e) regulate land-use planning and put in place oversight mechanisms to enforce proper land use (for example, based on remote sensing).

Rural land-use rights. Making existing legislation for recognition, demarcation, and registration of (digital) use rights to rural (and, in most cases, customary) land operation can help improve rural resilience, factor market functioning, land-use efficiency, and welfare. This work requires putting in place regulation for use rights management without mandatory conversion to title, clarifying in particular the (a) responsibility for documenting issuance and maintenance and digital interoperability with other registries, including farmer registries used to allocate agricultural support; (b) internal accountability and oversight, as well as external enforcement and mechanisms for appeal; (c) mechanisms for transferring land to outsiders, either individually or as a group; (d) links and interactions with local government (land-use planning and fees); and (e) enforcement and protection of the rights of women and outsiders.

This book discusses the available evidence on these issues, highlights examples of policy reforms in Africa and beyond to illustrate available opportunities for and benefits from reform, and identifies indicators and data sources to help identify a sequence of reforms and assess their progress and impact. This information will be of great interest to governments seeking to enhance their land institutions' performance; to their partners aiming to support such reform; and to policy makers, land professionals, scholars, and civil society aiming to lay the foundations for Africa to better utilize its economic, human, and ecological potential.

Abbreviations

ACLED	Armed Conflict Location & Event Data Project
BRT	bus rapid transit
CAMA	computer-assisted mass valuation
CAR	Cadastro Ambiental Rural (Rural Environmental Cadaster, Brazil)
CCRO	Certificate of Customary Rights of Occupancy (Tanzania)
CVL	Certificate of Village Land (Tanzania)
DECRG	Development Economics Research Group
GDP	gross domestic product
ha	hectares
KIP	Kampung Improvement Program (Indonesia)
LARP	land administration reform project (Lesotho)
LCMPA	Legal Capacity of Married Persons Act (Lesotho)
LSLBI	large-scale land-based investment
LUC	Land Use Charge (Nigeria)
OECD	Organisation for Economic Co-operation and Development
PES	payments for ecosystem services
PROCEDE	Programa de Certificación de Derechos Ejidales y Titulación de Solares (Program for the Certification of Ejido Rights and Titling of House Plots, Mexico)
RL	residential license (Tanzania)
SCC	social cost of carbon
SLM	sector land manager
SLR	sea-level rise
TFP	total factor productivity
TLMA	traditional land management authority (Malawi)
VLA	Village Land Act (Tanzania)
VLC	village land committee (Tanzania)
VLUP	village land-use plan (Tanzania)

Executive summary

In the coming decades, African countries will face four challenges that can be addressed more effectively if land institutions function well. First, rates of urbanization on the continent are among the highest globally, with Africa's urban population expected to triple to more than 1 billion by 2050. Urbanization can bring benefits and increase land values by capitalizing on skill-based human capital externalities and input sharing, labor market pooling, and knowledge exchange to boost productive job creation but also imposes costs from congestion, contagious disease, and crime. African cities' high land intensity increases the cost of accessing jobs and cities' carbon footprint. Clear land rights and institutions that allow exchange of such rights in land and financial markets increase incentives for investment in floorspace, public services, and mobility, the latter possibly financed via property taxes or other forms of land value capture.

Second, Africa's past agricultural output growth was largely driven by area expansion. Because it would affect increasingly marginal land, continuing this trend will become riskier, conflict with environmental goals, and trigger land degradation. The rural transformation strategies centered on large-scale land-based investment that were pursued by many African countries over the past decade largely failed to increase productivity or foster market integration and diversification of rural income sources and thus generate spillover benefits for

1

smallholders. A key reason was that ways to transfer land to investors were often centralized, nontransparent, and noncompetitive. Promoting operation of rural factor markets at the local level to reduce resource misallocation, substitute knowhow and capital for labor and land, and encourage long-term land transfers offers more promise of contributing to structural transformation.

Third, in much of Africa, climate change will increase variability of agricultural output and often also reduce mean yields. Greater frequency and severity of extreme weather events have in many instances already forced farmers to increase defensive spending or liquidate assets in ways that may impair investment, including in human capital and diversification. Where land or resource rights are not documented or local forums for negotiation are absent, climate shocks triggered persistent upticks in violent ethnic conflict at the frontier between pastoral and sedentary land use. Future land demand for renewable energy or climate finance may similarly set off speculative land acquisition that may weaken current users' position. The location of many cities on coasts or in floodplains increases their exposure to floods or sea-level rise. Land markets and the price signals they convey are critical to guide private and public adaptation investment and to facilitate insurance against such risks.

Last, but by no means least, changes in laws and customs that empowered women through asset ownership and control transformed economic activity in today's developed countries. Land and property account for 40 to 60 percent of household assets virtually everywhere. Yet, in most African countries, at most a quarter of formal land documents include a woman's name. Gender-sensitive efforts to document land rights increased this to more than 80 percent, improving women's agency, entrepreneurship, human capital investment, and land and financial market participation. Such economic empowerment can also help change customs that long discriminated against women and in doing so can improve overall welfare.

Benefits from land institutions

All over the world, land registries protect land rights and allow transfers at low cost to encourage investment and operation of land and financial markets while reducing the need for unproductive spending to defend or fight over rights in addition to providing public benefits. In many African countries, the high cost of land service delivery creates wealth and gender bias in access to documented land rights. This reduces trust and state capacity and limits the scope for financial market operation, property tax collection, and planning in urban areas and for better factor market functioning and long-term contracting in rural ones. Traditional institutions may fill this vacuum as long as economic activity remains localized and land transactions are short term. Effective land management and longer-term interaction with outsiders, including to address challenges of climate change, will, however, be contingent on having mechanisms in place to document, enforce, and transfer use or ownership rights to land. While reliance on accountable local institutions can help to establish such institutions in a cost-effective way, a false dichotomy between statutory and customary provisions has often prevented progress in this direction.

In rural areas, secure property rights reduce expropriation risk, thereby encouraging investment in land improvements, including via fallowing or manure application to restore soil fertility or planting perennials. In urban areas, where investments are more durable, documented land rights increased labor market participation and fostered housing investment, with benefits in terms of health and skill acquisition. If land rights are perceived to be contestable, individuals may spend resources on unproductive measures or fight over them rather than invest in productive activities. In urban settings, the need to guard property through physical presence may reduce women's labor market participation and children's school attendance.

The positive effects of documented rights on investment and sustainable resource management are not limited to individual rights. In fact, group rights have advantages if, as is the case for lands used for grazing, forest, biodiversity, or mineral extraction, gains from individual investment are modest and benefits from resource use accrue at a larger spatial scale so that the cost of defining individual rights may exceed incremental benefits. The case for group rights is strengthened if cohesive groups with clearly defined membership and internal as well as external accountability, including graduated sanctions, are in place.

While women's control of household assets is a key determinant of intra-household bargaining, limits on women's ability to own or bequeath land reduce productivity of land use in several African countries. Written documentation makes it easier for women to enforce their rights while still allowing flexibility in acknowledging social norms. Higher investment, productivity, market participation, credit access, and entrepreneurship due to more secure land rights helped empower women economically in many settings.

By increasing individuals' and households' capacity to smooth consumption and pursue economic strategies with higher risk but also higher return, secure rights to land provide implicit insurance. Its immobile and virtually indestructible nature makes land ideal collateral. Registration of rural land has encouraged nonfarm enterprise start-ups, market-based land transfers to more able farmers, and shifts to higher value-added crops. Exogenous differences in the ability to mortgage land increased land values and owners' propensity to take up entrepreneurship and establish larger firms. At the same time, illiquid land markets, high cost of registering mortgages, or limits to the ability to foreclose in case of default often undermined credit market effects of rural or periurban land titling, pointing toward registered land rights as a necessary but not sufficient condition for the realization of credit effects.

Land registries also generate public benefits, chief among them the provision of price signals, the publicity of which can reduce price dispersion and, by making property appraisal easier, improve credit access. Data from land registries are critical to effectively manage public land, regulate land use and manage externalities, and reduce the scope for fraud and money laundering in the real estate sector.

Location-specific public goods such as access to infrastructure, services, or amenities will be capitalized into land values. Because land is immobile, taxing it will generate fewer distortions than taxes on more mobile factors such as labor or capital. Recurrent land taxes and surcharges to capture appreciation of land due to public investment are ideally suited to finance local public goods, strengthen accountability through the social contract, and provide resources for urban expansion. As institutions mature, future land tax receipts can be used as collateral for bonds, providing an efficient way to fund long-term infrastructure projects.

Delays in land acquisition or permitting pose bottlenecks to infrastructure construction in many countries. Clear land records and publicity of land prices to allow transparent valuation can help discern projects with large public benefits from mediocre ones and prevent the former from being derailed by holdouts, political interference, or spurious litigation. Public availability of information on land rights also makes it easier to implement mechanisms such as land sharing, mixed-income developments, or in-kind compensation to help those who lose land to investment but have limited capacity to capitalize on cash-only compensation to maintain their living standards.

Institutional preconditions

Realizing the benefits from clear and transferable land rights requires public land registries to make available to interested parties reliable, complete, and enforceable information on rights and encumbrances (mortgages, court cases, pending land acquisition, and so on) on any land parcel. Such institutions, the establishment of which often required decades or centuries in today's developed countries, comprise a spatial and a textual component. The latter, called the *register*, documents the rights to land parcels held in order of priority, while the former, referred to as the *cadaster*, describes the boundaries of land to which rights are defined. Publicity of information on objects, subjects, and types of rights and the ability to use the power of the state to enforce these if needed reduce transaction costs in land and financial markets because parties need to spend less resources to check the authenticity of rights they might acquire or to enforce them. This expands the range of potential market participants, the complexity of rights that can be held or transacted, the length of time for which contracts can be entered into and enforced, and the scope for welfare-enhancing transfers.

In many African countries, the high cost of acquiring, transferring, or enforcing documented rights has led to strong wealth and gender bias in access to documented urban rights that undermine the quality, coverage, and publicity of documented rights. The cost of title acquisition, largely due to regulations requiring a high-precision survey and physical monumentation before rights can be registered, is a key reason. Regulatory change to adjust survey standards is thus an important step to make registration of land rights more affordable. The United Kingdom, which has, for over a century, used topographical maps rather than high-precision surveys to maintain a title registry, shows this is possible. In Africa, Rwanda adopted regulations allowing the use of high-resolution satellite imagery (under a "general boundary" concept) to issue titles to 11 million parcels at a unit cost of less than US$6 over two to three years, highlighting the scope for making documented land rights more affordable, especially in urban areas where a cost of US$10–20 seems in line with willingness to pay for title even by low-income households as documented in the Democratic Republic of Congo, Ghana, Tanzania, and Zambia.

Issuance of titles will also be unsustainable and will not yield the expected benefits if the cost of registering subsequent transfers (or mortgages) is not affordable or commensurate with associated benefits. A high cost of service delivery often impeded registry sustainability after titling programs and, together with wealth or gender bias in the ability to access documented rights, may have undermined the value of such documents and trust in centralized registries more broadly. Avoiding such an outcome requires a low cost of service delivery that is passed on to customers and the establishment of formal registries, first in locations where benefits from transferable land rights are high. Coverage can then be expanded from there, possibly with lower-cost options to document use rights in rural areas that involve local authorities, as experience is accumulated.

The role of traditional institutions

In many parts of rural Africa, customary institutions that, through chiefs, manage use of common land such as pasture and forest for joint benefit and allocate arable land for cultivation under secure long-term rights have long administered land in a more cost-effective and flexible way than formal institutions. Continued support for customary institutions is rooted in the fact that, even in settings where the cost of establishing formal registries for individual rights exceeds the benefits, they provide lineage members with land-use rights to arable land that can be transferred via local rental and act as a safety net. Their local presence often creates informal channels of accountability and allows chiefs to access information that enables them to resolve local disputes quickly, fairly, and without demanding bribes.

Recognition of the advantages of traditional authorities triggered a wave of laws in the early 2000s to recognize customary tenure across Africa.

However, regulations have been lacking to guide the implementation of such laws by clarifying how to demarcate chiefs' area of influence and link it to formal systems and how lineage members' and outsiders' rights would be managed and accountability ensured. As land values and demand for land by outsiders increase, lack of regulations may result in parallel systems and reinforce wealth bias because affluent or influential individuals may resort to "forum shopping" (that is, they may pursue land claims with formal and customary institutions in parallel). Three issues are of particular importance:

Accountability. Colonial interventions, land concessions, or co-optation often weakened traditional leaders' downward accountability, reduced locals' voice, and worsened resource management and governance. Without such accountability, chiefs may be encouraged to behave like owners rather than custodians of land as land values increase by transferring land to wealthy outsiders for personal rather than the group's benefit, even if such transfers reduce social welfare and are difficult to enforce. They may also start to charge for services they had earlier provided for free, as in Ghana, Uganda, and Zambia, with negative equity impact.

Contract enforcement with outsiders. In West Africa, migrants received perpetual use rights to incentivize cash crop investment when land was abundant but saw agreements reinterpreted or revoked with greater land scarcity. The threat of having land rights challenged triggered defensive but unproductive investment by migrants, reducing productivity of land use and provoking conflict in several African countries.

Traditionally, as land became scarcer or transactions with outsiders created opportunities to access markets or technology, customary systems tended to gradually individualize. Yet land users, especially if they are outsiders, will make "optimum" levels of investment in soil fertility or irrigation and drainage only if their rights are secure and can be enforced. To ensure optimum investment, regulation is needed to define what type of rights can be transferred to group members or outsiders and how such transfers are to be documented and enforced.

Managing local resources and resolving conflict. Sedentary and pastoral groups have long engaged in a mutually beneficial symbiotic relationship whereby transhumant pastoralists would access floodplains or wetlands during the dry season for their animals to graze on crop residues and leave manure to fertilize fields. Unforeseen droughts or unilateral withdrawal of access to critical resources (for example, watering holes or migration routes) can transform this relationship from complementary to confrontational. Data for almost three decades in Africa show that, by exacerbating competition over scarce wetlands during the dry season, droughts in pastoral areas triggered agropastoral conflict in neighboring agricultural areas. Political participation and access to forums for land dispute resolution reduced this effect, highlighting the importance of forums for negotiation or conflict resolution.

New opportunities and examples of reform

Digital interoperability, connectivity, and use of remotely sensed data can help to reduce the cost of registry establishment and maintenance while increasing quality of land records, the uses to which they can be put, and the ease with which rights holders can update or exchange rights. Reforms in select countries and global experience illustrate the benefits from harnessing this potential if the regulatory framework is appropriate while showing that, without proper regulations, reform efforts may be ineffective, costly, or unsustainable.

The potential of digital technologies

Advances in cloud computing and digital interoperability, use of remote sensing, and connectivity create opportunities to reduce the cost of establishing and running registries, improve the quality and publicity of land records, and establish such records as a foundational layer for a national spatial data infrastructure to complement benefits from digital IDs for transparent implementation of public programs.

Digitization and interoperability can reduce the cost of establishing, maintaining, and accessing land registries while increasing publicity and transparency through auditable workflows. Easier record access via digitization of legacy records increased mortgage registration, urban credit access, and rural structural transformation in many regions globally. Unambiguous identification of land parcels and automatic digital links with the civil registry or with registries for mortgages, court decisions, legal entities, or building permits can improve quality and reduce the cost of maintaining land records. It does so by ensuring information is consistent or by automatically requiring action if, for example, the registered landowner's civil status changes.

Digitization of spatial data adds to the above in two respects. First, in many countries, documents conveying rights to land were in the past issued by different entities, creating overlapping rights. Digitally overlaying the maps or plans substantiating such rights is the fastest way to identify competing claims or boundary disputes and wherever possible adjust documentation to reflect actual use based on local consultation before conflicts arise. Dormant but unused rights can be extinguished in a similar fashion. Second, land-use classification based on remote sensing, combined with digital boundaries, can help ascertain if or how land is used in near real time. Even if public land is not mapped, this allows identifying cultivated land at scale and, if it is not privately owned, mark it as potential encroachment and measures can be taken to reduce tenure insecurity and ensure that the potentially large benefits from such land accrue to the public.

Remote sensing. The use of high-resolution satellite or drone imagery reduces the cost of documenting land rights by allowing easier identification of property boundaries for local confirmation in a participatory adjudication process. Free, remotely sensed imagery dating back to the late 1970s allows monitoring of land-use changes over a long time at scale as a basis for climate finance, including the monitoring of forest cover or carbon stocks for traceability and climate finance, as illustrated, for example, by Brazil's system that combines satellite-based near-real-time monitoring with economic incentives (for example, farms' credit access or local governments' "blacklisting") to reduce deforestation. Remotely sensed data also provide estimates of urban floorspace based on building footprints and height that will be of great importance for planning urban land use and housing provision. If combined with maps of environmental risk, this allows an estimate of the likely property damage from adverse events such as floods, hillslides, or, in the longer term, sea level rise to the existing building stock. Risk maps, together with information on land prices, are needed to allow private sector insurance against such hazards and for adaptation based on informing land users of the risks of building in vulnerable areas and use of regulatory or fiscal instruments to bring social and private cost of construction in such areas closer to each other. If property prices and land prices are available, it would be possible to insure against such events.

Connectivity. The recent expansion of mobile phone ownership and coverage provides additional benefits by facilitating enforcement of joint or group rights by requiring digital consent from all co-owners before allowing any transaction to be registered—and depositing one-time or recurrent payments automatically in the co-owners' account. It also reduces the transaction cost of participation in land and other factor markets via digital interaction, allows more complex contracts such as weather-based index insurance and supply chain certification or payment for environmental services that are based on patterns of land use (for example, keeping trees) that can be monitored remotely that may be conditional on land use. It also allows for an increase in benefits from public land management via transparent auctions with a larger number of participants and publicity of relevant contractual details.

Examples of institutional and regulatory reform

Rwanda is the only African country with a fully digital nationwide registry and cadaster. After the 1994 genocide that partly originated in contests for land, Rwanda completely revised its legal framework (including for women), conducted a carefully evaluated pilot, and ensured that regulations could be drafted and passed quickly to respond to issues as they emerged. Issuing titles to all the country's land parcels from 2011 to 2013 on this basis provided clear benefits: for 86 percent of parcels, ownership documents included a woman, and soil conservation investment and activity in land and mortgage markets increased markedly and moved the country from rank 137 to the top of the "Registering Property" part of the World Bank's Doing Business ranking between 2005 and 2015. The program also improved state capacity: incremental urban property tax revenue from properties that were added to the registry under the program would allow recouping all program costs in three years, with rates uniformly set at 1 percent of property value, and the system is interoperable with the national ID; the mortgage registry; and valuation, building permitting, and land-use control systems. The ability to get information on rights to any land parcel via SMS enhances publicity, and efforts to move toward fully paperless titling are under way.

In Lesotho, women had very few rights until a 2006 law allowed them to own property independently. Two acts passed in 2010 then provided the basis for institutional and regulatory reform to, among other changes, link registry and cadaster, simplify workflows, reduce time required for registration as well as its cost, and strengthen women's rights via a presumption of joint ownership for property acquired in marriage under community of property, a reform followed by systematic registration of rights in informal urban settlements. Two decades (2000–2019) of registry data show that (a) in the short term (2007–14), policy reform triggered a ninefold and fourfold increase in land and mortgage market participation, respectively, largely by reducing transaction cost; (b) in the longer term (2000–2019), policy reform and titling together increased credit market access with effects of policy reform larger than those of titling; and (c) changes in the law to allow female land ownership had an independent effect and benefited women once registration was affordable.

The case of Nigeria illustrates how, if regulatory reform is difficult, updating the tax roll can help increase revenue, quality of service delivery, and demand for land rights documentation. Building on Lagos state's experience of streamlining and simplifying property tax collection, a World Bank–supported "program for results" aimed to incentivize states to collect data on owners, parcel, and structure characteristics for at least 50 percent of urban structures and provided technical support. In about 12 months, 34 of 36 states collected data on more than 8 million properties that are now used to plan and improve public service delivery and collect property taxes, an action that has already given rise to demands for documented land rights.

In a rural setting, Mexico shows how a regulatory framework to document individual as well as community rights can be implemented in a decentralized and sustainable way to show impact in several dimensions. The country documented customary rights by groups (*ejidos*) to more than 100 million hectares (ha) in the early 2000s in three steps.[1] First, ejidos were registered as legal entities with clearly defined statutes and organs of self-governance (the executive, assembly, and an oversight committee) to streamline internal governance and allow entering enforceable contracts with outsiders as a group based on assembly decisions. Second, external borders of the ejidos' landholdings were drawn, and community and individual agricultural or housing parcels were demarcated locally and registered in the central National Agrarian Registry

(Registro Agrario Nacional). Third, all decisions were ratified by the assembly and supervised by a network of independent paralegals from the publicly supported Land Attorney's office (Procuraduría Agraria), with enforcement through a dedicated set of courts in each state.

A procedure for ejidos to exit the customary regime and move to the private system by individualizing land rights was also put in place, together with safeguards—in particular, a requirement for such decisions to be approved by 75 percent of members in a centrally supervised vote. In practice, less than 10 percent of ejidos, mostly those closer to cities and with higher incomes, levels of literacy, and reliance on industry and services, exercised this right. Although under the customary regime, individual land cannot be transferred to outsiders or used as collateral, clear assignment of rights through the reforms provided large economic benefits as the program facilitated mechanization and increased productivity, fostered structural transformation via migration and investment, changed local political dynamics, and reduced violence by constraining authorities' discretion in reallocating land rights.

The scope to scale up decentralized approaches quickly and equitably is illustrated by the case of Ethiopia, where, from 2003 to 2005, land-use certificates were issued to more than 18 million parcels by 6 million households at low cost (<US$1 per parcel) in an equitable way led by elected councils. This supported climate change adaptation, women's empowerment, and land-related investment, although some market restrictions remain in place. A follow-up "second-round" certification created a computerized and fully georeferenced registry with more than 22 million records of public and private land that has been used in 350 woreda (county) offices to register more than 750,000 transactions of different types using digital workflows that incorporate regulatory differences across regions. Establishment of digital connectivity to farmers; linking the land registry to the national ID; and use of land registry data as a basis for farmer-specific agricultural advice, public land-use monitoring, and expansion of coverage into urban areas are planned and will be possible if the regulatory framework is adjusted accordingly.

In Benin, low-cost demarcation of village boundaries, followed by elaboration of rural land-use plans and demarcation of individual parcels in 300 villages from 2008 to 2011, reduced tree cover loss, fires, clearing, and intervillage border conflicts while increasing trust in local institutions, land resource management, and investment in tree planting and fallowing, especially by women. Yet, as access to full title was conditional on conversion via a costly and often discretionary process over a short time span following demarcation, a condition that remained out of reach for many, long-term impacts were less positive: the program increased land conflict and had no impact on income, education, credit access, migration, or altruism. Regional heterogeneity between the north and the south of the country was also important, suggesting that a more gradual and regionally differentiated approach may be more sustainable and affordable.

Tanzania's 1999 Village Land Act, hailed as one of the most progressive African land laws at the time of its passage, illustrates that legal provisions can easily be rendered ineffective by costly and often unclear implementation that favors the wealthy and creates space for discretion by officials, failure to publicize rights, and unclear enforcement. Complex requirements for preparing village land-use plans as a first step toward a Certificate of Village Land that can then provide the basis for individual use right issuance imply that almost two decades after the act was passed, less than 10 percent of villages had plans. In several cases, plans seem to have changed to reduce pastoralists' rights without their consent. Government's refusal to enforce registered village land boundaries if land was considered "unused" reduced confidence in registered rights. Moreover, as the process and cost of issuing individual use rights on village land are virtually undistinguishable from those for formal title, having separate laws and institutions for village and general land does little to allay wealth and gender bias in access to documented land rights.

Lack of implementing regulations led to similar challenges in Mozambique, where efforts to document community rights, although strongly supported by donors, had a limited impact and in Uganda, where regulations to govern issuance of "low-cost" use rights under the 1998 Land Act envisaged a complex and costly bureaucracy for which resources are not available. In Zambia, lack of legal provisions to accept electronic signatures has held up private-sector efforts to expand the supply of land documents for years.

In Kenya, far-reaching decentralization of land administration, as envisaged in the 2010 Constitution, was not fully implemented partly due to limited information sharing. Implementation of the 2016 Community Land Act, legislation passed with high expectations, has been held up by a lack of regulatory clarity. Without clear regulation, computerization of land records, which some see as a solution, may not live up to its potential.

Malawi's 2016 Land Law puts all customary land under traditional land management authorities (TLMAs) and mandates demarcation of TLMAs' land as a first step toward low-cost use rights certificate issuance. TLMA demarcation was important to create trust by traditional authorities who doubted the government's intention. All TLMAs were demarcated in 2018, partly with World Bank support, clearing the path for a rollout of a digital registration system and local administrative structures.

Harnessing land policies for broader socioeconomic development

Complementary policies can enhance the benefits from land registries and offer independent entry points for reform. Enabling local governments to collect data that allow them to use property records for property taxation, land value capture, and planning, including for urban expansion, can help them to more effectively provide local services, improve urban mobility, and increase urban job growth. Removing obstacles to rural factor market functioning, encouraging intergenerational transfers of use rights, and improving the scope for contracting with private parties higher up in the value chain can foster structural change in rural areas. Clarifying rights—including to public land—to foster investment, integration into larger markets, and insurance and publication of land price and climate risk information can strengthen resilience and encourage private adaptation efforts.

Urban property taxation, service delivery, and expansion

As land is immobile, taxing it allows raising revenue to finance local public goods in a way that is less distortive and, if the rich hold more of their wealth in land, more progressive than taxes on mobile factors such as capital and labor. Property taxes also increase owners' incentives to use land effectively, discourage speculation, and encourage compact urban development. As local public goods will increase land values, use of property taxes to finance them is appropriate and can strengthen the social contract between state and taxpayers. Collection of property tax increased participation and accountability even in fragile, low-capacity African settings, with the willingness to pay such taxes enhanced by better service delivery. In the longer term, the relative stability of property tax revenue allows it to be used to service municipal bonds that, among others, can generate resources to invest in infrastructure for urban expansion.

In virtually all African countries, levels of property tax collection are at 10 to 20 percent of potential. To address this and better capture the enormous potential of up to US$50 billion per year Africa-wide, there is need to (a) establish an urban tax roll with full coverage, (b) put in place market-based valuation that is regularly updated to ensure buoyancy, (c) minimize exemptions (for example, for untitled or owner-occupied properties) that are difficult to justify as tax-financed local services benefit all residents, and (d) ensure credible enforcement (for example, by requiring submission of a tax clearance certificate to register any subsequent registration for a given parcel). If regulatory reform as a basis for urban titling is not viable in the short term, establishing a fiscal cadaster can be an attractive option to increase own-source revenue, reduce or remove transaction taxes that would be a major obstacle to registry sustainability, generate the data needed to award more secure rights, and allow demand for such rights to be articulated and voiced more effectively.

Transaction taxes ("stamp duties") have been widely used historically because they allow collecting land revenue without incurring the high cost of maintaining a tax map in a paper-based environment. The ability to access satellite imagery and mass valuation techniques has drastically reduced this cost, making land value capture much easier. Regulatory changes needed to take advantage of such technology to establish systems to effectively collect recurrent land taxes have been slow. As a result, transaction taxes continue to make registering land transfers in Africa more expensive than in all other regions. While the revenue, net of collection cost, they generate is often modest, the distortions they generate are large. In addition, transfer taxes push transactions into informality so that registries lose currency and foster underreporting of transaction prices so that the reported price no longer conveys meaningful information. Replacing them with an equivalent recurrent land tax on a much larger base is easy technically, especially if provisions such as deferral for high-value properties owned by individuals with low liquid wealth are made; can increase revenue, welfare, efficiency, and transparency; and could be very attractive politically.

In cities, deploying arterial infrastructure ahead of development allows public services to be provided much more cost-effectively than doing so ex post, resulting in often dramatic increases of land values. However, in African countries where the absence of at least a fiscal cadaster that identifies land users and provides the basis for use of land value capture instruments, such benefits accrue exclusively to private landowners. This will deprive governments of the resources required to finance investment in infrastructure and services as a basis for productive job creation or force them to resort to much more distortionary instruments to finance such investment, reducing efficiency and widening inequality. Patterns of public land use and infrastructure persist over time and can leverage private investment: in Tanzania, provision of arterial infrastructure and basic infrastructure under "site and service" projects that combined mixed-income zoning with access to jobs and mobility in the 1970s allowed owners to incrementally upgrade structures so that three to four decades after the program, treated areas had larger buildings, better electricity access, and socioeconomic outcomes that were superior to those in untreated areas or in slums that had been upgraded at a much higher cost.

In African cities, the impact of ill-functioning land registries may be compounded by planning rules that make conversion from agricultural to nonagricultural use difficult or that, by stipulating minimum lot sizes or limits on floor-area ratios, may impede job creation and urban floorspace investment. This increases housing costs, constrains economic opportunities by pushing individuals into informality, and, because many structures are out of compliance, creates scope for rent seeking while also making it more difficult to implement needed planning regulations that could help make cities more resilient to climatic shocks.

Lack of affordable housing, often driven by high cost of urban floorspace, encourages informal settlement formation at cities' fringes with poor access to services, often in hazardous locations. Especially if organized partly by influential individuals for noneconomic reasons, slums may persist even though redevelopment could generate net benefits. In Kibera, Nairobi's main slum, benefits from redevelopment are estimated to be more than 30 times the total annual rent payments, even after fully compensating landlords, but redevelopment is prevented by noneconomic frictions.

A combination of tenure regularization and better service provision is often suggested to improve slum conditions. Such policies need to be carefully designed to avoid creating moral hazard and incentives for more invasions of public land, providing transferable rights is preferable: in Latin America, housing upgrading programs that did not include property rights had no impact on asset ownership or labor market outcomes in the medium term, and in Indonesia, restrictions on the transferability of land rights given to upgrading program beneficiaries seem to have inadvertently blocked future development.

Improved rural factor market functioning

In rural areas, immobility of land, informational imperfections, and enforcement cost create land market frictions that often interact with imperfections in other factor markets. In a nonmechanized environment, labor market imperfections arising from the seasonal nature and spatial dispersion of agricultural activities can lead to a negative relationship between land size and productivity, implying lower costs for owner-operated as compared to wage labor–operated farms. If farm size is too small to fully employ owners' family, frictions associated with participation in off-farm labor markets may lead to seasonal underemployment and prompt farmers to work on their farm even at returns below the market wage.

As the price of capital relative to labor declines, indivisibility of machinery may counter family farmers' labor cost advantages and lead to a positive relationship between farm size and productivity. A combination of imperfections in labor and capital markets can give rise to a U-shaped relationship between farm size and productivity. In such a situation, reducing land market frictions can increase productivity as in Kenya, where support to land rental allowed younger, land-poor, and more entrepreneurial farmers to increase value added via more intensive application of nonlabor inputs. In Ethiopia, allowing land transactions is equally estimated to have the potential to increase agricultural productivity and overall welfare in a way that is pro-poor and fosters structural transformation. Long-term contracts to transfer land to young farmers and allow them to invest even while their parents are still alive can contribute to such transformation. In India, land market frictions make it difficult to assemble parcels large enough to use machines, and eliminating such frictions could trigger large increases in rural workers' income and structural transformation.

A warming climate and more frequent extreme weather events may force farmers to increase defensive spending, adopt risk mitigation strategies, or liquidate assets (including by pulling children out of school) in ways that may compromise their long-term coping ability. Fragmentation of holdings to exploit micro-variation in climate allowed farmers in ecologically diverse settings to diversify risk at the cost of spending more time to move between parcels. Liquidity-constrained farmers unable to access other forms of insurance also often engage in sharecropping as a second-best risk-sharing mechanism, despite the associated and potentially large productivity losses that are widely documented, including in Africa. Improving access to credit or other means of insurance has been shown to prompt a switch toward more efficient cash rent contracts, and the same could possibly be achieved by bundling cash rent contracts with index insurance, especially if the location of farmers' fields can be unambiguously identified.

The surge in demand for large-scale land-based investment in the wake of the 2007–08 spike in food and commodity prices was expected to provide land-abundant African countries with opportunities to access knowhow and markets, as in other settings where such investment helped diversify rural economies and improved living standards, nutrition, and human capital formation. Yet, while Africa's cultivated area expanded by some 50 million ha from 2013 to 2019, benefits remained limited as large farm establishment failed to create jobs and had little effect on smallholders' access to technology or input and insurance markets while often competing for land. One reason was the use of centralized and noncompetitive mechanisms to transfer land that, together with formal land institutions' limited local presence, made it difficult to identify capable investors, enforce environmental and social safeguards, collect ground rent or other lease payments, and liquidate unsuccessful ventures, encouraging speculative land acquisition. Greater clarity on how land use regulations and contracts are to be enforced, together with increased emphasis on attracting upstream investment in marketing and processing rather than production, offers greater potential to link small and medium farmers to markets while capitalizing on their advantage in the production of high value-added products. Public investment in infrastructure such as roads is one way to increase attractiveness for upstream investors and will at the same time make it easier for small farmers to exit subsistence farming, bring perishable high-value crops to market, and obtain bulky inputs such as fertilizer at lower prices.

Increasing competitiveness of land-intensive forms of renewable energy and payments for ecosystem services (PES) can benefit current land users if land-use rights, held individually or as a group, are clear and can be transferred but can create a risk of dispossession if they are not. If land rights are contestable, efforts to promote renewables or PES that are sustainable, maximize additionality, and reduce leakage may need to be preceded by efforts to clarify use or management rights in ways that facilitate collective action and to ensure that procedures for contracting are transparent and competitive.

Resilience to climate change

Agricultural activities' spatial extension makes them more vulnerable to a changing climate and extreme weather events than those in industry or services. In fact, climate change is estimated to have already resulted in a significant reduction of agricultural productivity growth, especially in warmer regions. Short-term adaptation investment for better crop management or varietal choice, and better use of existing land and water resources, are likely to be contingent on secure rights, whereas longer-term adaptation via structural transformation or migration will be contingent on transferable rights. The importance of market integration is illustrated by analysis of drought impacts on African cities over five decades: cities with firms selling output to global markets were able to absorb shocks and even expand, while those dependent solely on local markets suffered declines as demand dried up. In Brazil, integration with other regions provided insurance for short-term climatic shocks. Where climate change triggered persistent productivity declines, they resulted in capital outflows and migration because local manufacturing could not absorb all displaced workers.

Higher frequency of extreme weather events such as storms or floods already affects many African cities. Higher temperatures and sea-level rise are likely to increase such vulnerabilities in the future. Yet, while areas at risk of flooding are easily identified and are often on public land, the housing stock susceptible to such risk keeps expanding, especially in low- and middle-income countries that make up more than 80 percent of the global increase. Improving documentation, publicity, and transferability of rights to guide investment incentives on private land; managing public land in ways that provide alternatives to such encroachment; and putting in place regulatory instruments to reduce negative externalities from private land-use decisions will be key elements of adaptation strategies.

In developed countries, extreme weather events influence property prices in a way that is often driven by insurers or mortgage lenders who, in an institutional framework that is not distorted, are often better placed at pricing risk objectively. Publicity of land price information and measures to ensure parties are aware of location-specific risk (for example, via disclosure laws) is thus important to drive private investment in adaptation and the propensity to insure against such risk. Because uninsured exposure to adverse events often results in political pressure for ex post disaster relief that is more costly and regressive than actuarially fair insurance ex ante, failure to provide home buyers with objective information on the risks they assume can be costly in the long term.

Subsidies that, prima facie, might be intended to promote adaptation may, by encouraging moral hazard, have the opposite effect. In the United Kingdom, flood insurance subsidies encouraged building in risk-prone areas and transferred significant wealth to the rich. Public wildfire protection for residential homes in the United States also encouraged moral hazard, as did subsidies to crop insurance in agriculture. Such effects are not limited to developed countries: plans to build a seawall in Jakarta have been shown to have resulted in moral hazard that crowded out private adaptation efforts. Fiscal instruments such as property tax surcharges levied in proportion to the benefits from such investment that accrue to individual land parcels may make commitment easier and, if used consistently in evaluating and debating large investments and their implications for local property values ex ante, also increase quality of investment decisions and the legitimacy and credibility of public commitment.

Policy implications

The fact that formally documented land rights are a precondition to use of land as collateral for long-term credit and financial market development has long provided a justification for efforts to expand access to formal rights via "'titling," often at subsidized rates in rural areas. Data suggest that, in most of Africa, such interventions failed to overcome high levels of informality, wealth and gender bias of formal registries, competition between customary and formal authorities, and weak public land management. To overcome the distrust in public land institutions, four aspects of the regulatory and institutional framework are key.

Urban property taxation: In many African cities, land values are increasing rapidly, but the implied potential for property tax revenue, estimated at US$60 billion annually, is severely underutilized, and existing taxes are often highly regressive. Reforms that allow cities to create a complete digital inventory of properties and users as a basis for a tax roll; use computer-assisted mass appraisal based on market prices as a basis for more progressive property valuation; set rates, minimize exemptions, and enforce payment can help tap into this potential. Such reforms can also strengthen the social contract, encourage subnational competition, and foster demand for moving to full rights in settings where reform of land institutions or regulations (for example, surveying standards) is not immediately viable politically.

Recurrent property taxes are more affordable than high up-front title fees, especially for credit-constrained households. They solve the issue of record maintenance that triggered almost universal return to informality by newly titled properties in low-income neighborhoods reported in the literature and, if property tax revenue is used to offset revenue losses from transfer tax reductions, can offer a politically viable path toward a land registry that is sustainable and affordable to poor landowners. A property tax map will also generate data to assess compliance with existing land-use regulations; allow use of fiscal instruments instead of more blunt command-and-control approaches to regulate land use; and point to legal gaps (for example, lack of provisions for sectional title) that might impede urban densification.

Registry service delivery: Digital technology can improve quality, coverage, affordability, and usefulness of registries for private land rights and help activate land and financial markets especially in urban areas only if the legal basis for doing so exists. Key regulations needed to allow this include (a) digitizing all property records and abolishing manual ones; (b) improving registry access and publicity of data via digital connectivity and reengineering of workflows to reduce cost and improve transparency; and (c) enhancing data quality and currency via interoperability with other registries (IDs, firm and mortgage registries, courts, building permits) and routine use of (free) remotely sensed imagery to centrally monitor land use, enforce environmental restrictions, and make information on rights, use, and prices publicly available at parcel or more aggregate level.

Rural factor market functioning: Frictions in rural factor markets tend to increase households' vulnerability to shocks and reduce the scope for diversification and structural transformation. Regulating issuance and use of georeferenced digital land-use rights documents that are interoperable with other registries offers opportunities to improve access to and competition in local markets including those for inputs, output, insurance, or long-term land transfers for generational change in ways that are yet to be fully explored.

One opportunity to establish registries of rural use rights quickly and cost-effectively would be to require coordinates of parcels cultivated by farmers to be added to digital farmer registries that many African countries have put in place to transparently transfer subsidies. This could help to better target support, maximize its impact by testing and evaluating different design options, and help improve land management by using spatial data to monitor land use, including compliance with environmental rules, as is routinely done in the European Union using land parcel information systems that are often generated in similar ways.

To make this feasible, regulation needs to clarify, among others (a) the procedure for registering use rights and the rights associated with registering them; (b) the type, spatial demarcation, rights, and responsibilities of local bodies or traditional authorities involved, and standards of internal and external accountability they need to meet to avoid conflicts of interest or abuse of power; (c) how local issuance and maintenance links to a central database and how such data can be accessed digitally by public sector and private parties.

Public land management: Public land provides amenities including habitats, biodiversity, or hydrological services, and land for future uses that could potentially be lost irreversibly via private encroachment. To prevent such loss, possibly motivated by the expectation of future legalization of claims, demarcation of public land is a necessary first step. Transparency and the ability to capitalize on services from public land can be enhanced if management is decentralized to local bodies with appropriate incentives that are subject to central oversight. This requires to (a) identify the public or traditional authority (or authorities) that is responsible for managing such land and can derive benefits such as user fees from it; (b) ensure any transfer of rights to public land is fully transparent and competitive; and (c) establish routine centralized monitoring of land use and remedies or sanctions for violations.

By affecting demand for documented land rights, the uses to which these can be put, and institutions' ability to supply them, regulatory and institutional reforms on property taxation, formal land service delivery, rural land-use rights, and public land demarcation and management can create a basis for sustainable resource management, resilient and equitable growth, and the social contract. Reference to global benchmarks can help motivate such reforms and communicate their results.

Note

1 | By 2008, the voluntary Program for the Certification of Ejido Rights and Titling of House Plots (Programa de Certificación de Derechos Ejidales y Titulación de Solares) had certified 98 percent of ejidos, with more than 100 million ha based on community requests.

1. Land institutions

Land is a central determinant of individuals' ability to earn a livelihood, take advantage of economic opportunities, and contribute to public goods to develop identity and a sense of belonging. Development economists have long highlighted the central role of institutions—that is, socially imposed constraints on human interaction that structure incentives in any exchange—in shaping growth and the distribution of associated gains among the population (Greif 1993; North 1971). Land institutions govern (a) how land can be accessed and used, including who has the right to associated benefit streams (Sjaastad and Bromley 2000); (b) how rights to land are documented and can be exchanged, as well as how the state or local communities will protect and enforce them; and (c) what obligations are associated with landownership and use and how such rights can be enforced (Behrer et al. 2021).

This chapter discusses the range of private and public benefits from effective land institutions, the channels through which they materialize, and the difference between group and individual rights. It explores the advantages and challenges of customary land institutions; reviews experiences with formalizing them; and discusses the nature of formal registries, the challenges they face in the African context, and the importance of regulatory reform and institutional restructuring in recent examples in which their functioning has been improved.

Three main conclusions emerge. First, there is scope for regulatory and institutional reform to significantly reduce the cost of documenting and registering land ownership and use rights in a way that allows these rights to be transacted and improves record quality and the ability to enforce documented rights. Fully digitizing legacy records, reengineering workflows to be in line with a digital setting, and improving access to information and services via digital means will make it possible to register all urban land rights formally (including elaboration of spatial plans) at a cost of at most US$12–15 per parcel in a way that largely can be subcontracted to the private sector. Given the levels of resources individuals are willing to pay for titles in urban Africa documented in the literature, this would allow almost full cost recovery, give a boost to land and financial markets, and reduce the wealth bias that in the past precluded registration of land and its use as collateral. The sustainability, fiscal attractiveness, and equity impact of such a step, including for decentralized governance by local governments, can be enhanced by linking registration of rights with a reduction of transfer taxes and adoption of a recurrent property tax based on market value.

Second, although most African countries recognize customary tenure by law, lack of implementing regulations to allow low-cost documentation of such rights (at the group level and then at the individual level within groups) made it impossible to harness synergies between customary and statutory rights and may have increased insecurity and contestability instead. Regulating issuance and management of use rights in ways that recognize such rights as valuable on their own, and allowing transfers (possibly at the group level) and links to digital farmer registries and new approaches to monitor land use based on remote sensing, offers opportunities to improve the functioning of rural factor markets (Benami and Carter 2021), often in a less costly and more sustainable way than could be achieved by full titling.

Third, the importance of private rights should not obscure the fact that large tracts of land, in both urban and rural areas, remain under public ownership. The importance of local and global public goods derived from such land is likely to increase over time. To ensure that this asset provides maximum local benefits in the long term and to leverage new opportunities such as climate finance, it is essential to have all public land demarcated and registered; eliminate conflicts of interest arising from the overlap between the institutions that formally own, manage, regulate, or transfer public land; and conduct any transfer of public land to private interests transparently with full contract disclosure and competitively with local participation and benefit sharing subject to central oversight, for example, via satellite-based monitoring of land use to ensure regulations mandating sustainable resource management are adhered to.

Why land institutions matter

Well-functioning land institutions affect landowners' incentives to make long-term investments in land and their ability to rely on it as a safety net and use it for secondary transactions, such as collateral to access credit; the productivity of land use; the spatial organization of economic activity; social structures; economic growth; and equity.

Land institutions that effectively protect rights and the ability to transfer them at low cost encourage investment, reduce the need for defensive but unproductive spending to secure rights, and allow short-term productivity-enhancing transfers through rental markets by ensuring secure tenure and guarding against expropriation risk. Documentation, even if only at the local level, helps empower rights holders, especially women, by making rights that are otherwise often ignored easier to enforce and allows long-term land transfers. Formal documentation in a central registry adds scope for credit effects, housing investment, and greater risk taking and entrepreneurship.

Investment. Secure property rights have long been noted to facilitate investment in land improvement by eliminating the risk of losing rights once investments have been made in rural (Besley 1995) and urban (Lanjouw and Levy 2002) contexts. A large literature on rural areas focuses on different types of such investments. Fallowing as an important way of restoring soil fertility has been affected by higher levels of tenure security in Ghana (Goldstein and Udry 2008). In West Africa, more secure rights increased fallowing and tree planting, with a somewhat weaker effect on the use of labor, manure, and fertilizer (Fenske 2011). More secure tenure increased application of organic manure in Niger (Gavian and Fafchamps 1996), Zambia (Dillon and Voena 2018), China (Jacoby, Li, and Rozelle 2002), Pakistan (Jacoby and Mansuri 2008), and Thailand (Chankrajang 2015).[1]

In rural settings, investments due to more secure tenure increased productivity, as documented in Madagascar, where more secure rights increased the productivity of land use (Bellemare 2013), and in Benin, where owners of demarcated plots were more likely to invest in maintaining soil fertility than those working on rented or borrowed land (Lawin and Tamini 2019). In urban contexts, secure rights incentivized improvements in housing (Field 2005; Gandelman 2016) that can have health benefits (Vogl 2007). Having secure rights to an asset that can act as implicit insurance against starvation can allow individuals to pursue riskier income-generating activities with higher total returns. By contrast, unclear or insecure property rights, including land conflicts, deterred investment and impeded realization of the associated benefits in the US West, where property rights uncertainty at the end of the nineteenth century deterred irrigation investment and reduced economic activity by as much as 5 percent (Alston and Smith 2022).

Prevention of spending on securing rights. If rights are unclear, individuals or groups may also be motivated to spend resources on unproductive measures to defend such claims (De Meza and Gould 1992). Examples of such defensive spending are widely reported in the literature. In urban areas, protecting rights to land and associated property can require physical presence, often by women, who may need to stay home and guard land assets rather than participate in labor markets (Field 2007). This is socially wasteful and disadvantages the poor.

In rural areas, visible investment in trees may be undertaken to establish rights or demarcate boundaries (Brasselle, Gaspart, and Platteau 2002), a practice that is particularly widespread among groups with otherwise insecure rights (Djezou 2016), including migrants (Bros, Desdoigts, and Kouadio 2019) in West Africa.[2] Beyond potentially dissipating large amounts of resources, competition for property rights that are perceived as contestable can generate large and potentially persistent negative externalities if it involves violence, as in Kenya (Greiner 2017). In Brazil, measures to clarify property rights that eliminated such contestability almost completely stopped land-related violence (Fetzer and Marden 2017).

Productivity-enhancing land transfers. Short-term local land rental transactions enable efficient but land-poor farmers to expand their landholdings by cultivating land leased out by those with low farming skills who instead pursue nonagricultural activities (Deininger, Savastano, and Xia 2017). Studies in Uganda (Baland et al. 2007), Kenya (Jin and Jayne 2013), Ethiopia (Deininger and Jin 2006; Teklu and Lemi 2004), and Zambia and Malawi (Chamberlin and Ricker-Gilbert 2016) document the productivity benefits from land rental. Land rental normally also improves welfare as rents received by owners exceed what they could earn from self-cultivation (Deininger, Ali, and Alemu 2011), and women often benefit disproportionately (Wineman and Liverpool-Tasie 2017).[3]

Female empowerment. Although local recognition of rights, often without documents, is sufficient for some investment effects to materialize, longer-term investments often require land to be transferable (Deininger and Jin 2006). Having rights documented also improves the tenure security of individuals, such as women, migrants, or pastoralists, whose rights may otherwise be ignored or easily overridden. Households or individuals displaced by conflict generally will be able to maintain their rights only if they have documentary evidence (Joireman and Yoder 2016).

By providing implicit insurance, documented land rights, even if they fall short of full title, allow rights holders to pursue riskier projects with higher average returns. Women's land rights are traditionally often weak (Dokken 2015), and asset ownership affects bargaining power in many dimensions (Meinzen-Dick et al. 2019), including fertility choices (Chakrabarti 2018).[4] Having land rights documented rather than just defined in the abstract makes them easier to enforce, particularly for those who, without documentation, may have difficulty enforcing their rights.

Programs that issue documents in women's names have been shown to increase women's role in intrahousehold decision-making (Deininger et al. 2008; Melesse, Dabissa, and Bulte 2018; Muchomba 2017), bargaining power (Menon, van der Meulen Rodgers, and Kennedy 2017), and influence over spending decisions (Wang 2014); their investment and productivity (Ali, Deininger, and Goldstein 2014); and their participation in land (Holden, Deininger, and Ghebru 2011), labor (Field 2007; Goldstein et al. 2018), and financial (Ali and Deininger 2024) markets. Documentation was most effective if combined with legal changes, as in Ethiopia (Kumar and Quisumbing 2012) and Rwanda (Ali, Deininger, and Duponchel 2017).[5]

Long-term transfers and structural transformation. Although short-term local rentals are possible without documents, longer-term rentals that can support structural transformation and a gradual shift of employment from agriculture to nonagriculture usually require more formal documentation. Historically, reforms to replace oral short-term rental contracts with written ones for a longer term, together with a public body for enforcement, fostered tenants' investment in irrigation and drainage, leading to significant efficiency gains in Taiwan, China (Fan and Yeh 2019). Rural land record computerization that did not alter the nature of rights but only the ease with which they could be accessed increased the level of rental market activity and allocative efficiency in Pakistan by transferring land to more productive farmers (Beg 2022).

Documentation of land rights at the community level in Mexico that fell short of full titling facilitated long-term land rentals, occupational shifts to nonagriculture, and migration (de Janvry et al. 2015; Valsecchi 2014). Complete registration of all land and measures to ease transferability and eliminate restrictions on urban residence rights in China almost doubled the likelihood of nonfarm enterprise start-ups (Deininger et al. 2019) while increasing rental market transfers of land to more productive young producers, off-farm labor supply by older farmers, and profits through a shift from grains to vegetables and other higher-value crops (Deininger et al. 2020). Documentation of use rights activated rental markets in Ethiopia, increasing women's participation (Bezabih, Holden, and Mannberg 2016), significantly reducing levels of resource misallocation (Chen, Restuccia, and Santaeulàlia-Llopis 2022).

Housing investment. Documented and enforceable rights are key to incentivize investments in urban floorspace that are less divisible and more capital intensive and durable than those in rural areas, implying that, in addition to rights definition, the cost of enforcement becomes important. If enforcing contracts is costly, efficient markets for rental contracts may not develop (Casas-Arce and Saiz 2010). Across countries, leases have been shown to be longer and the share of high-rise office buildings with long-term tenants higher in countries with more efficient legal systems and less corruption (Titman and Twite 2013). In China, provinces with better institutions also attracted more firm investment (Liu and Yang 2022).

Risk taking, consumption smoothing, and entrepreneurship. Given the importance of land and associated property as an asset, landownership increases individuals' and households' capacity to smooth consumption and take risky entrepreneurial decisions. Titling programs have been shown to increase beneficiaries' risk taking in Argentina (Di Tella, Galiani, and Schargrodsky 2007) and Peru (Aragón, Molina, and Outes-León 2020). In China, land registration and associated better land and labor market functioning increased entrepreneurship and encouraged urban residents to start new businesses in rural areas, improving productivity (Bu and Liao 2022). In Singapore, credit card data show that a policy shift that reduced access to home equity triggered a negative consumption response that was particularly large for households with limited credit market access,[6] highlighting the role of home equity to self-insure and smooth consumption (Agarwal and Qian 2017).

Credit effects. Asymmetric information and risk lead to credit rationing, which can be reduced by using collateral (Stiglitz and Weiss 1981). While the immobility and indestructibility of land make it ideal collateral (de Soto 2000), banks will use it for this purpose at scale only if encumbrances such as mortgages can be entered in the registry at low cost, if registries provide reliable information on ownership and other rights, and if the threat of foreclosure in case of default can be enforced.[7] Regulatory reforms to lower the cost of registry operation or programs to register land rights can expand credit access if land markets are active, courts operate effectively, and creditworthy borrowers' ability to implement profitable investment projects is constrained. Hopes for land titling in rural areas of developing countries to trigger broad-based credit access were often disappointed as not all of these conditions were in place. The fixed-cost element associated with providing credit may also have limited such benefits to the better-off with larger loans, as in Paraguay (Carter and Olinto 2003) or China (Zhang et al. 2020).

Credit effects of registered land rights are evident in urban settings: in India, digitization of land records increased levels of urban mortgage registration, improving credit access by more than 10 percentage points (Deininger and Goyal 2012). Privatization of state housing in China alleviated credit constraints by allowing households to capitalize on the value of their real estate (Wang 2012). Formal homeownership caused households to move up the housing ladder, work harder, take more risks, and save more with clear evidence of a collateral effect (Sodini et al. 2016). Easier property appraisal has also been shown to increase loan-to-value ratios and improve mortgage access (Jiang and Zang 2022).

In the United States, legal changes that allowed the use of land as collateral in one state increased property values by 4 percent, pointing to a direct collateral effect (Zevelev 2021), and exogenous fluctuations in housing wealth improved financial well-being (Atalay and Edwards 2022). In France, exogenous shifts in collateral value increased the probability of becoming an entrepreneur for treated households compared with control groups of renters or homeowners who were constrained in mortgage markets. This effect is persistent as, conditional on entry, treated entrepreneurs used more debt, started and maintained larger firms, and increased property owners' propensity to take up entrepreneurship (Schmalz, Sraer, and Thesmar 2017).

Public benefits from effective land institutions

Beyond increasing incentives for better land management by individual landowners, formal registries also generate public benefits by providing the basis for land taxation, reducing the scope for money laundering, and, if prices are publicized, decreasing the transaction cost for land market operation. Land prices allow valuing location-specific amenities or risks, creating signals to guide and finance public investment via surcharges on land taxes (often referred to as betterment levies), and allow private sector insurance.

Public land management. In any given country, between 30 and 50 percent of land is under public ownership and used to deliver public services and amenities, such as infrastructure, schools, and parks, or to provide environmental services. If boundaries to such land are not demarcated and registered, it is impossible to manage it effectively or monitor and prevent loss of a valuable resource. If not addressed swiftly, encroachment or other ways of appropriating public land are difficult to reverse. Managing public land, protecting it against abuse or appropriation (often by or at the behest of powerful and politically connected individuals), or transferring rights to it in a transparent and competitive way is impossible if rights are not clearly defined or enforced (Kaganova and Kaw 2020).

Land taxation. Property registries are an essential component of state capacity (Besley and Persson 2009), as indicated by evidence from panel regressions for 160 countries that show a strong association between land registry development and economic growth over 1960–2015 (D'Arcy, Nistotskaya, and Olsson 2021). Land records are needed to raise resources via property taxation as a key part of the social contract whereby citizens hold government accountable in return for tax payments (Besley, Ilzetzki, and Persson 2013). Spatially referenced land documents, together with market-based land valuations, can also increase the effectiveness of public spending and the quality of regulation by providing the basis for plans that are realistic and enforceable, allowing assessment of the cost of regulation, and providing market price signals to indicate demand for specific types of public services.

Improved land market functioning. An oft-ignored benefit from land institutions is that, via transaction prices and valuations, they provide price signals. In rural settings, markets are often thin and different types of potential market participants have access to vastly different levels of information (Seifert, Kahle, and Hüttel 2021) so that access to better price data can improve competitiveness (Hüttel et al. 2013). In urban settings, mandatory publication of transaction prices has been shown to reduce price dispersion (Ben-Shahar and Golan 2019) and market frictions (Eerola and Lyytikainen 2015). Publicity of land prices also helps properly value real estate assets posted as collateral for loans to increase loan-to-value ratios and allow banks to comply with macro-prudential regulations.

Easier land acquisition for public investment. In many developing country settings, acquiring land for public infrastructure or private ventures has emerged as a key bottleneck for investment, including for adaptation to climate change. If rights are clear and valuations public, it is easier to prevent projects that may provide large benefits to the public from being derailed by holdouts (Schafer and Singh 2018), political interference (Ghatak et al. 2013), or litigation (Gandhi et al. 2021). Clear land rights will also make it easier to implement approaches such as land sharing (Lozano-Gracia et al. 2013) or auctions (Ghatak and Ghosh 2011; Grossman et al. 2019; Zakharenko 2021). Such approaches as well as setting aside land for mixed income development (Blanco and Neri 2022) increase the likelihood that those who are affected by redevelopment will be able to maintain their level of welfare, an outcome not always achieved through cash-only compensation (Mezgebo and Porter 2020; Sha 2022).

Governance and prevention of money laundering. Data on property transactions, possibly linked to other administrative records, can overcome shortcomings of household surveys such as high nonresponse rates by the very wealthy (Brummet et al. 2018), so that consumption (Eika, Mogstad, and Vestad 2020) or wealth (Fagereng, Holm, and Torstensen 2020) can be measured more reliably. This allows to better document wealth inequality by gender (Frémeaux and Leturcq 2020) or the impact of public policies such as safety nets (Kolsrud, Landais, and Spinnewijn 2020). Land registries, ideally joint with registries of beneficial company ownership (Neef et al. 2022), are also key for monitoring foreign real estate investment (Alstadsæter and Økland 2022), an asset class that, with stricter monitoring of cross-border capital flows (Johannesen et al. 2020), is more frequently used for money laundering.[8]

Valuing the effects of regulation and amenities. Land price data can be used to value public goods such as road maintenance (Gertler et al. 2022) and broadband access (Ahlfeldt, Koutroumpis, and Valletti 2017), urban amenities (Bieri, Kuminoff, and Pope 2023) such as trees (Han et al. 2021) or coastal preservation (Severen and Plantinga 2018), and hazards such as air pollution (Chang and Li 2021), radon exposure (Pinchbeck et al. 2020), proximity to nuclear plants (Coulomb and Zylberberg 2021), or earthquake risk (Singh 2019). They also shed light on the cost of regulations, such as historical preservation standards (Hilber, Palmer, and Pinchbeck 2019), density restrictions (Hilber and

Vermeulen 2016), and restrictions on participants in land markets (Hartley et al. 2023; Lawley 2018). This can not only motivate calls for policy change, but also guide public investment and arrangements for financing or cost recovery, including by issuing bonds against future tax revenues or transport interventions such as congestion pricing (Tang 2021).

Quantifying climate risks. Property prices reflect people's willingness to pay for protection from flood risk in a specific location (Bosker et al. 2019) or climate-related expected exposure to sea-level rise (Goldsmith-Pinkham et al. 2021). They thus provide a consensus view on likely climate effects that can create incentives for private adaptation, allow prioritizing and financing (via property taxes) of public adaptation investment that affects locations differentially, and obtain actuarially fair insurance. Along the same lines, differential changes in property prices for different types of real estate in response to shocks such as COVID-19 can help guide private responses to these (Rosenthal, Strange, and Urrego 2022).

Individual versus group rights

Although most of the discussion in the literature focuses on individual rights, group rights can be an effective arrangement if group membership, individuals' responsibilities, and mechanisms for enforcement and external accountability are defined. In fact, they will have advantages if (a) benefits from resource use accrue at a larger spatial scale as is the case for biodiversity and ecosystem services, among others (Leonard et al. 2021)[9]; (b) cohesive groups with clearly defined membership exist and are legally defined (Kotchen and Segerson 2020); and (c) outcomes can be observed easily and mechanisms for internal decision-making, use of graduated sanctions, and equitable sharing of benefits from effective land management among members are available.

There are many uses of land that is only marginally suited for crop cultivation, such as for grazing, forest, or pastures that benefit from economics of density where average cost decreases with the size of the area used. Preservation of biodiversity, mineral extraction, and urban development fall in the same category. Analysis of all land under Indian reservations in the United States finds that after more than a century, land of relatively low productivity had better economic outcomes if it was left under tribal ownership than if it was allotted to individuals with restrictions on rights to transferability (Leonard, Parker, and Anderson 2020). The reason is that for such land, a parcel's suitability will depend on the attributes of all parcels adjoining it, and assembly will be costly, especially if private parcels are small, jointly owned by many individuals (for example, because of a history of undivided inheritance), or interspersed with public land (Leonard and Parker 2021). Clarifying access rights to publicly owned grazing land in the US West similarly increased productivity and use of fallowing as much as privatization (Bühler 2023).

Legally valid demarcation of indigenous lands indeed reduced deforestation on a large scale in Brazil (Baragwanath and Bayi 2020), to the extent that it has been argued that shifting from indigenous to individual tenure (or protected areas that are difficult to enforce) could result in a net loss of forest cover (Pacheco and Meyer 2022). Recognition of indigenous rights also improved conservation outcomes (Blackman et al. 2017), the quality of land management, or income (Peña et al. 2017; Vélez et al. 2020).[10]

Establishment of legal entities is one way to formalize group membership, establish internal control mechanisms, and define ways in which groups interact with nonmembers and be regulated externally. Ways in which groups and their members can benefit from effective resource management (for example, by being able to retain all or most of the resources obtained from land-use contracts with outsiders) can provide an important incentive. The Mexico example (spotlight 1.5) illustrates how this can be done, with group rights integrated into a formal cadaster in a way that provides groups with flexibility in the choice of specific tenure forms or ways of land use. Similar structures have been described for common land management by youth groups in Ethiopia (Holden and Tilahun 2018) and management of community forest resources in Nepal (Baland et al. 2010).[11] While limited observability of outcomes has often been a key obstacle to group rights effectiveness, availability of remote sensing products that allow measuring not only forest cover (Hansen et al. 2013) but also aboveground carbon stocks (Csillik et al. 2019) and forest-related greenhouse gas emissions (Harris et al. 2021) makes it possible to observe and quantify outcomes, including the climate change mitigation services provided by forests.

Traditional land institutions

Most rural land in Africa continues to be managed by traditional "customary" institutions that limit land transfers to nonlineage members. If outside demand for land remains low, risk high, and local state presence weak, customary arrangements offer high tenure security, effective land management, dispute resolution, and a social safety net in a way that is more accessible and less costly than available alternatives, and limits on transferability may not be a binding constraint. However, as land values and thus the benefits from land transactions with outsiders increase, customary institutions' internal and external accountability may need to be strengthened to ensure that chiefs act as custodians of land rather than as owners and that the rights of women and nonlineage members are respected to ensure equity and efficiency of land use.

Acknowledging the advantages of customary tenure under low population density, most African countries passed laws that recognized it in the late 1990s and early 2000s. To ensure that such laws will be effective in ensuring productive use of land, especially as land becomes scarcer and more valuable, regulation is needed on how traditional use rights relate to formal titles, are to be managed internally, and can mature into formal rights. Evidence suggests that failure to enact such legislation risks that coexistence, and competition between customary and formal tenure will make property rights more contestable and foster insecurity and risk of conflict rather than productivity-enhancing investment.

Characteristics and advantages of customary institutions

Property rights and the institutions governing them emerged to incentivize investment in restoring soil fertility (spotlight 3.1 in chapter 3). A defining characteristic of land tenure in Africa is that most rural land is held under customary tenure, an arrangement whereby traditional authorities ("chiefs") long acted as custodians of land on behalf of the community by allocating land to individuals or lineages for cultivation, often in return for tokens of appreciation in an equitable, accessible, and cost-effective way. In such systems, the use of common land, such as pasture and forest, is managed for joint benefit while arable land is given to households under secure long-term rights. Disputes are adjudicated quickly, following rules that evolved in adaptation to local conditions over long periods. If land is relatively abundant, risk is high, and resource value is modest, managing larger spatial units allows traditional institutions to internalize externalities that private landowners might ignore by adjusting behavior to match resource availability. In such settings, efforts to replace customary with individualized arrangements often proved unsustainable because of higher cost and less flexibility (Nugent and Sanchez 1998).

Safety net. Customary tenure's defining characteristic is that members of the lineage have an innate right to be assigned land but that permanent transfers of land to outsiders are not allowed. Although some suggest that this may encourage population growth (for a summary of recent studies, see Ali, Deininger, and Kemper 2022), access to customary land provides a safety net that, at low levels of income, is more incentive compatible and affordable than alternatives (Baland and Francois 2005) as documented for Uganda (de Haas 2022) and elsewhere.[12]

Restrictions on permanent land transfers to outsiders, the defining characteristic of customary tenure, can be understood as a measure to eliminate moral hazard by individuals that could otherwise undermine the long-term viability of customary tenure (Andolfatto 2002). Such restrictions are unlikely to be a binding constraint if land demand by outsiders is limited, investment is labor rather than capital intensive, and migration low so that contracts remain short term, the range of potential contractual partners stays small, and use of land as collateral is unrealistic because even banks accepting it would not be able to foreclose in case of default.[13]

Where land became scarcer, external demand for it increased, or long-term individual land transactions with outsiders offered advantages such as access to markets, technology, or other factors of production (Fenske 2014), customary systems often individualized in a gradual manner (Guirkinger and Platteau 2014). Such transitions were more rapid if other means to smooth consumption or manage externalities became available (Delpierre, Guirkinger, and Platteau 2019). The strength of customary systems may vary even in the same country: in The Gambia, for example, informal land exchanges that help insure against idiosyncratic shocks are encountered frequently (Beck, Bjerge, and Fafchamps 2019) but most likely in ethnically homogeneous villages where land is relatively abundant (Beck and Bjerge 2017). In China, adoption of full transferability, which eliminated the threat of periodic land reallocation, increased off-farm labor by 7 percent and incomes by 6.5 percent but also increased intravillage inequality (Zhao 2020), suggesting that moving from customary to individual tenure involves a trade-off that is best evaluated in light of risk mitigation and market access opportunities available locally.

Cost-effective administration. Local presence provides customary chiefs with access to private information that makes customary systems less costly to administer and more resilient than formal ones (Boone 2017). By relying on information not normally available to outsiders, chiefs have been shown to be able to improve the targeting of social assistance programs (Basurto, Dupas, and Robinson 2020), support local public good provision (Tourek et al. 2020), and assess individual demand and willingness to pay for land (Manara and Regan 2022). Local presence and trust also help explain traditional rulers' ability to dispense justice on land matters in a way that is faster, fairer, and less likely to require side payments than formal channels (Winters and Conroy-Krutz 2021).

Drawing on local information may increase welfare and efficiency of resource use at the local level (Casey et al. 2019), in line with evidence on the scope for complementarity between state and traditional authorities in the delivery of public goods in Africa (Henn 2020). Several studies point to the continued importance of traditional leaders. In Zambia, lapses in leadership that occurred after some leaders died in office are used as a natural experiment to suggest that chiefs but not members of parliament have a significant impact on the delivery of coproduced public goods, an effect that seems to be associated with chiefs' longer time horizons (Baldwin 2018).[14] Estimates from the Democratic Republic of Congo are consistent with complementarity between chiefs and formal state institutions (van der Windt et al. 2018). In Indonesia, reconstruction of the complete political and economic history of chiefs who had been elected between 1979 and 2014 suggests that villages' ability to attract capable chiefs via incentive-compatible contracts that provided them a share in land revenue led to permanent differences in socioeconomic outcomes, such as levels of education and overall economic development (Lim 2022).[15]

TABLE 1.1 Actual tasks and desired involvement by traditional leaders in African regions
share of respondents (%)

| Region | Traditional leaders' influence should | | Traditional leaders play a main role in | | | | Number of countries |
	Increase (1)	Increase a lot (2)	Dispute resolution (3)	Land allocation (4)	Governing the community (5)	Influencing people's vote (6)	
Central	65.3	26.5	31.9	23.2	19.6	18.1	2
East	51.4	27.2	48.8	24.9	29.7	15.8	3
North	51.8	29.3	31.6	15.6	27.2	19.6	1
South	55.6	23.1	52.1	31.0	45.3	13.1	5
West	54.3	25.0	52.2	35.9	36.6	21.1	12
Total	**55.1**	**25.2**	**49.0**	**31.4**	**35.7**	**18.3**	**23**

Source: World Bank computation from Afrobarometer Round 8 data.
Note: The figures in columns 3 through 6 are the share of respondents indicating that traditional leaders have "a lot" of influence over dispute resolution, land allocation, governing the community, or influencing people's vote, respectively.

Data from the Afrobarometer survey for 23 countries in table 1.1 show that traditional authorities are perceived to play an important role in dispute resolution (49 percent), community governance (36 percent), and land allocation (31 percent). More than half of the respondents in each region (55 percent overall) would like to see traditional leaders' influence increase (around a quarter by a lot). Across regions, traditional institutions are most influential in South Africa (52, 45, and 31 percent for dispute resolution, governance, and land allocation, respectively) and West Africa (52, 37, and 36 percent, respectively), slightly less important in East Africa (48, 30, and 25 percent, respectively), and less important in Central Africa (32, 20, and 23 percent, respectively) and North Africa (32, 27, and 16 percent, respectively).

Especially in settings where traditional leaders continue to play an important role, regulating existing laws recognizing customary tenure in a way that clarifies their functions and incentives in the area of land management and maintenance of land documents may thus be more effective than trying to replace them (Bruce and Knox 2009). To the extent that this would include providing capacity and access to information and technology such as digital land-use maps and real-time information on land use, it would allow capitalizing on the local trust that traditional leaders enjoy while improving accountability.

Challenges faced in formally recognizing customary tenure

Recognition of the advantages of traditional land management authorities in terms of cost and often also local accountability (Bruce and Migot-Adholla 1994) and the ability of tenure systems to evolve (Platteau 2000) triggered a wave of policies and laws recognizing customary systems that swept Africa in the early 2000s (Alden Wily 2018a). The importance of customary institutions is also recognized by the Framework and Guidelines for Land Policy that was adopted by African heads of state in 2010 and served as the basis for national and global land policy documents.[16]

However, failure to adopt implementing regulations for these laws has often reduced their relevance. Bubb (2013) demonstrates this by showing that, despite vast differences in legal provisions between Ghana and Côte d'Ivoire, local practices on either side of their common border differ little. This suggests that in practice, such laws are largely ignored, an issue that may lead to undesirable outcomes once land becomes scarcer (Chimhowu 2019). Key issues relate to accountability, especially in land disposal, respect for outsiders, and security of tenure for women.

Accountability. Historically, transfer of land to outsiders via concessions persistently weakened the power and downward accountability of traditional leaders. In the Democratic Republic of Congo, chiefs in villages just inside the perimeter of a historic rubber concession are elected less competitively and provide fewer public goods than those just outside it, resulting in significantly worse individual outcomes in terms of education, health, and wealth (Lowes and Montero 2020). Across chiefdoms in Sierra Leone, the lack of accountability and competition associated with hereditary rather than elected leadership makes it difficult for subjects to voice concerns and has been shown to reduce security of land rights, undermine broader development (Acemoglu, Reed, and Robinson 2014), and increase deforestation (Mihaylova 2023). Traditional leaders have also been reported to be co-opted by state institutions as in South Africa's former Bantustans where analysis suggests that support by chiefs significantly boosted the ruling party's vote share (de Kadt and Larreguy 2018) in return for the state guaranteeing their survival and access to rents.[17]

Traditional rulers' downward accountability was often weakened by colonial powers that tried to replace it with upward accountability. Differences between colonial powers have been used to document some of the impacts. Compared with individuals in former French territories, those in territories previously occupied by the British perceive corruption by chiefs to be much higher, are less likely to identify themselves in national than in ethnic terms, and perceive state capacity in terms of taxation, security, and chiefs' power to be weaker (Ali, Fjeldstad, and Shifa 2020). This holds not only across countries but also for historical tribal homelands that were split between British and French colonies, as well as for counties colonized by either of the two powers within Cameroon (Ali, Fjeldstad, et al. 2019).

Agreements with nonlineage members. As they represent a lineage, traditional leaders may discriminate against outsiders, as reported from West Africa, where migrants lacking consanguinity with autochthonous groups were often given "perpetual" use rights as an incentive to invest in cash crops such as cocoa. Such agreements may be reinterpreted or revoked (Woods 2003) as land becomes scarcer (Bambio and Bouayad Agha 2018). In Burkina Faso, migrants have suffered disproportionately from land conflicts, causing agricultural productivity to drop by more than 40 percent (Linkow 2016). In Côte d'Ivoire, "outsider" households have smaller landholdings and less complete rights over land than locals and, as a consequence, fallow a smaller proportion of their land and obtain lower yields (Fenske 2010).[18]

Pastoralists' use rights are time bound, and their effectiveness depends on access to transit routes and complementary resources such as watering holes that may be affected by agricultural intensification or climate change. Agreements on access to such passage rights or resources are easily ignored or altered by sedentary farmers, especially if land use intensifies and pastoralists lack voice in relevant forums (Bergius et al. 2020). Participatory planning to protect herd migration routes and resources (such as wetlands) is critical for dry season herd survival and can reduce the likelihood of conflict, as can recording of secondary rights (McPeak and Little 2018)[19] and venues for consultation and arbitration (Eberle, Rohner, and Thoenig 2020).

Systematically ignoring outsiders' rights may trigger conflict: in fact, some of Africa's most violent and enduring conflicts, as in Burundi, Rwanda, eastern Democratic Republic of Congo, northern Uganda, southwestern Côte d'Ivoire, and Senegal, have been argued to have their roots in land issues (Boone 2017). In Uganda, conflicts involving domestic migrants are the most important type in terms of numbers and productivity impacts, with parcels under such conflicts having 45 percent lower yields than those without (Mwesigye and Matsumoto 2016). As probability, length, and severity of conflicts between ethnic groups organized around segmentary lineages are well above the average (Moscona, Nunn, and Robinson 2020), mechanisms to avoid inter-ethnic land disputes that otherwise may escalate and be difficult to resolve given overlaps between tribal, ethnic, and religious identity (McGuirk and Nunn 2020) will be important.

Women's land rights. Although a number of studies link the strength of women's land rights and the nature of inheritance systems to women's role in the agricultural production process (spotlight 3.1 in chapter 3), these rights are often vulnerable as conditions change (Andersson Djurfeldt 2020), with consequences for women's agency and productivity of land use.[20] In many African countries, women's inheritance rights to land are weak de jure and de facto (Peterman 2012), and the ability to enforce such rights locally often remains fragile (Genicot and Hernandez-de-Benito 2022).

In Zambia, the threat of losing land upon widowhood in villages where custom does not let women inherit land decreased productivity by reducing women's fallowing, fertilizer application, and labor-intensive tillage techniques even while their husbands were still alive (Dillon and Voena 2018). In Malawi, fear of losing land in the near future is pervasive among women who, as a result, suffer reductions of output value by 12 percent and crop income by 30 percent (Deininger, Xia, and Holden 2019), and women's inheritance rights have been central to the debate on the country's land law for a long time (Peters 2010).

Although short-term control rights may not have strong productivity effects (Kang, Schwab, and Yu 2020), limits on women's rights to retain land in widowhood, which are widespread in Africa, are likely to reduce investment and agricultural productivity and have been argued to constrain entrepreneurship (Brixiova, Kangoye, and Tregenna 2020). In Malawi, women's rights to bequeath affect investment in land parcels, especially in patrilineal systems (Deininger et al. 2021). In Uganda, women are also likely to be involved in inheritance-related land disputes, reducing investment by close to 7 percent (Deininger and Castagnini 2006). Preceding land rights recognition with legislation to guarantee women's inheritance rights was critical to achieve benefits for women in cases of tenure documentation in Ethiopia and Rwanda.

Changes in family law could also be a first step toward shifting customary gender norms (Aldashev et al. 2012).[21] The importance of women's rights suggests that legal reforms to strengthen women's inheritance rights can have significant effects (Harari 2019), even if they seem to be poorly enforced in some areas (Linkow 2019) or overlap with cultural norms (La Ferrara and Milazzo 2017). This can involve training officials or providing information to women at key life events such as marriage (Field and Vyborny 2019) or (digital) access to legal services. Such an intervention in Kenya led to improved investment and credit access even though not all disputes were resolved (Aberra and Chemin 2021).

Examples for operationalizing and documenting traditional tenure

Ethiopia. In Ethiopia (spotlight 1.3), land-use certificates were issued in 2003–05 to more than 6 million households (18 million parcels) at low cost (<US$1 per parcel) via a decentralized process that used a description of neighboring plots as a geographical reference and was implemented by elected councils (Deininger et al. 2008). This illustrates the scope for scaling up quickly in a decentralized manner that draws on elected local bodies. As digital tools were not available then, this effort established paper-based local registers, with significant impact.

Studies show that the program reduced conflict (Di Falco et al. 2020), strengthened women's rights (Kumar and Quisumbing 2015) and bargaining power (Melesse, Dabissa, and Bulte 2018), and raised spending on food and health care (Muchomba 2017). It increased tenure security and investment in land improvements (Holden, Deininger, and Ghebru 2009), soil fertility (Melesse and Bulte 2015), and participation in informal rental markets (Holden, Deininger, and Ghebru 2011), with benefits that exceeded the cost (Deininger, Ali, and Alemu 2011). Although remaining restrictions on land sales and often also rentals reduced its impact, certification reform realized about one-fourth of the potential productivity gains from eliminating all types of factor misallocation (Chen, Restuccia, and Santaeulàlia-Llopis 2022).

Sustaining the progress was made difficult by two factors. First, limitations on transferability and recognition of rural land-use rights in cases of urban expansion, rooted in a dualistic system that strictly separates rural and urban land administration systems, reduced the value and usefulness of the certificates issued (Adam 2014). Second, as there was no regulation on how to keep the registries current, villages improvised to the best of their ability, resulting in highly variable procedures and quality of registry maintenance (Cochrane and Hadis 2019) and, as a result, the currency of local registries across the country. This triggered a push for "second-round" certification, that is, the creation of a computerized centralized registry for rural areas only. To unify procedures and prevent a reversion to informality, a program of "second round" certification created a computerized and fully georeferenced registry with more than 22 million records of public and private land at US$6 per parcel (Zein 2021). As land sales remain prohibited and many regions continue to restrict land rental (Holden and Ghebru 2016), interest in this "second-stage" certification (Bezu and Holden 2014) and short-term impact remained limited initially (Ghebru and Girmachew 2020). To address this, the government actively worked on establishing a fully digital system for processing transactions that now provides some 350 woreda (district) offices with access to use fully digital and auditable workflows that account for regional differences in regulations. While more than 750,000 transactions have been registered, efforts to improve access by distant villages via mobile service delivery, to increase the scope for certificates' transferability and their use as collateral and basis for insurance are under way. While limited network capacity precluded connecting directly to users' or service providers' mobile phones (to allow, for example, digital initiation of transactions or lodging of subdivision surveys), plans include linking the land registry to the national ID system, using it as a basis for farmer-specific agricultural advice and public land management, and expanding coverage into urban areas.

Benin. In Benin (spotlight 1.4), use rights were recognized by elaborating rural land-use plans and low-cost village boundary demarcation. Map 1.1 illustrates the boundaries of different types of individual and common land demarcated in this way, overlaid over satellite imagery. This intervention reduced tree cover loss and fires, land clearing, and intervillage border conflicts. It also increased trust in local institutions and improved local participation in managing communal areas and natural resources (Wren-Lewis, Becerra-Valbuena, and Houngbedji 2020). The program also systematically demarcated 70,000 individual parcels with the intention of eventually titling them. Demarcation increased perceived tenure security and investment in tree planting and fallowing, especially on parcels managed by women (Goldstein et al. 2018).

MAP 1.1   Examples of land demarcation in Benin's Plans Fonçiers Rural

a. Area marked as sacred ground in PFR

b. Demarcated landholdings with tree cover

c. Forest surrounded by demarcated landholdings

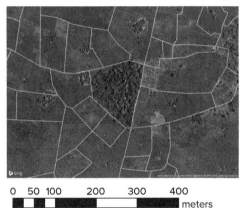

d. Forest between villages demarcated by the PFR

0   50 100   200   300   400

meters

Source: Wren-Lewis, Becerra-Valbuena, and Houngbedji 2020. CC BY 4.0 (https://creativecommons.org/licenses/by/4.0/).
Note: PFR = Plans Fonçiers Rural.

Benin's legal system, similar to that of other West African countries, views land-use certificates only as a temporary arrangement that will expire unless converted to title within a certain time frame. Moreover, documents issued under the project, which have legal value only if used as a basis for formal titling, were subsequently abolished and replaced with similar documents that cost about 10 times more (Lavigne Delville 2019). In the long term, the project affected attitudes to markets, a result driven by the country's more advanced Southern region, but did not yield economic benefits (Fabbri and Dari-Mattiacci 2021). To the contrary, it increased conflict (Arruñada, Fabbri, and Faure 2022) and raised suspicions about elite capture in communities less well connected to markets (Fabbri 2021).[22]

Similar arrangements in Côte d'Ivoire, where the requirement for universal titling can be interpreted as rendering existing informal agreements with outsiders "illegal," are reported to make it much easier for locals to renege on such informal contracts opportunistically (Colin 2013). In both cases, low-cost demarcation of use rights at the individual or family/village level, including documentation of arrangements with outsiders, could yield considerable benefits. A one-size-fits-all approach that tries to force formalization in rural areas where there is little demand for such an intervention may introduce wealth bias and increase rather than reduce inequality, impede rather than improve the functioning of markets, and reduce trust in property rights institutions. Especially if capacity and resources are limited, use of a lower-cost approach to documenting rural use rights while focusing efforts at issuance of title and activation of financial markets on urban areas, where benefits are likely to be larger and cost lower, may be warranted.

Mexico. Mexico (spotlight 1.5) provides an example of how individual and community rights can be recognized in a more decentralized and sustainable way. It combines a clear regulatory framework for documenting group rights with documented impact. Customary rights at the level of the group (*ejido*) were registered to more than 100 million hectares in the early 2000s in three steps.[23] First, the ejido was registered as a legal entity to engage with outsiders as a group with organs of self-governance (the executive, the assembly, and an oversight committee) that follow clear procedural rules and with its outer boundary demarcated. Second, internal boundaries of community land as well as individual agricultural and housing parcels were identified and registered centrally in the National Agrarian Registry (Registro Agrario Nacional [RAN]). Long-term transfers of land to outsiders under a range of options are similarly possible based on an assembly decision. Third, all decisions had to be ratified by the assembly, supervised by a network of independent paralegal teams via the publicly supported Land Attorney's office (Procuraduría Agraria) that provided on-demand access to legal advice and a dedicated court system in each of the country's states.

In addition to establishing clear procedures to register or transfer ejido land, there was no ambiguity on whether land tenure is governed by the social or the private system. Moreover, a procedure for communities to exit the customary regime and move to the private system by individualizing rights with proper safeguards, particularly the requirement for such decisions to be approved by 75 percent of members in a centrally supervised assembly vote, was put in place.[24] Studies show that the program facilitated mechanization and higher productivity (de Janvry et al. 2015), fostered structural transformation via migration (Valsecchi 2014) and investment (Dower and Pfutze 2013), and increased women's participation in leadership positions (García-Morán and Yates 2022).

This example illustrates that even without the possibility of transferring individual land to outsiders or to use it as collateral, documentation of use rights, establishment of a system to ensure internal and external accountability of local leaders, and greater transferability of land via group decision provided large economic benefits. Although it was important to provide an opportunity for groups to make the transition to fully transferable titles, less than 10 percent of communities, mostly in periurban areas, made use of this opportunity. Finally, women's co-ownership rights were recognized in principle, but better connectivity and widespread access to cell phones are likely to offer greater opportunities to document women's joint or individual rights in a way that translates into economic empowerment.

Tanzania. Tanzania adopted a Village Land Act in 1999 that was hailed as a major innovation at the time (Alden Wily 2003) because it contains many of the factors that made Mexico's experience a success. However, progress with implementation has been glacial (spotlight 1.6). Nearly two decades after passage of the law that would allow registration of villages' outer boundaries and issuance of a Certificate of Village Land (CVL), less than 10 percent of villages were able to establish a village land-use plan as the first of several steps toward CVL issuance (Huggins 2018). Moreover, rights granted via registered CVLs or (unregistered) village land-use plans are often unenforceable because they are not public and commitment to enforcement is weak: village land-use plans were repeatedly changed in ways that, in their absence, reduced pastoralists' rights.

Failure to honor boundaries registered in CVLs if land is considered "unused" or subject to investor interest (Bluwstein et al. 2018; Engström and Hajdu 2018), an issue that is now before the courts, created doubt about the government's willingness to enforce, raising concern about the security of rights received by outside investors. Finally, the regulations governing issuance of use rights on village land mandate a process that is virtually undistinguishable from that for issuing formal title, with costs of several hundred dollars (Stein et al. 2016). They thus replicate the wealth bias inherent in titling that motivated adoption of a separate act to govern village land and, via on-demand "titling" of individual parcels rather than comprehensive issuance of use right documents for all villagers, threatens to increase inequality and hollow out the concept of village land from within (Mramba 2023).[25]

Two lessons emerge from the Tanzania example. First, procedural obstacles such as unaffordable standards and staffing requirements, vague definition of rights, and overlaps in institutional mandates between local and central authorities can frustrate implementation of progressive laws for low-cost documentation of use rights and generate significant rents (Deininger 2023). Second, slow progress in documenting use rights may be due less to the technical difficulty of doing so than to a concerns that ceding control over use and disposal of public land may give rise to capture by local elites, concern that is best addressed through regulations including land-use monitoring using modern technology to avoid abuse and formulas for taxation and revenue sharing between local and central bodies that create incentives for promoting investment and effective land use.

Other African countries. Despite large amounts of donor support and attention, efforts to translate legal recognition of community rights in Mozambique into actual control suffered a fate similar to that of Tanzania (Quan, Monteiro, and Mole 2013). In Uganda, regulations for issuance of "low-cost" use rights ended up with complex procedures and staffing needs that are impossible to justify economically (Hunt 2004).[26]

In Kenya, far-reaching changes to decentralize land administration written in the 2010 Constitution faced delays in implementation (D'Arcy and Nistotskaya 2019) partly because of lack of information sharing (Boone et al. 2019). Implementation of the country's 2016 Community Land Act, a piece of legislation passed with high expectations (Alden Wily 2018c), was similarly impeded by a lack of regulatory clarity (Odote, Hassan, and Mubarak 2021).[27] While the ongoing land records computerization program could in principle overcome past tendencies of using land rights for political patronage (Hassan and Klaus 2020) via competition among local governments (Dyzenhaus 2021), technical difficulties have thus far prevented full implementation of this system even in the capital.

Malawi's 2016 Land Law is similar to those discussed earlier in that it puts all customary land under traditional land management authorities and mandates their recognition and demarcation on the ground as the first step toward issuance of low-cost use right certificates. Although the legislation was fiercely debated and its passage delayed (Chikaya-Banda and Chilonga 2021), full demarcation of traditional land management authorities was achieved by 2018. One reason was that, given its importance for making the law effective and avoiding confusion and conflict between different types of registries, complete demarcation had been agreed to serve as a trigger in a World Bank Development Policy Loan, making it of interest to institutions well beyond the ministry responsible for land. Full demarcation of traditional land management areas clears the way for clarifying the status of expired estate leases within such areas and subsequent issuance of customary land-use rights certificates.

Formal land registries

Centralized formal registries provide public notice of the status of rights to land, thereby (a) reducing the cost of land transactions with strangers, (b) lowering enforcement and information cost, and (c) creating the basis for secondary land transactions (for example, as collateral for credit). Although their costs of operation exceed that of customary institutions, in urban and more commercially oriented settings, these costs will often be only a fraction of the possible benefits.

However, in many African countries, high cost of first-time title issuance and registration of subsequent transactions, together with limited quality, coverage, and currency of formal systems, limit outreach, usefulness, and trust in modern systems and impeded realization of these benefits. Regulatory and institutional reforms to lower the cost and improve the quality of service delivery are needed to realize the benefits from formal land rights documentation, starting in urban settings and expanding from there toward rural ones.

Advantages of formal property registries

Formal registries provide legal protection to a range of interests in a piece of land, such as rights of ownership, use, or mortgage that by law can or must be registered. The key difference compared to customary rights is the ability to enforce such rights with the help of the state (Firmin-Sellers 1995). In contrast to contractual rights, enforcement is in rem and can be affected only with rights holders' consent, thus protecting third parties. Rights are unambiguously defined, and multiple rights to the same parcel can be held if registries have a territorial monopoly (Arruñada 2003).

The two most popular systems of registering rights differ in whether legal protection is based on a document lodged for registration (in a system of deeds) or the act of registration itself (in a title registration system).[28] Title registration systems often back the information provided with a state guarantee, whereas in recording or deed systems, the law regulates only the assignment of priority between registry entries. Although the due diligence to be performed upon registration in a title system implies higher up-front cost, a title search is more demanding in a deed system.

Technically, land registries comprise a spatial component and a textual part. The former, normally referred to as the cadaster, describes the boundaries of the objects (land parcels) over which rights are defined. The textual part, referred to as the register of rights, provides public evidence of registrable rights held by individuals or legal entities and assigns priority among them. Complete cadastral and registry coverage for a territorial unit provides a base layer of information that can be used by a wide range of institutions for planning and public good provision.[29]

A public registry has two main advantages. First, by making information on ownership rights and any encumbrances pertaining to a specific parcel available publicly, it reduces the scope for moral hazard caused by asymmetric information, thus expanding the range of potential contractual partners to a transaction beyond those who, for example, due to social ties or local presence, can unambiguously ascertain the status of such rights at low cost. Second, by allowing transfer of rights to land independently from the underlying asset and protecting third parties' rights *in rem* (Arruñada, Zanarone, and Garoupa 2019), a public registry allows recourse to the enforcement organs of the state for enforcing rights as a last resort. This creates scope for secondary transactions, including use of land as collateral for credit.

Challenges for Africa's formal property registries

The above benefits will be maximized if the cost of registration is low and reliable information on rights or encumbrances to any given piece of land and attached real estate can be accessed publicly, ideally in electronic form. In Africa, the coverage and currency of land registries has been reduced by the cost of boundary demarcation, which mainly derives from the requirement to conduct a high-precision survey and emplace markers, often still made of concrete; elevated registration fees, much of which can be attributed to high transfer taxes; and costly, often still manual processes that limit interoperability and effective service delivery but create opportunities for corruption. All of these can be reduced by institutional reform, a move toward fully digital service delivery, and the adoption of streamlined restructured workflows. Failure to address such institutional issues up front has undermined many rural titling programs' sustainability and ability to achieve their objectives.

Cost of surveying. In many African countries, coverage with registered rights and the usefulness of land registries are reduced by the cost of first-time or subsequent registration of rights. Acquiring such rights on a case-by-case basis via demand-driven "sporadic registration" is reported to cost far more than US$1,000 in Madagascar (Jacoby and Minten 2007) and even more in rural Ghana (Agyei-Holmes et al. 2020). Formal fees for obtaining a title are estimated to be close to US$500 in Benin (Mekking, Kougblenou, and Kossou 2021) and Zambia (Honig 2021). A key reason for such high cost is the need for a high-precision survey of the property. Relaxing precision requirements or other regulatory constraints that limit competition in the survey sector is thus one of the easiest ways to make documented land rights more affordable.

While a description of the boundaries of the property to which rights are registered is an essential part of a property record,[30] low-cost options to accomplish this are available. Experience from developed and developing countries suggests that an index map that depicts property boundaries on a current satellite image, together with GPS coordinates with meter accuracy, which can be acquired for US$1–2, can provide the basis for confirmation of rights by neighbors and other stakeholders. Developed countries such as the United Kingdom continue to rely on topographic maps rather than high-precision surveys to identify property without negatively affecting a thriving real estate market.[31]

High survey cost has been found to be a significant factor in explaining the limited coverage, wealth bias, and potential negative equity impact of land titling interventions. Studies found land titling to have favored speculative land acquisition (Sitko and Jayne 2014) by elites and politicians (Njoh 2013) in ways that marginalize traditional rights holders (Jansen and Roquas 1998) and were associated with high corruption risk (Benjaminsen and Sjaastad 2002; Peters 2004). The high cost can also explain why many landowners abandon the titling process halfway after having made the first step (Ali and Deininger 2022) or resort to informal substitutes (Chimhowu and Woodhouse 2005), including sales contracts (Lavigne Delville 2002), tax receipts (Goodfellow and Owen 2020), or reliance on "experts" (Ehwi, Morrison, and Tyler 2021).

Beyond increasing the cost of title issuance, a focus on precisely demarcating boundaries may distract from the need to conduct a thorough investigation of rights in the field to determine that there are no potentially contradicting or overlapping claims.[32] It may also trigger conflicts where none had existed before (Arruñada 2018).[33] Requiring high-precision surveys and physical boundary monumentation may lead to a lock-in effect similar to what was found for lands settled in 1862–1940 in the United States (Allen and Leonard 2021).[34]

The literature suggests that willingness to pay for land documents in urban settings is quite high: almost all residents of low-income, unplanned settlements in Dar es Salaam participated in a saving scheme to accumulate resources to acquire title, with a mean willingness to pay of US$35 and strong interest to register women as co-owners (Ali et al. 2016).[35] Private information by local chiefs in the same setting suggests a willingness to pay of US$200 for title (Manara and Regan 2022).[36] Informal residents' willingness to pay for title was also high in urban areas of the Democratic Republic of Congo (Balan et al. 2020), Zambia (Ali, Deininger, et al. 2019), Ghana (Ehwi, Morrison, and Tyler 2021), and Nigeria (Goodfellow and Owen 2020).

Cost of subsequent registration. The fact that there are synergies and cost savings from systematic acquisition of boundary information for all properties in a territorial unit led to the adoption of "systematic" campaign-style first registration for free or at highly subsidized rates in most donor-funded projects. Even with such savings, mapping routinely accounted for more than half the total cost (Burns 2007). If not accompanied by a reduction of the cost of service delivery to allow the registry to sustain itself from recurrent user fees (in terms of the monetary outlay for registration and the travel time required) at the level commensurate with the associated private benefits, the impact of such initiatives was often short-lived as the gains in formality were not sustained and landowners reverted to informality (Atwood 1990; Pinckney and Kimuyu 1994).

Evidence of such a return to informality is not limited to Africa: in Argentina, where titling positively affected labor market outcomes (Galiani and Schargrodsky 2010), the high cost of subsequent registration triggered "de-formalization" (Galiani and Schargrodsky 2016). The role and the associated political economy and distributional aspects are illustrated by the case of Peru. In this country, a functional, low-cost registry that had been established to cater to low-income households is reported to have been shut down in response to political pressure from notaries whose business model was undercut by such "unfair" competition (Gutierrez and Molina 2020).[37]

Formal recognition of customary tenure. In settings where customary rights enjoy legal protection, clarity is needed on how formal and customary systems interact, particularly how customary land is represented in the registry and cadaster (that is, in whose name customary land is registered and how its outer boundaries are determined), and whether a transition from customary to formal tenure can be made at the individual or group level. In the absence of such clarity, recognizing customary tenure may make rights more rather than less contestable by creating two parallel systems and encouraging the wealthy to engage in "forum shopping," that is, to pursue claims with formal and customary institutions in parallel (Eck 2014).

Such dualism between modern and traditional systems is reported in the literature for Uganda (Gochberg 2021), Zambia (Honig 2017), and Ghana (Lentz 2010). It may be associated with phenomena such as chiefs "privatizing" land and making it available to wealthy outsiders (Chimhowu 2019), even if doing so reduces social welfare (Leeson and Harris 2018). With increased land pressure, chiefs may also start to charge high fees (Honig 2021) for services that they earlier provided for free and come to see themselves as owners rather than custodians of land (Lanz, Gerber, and Haller 2018). This has widened inequality even in donor-supported interventions in Ghana (Adam, Adams, and Gerber 2021) and Zambia (Green and Norberg 2018).

Beyond dissipating resources that could be used more productively, legal dualism can also exacerbate inequality, reduce trust, hollow out traditional systems from inside, and, in the extreme—if alternative ways of asserting property rights are not available—trigger conflict (Greiner 2017). Unclear rules have been reported to increase rather than reduce insecurity (Tchatchoua-Djomo, van Leeuwen, and van der Haar 2020), especially if they provide a basis for opportunistic action by the well-connected (Colin 2013). Unless the legal environment is clear, spending resources to issue use rights certificates that lack legal backing may not have any economic impact, as happened in Zambia (Huntington and Shenoy 2021). To see whether such concerns are justified, data are needed.

Evidence on registry capacity, performance, and challenges

Limited wealth- and gender-biased access to formal land documents. Data from household surveys, as reported in table 1.2, document limited access to formal documentation of land rights that is often biased by gender and wealth. For urban residential land (columns 1 through 8), the share of owners with title ranges from 11.1 percent in Niger to 55.7 percent in Senegal, but of these, only between 27 percent (in Benin) and 63 percent (in Togo) are up to date, as proxied by being in the name of a household member.[38] This points to a share of urban landowners with current title below 10 percent in three countries (Chad, Niger, and Benin), between 10 and 20 percent in five (Togo, Mali, Guinea-Bissau, Burkina Faso, and Côte d'Ivoire), and close to 30 percent in Senegal. More than 70 percent of residential titles are exclusively in the name of males, and households in the top quartile of the expenditure distribution are more likely to have

TABLE 1.2 Access to title for residential and agricultural land in select countries share of respondents (%)

Country	Residential land								Agricultural land				
	Own (1)	Title (2)	Updated (3)	Male (4)	Q1 (5)	Q2 (6)	Q3 (7)	Q4 (8)	Own (9)	Rent (10)	Free (11)	Title (12)	Risk (13)
Benin	53.6	32.4	27.0	75.1	16.3	25.6	35.8	58.9	68.4	10.3	29.5	1.2	1.8
Burkina Faso	74.0	27.1	65.9	86.6	15.3	23.1	24.4	58.2	77.6	2.5	36.1	2.4	3.3
Chad	83.0	12.3	43.8	71.4	6.1	11.5	14.2	24.7	—	—	—	1.2	—
Côte d'Ivoire	43.0	36.1	52.9	80.8	26.5	32.7	40.0	52.4	86.0	8.1	15.5	7.6	4.1
Ethiopia	—	—	—	—	—	—	—	—	—	—	—	60.2	—
Guinea-Bissau	72.0	32.7	52.6	72.2	21.0	28.0	35.9	50.8	91.1	3.7	21.5	4.3	3.8
Mali	79.4	32.7	51.7	88.0	13.8	24.3	40.9	66.7	89.9	2.2	11.8	1.0	4.0
Niger	81.3	11.1	62.7	84.0	3.1	6.4	12.2	34.3	84.3	5.2	21.9	1.5	3.2
Senegal	71.7	55.7	53.3	78.3	32.7	49.2	62.0	80.5	81.3	4.5	30.2	1.8	15.0
Togo	43.2	24.8	63.3	71.6	9.6	15.1	25.7	52.9	57.7	20.4	34.1	1.3	3.5

Source: Calculations using data from West African Economic and Monetary Union surveys.

Note: — = not available. Q1–Q4 refer to the household's quartile of per capita expenditure. For agricultural land, *own, rent,* and *free* denote the modality of land access, and *risk* refers to the perceived risk of losing land within the next five years. For Ethiopia, the "Title" column refers to documented rights from first-stage certification (refer to spotlight 1.3 for a more detailed discussion).

access to titles everywhere. Access is most unequal in Niger, where members of the top quartile are 11 times more likely to have title than those in the bottom quartile, and least unequal in Côte d'Ivoire.

For agricultural land (columns 9 through 13), the share of those who own land ranges from 58 percent in Togo to 91 percent in Guinea-Bissau, while the share of those accessing land for free, mostly through intrafamily transactions, exceeds that of renters everywhere, ranging from 12 percent in Mali to 36 percent in Burkina Faso, with renters' share ranging from 2.2 percent in Mali to 20 percent in Togo. Of those who own agricultural land, the share with title remains below 2 percent in six of the countries considered (Benin, Chad, Mali, Niger, Senegal, and Togo), with 2.4 percent in Burkina Faso, 4.3 percent in Guinea-Bissau, and 7.6 percent in Côte d'Ivoire. However, the fact that at 4.1 percent, perceived risk of land loss is the second highest in Côte d'Ivoire (after Senegal, at 15 percent) suggests that the presence of a title is not the only and possibly not the most important factor affecting this variable.

Quality of land service delivery. Even if registries deliver services at high cost, the quality of such services may be poor if costs are driven by excessive survey standards, transaction taxes, and high-cost service delivery models that do little to improve quality. Table 1.3 points toward three main dimensions of registry quality on which globally comparable data have been collected by the World Bank's Doing Business project (Djankov et al. 2020).

First, digital textual and spatial records that are fully integrated and interoperable with other registries improve the quality, security, and usefulness of land records by providing relevant information on rights to land. Other registries may include the civil or company registry including for digital personal ID, the mortgage registry, the registry of court decisions, and municipal registers for building permits or property taxes. Digital interoperability can increase trust and reduce processing time and the scope for fraud and discretion via fully digital and auditable workflows and can harness synergies across registries (for example, via automatic alerts in case a landowner's or parcel's status changes in one registry) to improve record quality.

Of 53 African countries, only 3.8 percent report having a digital system that integrates the cadaster and registry (table 1.3, column 4), but of these, only Rwanda's is fully functional, while those in other countries still lack national coverage. While the scope to digitize records and workflows, starting with urban land, is thus immense, it may be resisted by groups that benefit from paper records being more easily manipulated and prevent efforts at digitization in other regions of the world.

Second, having at least a minimum level of coverage is important for markets to function and for the public sector to use registry and cadastral information for planning, permitting, or tax collection. It will also help the private sector to add location-based services and make it worthwhile for banks to invest in developing workflows and instruments for mortgage lending. An up-to-date

TABLE 1.3 Key attributes of land administration systems in African and world regions

percent

Region	Registration cost (1)	Digital records			Main city covered		Court decision in <1 year (7)	Number of countries (8)
		Registry (2)	Cadaster (3)	Linked (4)	Registry (5)	Cadaster (6)		
Africa, Central	9.3	8.3	8.3	8.3	8.3	8.3	8.3	12
Africa, East	5.3	14.3	14.3	14.3	0.0	0.0	14.3	7
Africa, North	4.7	0.0	16.7	0.0	0.0	16.7	0.0	6
Africa, South	6.9	8.3	0.0	0.0	33.3	25.0	8.3	12
Africa, West	7.2	0.0	6.3	0.0	6.3	6.3	6.3	16
EAP	4.5	20.8	33.3	20.8	58.3	54.2	29.2	24
ECA	2.7	43.5	52.2	30.4	60.9	69.6	39.1	23
LAC	5.9	3.1	31.3	3.1	15.6	31.3	3.1	32
ME	5.8	28.6	28.6	14.3	71.4	64.3	7.1	14
SAS	7.0	12.5	25.0	12.5	25.0	25.0	12.5	8
SSA	7.02	5.7	7.5	3.8	11.3	11.3	7.5	53
WENA	4.2	58.8	88.2	55.9	91.2	97.1	29.4	34
World	**5.4**	**23.4**	**37.2**	**19.7**	**43.6**	**47.3**	**17.6**	**188**

Source: Calculations using data from 2020 Registering Property indicator of the World Bank's Doing Business project.
Note: Registration cost in column 1 is defined as a percentage of average land value. The figures in columns 2 through 7 refer to the percentage of countries that score on the respective indicator (for example, 8.3 in line 1, column 2, means that 8.3 percent of the 12 countries in Central Africa (that is, one country) has a digital registry. Court decision in <1 year means that a first-instance court decision for the most common type of land dispute can be obtained in less than one year. EAP = East Asia and Pacific; ECA = Eastern Europe and Central Asia; LAC = Latin America and the Caribbean; ME = Middle East; SAS = South Asia; SSA = Sub-Saharan Africa; WENA = Western Europe and North America.

registry will also help to generate price data to be made available publicly, easing price discovery in land markets and allowing increasing loan-to-value ratios in mortgage markets by more accurately reflecting the value of land pledged as collateral.

Table 1.3 points toward limited coverage of the registry or cadaster even for the main city. Beyond Rwanda's nationwide digital registry and cadaster, Botswana, Malawi, and The Gambia have a paper registry and cadaster, Eswatini and Mauritius a paper registry, and South Africa and Morocco paper cadasters for the main city. As paper maps are often out of date and lack interoperability, for example with land-use planning, this implies that virtually all African cities lack the foundation for a vibrant land and mortgage market or the tools to regulate and plan land use in a way that can be enforced in a fair and transparent manner at reasonable cost.

Third, land and mortgage markets will operate smoothly only if rights can be enforced at low cost. Foreclosure of land pledged as collateral normally requires a court decision. If, for example, due to the difficulty of obtaining needed (paper) documents, it takes too long for such decisions to be made, the benefit from using land as collateral will decrease. Data in table 1.3 show that in only four African countries a first-instance decision for a "standard" land case can be obtained in less than a year. This is likely to reduce not only the ability to use land as collateral, but also overall investment.

The weak technical and institutional foundations for documenting and enforcing land rights imply that access and regulatory issues related to land may constrain job growth. Table 1.4 shows that 26 percent of firms in Sub-Saharan Africa (30 and 27 percent in West and Central Africa, respectively) perceive land as a major constraint to enterprise growth, more than in any other region except the Middle East (28 percent). Such constraints are most severe for large firms. Although land constraints apply equally in cities of all sizes in West Africa, they are severer in large cities and capitals in South and Central Africa and in smaller cities in East Africa.

Beyond economic impacts, high cost and low quality of land registries also undermine trust in such institutions: data from 34 African countries as summarized in table 1.5 suggest that less than 20 percent of respondents are confident that a visit to the local land registry office would allow them to identify the owner of a specific land parcel. Instead, land registries are perceived to be wealth biased and corruption-prone: 61 percent of respondents (75 percent in Central Africa) think that rich people can fraudulently register land that does not belong to them, while only 17 percent believe the same to be true for ordinary people.

TABLE 1.4 Share of firms viewing land as a severe or very severe constraint to enterprise growth in African and world regions

Region	Total (%)	By firm size (employees) (%)			Number of	
		>100	20–99	5–19	Countries	Firms
Africa, Central	27.3	28.0	27.4	20.9	10	5,498
Africa, East	21.9	22.8	20.8	18.0	6	6,933
Africa, North	16.7	17.2	17.7	16.3	4	11,158
Africa, South	22.0	24.1	20.4	16.7	11	10,443
Africa, West	29.7	31.3	27.8	24.0	16	12,113
EAP	14.9	14.3	13.4	19.1	17	17,505
ECA	12.3	12.0	12.6	12.6	29	46,941
LAC	13.1	13.8	12.6	12.5	31	32,331
ME	28.4	29.5	24.5	22.9	5	4,652
SAS	24.0	25.8	23.9	20.7	7	17,317
SSA	26.1	27.5	24.9	21.0	43	35,383
WENA	9.0	9.0	10.3	6.5	14	9,130
World	**17.6**	**18.1**	**17.0**	**15.9**	**151**	**174,021**

Source: Calculations using data from World Bank Business Enabling Environment (BEE) surveys.
Note: EAP = East Asia and Pacific; ECA = Eastern Europe and Central Asia; LAC = Latin America and the Caribbean; ME = Middle East; SAS = South Asia; SSA = Sub-Saharan Africa; WENA = Western Europe and North America.

TABLE 1.5 Perceptions of reliability and transparency of land administration in African regions

share of respondents (%)

Region	Can get land information	Fraudulent registration possible by		Number of countries
		Ordinary people	Rich people	
Central	19.7	15.8	75.4	3
East	20.8	12.0	65.6	3
North	9.3	16.7	53.8	3
South	21.0	19.4	60.3	10
West	18.9	16.1	59.8	15
Total	**18.9**	**16.7**	**61.3**	**34**

Source: Afrobarometer Round 7.
Note: Can get land information is the share responding "very likely" to the question, "If you went to the local lands office to find out who owns a piece of land in your community, how likely is it that you could get this information?" *Fraudulent registration* (*ordinary* and *rich*) tabulates the share of respondents who think it is very likely for an ordinary person or a rich person, respectively, to "pay a bribe or use personal connections to get away with registering land that does not belong to them."

TABLE 1.6 Share of violent conflicts related to land and natural resources in African regions and fatalities in these events

Region	Violent events			Fatalities in these events		
	2007–12	2013–17	2018–22	2007–12	2013–17	2018–22
Central	2.1	4.9	8.3	6.9	8.6	13.9
East	4.7	6.0	7.2	5.5	6.4	6.1
North	2.2	4.1	4.7	6.7	5.1	12.6
South	2.9	3.7	5.4	15.6	10.1	6.9
West	2.7	5.2	9.8	6.2	7.3	11.4
Total	**3.2**	**4.8**	**7.3**	**6.5**	**7.0**	**10.8**

Source: Calculations based on data from the Armed Conflict Location & Event Data Project.

Distrust in land institutions, increasing land scarcity, and greater variability of returns from land due to extreme weather events risk increasing land-related conflict. Data from the Armed Conflict Location & Event Data Project (ACLED)[39] on violent conflict include information on reasons for conflict, which allows identifying those related to land or resources directly linked to land.[40] Table 1.6 reports the share of violent conflicts related to land and natural resources, as well as fatalities in all violent conflicts for three periods from 2007 to 2022.[41] It shows that the relative frequency of such conflicts more than doubled overall and almost quadrupled in West and Central Africa, where droughts and climate-related weather events were particularly frequent. Greater decentralization and access to venues for conflict resolution, if complemented by efforts toward better documentation of resource rights using locally accepted means, have been shown to reduce such conflict.

Examples of reform

Rwanda. As spotlight 1.1 illustrates, Rwanda is the only African country with a nationwide fully digital registry and cadaster. It titled all the country's 11.5 million parcels from 2011 to 2013 at a unit cost of less than US$6 (Nkurunziza 2015), building on a completely revised legal and regulatory framework, a carefully evaluated pilot, and the ability to pass implementing regulations to respond quickly to problems as they emerged (Ngoga 2018).

Beyond showing that obstacles to systematically registering land at scale in Africa are often more political than technical in nature, spotlight 1.1 also demonstrates the benefits from such action: 86 percent of land parcels were individually or jointly owned by a woman (Ali, Deininger, and Duponchel 2017), and soil conservation investment (Ali, Deininger, and Goldstein 2014) as well as land and mortgage market activity increased (Ali et al. 2015). The move to a flat fee radically reduced the cost of registration and helped the country move from being ranked 137 in the Registering Property part of the World Bank's Doing Business ranking in 2005 to the top in 2015.

The program also improved state capacity: the incremental urban property tax revenue from properties added to the registry under the program would allow the program cost to be recouped in less than a decade or three years with rates unchanged or uniformly set at 1 percent of property value, respectively (Ali et al. 2021). The flat registration fees implied that registration cost, relative to property value, was disproportionately high for rural land. A survey showed that this indeed led to informality in rural areas and, by collecting evidence on willingness to pay, helped identify options to adjust fee structures to help deal with this without jeopardizing the registry's ability to sustain itself from fee revenue (Ali et al. 2021).

Lesotho. The case of Lesotho (spotlight 1.2) illustrates how, following reductions in administrative requirements for registering mortgages, urban land titling increased credit supply, especially for women. Regulatory reform in 2010 that, among other things, simplified procedures (including the need for ministerial consent) to register mortgages was followed by systematic titling in 2011–13 (Ali and Deininger 2024). Building on a 2006 law that, for the first time, allowed married women to own assets independently, procedural reform and titling increased women's level of registered rights in the short term.[42]

Regulatory reform and institutional restructuring improved market functioning, particularly mortgage markets, an effect that materialized quickly and was large for already registered parcels but took longer and remained smaller for land formalized via the systematic land registration program.

The stock of systematically and sporadically registered parcels significantly increased mortgage market activity. Reforms triggered a marked reduction in transaction cost and an increase in registered transfers and mortgages, especially in the name of women. Partly because of systematic differences in parcel characteristics that affected their marketability and suitability as collateral, the estimated impact of the stock of sporadically registered parcels remained larger than that of systematically registered ones seven years after the end of the program by between 4 and 10 times, pointing toward a large impact on potential taxes.

These examples illustrate that beyond making first registration of rights affordable by lowering mapping standards, improving formal titling systems will require (a) adjusting regulations to simplify procedures and establish fully digital workflows for creating and transferring land records; (b) reducing the cost of registering rights for the first time and of subsequent transactions and ideally making the registry and cadaster financially self-sustaining; (c) digitizing legacy records before doing any new registration to avoid creating overlaps, allowing transactions to increase immediately, and enhancing confidence in the registry; and (d) ensuring that cadastral and registry records are fully interoperable and can be accessed as needed by both private and public institutions. Given low coverage with formal rights and the fact that mortgage lending is hardly observed in most African cities, the potential for improvement is immense. However, regulatory reform to address these issues will be a precondition for realizing this potential.

Implications for policy

The previous discussion suggests that instead of advocating a "one-size-fits-all" approach that aims to promote abstract principles, such as titling or land markets, irrespective of local context and opportunities, efforts to improve the functioning of land institutions in Africa will be most effective if they take account of context and economic potential. Regulatory change to improve transparency and quality of service delivery will be important to harness opportunities from data management, and interoperability will be key to unlock benefits from improved land management that will transcend the land sector. Such change would be aimed to (a) establish a functional, fully digital and interoperable urban land registry that can be maintained based on user charges based on full coverage with title documents in urban areas; (b) support rural factor market operation by operationalizing use rights via participatory mechanisms to demarcate, document, and maintain rights short of full title that are more easily issued and managed locally, can be linked to georeferenced digital farmer registries, and offer scope to mature into full title via group decision; and (c) complete mapping and registration of public land, institutional reform to eliminate conflict of interest by institutions managing such land, and establishment of processes to ensure that such land benefits local communities and that any transfers are fully transparent and competitive. Progress toward these objectives can be monitored using a combination of data sources.

Reduce cost of land service delivery. To eliminate wealth bias in access to the registry and make full coverage with registered rights affordable and sustainable, there is need to (a) fully harness the advantages of a digitally interoperable registry and pass cost savings to customers in the form of reduced fees, (b) adjust survey and planning standards to be fit for purpose and affordable, and (c) eliminate transfer taxes that drive transactions into informality, possibly via a revenue-neutral shift to a recurrent property tax. If these adjustments are made, the added value from formal title should be enough to finance the property registry's recurrent cost via user fees, possibly with a modest subsidy from urban to rural areas, and lesser rights that can mature over time should be considered for areas where this is not the case.

Improve quality and usefulness of registry information via digital interoperability. Enhancing the quality and usefulness of registry information is essential to counter the pervasive lack of trust in land registries. This requires (a) moving toward a fully digital system, including digitization of all legacy data and taking measures to ascertain their validity and cancel documents that are no longer valid[43]; (b) putting in place streamlined and fully automated digital workflows that reduce transaction cost through document processing via digital electronic signature and enhance transparency via digital audit trails and performance benchmarks; (c) establishing full interoperability with other registries, managed at the national level (personal ID, legal entities, mortgages, and court decisions) or local government level (tax rolls, plans, and building permits) using unique parcel identifiers and ensuring registry currency by automatically raising flags in the registry or triggering notices to affected people if changes are made in other registries (for example, the civil registry); (d) leveraging interoperability by putting in place restrictions (such as co-owners' electronic consent and presence of a tax clearance certificate) to reduce the scope for fraudulent land transactions and ensure compliance with existing laws and regulations; and (e) linking digital data on boundaries of land parcels (whether publicly or privately owned) to satellite imagery to monitor land use and take action when existing restrictions have been violated.

Improve publicity of registry information. To remove obstacles in accessing information on land rights and prices as a key output from land registries, there is need to (a) harness digital connectivity to make it easier to access registry information, use this information for private contracting, and improve security of rights by automatically issuing notices to holders of secondary rights when any modification requires their consent; (b) foster decentralization in land management and service delivery by combining central data maintenance with access to landownership data by local government bodies to improve land management and planning, as well as collection of land-based revenue to improve efficiency of land use; (c) routinely disseminate data (for example, on prices) at a granular level to provide a benchmark to improve functioning of real estate markets; and (d) establish mechanisms to share, with owners' consent, information on landownership and use at the parcel level with interested parties to document historical land use and allow use of such information in private contracts, including for resource transfers via mobile money.

Full coverage with formally registered rights and link to land value capture in urban areas

Documentation of urban ownership or use rights. Rather than starting in rural areas where comparatively low land values and thin markets will reduce the benefits from titling and make use of land as collateral difficult, establishing well-functioning registries in urban areas and expanding from there will have higher potential to foster women's entrepreneurship, improve the operation of land and financial markets, and increase investment. The example of Lesotho and the high demand for secure rights in urban areas of other countries suggest that if a functional registry is in place, regulatory change that reduces operational cost and passes savings on to customers via lower registration costs and improved record quality (for example, via interoperability that allows banks to register mortgages automatically) within a sustainable model of financing recurrent costs (ideally based on user fees) will trigger registrations by landowners.[44]

Ensuring a self-sustaining business model. In Rwanda, the total cost of a nationwide land tenure regularization program was US$6 per document, not including physical planning. If relevant regulations are in place, costs for first registration of less than US$20 per document for data collection, elaboration of planning documentation, and, where needed, integration with tax mapping, valuation, and billing in an integrated software package with digital interfaces for the public are reasonable. If the estimates of willingness to pay that are reported in the literature are to be believed, such a program could be implemented with close to full cost recovery in urban areas. It would generate almost all the data needed for a revenue-neutral elimination of transfer taxes in return for a recurrent land tax based on market values of land, implying that subsidized first registration together with a marked reduction of transfer taxes in lieu of recurrent property taxes at market value could command broad political support. By ensuring currency of documents, this would also be more sustainable, equitable, and transparent than current approaches and would most likely generate much higher levels of revenue. Although the quasi-judicial process of adjudicating rights will need to be performed by the public sector, experience from Africa and elsewhere shows that data collection and software development can be outsourced to the private sector.[45]

Increase capacity and competition by private land professionals. The private sector will, however, be able to implement these tasks only if the regulatory framework is in place; in fact, basic regulatory issues, such as the lack of regulation for accepting electronic signatures, have held up private-sector efforts for years (Sagashya and Tembo 2022). Key elements of the regulatory and institutional reforms needed to enable private-sector efforts include measures to (a) reduce the cost and improve the quality of service delivery by shifting to a fully digital system that is interoperable electronically with other public registries (individuals and digital ID, legal entities, mortgages, court decisions, taxes, building permits, and so forth) and uses reengineered workflows and procedures; (b) revise the procedure for first-time registration to use index maps, ideally based on drone imagery, and gender-sensitive procedures (for example, joint registration of property as the default for married couples) based on local customs and preferences; and (c) reduce the cost of any subsequent registration by dropping fees and eliminating transaction taxes, possibly replacing them with a recurrent property tax, which would also help with maintenance (for additional details, see chapter 2, "Key issues to be addressed to facilitate the use of property taxes").

Operationalizing rural use rights

Harness interoperability. The evidence above suggests that in rural locations where full coverage with formal titles is not viable in the short term, regulating laws that recognize customary tenure and foresee issuance of low-cost use rights certificates may, in a digital environment, achieve many of the benefits expected from titles in activating rural factor markets. Opportunities for achieving this objective can be maximized and the cost of issuing and maintaining such documents reduced through interoperability, for example, with digital farmer registries or land-use planning by including georeferenced parcel boundaries (which can be generated using machine learning approaches) and making the information from such registries available to the private sector to link farmers to markets.

Focus on transferable use rights. Issuance of use rights rather than full titles may come with some restrictions on land transactions. In the example of Mexico (spotlight 1.5), such restrictions did not preclude large economic impacts and contribution to structural change via longer-term leases and migration as ways to enter into transactions with outsiders or make the transition to full title at the community level were clearly specified. While mechanisms for internal management will need to be defined on a case-by-case basis, digital interoperability greatly increases the scope for doing so.

Leverage Earth observation for land-use planning and monitoring. Digital connectivity and the use of parcel boundaries further enhance the scope for exploring opportunities to use documentation of use rights to (a) link certificates to evidence of actual land use based on remote sensing, as illustrated by the example of Brazil (see chapter 4); (b) reduce frictions in rural factor markets, including those for insurance, by combining authenticated data from use rights registers with digital marketplaces; and (c) empower women by documenting their land rights, as illustrated by the case of Ethiopia (spotlight 1.3), and expand issuance of documented rights to other holders of secondary land rights.

Clarify interaction between customary and statutory systems. Harnessing this potential will require clarifying issues related to (a) the legal status of the community, its representation toward the outside, and mechanisms of internal accountability and oversight; (b) low-cost, decentralized procedures to map, register, and manage community land rights (for example, by demarcating outer boundaries of the customary domain within which individual rights can be managed locally) and ensuring (digital) updating; (c) ways to engage with outsiders, including investors, that provide benefits to all parties; (d) mechanisms for intercommunity collaboration, external accountability, appeals, and oversight; (e) avenues through which communities and their leaders can benefit from improving land use and that can thus incentivize such actions; and (f) mechanisms to allow making the transition to full title at the group rather than the individual level to avoid wealth bias and corruption.

Public land management

Demarcate and register all public land. Although private land is of great importance, large tracts of land that are important for biodiversity, potential agricultural expansion, or nonagricultural use remain public. In addition to ensuring that public land provides benefits to the public at large rather than specific individuals, there is need to ensure that (a) conflict of interest, which in many settings is caused by having institutions that formally own public land also regulate its use and often control its disposal, is eliminated; (b) all public land is registered, public ownership is justified by provision of public goods, management responsibility is aligned with the ability to provide these (which usually means delegation to lower levels with proper oversight), effectiveness of land management and adherence to public regulations are monitored independently using remote sensing, and action is taken swiftly in case of abuse; and (c) if rights to public land are transferred to private parties (especially for commercial purposes), transfers are transparent and competitive, with contractual provisions public to facilitate third-party monitoring, and compliance with contractual provisions is routinely monitored and reported.

Decentralize public land management and ensure transparent rights transfer and objective land-use monitoring. Ideally, such steps would be combined with decentralization of management responsibility for public land to local institutions that would be allowed to keep all or part of the proceeds from disposing of such land. The potential for competitive, market-driven processes to increase revenue generation from unoccupied public land is illustrated by analysis of the impact of a legal reform in Ukraine. After earlier digitization efforts did not produce the desired results, the legal reform in 2021 mandated the use of transparent online auctions by local governments rather than a central agency to lease rights to public agricultural land. Using the preferred specification, the shift to a collusion-proof electronic auction platform immediately increased lease revenue by 175 percent. Had all the public land that was transferred to private ownership in Ukraine since 2015 been auctioned using this postreform mechanism, local governments would have received incremental lease revenue of US$500 million per year (Deininger, Ali, and Neyter 2022). This suggests that where public land is important, legal reform to ensure that rights to such land are allocated transparently, competitively, and in a decentralized way is essential to ensure proper use of such land and improve social, economic, and environmental outcomes.

Global benchmarking and information access

Although information on the rights to specific land parcels is a key output from land registries, access to such information is often restricted, creating considerable transaction cost for potential investors and making it more difficult to identify areas for reform.[46] If the challenges inherent to global comparisons (Arrunada 2007) are addressed, comparing the quality of land institutions across countries could reduce informational imperfections and enhance the impact of reforms (and the speed with which they materialize) by informing private-sector players in a consistent and objective way. It would allow countries to assess progress on reforms objectively and defend such reforms against opposition from stakeholders who may stand to lose rents. Documenting regulatory quality can help objectively measure the quality of land institutions, identify the scope for reforms, document and communicate effectiveness of reform, and allow learning from other countries that implemented similar reforms earlier. Combining indicators of regulatory quality with data from administrative sources (including land transaction prices) allows identifying high-level issues and, together with data from (free) satellite imagery or household surveys, analyzing economic, social, and environmental impacts of reform.

Indicators of regulatory quality. Key indicators of regulatory quality include whether (a) registry and cadaster are integrated digitally and can be accessed by interested parties, (b) all registration workflows are digital and auditable, (c) the registry is digitally linked to and fully interoperable with other public registers (individuals including digital ID, legal entities, mortgages, tax, and court decisions) in a way that issues notices in case changes in one registry require updates elsewhere, (d) a recurrent property tax is in place and prices for land transactions and valuations of land and properties for tax purposes are public, (e) a complete inventory of public land together with mechanisms to monitor land-use change on the ground and act on changes such as encroachment or other unauthorized activity is in place, and (f) public land transfers to private parties, especially for commercial purposes, are done competitively and information on terms of such transfers is available.[47]

Administrative data. Regulatory and institutional reforms are necessary but not sufficient to improve land record quality and use of such records by private parties. Quantitative data from the registry on each of the above broad areas can help provide actionable recommendations by assessing if reforms have their desired impact and how use of the registries varies across space and type of property owners. Examples include (a) the level of coverage with registered rights (number of registry records and share of women (co)owners for those related to a physical person as well as area covered with such rights for different administrative units); (b) the number of registered mortgages, land sales (and prices for these) as an indicator for market functioning, and the share of registered transfers through inheritance to assess currency); (c) the number of properties on the tax roll and the assessed and actually collected property tax revenue from these; (d) the stock and flow of land-related court cases to assess the broad adequacy of the legal environment and the ability of the judicial system to handle these; and (e) the amount of public land disposed through competitive auction.

Although aggregate information on the above will allow overall tracking of reform progress, having data disaggregated for lower administrative units can, by revealing detail on differentiated reform impacts, help to adjust and fine-tune policy interventions to local conditions and better inform private parties. Several countries, including the United Kingdom, have recently started to publish prices for land and associated property for individual transactions. Doing so not only improves the basis for private decision-making but also allows more transparent valuation of land for purposes of taxation, a benchmark for land acquisition, and the evaluation of policies affecting land rights or land use.

Household survey data for policy analysis. To measure access to documented land rights at the individual level and the impact of such actions on empowerment, investment, and economic welfare in a reliable, objective, and comparable way, household survey data based on a proper sample frame and quality control are needed. Although use of such surveys has become standard, information on landownership and use has often been omitted or collected in ways that make comparable analysis, especially of gender differences in land access and its impact on welfare and productivity, nearly impossible. To support national statistical institutes' reporting on land-related indicators in the Sustainable Development Goals, the World Bank, the Food and Agriculture Organization, and UN-Habitat developed a land tenure module for incorporation into Living Standards Measurement Study–type questionnaires.[48] Use of the questions included in this module will be essential to appreciate equity impacts of policy and institutional reforms and, especially if combined with administrative data, to document the links between land policy reforms, access to finance, and structural transformation.

Household surveys have traditionally also been used to make inferences on agricultural production. This is appropriate if household-based enterprises located adjacent to a household's primary residence account for all or most agricultural production. If, as in several African countries, this condition no longer holds, capturing agricultural enterprises, even if they are far from a household's main residence or operated by legal entities, will be important. If the registry is complete and up to date, it can be the basis for a sample frame to conduct such a survey (Deininger and Xia 2021); if not, census listings (Ali and Deininger 2022) or area frames, possibly complemented with crop maps, can provide such a basis.

SPOTLIGHTS

Spotlight 1.1: Modalities and impacts of land tenure regularization in Rwanda

In Rwanda, Africa's most densely populated country (470 inhabitants/km^2 overall and 635 inhabitants/km^2 of agricultural land), where land scarcity and insecure tenure had been identified as one of the reasons for the 1994 genocide (Andre and Platteau 1998), addressing land tenure has long been a key concern. Starting with virtually no legal framework and ranked 137 in the World Bank's 2005 Doing Business ranking, the country set out to improve land registration and management. To eliminate bias against women's landownership, the government passed an inheritance law in 1999 (Daley, Dore-Weeks, and Umuhoza 2010), followed in 2004 by a land policy, and in 2005 by an organic land law and administrative structures for land management and administration at the national and local levels down to the cell as the lowest administrative unit. Because there was no experience to go by, in 2007–10, a pilot to register some 15,000 parcels was undertaken in four cells that reflected the country's diversity. Careful analysis and review of the pilot at each step, together with an impact evaluation, allowed the administration to draft regulations governing how the land law should operate in a problem-solving mode based on feedback from the field rather than on abstract reasoning.

Evaluation of the pilot program by Ali, Deininger, and Goldstein (2014) finds impacts in three areas: (a) land access improved for legally married women, although women who were not legally married saw their property rights diminished, an issue corrected before the national rollout; (b) investment increased significantly, with a doubling of the overall propensity to invest in soil conservation measures and a tripling for female-headed households, in line with the notion that they had previously suffered from more insecurity; and (c) fears that land regularization would trigger distress sales proved unfounded—to the contrary, further study (Ali et al. 2015) showed that land registration improved the functioning of the land rental markets and increased the volume of efficiency-enhancing land transfers in the short term.

The ability to develop regulations informed by piloting paid off by facilitating rapid scaleup and national rollout: virtually all of the country's 11.5 million land parcels were registered in fewer than three years (2011 to 2013) and at a unit cost of less than US$6 per parcel (Nkurunziza 2015). Trained local "parasurveyors" used high-resolution satellite imagery to record parcel boundaries and ownership in a public process with the mandatory presence of neighbors and local authorities, possibly after disputes had been resolved with elders' support. Results were publicly displayed locally for at least a month to hear any objections and make corrections. Once this process was completed, titles and lease certificates were distributed to landowners.[49]

Beyond survey-based studies supporting the program's positive gender impact (Santos, Fletschner, and Daconto 2014), having a complete registry makes it possible to use administrative data to document accomplishments. Ali, Deininger, and Duponchel (2017) show that three aspects stood out already in 2015: (a) of the parcels owned by natural persons, 86 percent had a woman owner, either in joint (61 percent) or individual (25 percent) ownership; (b) having a complete registry and a unique parcel identifier made it much easier for banks to ascertain whether there were competing claims, and US$2.6 billion in mortgage lending was secured by some 50,000 loans (65 percent residential, 30 percent agricultural, and 5 percent commercial land); and (c) contrary to concerns about markets leading to greater inequality, land sale transactions made access to land in rural areas more equal, possibly because of broad initial landownership. The registry is also fully digitally linked to the National ID system, the mortgage registry, the valuation system, the building permitting system, and land-use control. Users can obtain information on any land parcel via SMS, and efforts to move toward paperless titling are under way (Akumuntu and Potel 2022).

While it demonstrates the viability of low-cost registration of rights at scale, Rwanda's experience also highlights the importance of regularly monitoring transaction volume to assess sustainability. Ali et al. (2021) use registry data to show great differences in the registration of subsequent transactions across regions and types of property: while 5.6 percent of registered residential parcels and 1.5 percent of agricultural parcels were transferred annually via registered sale in Kigali, the figures for the rest of the country were 0.3 percent for residential parcels and 0.06 percent for agricultural parcels. To assess whether this can be attributed to lower transaction volume or informal transactions, they conducted a nationwide survey of 100 rural villages in 2018. Results suggest that with 5.3 percent of rural parcels changing hands every year, most transactions are indeed informal, threatening to undermine registered landownership by women in particular.

As publicity campaigns and placement of sector land managers (SLMs) had already improved access to information and formal institutions,[50] fees and subdivision restrictions are a possible reason for such high levels of informality. Indeed, the flat registration fees charged are highly regressive: for the median rural land parcel, the fee required to register a transaction would be equivalent to 22.6 percent of property value, whereas for the median urban parcel in Kigali, it would be just 0.64 percent of property value. Of those who failed to register a transaction, 83 percent quoted high fees as the reason and indicated a willingness to pay of 2 to 4 percent of property value to do so.

Ali et al. (2021) explore alternative options for covering the registry's current operational costs in the short term. Their preferred option would combine three elements: (a) eliminating fees for registering transfers due to inheritance or marriage and exempting the 40 percent poorest landowners (who can be identified from a national database),[51] (b) keeping costs for urban parcels at the current level, and (c) reducing registration fees in rural areas to levels in line with respondents' willingness to pay. Implementing the associated resource transfers in a digital environment is simple and in the medium term, options to charge the private sector (for example, for mortgage registration) or other government departments for data access could also be considered.

One illustration of this potential is to link the land registry with data on lease property taxation: Ali, Deininger, and Goldstein (2014) compare the registry to the valuation roll to show that only one-third of nonexempt residential properties in urban Kigali paid lease fees, resulting in lost national revenue of some US$4.8 million. Using registry information for automatic billing would, with full payment, generate benefits that would allow the total cost of establishing the registry to be recouped in about 10 years. Moving to a 1 percent property tax on the value of land and buildings would not only avoid the regressive character of lease fees but also allow increasing property tax revenue to US$19.3 million—almost 10 times the current collection.

Spotlight 1.2: Gendered credit market effects of land registry reform and titling in Lesotho

The importance of regulatory reforms is illustrated by Deininger and Ali (2022) for the case of Lesotho. They use complete registry data from 1980 to 2019, rather than survey data, to analyze the short- and longer-term effects of a program to support comprehensive regulatory reform followed by titling that was implemented in 2010–13. Titling increased access to registered rights, especially by women, in the short term. Policy reform had, however, larger effects on activity and female participation in land and credit markets throughout and was a precondition for earlier legislation that made independent asset ownership by women possible to have any effect.

In Lesotho, women had very few rights until the 2006 Legal Capacity of Married Persons Act (LCMPA) removed the minority status of married women and the powers a husband had over the person and property of his wife, in a reform similar in scope to the demise of coverture in the United States in the 1850s (Hazan, Weiss, and Zoabi 2019). Building on the LCMPA, a land administration reform project (LARP) supported legal and regulatory reform through passage of the 2010 Land Act and the Land Administration Authority Act and associated regulations to reduce barriers to registering land rights by, for example, linking the registry and cadaster, simplifying workflows, and strengthening women's rights through a presumption of joint ownership for any property acquired in marriage under community of property. This was combined with a program of systematic first registration of rights.

Registry data from 1980 to 2019 provide three insights: First, regulatory reforms had a near-immediate effect by reducing processing time and increasing women's access to land. This suggests that land registry data can be used to provide real-time information on the effect of interventions related to land. Systematic use and dissemination of such data would make it possible to identify potential problems quickly so that, if needed, corrective action can be taken, thus greatly increasing the likelihood that interventions would achieve their targets sustainably.

Second, the time gap between passage of the LCMPA and the project intervention can help to identify whether legal change is enough to empower women. The LCMPA alone had virtually no impact on female co-ownership of land. However, regulatory changes that made co-ownership of land the default option for common-law marriages, the adjustment of workflows for systematic first registration to put such rights into practice by obtaining women's explicit consent, and dissemination events dramatically increased women's access to registered co-ownership. This effect also applied to land registered outside project areas and persisted after the project ended in 2013.

Finally, the fact that (sporadic) registrations took place outside the project area and after the project ended makes it possible to distinguish short- and medium-term effects and to separate the impact of titling from that of regulatory reform. In line with previous analyses, the study finds that LARP's main short-term impacts, especially for women, derive from systematic first registration of rights. At the same time, policy reform was instrumental to expand the number of registered mortgages and land sales, especially by female co-owners. In other words, without regulatory reform ahead of commencing systematic registration, neither sustainability of effects nor impacts on land sales and mortgage markets would have been ensured. In the medium term, the impact of policy reform on land and mortgage market activity was between 4 and 10 times more important than that of systematic titling because of differences in the characteristics of parcels targeted by the two programs.

Beyond highlighting the synergies between policy reform and titling, the importance of policy reforms, and the establishment of a sustainable registry before engaging in systematic (subsidized) registration of land rights, this example also shows that a focus on urban rather than rural areas may be more suitable to establish the basis for an effective and sustainable land registry.

Spotlight 1.3: Registration of rural land in Ethiopia

Motivated in part by the results of issuance of land-use certificates to some 630,000 households in Tigray in 1998–99, a nationwide effort issued land-use certificates to more than 6 million households (18 million plots) in 2003–05. The process started with local awareness campaigns, followed by election of land-use committees in each village. After these committees had been trained, with the assistance of elders as needed, they systematically resolved conflicts, referring cases that could not be settled locally to the courts. This was followed by demarcation and low-cost surveying of undisputed private plots and often also common resources in the presence of neighbors, and issuance of land-use certificates, which, for married couples, included the names and pictures of both spouses. The highly decentralized approach allowed the program to adapt to local conditions while still making rapid progress. National survey data make it clear that procedures were adhered to, implementation was not biased against the poor, and recipients appreciated their certificates (Deininger et al. 2008).

Several studies illustrate how the program activated rental markets, increased productivity, and empowered women both nationally and regionally. A four-period panel study from Amhara, where, unlike in other regions, rental markets can operate freely, allows use of a pipeline and a difference-in-differences approach to assess impacts of land certification there. It suggests that the program increased tenure security, land-related investment, and rental market participation, yielding benefits well above its cost (Deininger, Ali, and Alemu 2011). For Tigray, there is also evidence that certification enhanced participation in the land rental market of potential tenants and landlord households, especially those headed by women (Holden, Deininger, and Ghebru 2011); the marginal effect of certification on productivity was higher for households headed by women than those headed by men (Bezabih, Holden, and Mannberg 2016).

On investment and productivity effects, long panel data from the Tigray region illustrate the substantial positive impacts of certification on maintenance of soil conservation structures, investment in trees, and land productivity (Holden, Deininger, and Ghebru 2009). Nationally, households with land certificates were more likely to adopt soil fertility management strategies than households without certificates (Melesse and Bulte 2015). Access to secure property rights also seemed to encourage household take-up of agricultural development interventions such as chemical fertilizers, agricultural extension services, and sustainable land and water management (Adamie 2021).

Amplified by changes in the Family Code passed in 2000, land certification had positive impacts on women's rights and welfare (Kumar and Quisumbing 2015). Joint land certification was associated with increased spending on women's goods and higher food consumption and use of health care, indicative of strong female empowerment effects (Muchomba 2017). Survey data and field experiments support this conclusion; they indicate that joint land certification has significant impacts on women's empowerment, especially to assume roles outside the home (Melesse, Dabissa, and Bulte 2018), and some impact on education (Congdon Fors, Houngbedji, and Lindskog 2019).

Land records generated during certification included neighbors' names, but neither sketches nor coordinates of field boundaries provide a spatial reference. Concerns that this lack of spatial detail might compromise tenure security and investment prompted the launch of a program of second-level certification to add this information and move to computerized record management; this was done in 2014–20 at a cost of about US$6 per parcel (Zein 2021). The system is now operational in six regions and has been used by some 350 *woreda* (county) offices to register more than 750,000 transactions using a fully digital and auditable workflow that accounts for and enforces differences in regulatory frameworks across regions. Registry information is also increasingly used for analytical purposes (Holden and Tilahun 2020).

If regulatory issues regarding the dualism between rural and urban land administration institutions (Adam 2014) can be resolved, extending this system to cover urban areas would be straightforward and could greatly enhance benefits from second-stage certification. Doing so could also allow to explore options for cost recovery from user fees in urban areas, connecting directly to users' or service providers' mobile phones (to allow, for example, digital initiation of transactions or lodging of subdivision surveys), linking the land registry to the national ID system, and using the system as a basis for farmer-specific agricultural advice and public land management.

Spotlight 1.4: Impacts and sustainability challenges of land tenure formalization in Benin

In Benin, village boundaries were demarcated as part of drafting local land management plans to improve management of common resources and as a precondition for demarcation of individual parcels in 300 villages from 2008 to 2011. Random selection of villages avoids the selection issues that tend to affect evaluation of nationwide programs elsewhere and allows results from comparing treated and untreated groups to be interpreted as causal effects.[52] Using annual satellite data on forest loss and forest fires between 2000 and 2017 for treated villages and a 5-kilometer buffer surrounding them, Wren-Lewis, Becerra-Valbuena, and Houngbedji (2020) find evidence of program-induced reductions of tree cover loss of around 20 percent and of fires of approximately

5 percent because of the program. There is no evidence of spillovers or anticipatory deforestation.

Evidence from satellite imagery is supported by village surveys in 2011, shortly after the program ended, suggesting significant reductions of 14 percentage points in intervillage border conflicts, 9 percentage points in farmers clearing land for additional tillage, and 2 percentage points in the share of households reporting a border conflict. Trust in local institutions to resolve land disputes rose by 9 percentage points. In villages with communal or forest areas, the share with committees managing access to communal areas went up by 8 percentage points and to community forest rose by 6 percentage points. This suggests that clarifying and formalizing customary rights in rural land can be effective in reducing forest loss.

The program also systematically registered about 70,000 individual parcels. Because formalization had not yet been completed in 2011,[53] Goldstein et al. (2018), using household panel data from 2006 and 2011, found that demarcation increased perceived tenure security and investment in tree planting and fallowing, especially on female-managed plots. Although this suggests the program enhanced the security of groups such as women, whose rights had been weak, productivity was not affected; rather, the program significantly reduced yields for female-headed households.[54]

Exploring whether program-induced strengthening of land rights affected perceptions, a follow-up survey of close to 600 individuals in 43 treatment and control villages six years after the intervention suggests the program had no effect on incomes, education, credit access, migration, altruism, or the number of land disputes. It did, however, increase respect for abstract property rights and the rule of law, a result driven by the more commercially oriented southern part of the country (Fabbri and Dari-Mattiacci 2021).

At the same time, the program increased land conflicts over a period of 10 years (Arruñada, Fabbri, and Faure 2022), possibly because the land code it introduced prohibited any sale of a plot without a title (Lavigne Delville 2019), thereby impeding rather than encouraging land transfers. The project also did not increase trust in the "modern" institutions it supported: in both treatment and control villages, some 90 percent of respondents preferred traditional authorities to formal courts for resolving disputes—an attitude that may be partly explained by the belief, held by 84 percent of respondents, that only wealthy and powerful people can afford accessing formal courts to dispute rulings by traditional authorities unfavorable to them. Closely related, Fabbri (2021) finds that support for land markets and associated institutions did not increase in treatment villages generally and fell considerably in those that were more remote. In fact, the program seems to have increased support for a ban on land markets and for customary rather than modern institutions and norms, highlighting the continued importance of local institutions.[55]

One reason for limited impact seems to be lack of community involvement and outreach: at closing in 2013, the program had issued only some 5,000 of the expected 72,422 titles (Lavigne Delville 2019). Moreover, the land certificates issued under the project were abolished in 2017 and replaced with a legally similar document with a price between 7 and 15 times that of the earlier land certificates. The positive impacts of initial demarcation activities suggest that a focus on recognition and management of local use rights, to be upgraded if and when needed, might have been less costly and more sustainable in the long term.

Spotlight 1.5: Modalities and impacts of recognizing neo-customary land institutions in Mexico

Legal and institutional reforms to increase income in Mexico's *ejidos*—communities modeled on traditional indigenous institutions established by the country's 1917 land reform—that were decreed in the early 1990s illustrate one option for how traditional institutions and a modern land registry can be combined. The reform put all members of the general assembly in charge of choosing tenure regimes (purely communal, mixed communal/individual, or purely individual) for different parts of the ejidal land, facilitated land rental and contribution of ejido land to joint ventures with outsiders, but limited sales to members. It also allowed the assembly to make the transition to unrestricted individual property rights (*dominio pleno*), thus providing an exit option by moving to fully transferable and mortgageable individual rights. To make this operational, it was essential to formalize and strengthen self-governance by giving the ejido legal personality and establishing different organs of self-governance (the executive, the assembly, and an oversight committee), each with well-defined roles to separate powers within the ejido and clear decision-making procedures.

To accomplish this, three elements were key in 1998–2008:

(a) An ombudsman office (Procurador Agrario), supported by an agrarian justice structure in the states, was created to clear a backlog of land conflicts (more than 350,000 were resolved between 1992 and 1999), educate landowners about their rights, provide paralegal assistance, and process complaints about procedures.

(b) A standardized workflow was designed for certifying ejidos, and a voluntary certification program, Programa de Certificación de Derechos Ejidales y Titulación de Solares (PROCEDE), was rolled out nationally. By 2008, more than 98 percent of ejidos on an area of more than 100 million hectares had been certified by PROCEDE.

(c) Finally, to allow verification of property rights and subsequent land transactions, a central registry (RAN) was created with branches in each of the states.[56]

An interesting aspect of this reform is that more than a decade after certification had been completed, only about 9 percent of ejidos had opted to adopt dominio pleno; these were mostly located closer to cities, had higher incomes, were more literate, and relied on industry and services rather than agriculture for income (Ramírez-Álvarez 2019). This suggests that although it is important to have an option to end the communal property regime that can be exercised based on local conditions, for most locations, the benefits from moving to such a system would exceed the associated cost, even in an upper-middle-income country such as Mexico.

The literature identifies three impacts of the reform:

(a) By making land transfers legally possible and having a mechanism to register them, the program fostered structural transformation via outmigration and—through market-based consolidation—affected productivity. After getting a certificate, households were 28 percent more likely to have a member migrate, an effect that is stronger for those with more initial insecurity and below-average land quality and area due to land transferability rather than relaxation of credit constraints. The area cultivated remained almost unchanged, but land consolidation facilitated mechanization and higher productivity (de Janvry et al. 2015). The estimated program effects are particularly pronounced for international migration, where the program explains more than one-fourth of the increase in international emigrants from ejidos in the mid-1990s (Valsecchi 2014) and agricultural investment was increased (Dower and Pfutze 2013).

(b) In line with evidence that the power of the ruling party to allocate land before property reform served political ends at considerable economic cost (Albertus et al. 2016) and that secure rights to land will reduce the scope for clientelist networks to exercise political power,[57] reforms reduced electoral support for the ruling party (de Janvry, Gonzalez-Navarro, and Sadoulet 2014).

(c) Finally, by using political intervention to reduce the potential gains from violence, the reform reined in violence, as measured by the number of murders (Murphy and Rossi 2016). Immediate certification of all land in 1993 would have led to an estimated 12.8 percent reduction in homicides. The fact that this effect is present only in municipalities where the dominant party had never lost an election suggests that the reduction was driven entirely by reducing the power of political authorities to reallocate land rights (Castañeda Dower and Pfutze 2020).

Spotlight 1.6: Village land management in Tanzania

After significant debate (Shivji 1998) and with international support (McAuslan 2013), in 1999 Tanzania adopted two voluminous laws, the Land Act and the Village Land Act (VLA), which were hailed by observers at the time as among the most progressive pieces of legislation in Africa (Alden Wily 2003). Land was divided into general (urban) and village (rural) land. The former was fully transferable and mortgageable and to be titled, whereas the latter was to be managed at the village level based on demarcation of village boundaries supervised by elected village land committees (VLCs) with both genders represented equally. This was expected to be carried out after a simple, locally driven process of land-use planning to be overseen by the VLC and culminating in production of a village land-use plan (VLUP) and issuance of a CVL as a precondition for issuing Certificates of Customary Rights of Occupancy (CCROs) to individual owners.

In practice, the objective of securing tenure and improving land use was not achieved, for several reasons:

(a) Exacting planning and survey standards and extremely centralized manual processes for title issuance[58] made it nearly impossible to respond to high demand (and willingness to pay) for urban land titles and increase formalization, estimated at less than 30 percent even in the capital. Rather than reform the system, renewable residential licenses (RLs; originally valid for two years, then extended to five) were introduced to confirm occupancy in return for tax payment, although with less than 5 percent of RLs including a woman's name, without overcoming male bias (Kironde 2006). The low cost of these documents was matched by their quality; anecdotal evidence suggests that sometimes RLs were issued to tenants claiming ownership, procedures to register changes were never clearly defined, registry operation remained haphazard, and several banks were unable to foreclose on land pledged as security for loans on the basis of such documents (Kusiluka and Chiwambo 2019). Despite strong demand for formalization overall, there is virtually no interest in this type of document, even in low-income neighborhoods (Manara 2022).

(b) The VLA's participatory spirit was largely undermined by regulations mandating costly and complex procedures. For example, regulations for participatory village land-use planning, reinforced by the 2007 Land Use Planning Act, replaced the simple process envisaged by the VLA with a complex and elaborate process requiring external expertise, costly high-precision surveying of village boundaries, and established access to a dedicated registry building to store documents as a precondition to recognize village boundaries. More than a decade after the VLA had been passed, less than 10 percent of villages had a VLUP approved and were thus able to issue CCROs (Huggins 2018). The technocratic focus seems to have come at the cost of participation, especially limiting the scope for involving pastoralists, who were often not consulted in developing such plans, resulting in incorrect representation of their rights (Bergius et al. 2020).

(c) Despite the complex and costly process of elaborating VLUPs, surveying village boundaries, and issuing CVLs, the legal value of these documents was put in doubt by government pronouncements that such certificates would be valid only if land was "used" productively. Reports of the central government ignoring these rights and directly transferring registered village land it considered "unused" to investors in the Southern Agricultural Growth Corridor reduced confidence in such documents not only by villagers but also by investors (Bluwstein et al. 2018).[59]

(d) Not unlike in neighboring countries such as Uganda, where legislation intended to provide simpler alternatives to title, regulations for issuance of CCROs on village land are virtually undistinguishable from the process for issuing formal titles. This defeats the purpose as costs are reported to run up to hundreds of dollars in application fees, technician fees for plot surveys, "facilitation" costs to the village land committee and district land registrar, court registration fees, lawyers' fees and travel, and time requirements that can take months or years (Stein et al. 2016).

The possibility of having CCROs issued on demand rather than systematically village by village creates serious governance challenges as well-informed agents may try to appropriate large amounts of land in less than fully transparent or competitive ways, threatening village-level governance more broadly, a danger that will be particularly acute if the possibility of removing "unused" land from village control is upheld by the courts.

Notes

1 | Lawry et al. (2017) provide a summary of the literature, with earlier studies documenting the investment impacts of tenure security in Viet Nam (Do and Iyer 2008), Thailand (Feder et al. 1988), Nicaragua (Bandiera 2007), and Eastern Europe (Rozelle and Swinnen 2004).

2 | In Ethiopia, some types of trees are indeed used to demarcate borders and thus claim ownership rights (Deininger and Jin 2006), but in many other investments, most prominently investments in soil fertility, this does not apply.

3 | Although tenants may be less inclined to invest in leased land, this is not necessarily the case. For example, in Burkina Faso, the level of soil conservation investments or fallowing is found to be no different from that on own inherited land (Kusunose, Theriault, and Alia 2020).

4 | Hazan, Weiss, and Zoabi (2019) used the staggered demise of coverture across states in the United States to show that women's rights led to shifts in household portfolios, a positive shock to the supply of credit, and a reallocation of labor toward sectors other than agriculture and capital-intensive industries that deepened financial markets and promoted industrialization.

5 | Demographic and Health Survey data for 15 African countries show that there are only two countries (Rwanda and Senegal) where widows and their children inherit most of a deceased individual's assets, whereas in more than half the countries (Benin, the Democratic Republic of Congo, Guinea, Mali, Namibia, Niger, Nigeria, Sierra Leone, Tanzania, Uganda, Zambia, and Zimbabwe), widows report no inheritance of assets whatsoever.

6 | To cool the housing market, the country's Housing and Development Board increased the minimum occupation period for resale of apartments in the public housing market from three to five years, affecting public housing owners' home equity due to a prohibition on cash-out refinancing.

7 | Between 1995 and 2010, American Indian reservations in the United States either adopted secured transaction laws and filing systems from neighboring states or wrote their own laws and put in place registries. The intensity of night lights at reservation boundaries is used to argue that secure-transaction laws backed by registries helped foster economic activity (Dippel et al. 2021), but no difference in performance is found between reservations that adopted laws from neighboring states and those that drafted their own.

8 | Administrative data on property purchases by foreign companies in the United Kingdom suggest that the Common Reporting Standard (CRS) that required automatic reporting of cross-border flows for financial but not real estate assets led to a clear increase in real estate investments by companies incorporated in tax havens targeted by the policy. A quarter of the money that fled taxes after the CRS is estimated to have been invested in property, equivalent to between £16 billion and £19 billion of UK real estate purchases in 2013–16 (Jeanne and Le Guern Herry 2022).

9 | This effect is quantified for shale gas extraction from an Indian reservation on the Bakken shale reserve in the United States, where land parcels of different sizes can be owned privately (in trust or under fee simple), by tribes, or by the federal government. Leonard and Parker (2021) develop and estimate a transaction cost model in which the expected production from a parcel declines with the number of contracting parties, showing that undivided ownership increases productivity by about one-third.

10 | Defining group membership and establishing mechanisms to ensure accountability for resource use is not too difficult in the case of indigenous people's rights as existing arrangements can be drawn upon. It is for this reason that legal recognition of such groups and demarcation of their lands has long been argued to be an effective way to improve conservation outcomes (Ginsburg and Keene 2020).

11 | In Viet Nam, public good contributions are negatively affected by inequality, an effect that is particularly large in corrupt environments (Markussen et al. 2021).

12 | In the Russian Federation, the military draft for World War I dramatically reduced cultivated area. Communal tenure farms were more resilient as they reallocated labor in favor of the commune due to the increased attractiveness of its nonmarket access to land and social insurance (Dower and Markevich 2018).

13 | Zhao (2020) discusses and quantifies the trade-off between equity (in a system with periodic redistribution) and higher incomes under a system where such redistribution is not available for China. Montero (2022) discusses the same trade-off for land reform cooperatives in El Salvador.

14 | Traditional political institutions can be compatible with democracy and accountable to citizens if they use inclusive decision-making processes and leaders have strong nonelectoral connections to the communities they represent (Baldwin and Holzinger 2019).

15 | This mirrors findings showing that a higher wage attracts more-educated candidates who improve the efficiency of service delivery, an effect that seems to be driven more by selection of competent politicians rather than by the incentive to be re-elected (Gagliarducci and Nannicini 2013).

16 | The Framework and Guidelines on Land Policy was spearheaded by the Africa Land Policy Initiative, which brings together the African Union Commission, the United Nations Economic Commission, and the African Development Bank (see https://www.un.org/en/land-natural-resources-conflict /pdfs/35-EN-%20Land%20Policy%20Report_ENG%20181010pdf.pdf). The Food and Agriculture Organization's voluntary guidelines on responsible governance of tenure (https://www.fao.org/3 /i2801e/i2801e.pdf) build on this in reaffirming the importance of customary tenure.

17 | Empowering unaccountable local chiefs whose powers had been strengthened under apartheid rather than having them elected has been a major issue in South Africa (Ntsebeza 2004). The country's 2004 Communal Land Rights Act (CLARA) was heavily criticized for giving chiefs more powers over land than they had even in colonial times, undermining downward accountability and failing to address gross gender inequity (Claassens and Cousins 2009). When it was struck down by the country's High Court in 2010, no successor legislation was put in place.

18 | The importance of social norms is illustrated by regional differences. In traditionally settled forest areas, land "sales" are governed by traditional patterns. Pioneers on previously unsettled land can acquire full private rights; however, once inherited, these rights are interpreted according to the social norms prevalent in the rest of the country (Colin and Ayouz 2006).

19 | If their ability to access critical resources such as watering holes is respected, pastoralists use a range of strategies to cope with the disappearance of grazing lands in periurban areas (Moritz 2008).

20 | The tendency of customary institutions to limit women's property rights is not restricted to Africa: Casari and Lisciandra (2016) rely on data from inheritance contracts to show that from the thirteenth to nineteenth centuries, women's inheritance rights to common land in the Italian Alps were gradually

eroded to preserve the wealth of village insiders, affecting population growth, marriage strategies, and the ability to diversify risk.

21 | Bias against women's rights, however, is not inherent to all customary systems: in the case of nineteenth-century Bangkok, women's (documented) land-use rights were upheld in courts and triggered higher agricultural investment and living standards than for men (Chankrajang and Vechbanyongratana 2021).

22 | In both treatment and control villages, some 90 percent of respondents preferred traditional authorities to formal courts for resolving disputes—an attitude that may be partly explained by the belief, held by 84 percent of respondents, that only wealthy and powerful people can afford accessing formal courts to dispute rulings by traditional authorities unfavorable to them.

23 | By 2008, the voluntary Program for the Certification of Ejido Rights and Titling of House Plots (Programa de Certificación de Derechos Ejidales y Titulación de Solares [PROCEDE]) had certified 98 percent of ejidos with an area of more than 100 million hectares based on the request of communities.

24 | Only about 9 percent of ejidos, mostly located closer to cities and with higher incomes, levels of literacy, and reliance on industry and services rather than agriculture for income, exercised this right (Ramírez-Álvarez 2019). This contrasts with "on-demand" opportunities for exit by individuals via private titling that is practiced in many African countries, which hollow out the system from within and tend to give rise to rent seeking and may foster inequality.

25 | In Thailand, incomplete and uneven adoption of the Torrens system is argued to have increased rather than reduced tenure insecurity and conflict (Vechbanyongratana and Niwatananun 2020).

26 | Basnyat et al. (2018) document a similar process of "legal-sounding re-centralization" that shifted control from local user groups in Nepal by requiring regular revisions of community forest management plans. Although new plans were virtually identical to existing ones because stipulated scientific standards or participatory processes were often not applied, it empowered bureaucrats who oversaw the process or acted as consultants.

27 | Key factors are (a) doubts about coverage, particularly regarding forestlands and gender provisions that may require legal review (Mwathane et al. 2022) or even judicial inquiry of the constitution (Alden Wily 2018b); (b) unclear, overlapping institutional responsibilities; and (c) lack of costed procedures and reliance on a demand-driven approach that requires a level of organizational and financial capacity beyond the reach of most communities and makes implementation dependent on donor funding.

28 | Such protection is based on either a document lodged for registration and a way to prioritize among documents (often based on the time of registration) in a system of deeds or a search by the registrar at the point of registration (in a title registration system). See Arruñada and Garoupa (2005) for a conceptual comparison and economic evaluation of different registration systems and Arruñada (2012) for the importance of registries for impersonal exchange with third parties.

29 | The way in which land is demarcated will affect the transaction cost of land assembly and land-use change (Dippel, Frye, and Leonard 2020). For the United States, having land demarcated in a predictable rectangular pattern has been shown to increase land values and reduce the incidence of land disputes over long time horizons (Libecap and Lueck 2011).

30 | Historically, state capacity often explained differences in map accuracy as documented for different states in modern-day South Africa (Dimitruk, Du Plessis, and Du Plessis 2021).

31 | Owners who think that the benefits from having a professional survey done exceed the cost—or who like to have surveyors or other officials emplace permanent boundary markers on their property—can always do so at their own cost.

32 | The survey profession has equally recognized the need for "fit-for-purpose" survey standards (Enemark et al. 2014).

33 | Although some of the associated tasks can be subcontracted to the private sector, determination of rights is a judicial process that requires the public sector to take responsibility for the results and thus cannot be delegated.

34 | A negative effect of homesteading on modern land use cannot be explained by land quality, title details, or unobserved settler characteristics, suggesting that how land was settled created a path dependence in land-use decisions for homesteads despite equivalent legal rights.

35 | Although few male owners had planned to include their spouses on the title originally, the response to nudges via awareness raising, complemented by small price discounts to include women as co-owners, was high.

36 | Even after paying this amount, less than half of those interested could get title within two years, suggesting that bureaucratic supply-side constraints may be as or even more important and binding than price and reinforcing the need for regulatory reform to improve access to titles.

37 | Lack of attention to costs for subsequent registration impeded broad coverage in the Philippines (Maurer and Iyer 2008) and is also reported from Jamaica (Barnes and Griffith-Charles 2007).

38 | As table 1.2 illustrates, the share of owners ranges from 43 percent in Togo and Côte d'Ivoire to 83 percent in Chad and 81 percent in Niger.

39 | ACLED data are available publicly at http://www.acleddata.com, for a total of 281,311 violent conflicts (defined as involving at least one fatality) in Africa between January 1, 1997, and May 27, 2022. They provide information on reason, location, and number of fatalities. See Raleigh et al. (2010) for a more detailed description.

40 | Here, a violent conflict is classified as land related if the event description includes "land" but not "landmines" or "landed" and as resource related if the description includes "farm," "crop," "harvest," "pastoral," "livestock," "grazing," "pasture," "cattle," or "cow." This provides a total of 4,110 violent clashes over land and 11,891 clashes over natural resources, with an overlap of 705.

41 | Here, the share is used to account for the fact that, because of better access to social media, the number of violent conflicts reported in the ACLED data increased dramatically between 2007–12 and 2017–22.

42 | Consistent with evidence on ambiguous effects of legal reforms not backed by regulation in patriarchal societies such as India (Anderson and Genicot 2015) or Pakistan (Beg et al. 2021), the 2006 law alone did not affect women's access to registered land rights.

43 | Both self-registration and presumptive titles can be used in this context, as illustrated by the example of *Terra Legal*.

44 | It has been argued that in Peru, urban titling programs can be self-financing if, instead of high up-front fees that credit-constrained households cannot afford, a small fraction of the associated increases in land values is captured ex post via land taxes (Hawley, Miranda, and Sawyer 2018).

45 | In India, computerization of legacy records was implemented entirely via subcontracting over a decade ago (Deininger 2007). An ambitious scheme (Survey of Villages Abadi and Mapping with Improvised Technology in Village Areas) to collect the information needed to issue landownership documents to all rural residential areas nationwide (https://svamitva.nic.in/svamitva/index.html) is also contracted out to private-sector service providers.

46 | The "Registering Property" indicator under the World Bank's Doing Business project has collected information on indicators of registry quality as part of a Land Administration Quality Index since 2015. Although lack of granularity, together with the limited number of large policy changes, limits use of the data to the cross section, studies linked these data to overall economic growth (D'Arcy, Nistotskaya, and Olsson 2021) and urban form (Djankov et al. 2021).

47 | Indicators of regulatory quality can be complemented with opinion surveys such as Afrobarometer or Prindex for a subjective assessment that also highlights distributional issues associated with land policy reform. Comparing survey-based indicators to information on perceived security of rights and actual documentation points toward enormous differences (Huntington and Stevens 2023) that are attributable to differences in sampling (Ali, Deininger, et al. 2019) and often limited awareness by households of the difference between formal and informal certificates.

48 | See https://openknowledge.worldbank.org/server/api/core/bitstreams/fe30d845-4dac-56d8-b69a -c20b1f437e12/content.

49 | Advances in technology and smartphone penetration since 2013 would allow further streamlining of this process and reduce cost, for example, by eliminating the digitization phase and complementing the objection and correction process based on physical display of paper maps with an app-based one.

50 | Ali, Deininger, and Duponchel (2017) use the phased rollout of SLM placement to show that having an SLM installed in a sector significantly increased the level of registered land transactions.

51 | If proposals to establish interoperability between the land registry, the national ID database, and the court registry were implemented, it would be possible to effect such registrations in a way that is fully integrated into the workflows associated with these life events.

52 | Villages to be treated were randomly selected from 576 applicant villages—1,543 targeted villages, of which 1,235 applied for the program—that met the participation criteria. Of course, the deforestation analysis could be done for the entire sample.

53 | As such formalization is costly (with rates varying across local governments), it is unclear how much formalization will actually result from the project. Lavigne Delville (2019) discusses some of the broader challenges and institutional changes of titling in the context of Benin's land policy.

54 | Goldstein et al. (2018) explain this as indicating that women respond to exogenous tenure security changes by shifting investment away from relatively secure, demarcated land toward less secure land outside the village (not demarcated under the program), although bias against female-headed households may also be an issue as border security effects are less pronounced for these.

55 | The two hypothetical situations presented involved a challenge to customary norms by a villager either wanting to transfer land outside the village or to sell land with a sitting tenant. In both cases, the coefficient on banning the land market is positive and statistically significant at 1 percent for more remote treated villages and positive but insignificant overall or in a subsample of less remote villages. See table 3 in Fabbri (2021) for details.

56 | The Registro Agrario Nacional issues certificates documenting a household's entitlement to its habitation plots, agricultural parcels, and *certificados de derecho al uso comun* documenting a household's right to the proportional use of common lands in case the assembly has decided in favor of common use and titles for dominio pleno by individuals in ejidos who adopt it.

57 | Larreguy, Marshall, and Trucco (2018) use Mexico's urban land titling program implemented by CORETT (Comisión para la Regularización de la Tenencia de la Tierra) to illustrate the trade-off faced by incumbents who are likely to reap political rewards from implementing land titling but at the same time also risk the breakdown of clientelist ties, noting that titling reforms are most likely to be chosen by incumbents who risk losing power.

58 | See Sundet (2004) for a detailed critique of the Land Act and the Village Land Act, including a discussion of how discretionary powers by the Ministry of Land, Housing, and Human Settlements Development impeded land market operation.

59 | Defining "productive use" is particularly difficult where pastoralism and shifting cultivation are practiced (Blache 2019).

References

Aberra, A., and M. Chemin. 2021. "Does Legal Representation Increase Investment? Evidence from a Field Experiment in Kenya." *Journal of Development Economics* 150: 102612.

Acemoglu, D., T. Reed, and J. A. Robinson. 2014. "Chiefs: Economic Development and Elite Control of Civil Society in Sierra Leone." *Journal of Political Economy* 122 (2): 319–68.

Adam, A. G. 2014. "Land Tenure in the Changing Peri-Urban Areas of Ethiopia: The Case of Bahir Dar City." *International Journal of Urban and Regional Research* 38 (6): 1970–84.

Adam, J. N., T. Adams, and J.-D. Gerber. 2021. "The Politics of Decentralization: Competition in Land Administration and Management in Ghana." *Land* 10 (9): 948.

Adamie, B. A. 2021. "Land Property Rights and Household Take-Up of Development Programs: Evidence from Land Certification Program in Ethiopia." *World Development* 147: 105626.

Agarwal, S., and W. Qian. 2017. "Access to Home Equity and Consumption: Evidence from a Policy Experiment." *Review of Economics and Statistics* 99 (1): 40–52.

Agyei-Holmes, A., N. Buehren, M. Goldstein, R. Osei, I. Osei-Akoto, and C. Udry. 2020. "The Effects of Land Title Registration on Tenure Security, Investment and the Allocation of Productive Resources: Evidence from Ghana." Policy Research Working Paper 9376, World Bank, Washington, DC.

Ahlfeldt, G., P. Koutroumpis, and T. Valletti. 2017. "Speed 2.0: Evaluating Access to Universal Digital Highways." *Journal of the European Economic Association* 15 (3): 586–625.

Akumuntu, A., and J. Potel. 2022. "Electronic Land Titling (E-Titling) in Land Administration and Economic Ecosystems in Rwanda." *African Journal on Land Policy and Geospatial Sciences* 5 (4): 832–47.

Albertus, M., A. Diaz-Cayeros, B. Magaloni, and B. R. Weingast. 2016. "Authoritarian Survival and Poverty Traps: Land Reform in Mexico." *World Development* 77: 154–70.

Aldashev, G., I. Chaara, J. P. Platteau, and Z. Wahhaj. 2012. "Using the Law to Change the Custom." *Journal of Development Economics* 97 (2): 182–200.

Alden Wily, L. 2003. "Community-Based Land Tenure Management: Questions and Answers about Tanzania's New Village Land Act, 1999." IIED Issue Paper 120, International Institute for Environment and Development, London.

Alden Wily, L. 2018a. "Collective Land Ownership in the 21st Century: Overview of Global Trends." *Land* 7 (2): 68.

Alden Wily, L. 2018b. "The Community Land Act in Kenya: Opportunities and Challenges for Communities." *Land* 7 (1): 12.

Alden Wily, L. 2018c. "Risks to the Sanctity of Community Lands in Kenya: A Critical Assessment of New Legislation with Reference to Forestlands." *Land Use Policy* 75: 661–72.

Ali, D. A., M. Collin, K. Deininger, S. Dercon, J. Sandefur, and A. Zeitlin. 2016. "Small Price Incentives Increase Women's Access to Land Titles in Tanzania." *Journal of Development Economics* 123 (C): 107–22.

Ali, D. A., and K. Deininger. 2022. "Institutional Determinants of Large Land-Based Investments' Performance in Zambia: Does Title Enhance Productivity and Structural Transformation?" *World Development* 157 (6): 105932.

Ali, D. A., and K. Deininger. 2024. "Using Registry Data to Assess Gender-Differentiated Land and Credit Market Effects of Urban Land Policy Reform: Evidence from Lesotho." *World Development* 175: 106478.

Ali, D. A., K. Deininger, and M. Duponchel. 2017. "New Ways to Assess and Enhance Land Registry Sustainability: Evidence from Rwanda." *World Development* 99: 377–94.

Ali, D. A., K. Deininger, and M. Goldstein. 2014. "Environmental and Gender Impacts of Land Tenure Regularization in Africa: Pilot Evidence from Rwanda." *Journal of Development Economics* 110: 262–75.

Ali, D. A., K. Deininger, M. Goldstein, and E. La Ferrara. 2015. "Investment and Market Impacts of Land Tenure Regularization in Rwanda." Policy research paper, World Bank, Washington, DC.

Ali, D. A., K. Deininger, T. Hilhorst, F. Kakungu, and Y. Yi. 2019. "Making Secure Land Tenure Count for Global Development Goals and National Policy: Evidence from Zambia." Policy Research Working Paper 8912, World Bank, Washington, DC.

Ali, D. A., K. Deininger, and N. Kemper. 2022. "Pronatal Property Rights over Land and Fertility Outcomes: Evidence from a Natural Experiment in Ethiopia." *Journal of Development Studies* 58 (5): 951–67.

Ali, D. A., K. Deininger, G. Mahofa, and R. Nyakulama. 2021. "Sustaining Land Registration Benefits by Addressing the Challenges of Reversion to Informality in Rwanda." *Land Use Policy* 110: 104317.

Ali, M., O.-H. Fjeldstad, B. Jiang, and A. B. Shifa. 2019. "Colonial Legacy, State-Building and the Salience of Ethnicity in Sub-Saharan Africa." *Economic Journal* 129 (619): 1048–81.

Ali, M., O.-H. Fjeldstad, and A. B. Shifa. 2020. "European Colonization and the Corruption of Local Elites: The Case of Chiefs in Africa." *Journal of Economic Behavior and Organization* 179: 80–100.

Allen, D. W., and B. Leonard. 2021. "Property Right Acquisition and Path Dependence: Nineteenth-Century Land Policy and Modern Economic Outcomes." *Economic Journal* 131 (640): 3073–102.

Alstadsæter, A., and A. Økland. 2022. "Hidden in Plain Sight: Offshore Ownership of Norwegian Real Estate." Norwegian University of Life Sciences, Ås, Norway.

Alston, E., and S. M. Smith. 2022. "Development Derailed: Policy Uncertainty and Coordinated Investment." *Journal of Law and Economics* 65 (1): 39–76.

Anderson, S., and G. Genicot. 2015. "Suicide and Property Rights in India." *Journal of Development Economics* 114: 64–78.

Andersson Djurfeldt, A. 2020. "Gendered Land Rights, Legal Reform and Social Norms in the Context of Land Fragmentation: A Review of the Literature for Kenya, Rwanda and Uganda." *Land Use Policy* 90: 104305.

Andolfatto, D. 2002. "A Theory of Inalienable Property Rights." *Journal of Political Economy* 110 (2): 382–93.

Andre, C., and J. P. Platteau. 1998. "Land Relations under Unbearable Stress: Rwanda Caught in the Malthusian Trap." *Journal of Economic Behavior and Organization* 34 (1): 1–47.

Aragón, F. M., O. Molina, and I. W. Outes-León. 2020. "Property Rights and Risk Aversion: Evidence from a Titling Program." *World Development* 134: 105020.

Arruñada, B. 2003. "Property Enforcement as Organized Consent." *Journal of Law, Economics, and Organization* 19 (2): 401–44.

Arruñada, B. 2007. "Pitfalls to Avoid When Measuring Institutions: Is Doing Business Damaging Business?" *Journal of Comparative Economics* 35 (4): 729–47.

Arruñada, B. 2012. *Institutional Foundations of Impersonal Exchange: Theory and Policy of Contractual Registries.* Chicago: University of Chicago Press.

Arruñada, B. 2018. "Evolving Practice in Land Demarcation." *Land Use Policy* 77: 661–75.

Arruñada, B., M. Fabbri, and M. Faure. 2022. "Land Titling and Litigation." *Journal of Law and Economics* 65 (1): 131–56.

Arruñada, B., and N. Garoupa. 2005. "The Choice of Titling System in Land." *Journal of Law and Economics* 48 (2): 709–27.

Arrunada, B., G. Zanarone, and N. Garoupa. 2019. "Property Rights in Sequential Exchange." *Journal of Law, Economics, and Organization* 35 (1): 127–53.

Atalay, K., and R. Edwards. 2022. "House Prices, Housing Wealth and Financial Well-Being." *Journal of Urban Economics* 129: 103438.

Atwood, D. A. 1990. "Land Registration in Africa: The Impact on Agricultural Production." *World Development* 18 (5): 659–71.

Balan, P., A. Bergeron, G. Tourek, and J. Weigel. 2020. "Land Formalization in Weak States: Experimental Evidence from Urban Property Titling in the D.R. Congo." Working paper, Harvard University, Cambridge, MA.

Baland, J.-M., P. Bardhan, S. Das, and D. Mookherjee. 2010. "Forests to the People: Decentralization and Forest Degradation in the Indian Himalayas." *World Development* 38 (11): 1642–56.

Baland, J. M., and P. Francois. 2005. "Commons as Insurance and the Welfare Impact of Privatization." *Journal of Public Economics* 89 (2–3): 211–31.

Baland, J.-M., F. Gaspart, J. P. Platteau, and F. Place. 2007. "The Distributive Impact of Land Markets in Uganda." *Economic Development and Cultural Change* 55 (2): 283–311.

Baldwin, K. 2018. "Elected MPs, Traditional Chiefs, and Local Public Goods: Evidence on the Role of Leaders in Co-production from Rural Zambia." *Comparative Political Studies* 52 (12): 1925–56.

Baldwin, K., and K. Holzinger. 2019. "Traditional Political Institutions and Democracy: Reassessing Their Compatibility and Accountability." *Comparative Political Studies* 52 (12): 1747–74.

Bambio, Y., and S. Bouayad Agha. 2018. "Land Tenure Security and Investment: Does Strength of Land Right Really Matter in Rural Burkina Faso?" *World Development* 111: 130–47.

Bandiera, O. 2007. "Land Tenure, Investment Incentives, and the Choice of Techniques: Evidence from Nicaragua." *World Bank Economic Review* 21 (3): 487–508.

Baragwanath, K., and E. Bayi. 2020. "Collective Property Rights Reduce Deforestation in the Brazilian Amazon." *Proceedings of the National Academy of Sciences* 117 (34): 20495.

Barnes, G., and C. Griffith-Charles. 2007. "Assessing the Formal Land Market and Deformalization of Property in St. Lucia." *Land Use Policy* 24 (2): 494–501.

Basnyat, B., T. Treue, R. K. Pokharel, L. N. Lamsal, and S. Rayamajhi. 2018. "Legal-Sounding Bureaucratic Re-centralisation of Community Forestry in Nepal." *Forest Policy and Economics* 91: 5–18.

Basurto, M. P., P. Dupas, and J. Robinson. 2020. "Decentralization and Efficiency of Subsidy Targeting: Evidence from Chiefs in Rural Malawi." *Journal of Public Economics* 185: 104047.

Beck, U., and B. Bjerge. 2017. "Pro-Poor Land Transfers and the Importance of Land Abundance and Ethnicity in The Gambia." *World Development* 99: 122–40.

Beck, U., B. Bjerge, and M. Fafchamps. 2019. "The Role of Social Ties in Factor Allocation." *World Bank Economic Review* 33 (3): 598–621.

Beg, S. 2022. "Digitization and Development: Property Rights Security, and Land and Labor Markets." *Journal of the European Economic Association* 20 (1): 395–429.

Beg, S., E. Field, J. Lebow, and K. Vyborny. 2021. "Identity-Verified Land Records and Female Access to Land and Inheritance." Working paper, Duke University, Chapel Hill, NC.

Behrer, A. P., E. L. Glaeser, G. A. M. Ponzetto, and A. Shleifer. 2021. "Securing Property Rights." *Journal of Political Economy* 129 (4): 1157–92.

Bellemare, M. F. 2013. "The Productivity Impacts of Formal and Informal Land Rights: Evidence from Madagascar." *Land Economics* 89 (2): 272–90.

Ben-Shahar, D., and R. Golan. 2019. "Improved Information Shock and Price Dispersion: A Natural Experiment in the Housing Market." *Journal of Urban Economics* 112: 70–84.

Benami, E., and M. R. Carter. 2021. "Can Digital Technologies Reshape Rural Microfinance? Implications for Savings, Credit, and Insurance." *Applied Economic Perspectives and Policy* 43 (4): 1196–220.

Benjaminsen, T. A., and E. Sjaastad. 2002. "Race for the Prize: Land Transactions and Rent Appropriation in the Malian Cotton Zone." *European Journal of Development Research* 14 (2): 129–52.

Bergius, M., T. A. Benjaminsen, F. Maganga, and H. Buhaug. 2020. "Green Economy, Degradation Narratives, and Land-Use Conflicts in Tanzania." *World Development* 129: 104850.

Besley, T. 1995. "Property Rights and Investment Incentives: Theory and Evidence from Ghana." *Journal of Political Economy* 103 (5): 903–37.

Besley, T., E. Ilzetzki, and T. Persson. 2013. "Weak States and Steady States: The Dynamics of Fiscal Capacity." *American Economic Journal: Macroeconomics* 5 (4): 205–35.

Besley, T., and T. Persson. 2009. "The Origins of State Capacity: Property Rights, Taxation, and Politics." *American Economic Review* 99 (4): 1218–44.

Bezabih, M., S. Holden, and A. Mannberg. 2016. "The Role of Land Certification in Reducing Gaps in Productivity between Male- and Female-Owned Farms in Rural Ethiopia." *Journal of Development Studies* 52 (3): 360–76.

Bezu, S., and S. Holden. 2014. "Demand for Second-Stage Land Certification in Ethiopia: Evidence from Household Panel Data." *Land Use Policy* 41: 193–205.

Bieri, D. S., N. V. Kuminoff, and J. C. Pope. 2023. "National Expenditures on Local Amenities." *Journal of Environmental Economics and Management* 117: 102717.

Blache, A. 2019. "Grabbing Land, Catching Votes! Land and the 2015 Election Campaign in Kilombero District, Tanzania." *Les Cahiers d'Afrique de l'Est* 53. https://doi.org/10.4000/eastafrica.791.

Blackman, A., L. Corral, E. S. Lima, and G. P. Asner. 2017. "Titling Indigenous Communities Protects Forests in the Peruvian Amazon." *Proceedings of the National Academy of Sciences* 114 (16): 4123.

Blanco, H., and L. Neri. 2022. "Knocking It Down and Mixing It Up: Spillover Effects of Public Housing Regenerations." IZA Discussion Paper No. 15855, Institute of Labor Economics, Bonn, Germany.

Bluwstein, J., J. F. Lund, K. Askew, H. Stein, C. Noe, R. Odgaard, F. Maganga, and L. Engström. 2018. "Between Dependence and Deprivation: The Interlocking Nature of Land Alienation in Tanzania." *Journal of Agrarian Change* 18 (4): 806–830.

Boone, C. 2017. "Sons of the Soil Conflict in Africa: Institutional Determinants of Ethnic Conflict over Land." *World Development* 96: 276–93.

Boone, C., A. Dyzenhaus, A. Manji, C. W. Gateri, S. Ouma, J. K. Owino, A. Gargule, and J. M. Klopp. 2019. "Land Law Reform in Kenya: Devolution, Veto Players, and the Limits of an Institutional Fix." *African Affairs* 118 (471): 215–37.

Bosker, M., H. Garretsen, G. Marlet, and C. V. Woerkens. 2019. "Nether Lands: Evidence on the Price and Perception of Rare Natural Disasters." *Journal of the European Economic Association* 17 (2): 413–53.

Brasselle, A. S., F. Gaspart, and J. P. Platteau. 2002. "Land Tenure Security and Investment Incentives: Puzzling Evidence from Burkina Faso." *Journal of Development Economics* 67 (2): 373–418.

Brixiova, Z., T. Kangoye, and F. Tregenna. 2020. "Enterprising Women in Southern Africa: When Does Land Ownership Matter?" *Journal of Family and Economic Issues* 41 (1): 37–51.

Bros, C., A. Desdoigts, and H. Kouadio. 2019. "Land Tenure Insecurity as an Investment Incentive: The Case of Migrant Cocoa Farmers and Settlers in Ivory Coast." *Journal of African Economies* 28 (2): 147–75.

Bruce, J. W., and A. Knox. 2009. "Structures and Stratagems: Making Decentralization of Authority over Land in Africa Cost-Effective." *World Development* 37 (8): 1360–9.

Bruce, J. W., and S. E. Migot-Adholla. 1994. *Searching for Land Tenure Security in Africa.* Dubuque, IA: Kendall/Hunt Publishers.

Brummet, Q., D. Flanagan-Doyle, J. Mitchell, J. Voorheis, L. Erhard, and B. McBride. 2018. "What Can Administrative Tax Information Tell Us about Income Measurement in Household Surveys? Evidence from the Consumer Expenditure Surveys." *Statistical Journal of the IAOS* 34 (4): 513–20.

Bu, D., and Y. Liao. 2022. "Land Property Rights and Rural Enterprise Growth: Evidence from Land Titling Reform in China." *Journal of Development Economics* 157: 102853.

Bubb, R. 2013. "The Evolution of Property Rights: State Law or Informal Norms?" *Journal of Law and Economics* 56 (3): 555–94.

Bühler, M. 2023. "On the Other Side of the Fence: Property Rights and Productivity in the United States." *Journal of the European Economic Association* 21 (1): 93–134.

Burns, T. 2007. "Land Administration Reform: Indicators of Success and Future Challenges." Agriculture and Rural Development Discussion Paper 37, World Bank, Washington, DC.

Carter, M. R., and P. Olinto. 2003. "Getting Institutions 'Right' for Whom? Credit Constraints and the Impact of Property Rights on the Quantity and Composition of Investment." *American Journal of Agricultural Economics* 85 (1): 173–86.

Casari, M., and M. Lisciandra. 2016. "Gender Discrimination in Property Rights: Six Centuries of Commons Governance in the Alps." *Journal of Economic History* 76 (2): 559–94.

Casas-Arce, P., and A. Saiz. 2010. "Owning versus Renting: Do Courts Matter?" *Journal of Law and Economics* 53 (1): 137–65.

Casey, K., R. Glennerster, E. Miguel, and M. Voors. 2019. "Skill versus Voice in Local Development." Research paper, Graduate School of Business, Stanford University.

Castañeda Dower, P., and T. Pfutze. 2020. "Land Titles and Violent Conflict in Rural Mexico." *Journal of Development Economics* 144: 102431.

Chakrabarti, A. 2018. "Female Land Ownership and Fertility in Nepal." *Journal of Development Studies* 54 (9): 1698–715.

Chamberlin, J., and J. Ricker-Gilbert. 2016. "Participation in Rural Land Rental Markets in Sub-Saharan Africa: Who Benefits and by How Much? Evidence from Malawi and Zambia." *American Journal of Agricultural Economics* 98 (5): 1507–28.

Chang, Z., and X. Li. 2021. "How Regulation on Environmental Information Disclosure Affects Brownfield Prices in China: A Difference-in-Differences (DID) Analysis." *Journal of Environmental Planning and Management* 64 (2): 308–33.

Chankrajang, T. 2015. "Partial Land Rights and Agricultural Outcomes: Evidence from Thailand." *Land Economics* 91 (1): 126–48.

Chankrajang, T., and J. Vechbanyongratana. 2021. "Land, Ladies, and the Law: A Case Study on Women's Land Rights and Welfare in Southeast Asia in the Nineteenth Century." *Economic History Review* 74 (1): 138–63.

Chen, C., D. Restuccia, and R. Santaeulàlia-Llopis. 2022. "The Effects of Land Markets on Resource Allocation and Agricultural Productivity." *Review of Economic Dynamics* 45: 41–54.

Chikaya-Banda, J., and D. Chilonga. 2021. "Key Challenges to Advancing Land Tenure Security through Land Governance in Malawi: Impact of Land Reform Processes on Implementation Efforts." *Land Use Policy* 110: 104994.

Chimhowu, A. 2019. "The 'New' African Customary Land Tenure: Characteristic, Features and Policy Implications of a New Paradigm." *Land Use Policy* 81: 897–903.

Chimhowu, A., and P. Woodhouse. 2005. "Vernacular Land Markets and the Changing Face of Customary Land Tenure in Africa." *Forum for Development Studies* 32 (2): 385–414.

Claassens, A., and B. Cousins. 2009. *Land, Power and Custom: Controversies Generated by South Africa's Communal Land Rights Act.* Athens, OH: Ohio University Press.

Cochrane, L., and S. Hadis. 2019. "Functionality of the Land Certification Program in Ethiopia: Exploratory Evaluation of the Processes of Updating Certificates." *Land* 8 (10): 149.

Colin, J.-P. 2013. "Securing Rural Land Transactions in Africa: An Ivorian Perspective." *Land Use Policy* 31: 430–40.

Colin, J.-P., and M. Ayouz. 2006. "The Development of a Land Market? Insights from Côte d'Ivoire." *Land Economics* 82 (3): 404–23.

Congdon Fors, H., K. Houngbedji, and A. Lindskog. 2019. "Land Certification and Schooling in Rural Ethiopia." *World Development* 115: 190–208.

Coulomb, R., and Y. Zylberberg. 2021. "Environmental Risk and the Anchoring Role of Mobility Rigidities." *Journal of the Association of Environmental and Resource Economists* 8 (3): 509–42.

Csillik, O., P. Kumar, J. Mascaro, T. O'Shea, and G. P. Asner. 2019. "Monitoring Tropical Forest Carbon Stocks and Emissions Using Planet Satellite Data." *Scientific Reports* 9 (1): 17831.

Daley, E., R. Dore-Weeks, and C. Umuhoza. 2010. "Ahead of the Game: Land Tenure Reform in Rwanda and the Process of Securing Women's Land Rights." *Journal of Eastern African Studies* 4 (1): 131–52.

D'Arcy, M., and M. Nistotskaya. 2019. "Intensified Local Grievances, Enduring National Control: The Politics of Land in the 2017 Kenyan Elections." *Journal of Eastern African Studies* 13 (2): 294–312.

D'Arcy, M., M. Nistotskaya, and O. Olsson. 2021. *Land Property Rights, Cadasters and Economic Growth: A Cross-Country Panel 1000–2015 CE,* University of Gothenburg, Gothenburg, Sweden.

de Haas, M. 2022. "Reconstructing Income Inequality in a Colonial Cash Crop Economy: Five Social Tables for Uganda, 1925–1965." *European Review of Economic History* 26 (2): 255–83.

de Janvry, A., K. Emerick, M. Gonzalez-Navarro, and E. Sadoulet. 2015. "Delinking Land Rights from Land Use: Certification and Migration in Mexico." *American Economic Review* 105 (10): 3125–49.

de Janvry, A., M. Gonzalez-Navarro, and E. Sadoulet. 2014. "Are Land Reforms Granting Complete Property Rights Politically Risky? Electoral Outcomes of Mexico's Certification Program." *Journal of Development Economics* 110: 216–25.

de Kadt, D., and H. A. Larreguy. 2018. "Agents of the Regime? Traditional Leaders and Electoral Politics in South Africa." *Journal of Politics* 80 (2): 382–99.

De Meza, D., and J. Gould. 1992. "The Social Efficiency of Private Decisions to Enforce Property Rights." *Journal of Political Economy* 100 (3): 561–80.

de Soto, H. 2000. *The Mystery of Capital: Why Capitalism Triumphs in the West and Fails Everywhere Else.* New York: Basic Books.

Deininger, K. 2007. *India: Land Policies for Growth and Poverty Reduction.* New Delhi: Oxford University Press and World Bank South Asia Region.

Deininger, K. 2023. "Through the Maze of Land Rights Laws: Discussion." In *State and Business in Tanzania's Development: An Institutional Diagnostic,* edited by F. Bourguignon and S. M. Wangwe, 257–61. Cambridge, UK: Cambridge University Press.

Deininger, K., and D. A. Ali. 2022. "How Urban Land Titling and Registry Reform Affect Land and Credit Markets: Evidence from Lesotho." Policy Research Working Paper 10043, World Bank, Washington, DC.

Deininger, K., D. A. Ali, and T. Alemu. 2011. "Impacts of Land Certification on Tenure Security, Investment, and Land Market Participation: Evidence from Ethiopia." *Land Economics* 87 (2): 312–34.

Deininger, K., D. A. Ali, S. Holden, and J. Zevenbergen. 2008. "Rural Land Certification in Ethiopia: Process, Initial Impact, and Implications for Other African Countries." *World Development* 36 (10): 1786–812.

Deininger, K., D. A. Ali, and R. Neyter. 2022. "Impacts of Transparent Online Auctions on Public Land Lease Revenue: Evidence from Legal and Administrative Changes in Ukraine." Policy Research Working Paper 10201, World Bank, Washington, DC.

Deininger, K., and R. Castagnini. 2006. "Incidence and Impact of Land Conflict in Uganda." *Journal of Economic Behavior and Organization* 60 (3): 321–45.

Deininger, K., and A. Goyal. 2012. "Going Digital: Credit Effects of Land Registry Computerization in India." *Journal of Development Economics* 99 (2): 236–43.

Deininger, K., and S. Jin. 2006. "Tenure Security and Land-Related Investment: Evidence from Ethiopia." *European Economic Review* 50 (5): 1245–77.

Deininger, K., S. Jin, S. Liu, T. Shao, and F. Xia. 2019. "Property Rights Reform to Support China's Rural–Urban Integration: Village-Level Evidence from the Chengdu Experiment." *Oxford Bulletin of Economics and Statistics* 81 (6): 1214–51.

Deininger, K., S. Jin, S. Liu, and F. Xia. 2020. "Property Rights Reform to Support China's Rural–Urban Integration: Household-Level Evidence from the Chengdu Experiment." *Australian Journal of Agricultural and Resource Economics* 64 (1): 30–54.

Deininger, K., S. Savastano, and F. Xia. 2017. "Smallholders' Land Access in Sub-Saharan Africa: A New Landscape?" *Food Policy* 67: 78–92.

Deininger, K., and F. Xia. 2021. "Productivity of Large and Small Farms and Plots in Malawi: Evidence and Possible Explanations." Policy Research Working Paper, World Bank, Washington, DC.

Deininger, K., F. Xia, and S. Holden. 2019. "Gendered Incidence and Impacts of Tenure Insecurity on Agricultural Performance in Malawi's Customary Tenure System." *Journal of Development Studies* 55 (4): 597–619.

Deininger, K., F. Xia, T. Kilic, and H. Moylan. 2021. "Investment Impacts of Gendered Land Rights in Customary Tenure Systems: Substantive and Methodological Insights from Malawi." *World Development* 147: 105654.

Delpierre, M., C. Guirkinger, and J.-P. Platteau. 2019. "Risk as Impediment to Privatization? The Role of Collective Fields in Extended Agricultural Households." *Economic Development and Cultural Change* 67 (4): 863–905.

Di Falco, S., J. Laurent-Lucchetti, M. Veronesi, and G. Kohlin. 2020. "Property Rights, Land Disputes and Water Scarcity: Empirical Evidence from Ethiopia." *American Journal of Agricultural Economics* 102 (1): 54–71.

Di Tella, R., S. Galiani, and E. Schargrodsky. 2007. "The Formation of Beliefs: Evidence from the Allocation of Land Titles to Squatters." *Quarterly Journal of Economics* 122 (1): 209–41.

Dillon, B., and A. Voena. 2018. "Widows' Land Rights and Agricultural Investment." *Journal of Development Economics* 135: 449–60.

Dimitruk, K., S. Du Plessis, and S. Du Plessis. 2021. "De Jure Property Rights and State Capacity: Evidence from Land Specification in the Boer Republics." *Journal of Institutional Economics* 17 (5): 764–80.

Dippel, C., D. Feir, B. Leonard, and M. Roark. 2021. "Secured Transactions Laws and Economic Development on American Indian Reservations." *AEA Papers and Proceedings* 111: 248–52.

Dippel, C., D. Frye, and B. Leonard. 2020. "Property Rights without Transfer Rights: A Study of Indian Land Allotment." NBER Working Paper 27479, National Bureau of Economic Research, Cambridge, MA.

Djankov, S., E. L. Glaeser, V. Perotti, and A. Shleifer. 2020. "Measuring Property Rights Institutions." NBER Working Paper 27839, National Bureau of Economic Research, Cambridge, MA.

Djankov, S., E. L. Glaeser, V. Perotti, and A. Shleifer. 2021. "Property Rights and Urban Form." NBER Working Paper 28793, National Bureau of Economic Research, Cambridge, MA.

Djezou, W. 2016. "Land Tenure Security and Deforestation: A Case Study of Forest Land Conversion to Perennial Crops in Côte d'Ivoire." *Economics Bulletin* 36 (1): 173–86.

Do, Q. T., and L. Iyer. 2008. "Land Titling and Rural Transition in Vietnam." *Economic Development and Cultural Change* 56 (3): 531–79.

Dokken, T. 2015. "Allocation of Land Tenure Rights in Tigray: How Large Is the Gender Bias?" *Land Economics* 91 (1): 106–25.

Dower, P. C., and A. Markevich. 2018. "Labor Misallocation and Mass Mobilization: Russian Agriculture during the Great War." *Review of Economics and Statistics* 100 (2): 245–59.

Dower, P. C., and T. Pfutze. 2013. "Specificity of Control: The Case of Mexico's Ejido Reform." *Journal of Economic Behavior and Organization* 91: 13–33.

Dyzenhaus, A. 2021. "Patronage or Policy? The Politics of Property Rights Formalization in Kenya." *World Development* 146: 105580.

Eberle, U. J., D. Rohner, and M. Thoenig. 2020. "Heat and Hate: Climate Security and Farmer-Herder Conflicts in Africa." CEPR Discussion Paper 15542, Center for Economic and Policy Research, Washington, DC.

Eck, K. 2014. "The Law of the Land: Communal Conflict and Legal Authority." *Journal of Peace Research* 51 (4): 441–54.

Eerola, E., and T. Lyytikainen. 2015. "On the Role of Public Price Information in Housing Markets." *Regional Science and Urban Economics* 53: 74–84.

Ehwi, R. J., N. Morrison, and P. Tyler. 2021. "Gated Communities and Land Administration Challenges in Ghana: Reappraising the Reasons Why People Move into Gated Communities." *Housing Studies* 36 (3): 307–35.

Eika, L., M. Mogstad, and O. L. Vestad. 2020. "What Can We Learn about Household Consumption Expenditure from Data on Income and Assets?" *Journal of Public Economics* 189: 104163.

Enemark, S., K. C. Bell, C. Lemmen, and R. McLaren. 2014. *Fit for Purpose Land Administration.* Frederiksberg, Denmark: International Federation of Surveyors and the World Bank.

Engström, L., and F. Hajdu. 2018. "Conjuring 'Win-World'—Resilient Development Narratives in a Large-Scale Agro-Investment in Tanzania." *Journal of Development Studies* 55: 1–20.

Fabbri, M. 2021. "Property Rights and Prosocial Behavior: Evidence from a Land Tenure Reform Implemented as Randomized Control-Trial." *Journal of Economic Behavior and Organization* 188: 552–66.

Fabbri, M., and G. Dari-Mattiacci. 2021. "The Virtuous Cycle of Property." *Review of Economics and Statistics* 103 (3): 413–27.

Fagereng, A., M. B. Holm, and K. N. Torstensen. 2020. "Housing Wealth in Norway, 1993–2015." *Journal of Economic and Social Measurement* 45 (1): 65–81.

Fan, E., and S. J. Yeh. 2019. "Tenure Security and Long-Term Investment on Tenanted Land: Evidence from Colonial Taiwan." *Pacific Economic Review* 24 (4): 570–87.

Feder, G., Y. Chalamwong, T. Onchan, and C. Hongladarom. 1988. *Land Policies and Farm Productivity in Thailand.* Baltimore, MD: Johns Hopkins University Press.

Fenske, J. 2010. "L'etranger: Status, Property Rights, and Investment Incentives in Côte d'Ivoire." *Land Economics* 86 (4): 621–44.

Fenske, J. 2011. "Land Tenure and Investment Incentives: Evidence from West Africa." *Journal of Development Economics* 95 (1): 137–56.

Fenske, J. 2014. "Trees, Tenure and Conflict: Rubber in Colonial Benin." *Journal of Development Economics* 110: 226–38.

Fetzer, T., and S. Marden. 2017. "Take What You Can: Property Rights, Contestability and Conflict." *Economic Journal* 127 (601): 757–83.

Field, E. 2005. "Property Rights and Investment in Urban Slums." *Journal of the European Economic Association* 3 (2–3): 279–90.

Field, E. 2007. "Entitled to Work: Urban Property Rights and Labor Supply in Peru." *Quarterly Journal of Economics* 122 (4): 1561–602.

Field, E., and K. Vyborny. 2019. "Information Gaps and De Jure Legal Rights: Evidence from Pakistan." EDI Working Paper, Economic Diversity Initiative, London.

Firmin-Sellers, K. 1995. "The Politics of Property Rights." *American Political Science Review* 89 (4): 867.

Frémeaux, N., and M. Leturcq. 2020. "Inequalities and the Individualization of Wealth." *Journal of Public Economics* 184: 104145.

Gagliarducci, S., and T. Nannicini. 2013. "Do Better Paid Politicians Perform Better? Disentangling Incentives from Selection." *Journal of the European Economic Association* 11 (2): 369–98.

Galiani, S., and E. Schargrodsky. 2010. "Property Rights for the Poor: Effects of Land Titling." *Journal of Public Economics* 94 (9–10): 700–29.

Galiani, S., and E. Schargrodsky. 2016. "The Deregularization of Land Titles." NBER Working Paper 22482, National Bureau of Economic Research, Cambridge, MA.

Gandelman, N. 2016. "Inter-generational Effects of Titling Programmes: Physical vs. Human Capital." *Journal of Development Studies* 52 (3): 331–42.

Gandhi, S., V. Tandel, A. Tabarrok, and S. Ravi. 2021. "Too Slow for the Urban March: Litigations and the Real Estate Market in Mumbai, India." *Journal of Urban Economics* 123: 103330.

García-Morán, A., and J. S. Yates. 2022. "In between Rights and Power: Women's Land Rights and the Gendered Politics of Land Ownership, Use, and Management in Mexican Ejidos." *World Development* 152: 105804.

Gavian, S., and M. Fafchamps. 1996. "Land Tenure and Allocative Efficiency in Niger." *American Journal of Agricultural Economics* 78 (2): 460–71.

Genicot, G., and M. Hernandez-de-Benito. 2022. "Women's Land Rights and Village Institutions in Tanzania." *World Development* 153: 105811.

Gertler, P. J., M. Gonzalez-Navarro, T. Gracner, and A. D. Rothenberg. 2022. *Road Maintenance and Local Economic Development: Evidence from Indonesia's Highways.* Berkeley: University of California.

Ghatak, M., and P. Ghosh. 2011. "The Land Acquisition Bill: A Critique and a Proposal." *Economic and Political Weekly* 46 (41): 65–72.

Ghatak, M., S. Mitra, D. Mookherjee, and A. Nath. 2013. "Land Acquisition and Compensation in Singur: What Really Happened?" London School of Economics, London.

Ghebru, H., and F. Girmachew. 2020. "Direct and Spillover Effects of Land Rights Formalization in Africa: A Case Study of the Second-Level Land Certification (SLLC) in Ethiopia." Working paper, International Food Policy Research Institute, Washington, DC.

Ginsburg, C., and S. Keene. 2020. "At a Crossroads: Consequential Trends in Recognition of Community-Based Forest Tenure from 2002–2017." *China Economic Journal* 13 (2): 223–48.

Gochberg, W. 2021. "The Social Costs of Titling Land: Evidence from Uganda." *World Development* 142: 105376.

Goldsmith-Pinkham, P., M. T. Gustafson, R. C. Lewis, and M. Schwert. 2021. "Sea Level Rise Exposure and Municipal Bond Yields." Working paper, Yale University, New Haven, CT.

Goldstein, M., K. Houngbedji, F. Kondylis, M. O'Sullivan, and H. Selod. 2018. "Formalization without Certification? Experimental Evidence on Property Rights and Investment." *Journal of Development Economics* 132: 57–74.

Goldstein, M., and C. Udry. 2008. "The Profits of Power: Land Rights and Agricultural Investment in Ghana." *Journal of Political Economy* 116 (6): 980–1022.

Goodfellow, T., and O. Owen. 2020. "Thick Claims and Thin Rights: Taxation and the Construction of Analogue Property Rights in Lagos." *Economy and Society* 49 (3): 406–32.

Green, E., and M. Norberg. 2018. "Traditional Landholding Certificates in Zambia: Preventing or Reinforcing Commodification and Inequality?" *Journal of Southern African Studies* 44 (4): 613–28.

Greif, A. 1993. "Contract Enforceability and Economic Institutions in Early Trade: The Maghribi Traders' Coalition." *American Economic Review* 83 (3): 525–48.

Greiner, C. 2017. "Pastoralism and Land-Tenure Change in Kenya: The Failure of Customary Institutions." *Development and Change* 48 (1): 78–97.

Grossman, Z., J. Pincus, P. Shapiro, and D. Yengin. 2019. "Second-Best Mechanisms for Land Assembly and Hold-Out Problems." *Journal of Public Economics* 175: 1–16.

Guirkinger, C., and J.-P. Platteau. 2014. "The Effect of Land Scarcity on Farm Structure: Empirical Evidence from Mali." *Economic Development and Cultural Change* 62 (2): 195–238.

Gutierrez, I. A., and O. Molina. 2020. "Reverting to Informality: Unregistered Property Transactions and the Erosion of the Titling Reform in Peru." *Economic Development and Cultural Change* 69 (1): 317–34.

Han, L., S. Heblich, C. Timmins, and Y. Zylberberg. 2021. "Cool Cities: The Value of Urban Trees." University of Wisconsin, Madison.

Hansen, M. C., P. V. Potapov, R. Moore, M. Hancher, S. A. Turubanova, A. Tyukavina, D. Thau, et al. 2013. "High-Resolution Global Maps of 21st-Century Forest Cover Change." *Science* 342 (6160): 850–53.

Harari, M. 2019. "Women's Inheritance Rights and Bargaining Power: Evidence from Kenya." *Economic Development and Cultural Change* 68 (1): 189–238.

Harris, N. L., D. A. Gibbs, A. Baccini, R. A. Birdsey, S. de Bruin, M. Farina, L. Fatoyinbo, et al. 2021. "Global Maps of Twenty-First Century Forest Carbon Fluxes." *Nature Climate Change* 11 (3): 234–40.

Hartley, J., L. Ma, S. Wachter, and A. A. Zevelev. 2023. "Do Foreign Buyer Taxes Affect House Prices?" Working paper, Stanford University, Stanford, CA.

Hassan, M., and K. Klaus. 2020. "Closing the Gap: The Politics of Property Rights in Kenya." University of Michigan, Ann Arbor.

Hawley, Z., J. J. Miranda, and W. C. Sawyer. 2018. "Land Values, Property Rights, and Home Ownership: Implications for Property Taxation in Peru." *Regional Science and Urban Economics* 69: 38–47.

Hazan, M., D. Weiss, and H. Zoabi. 2019. "Women's Liberation as a Financial Innovation." *Journal of Finance* 74 (6): 2915–56.

Henn, S. J. 2020. "The State, Chiefs, and Development: Evidence from Africa." Working paper, Boston University, Boston.

Hilber, C. A. L., C. Palmer, and E. W. Pinchbeck. 2019. "The Energy Costs of Historic Preservation." *Journal of Urban Economics* 114: 103197.

Hilber, C. A. L., and W. Vermeulen. 2016. "The Impact of Supply Constraints on House Prices in England." *Economic Journal* 126 (591): 358–405.

Holden, S. T., K. Deininger, and H. Ghebru. 2009. "Impacts of Low-Cost Land Certification on Investment and Productivity." *American Journal of Agricultural Economics* 91 (2): 359–73.

Holden, S. T., K. Deininger, and H. Ghebru. 2011. "Tenure Insecurity, Gender, Low-Cost Land Certification and Land Rental Market Participation in Ethiopia." *Journal of Development Studies* 47 (1): 31–47.

Holden, S. T., and H. Ghebru. 2016. "Land Rental Market Legal Restrictions in Northern Ethiopia." *Land Use Policy* 55: 212–21.

Holden, S. T., and M. Tilahun. 2018. "The Importance of Ostrom's Design Principles: Youth Group Performance in Northern Ethiopia." *World Development* 104: 10–30.

Holden, S. T., and M. Tilahun. 2020. "Farm Size and Gender Distribution of Land: Evidence from Ethiopian Land Registry Data." *World Development* 130: 104926.

Honig, L. 2017. "Selecting the State or Choosing the Chief? The Political Determinants of Smallholder Land Titling." *World Development* 100: 94–107.

Honig, L. 2021. "The Power of the Pen: Informal Property Rights Documents in Zambia." *African Affairs* 121 (482): 81–107.

Huggins, C. 2018. "Land-Use Planning, Digital Technologies, and Environmental Conservation in Tanzania." *Journal of Environment and Development* 27 (2): 210–35.

Hunt, D. 2004. "Unintended Consequences of Land Rights Reform: The Case of the 1998 Uganda Land Act." *Development Policy Review* 22 (2): 173–91.

Huntington, H., and A. Shenoy. 2021. "Does Insecure Land Tenure Deter Investment? Evidence from a Randomized Controlled Trial." *Journal of Development Economics* 150: 102632.

Huntington, H., and C. Stevens. 2023. "Taking Stock of Global Land Indicators: A Comparative Analysis of Approaches for a Globally Consistent Land Tenure Security Measure." *Land Use Policy* 124: 106376.

Hüttel, S., M. Odening, K. Kataria, and A. Balmann. 2013. "Price Formation on Land Market Auctions in East Germany: An Empirical Analysis." *German Journal of Agricultural Economics* 62 (2): 99–115.

Jacoby, H. G., G. Li, and S. Rozelle. 2002. "Hazards of Expropriation: Tenure Insecurity and Investment in Rural China." *American Economic Review* 92 (5): 1420–47.

Jacoby, H. G., and G. Mansuri. 2008. "Land Tenancy and Non-contractible Investment in Rural Pakistan." *Review of Economic Studies* 75 (3): 763–88.

Jacoby, H. G., and B. Minten. 2007. "Is Land Titling in Sub-Saharan Africa Cost-Effective? Evidence from Madagascar." *World Bank Economic Review* 21 (3): 461–85.

Jansen, K., and E. Roquas. 1998. "Modernizing Insecurity: The Land Titling Project in Honduras." *Development and Change* 29 (1): 81–106.

Jeanne, B., and S. Le Guern Herry. 2022. "Will We Ever Be Able to Track Offshore Wealth? Evidence from the Offshore Real Estate Market in the UK." Sciences Po Economics Discussion Paper 2022-10, Sciences Po Department of Economics, Paris.

Jiang, E. X., and A. L. Zang. 2022. "Collateral Value Uncertainty and Mortgage Credit Provision." University of Chicago.

Jin, S., and T. S. Jayne. 2013. "Land Rental Markets in Kenya: Implications for Efficiency, Equity, Household Income, and Poverty." *Land Economics* 89 (2): 246–71.

Johannesen, N., P. Langetieg, D. Reck, M. Risch, and J. Slemrod. 2020. "Taxing Hidden Wealth: The Consequences of US Enforcement Initiatives on Evasive Foreign Accounts." *American Economic Journal: Economic Policy* 12 (3): 312–46.

Joireman, S. F., and L. S. M. Yoder. 2016. "A Long Time Gone: Post-conflict Rural Property Restitution under Customary Law." *Development and Change* 47 (3): 563–85.

Kaganova, O., and J. K. Kaw. 2020. "An Asset Management Approach to Planning, Funding, and Managing Public Spaces." In *The Hidden Wealth of Cities: Creating, Financing, and Managing Public Spaces*, edited by J. K. Kaw, H. Lee, and S. Wahba, 55–93. Washington, DC: World Bank.

Kang, M., B. Schwab, and J. Yu. 2020. "Gender Differences in the Relationship between Land Ownership and Managerial Rights: Implications for Intrahousehold Farm Labor Allocation." *World Development* 125: 104669.

Kironde, L. 2006. *Issuing of Residential Licenses in Unplanned Settlements in Dar es Salaam, Tanzania.* Dar es Salaam: UN Habitat.

Kolsrud, J., C. Landais, and J. Spinnewijn. 2020. "The Value of Registry Data for Consumption Analysis: An Application to Health Shocks." *Journal of Public Economics* 189: 104088.

Kotchen, M. J., and K. Segerson. 2020. "The Use of Group-Level Approaches to Environmental and Natural Resource Policy." *Review of Environmental Economics and Policy* 14 (2): 173–93.

Kumar, N., and A. Quisumbing. 2012. "Inheritance Practices and Gender Differences in Poverty and Well-Being in Rural Ethiopia." *Development Policy Review* 30 (5): 573–95.

Kumar, N., and A. R. Quisumbing. 2015. "Policy Reform toward Gender Equality in Ethiopia: Little by Little the Egg Begins to Walk." *World Development* 67: 406–23.

Kusiluka, M. M., and D. M. Chiwambo. 2019. "Acceptability of Residential Licences as Quasi-Land Ownership Documents: Evidence from Tanzania." *Land Use Policy* 85: 176–82.

Kusunose, Y., V. Theriault, and D. Alia. 2020. "Can Customary Land Tenure Facilitate Agricultural Productivity Growth? Evidence from Burkina Faso." *Land Economics* 96 (3): 441–55.

La Ferrara, E., and A. Milazzo. 2017. "Customary Norms, Inheritance, and Human Capital: Evidence from a Reform of the Matrilineal System in Ghana." *American Economic Journal: Applied Economics* 9 (4): 166–85.

Lanjouw, J. O., and P. I. Levy. 2002. "Untitled: A Study of Formal and Informal Property Rights in Urban Ecuador." *Economic Journal* 112 (482): 986–1019.

Lanz, K., J.-D. Gerber, and T. Haller. 2018. "Land Grabbing, the State and Chiefs: The Politics of Extending Commercial Agriculture in Ghana." *Development and Change* 49 (6): 1526–52.

Larreguy, H., J. Marshall, and L. Trucco. 2018. "Breaking Clientelism or Rewarding Incumbents? Evidence from an Urban Titling Program in Mexico." Harvard University, Cambridge, MA.

Lavigne Delville, P. 2002. "When Farmers Use 'Pieces of Paper' to Record Their Land Transactions in Francophone Rural Africa: Insights into the Dynamics of Institutional Innovation." *European Journal of Development Research* 14 (2): 89–108.

Lavigne Delville, P. 2019. "History and Political Economy of Land Administration Reform in Benin." Working Paper WP19/BID08, Economic Development and Institutions, Oxford, UK.

Lawin, K. G., and L. D. Tamini. 2019. "Land Tenure Differences and Adoption of Agri-environmental Practices: Evidence from Benin." *Journal of Development Studies* 55 (2): 177–90.

Lawley, C. 2018. "Ownership Restrictions and Farmland Values: Evidence from the 2003 Saskatchewan Farm Security Act Amendment." *American Journal of Agricultural Economics* 100 (1): 311–37.

Lawry, S., C. Samii, R. Hall, A. Leopold, D. Hornby, and F. Mtero. 2017. "The Impact of Land Property Rights Interventions on Investment and Agricultural Productivity in Developing Countries: A Systematic Review." *Journal of Development Effectiveness* 9 (1): 61–81.

Leeson, P. T., and C. Harris. 2018. "Wealth-Destroying Private Property Rights." *World Development* 107: 1–9.

Lentz, C. 2010. "Land Inalienable? Historical and Current Debates on Land Transfers in Northern Ghana." *Africa* 80 (1): 56–80.

Leonard, B., and D. P. Parker. 2021. "Fragmented Ownership and Natural Resource Use: Evidence from the Bakken." *Economic Journal* 131 (635): 1215–49.

Leonard, B., D. P. Parker, and T. L. Anderson. 2020. "Land Quality, Land Rights, and Indigenous Poverty." *Journal of Development Economics* 143: 102435.

Leonard, B., S. Regan, C. Costello, S. Kerr, D. P. Parker, A. J. Plantinga, J. Salzman, V. K. Smith, and T. Stoellinger. 2021. "Allow 'Nonuse Rights' to Conserve Natural Resources." *Science* 373 (6558): 958–61.

Libecap, G. D., and D. Lueck. 2011. "The Demarcation of Land and the Role of Coordinating Property Institutions." *Journal of Political Economy* 119 (3): 426–67.

Lim, G. J. 2022. "Local Elites, Land Rents and Incentives for Development: Evidence from Village Chiefs in Indonesia." Working paper, University of Hong Kong, Hong Kong SAR, China.

Linkow, B. 2016. "Causes and Consequences of Perceived Land Tenure Insecurity: Survey Evidence from Burkina Faso." *Land Economics* 92 (2): 308–27.

Linkow, B. 2019. "Inheritance Practices, Investment Incentives and Women's Control over Land in Rural Kenya." *Journal of African Economies* 28 (3): 304–22.

Liu, X., and J. Yang. 2022. "The Cost of Poor Institutions: Estimations Based on Chinese Firm Flows." *Emerging Markets Finance and Trade* 58 (5): 1308–19.

Lowes, S., and E. Montero. 2020. "Concessions, Violence, and Indirect Rule: Evidence from the Congo Free State." Working paper, University of California, San Diego.

Lozano-Gracia, N., C. Young, S. V. Lall, and T. Vishwanath. 2013. "Leveraging Land to Enable Urban Transformation: Lessons from Global Experience." Policy Research Working Paper 6312, World Bank, Washington, DC.

Manara, M. 2022. "From Policy to Institution: Implementing Land Reform in Dar es Salaam's Unplanned Settlements." *Environment and Planning A* 54 (7): 1368–90.

Manara, M., and T. Regan. 2022. "Ask a Local: Improving the Public Pricing of Land Titles in Urban Tanzania." *Review of Economics and Statistics* 1–44.

Markussen, T., S. Sharma, S. Singhal, and F. Tarp. 2021. "Inequality, Institutions and Cooperation." *European Economic Review* 138: 103842.

Maurer, N., and L. Iyer. 2008. "The Cost of Property Rights: Establishing Institutions on the Philippine Frontier under American Rule, 1898–1918." NBER Working Paper 14298, National Bureau of Economic Research, Cambridge, MA.

McAuslan, P. 2013. *Land Law Reform in Eastern Africa: Traditional or Transformative? A Critical Review of 50 Years of Land Law Reform in Eastern Africa 1961–2011.* London: Routledge.

McGuirk, E. F., and N. Nunn. 2020. "Nomadic Pastoralism, Climate Change, and Conflict in Africa." NBER Working Paper 28243, National Bureau of Economic Research, Cambridge, MA.

McPeak, J. G., and P. D. Little. 2018. "Mobile Peoples, Contested Borders: Land Use Conflicts and Resolution Mechanisms among Borana and Guji Communities, Southern Ethiopia." *World Development* 103: 119–32.

Meinzen-Dick, R., A. Quisumbing, C. Doss, and S. Theis. 2019. "Women's Land Rights as a Pathway to Poverty Reduction: Framework and Review of Available Evidence." *Agricultural Systems* 172: 72–82.

Mekking, S., D. V. Kougblenou, and F. G. Kossou. 2021. "Fit-for-Purpose Upscaling Land Administration: A Case Study from Benin." *Land* 10 (5): 440.

Melesse, M. B., and E. Bulte. 2015. "Does Land Registration and Certification Boost Farm Productivity? Evidence from Ethiopia." *Agricultural Economics* 46 (6): 757–68.

Melesse, M. B., A. Dabissa, and E. Bulte. 2018. "Joint Land Certification Programmes and Women's Empowerment: Evidence from Ethiopia." *Journal of Development Studies* 54 (10): 1756–74.

Menon, N., Y. van der Meulen Rodgers, and A. R. Kennedy. 2017. "Land Reform and Welfare in Vietnam: Why Gender of the Land-Rights Holder Matters." *Journal of International Development* 29 (4): 454–72.

Mezgebo, T. G., and C. Porter. 2020. "From Rural to Urban, but Not through Migration: Household Livelihood Responses to Urban Reclassification in Northern Ethiopia." *Journal of African Economies* 29 (2): 173–91.

Mihaylova, I. 2023. "Perpetuating the Malign Legacy of Colonialism? Traditional Chiefs' Power and Deforestation in Sierra Leone." *World Development* 164: 106176.

Montero, E. 2022. "Cooperative Property Rights and Development: Evidence from Land Reform in El Salvador." *Journal of Political Economy* 130 (1): 48–93.

Moritz, M. 2008. "Competing Paradigms in Pastoral Development? A Perspective from the Far North of Cameroon." *World Development* 36 (11): 2243–54.

Moscona, J., N. Nunn, and J. A. Robinson. 2020. "Segmentary Lineage Organization and Conflict in Sub-Saharan Africa." *Econometrica* 88 (5): 1999–2036.

Mramba, S. J. 2023. "Through the Maze of Land Rights Laws." In *State and Business in Tanzania's Development: An Institutional Diagnostic*, edited by F. Bourguignon and S. M. Wangwe, 216–56. Cambridge, UK: Cambridge University Press.

Muchomba, F. M. 2017. "Women's Land Tenure Security and Household Human Capital: Evidence from Ethiopia's Land Certification." *World Development* 98: 310–24.

Murphy, T. E., and M. A. Rossi. 2016. "Land Reform and Violence: Evidence from Mexico." *Journal of Economic Behavior and Organization* 131: 106–13.

Mwathane, I., M. Makathimo, R. Kibugi, and E. Nyukuri. 2022. "Securing and Managing Community Land: Lessons from Kenya." *African Journal on Land Policy and Geospatial Sciences* 5 (4): 753–66.

Mwesigye, F., and T. Matsumoto. 2016. "The Effect of Population Pressure and Internal Migration on Land Conflicts: Implications for Agricultural Productivity in Uganda." *World Development* 79: 25–39.

Neef, T., P. Nicolaides, L. Chancel, T. Piketty, and G. Zucman. 2022. "Effective Sanctions against Oligarchs and the Role of a European Asset Registry." EU Tax Observatory and World Inequality Lab, Paris. https://wid.world/document/effective-sanctions-against-russian-oligarchs-and-the-role-of-a -european-asset-registry/.

Ngoga, T. H. 2018. *Rwanda's Land Tenure Reform: Non-existent to Best Practice.* Wallingford, CT: CABI International.

Njoh, A. J. 2013. "Equity, Fairness and Justice Implications of Land Tenure Formalization in Cameroon." *International Journal of Urban and Regional Research* 37 (2): 750–68.

Nkurunziza, E. 2015. "Implementing and Sustaining Land Tenure Regularization in Rwanda." In *How Innovations in Land Administration Reform Improve on "Doing Business,"* edited by T. Hilhorst and F. Meunier, 10–19. Washington, DC: World Bank.

North, D. C. 1971. *Structure and Change in Economic History.* New York: W. W. Norton.

Ntsebeza, L. 2004. "Democratic Decentralisation and Traditional Authority: Dilemmas of Land Administration in Rural South Africa." *European Journal of Development Research* 16 (1): 71–89.

Nugent, J. B., and N. Sanchez. 1998. "Common Property Rights as an Endogenous Response to Risk." *American Journal of Agricultural Economics* 80 (3): 651–7.

Odote, C. O., R. Hassan, and H. Mubarak. 2021. "Over Promising while Under Delivering: Implementation of Kenya's Community Land Act." *African Journal on Land Policy and Geospatial Sciences* 4 (2): 292–307.

Pacheco, A., and C. Meyer. 2022. "Land Tenure Drives Brazil's Deforestation Rates across Socio-environmental Contexts." *Nature Communications* 13 (1): 5759.

Peña, X., M. A. Vélez, J. C. Cárdenas, N. Perdomo, and C. Matajira. 2017. "Collective Property Leads to Household Investments: Lessons from Land Titling in Afro-Colombian Communities." *World Development* 97: 27–48.

Peterman, A. 2012. "Widowhood and Asset Inheritance in Sub-Saharan Africa: Empirical Evidence from 15 Countries." *Development Policy Review* 30 (5): 543–71.

Peters, P. 2004. "Inequality and Social Conflict over Land in Africa." *Journal of Agrarian Change* 4 (3): 269–314.

Peters, P. E. 2010. "'Our Daughters Inherit Our Land, but Our Sons Use Their Wives' Fields': Matrilineal-Matrilocal Land Tenure and the New Land Policy in Malawi." *Journal of Eastern African Studies* 4 (1): 179–99.

Pinchbeck, E. W., S. Roth, N. Szumilo, and E. Vanino. 2020. "The Price of Indoor Air Pollution: Evidence from Radon Maps and the Housing Market." IZA Discussion Paper No. 13655, Institute of Labor Economics, Bonn Germany.

Pinckney, T. C., and P. K. Kimuyu. 1994. "Land Tenure Reform in East Africa: Good, Bad or Unimportant?" *Journal of African Economies* 3 (1): 1–28.

Platteau, J.-P. 2000. "Allocating and Enforcing Property Rights in Land: Informal versus Formal Mechanisms in Subsaharan Africa." *Nordic Journal of Political Economy* 26 (1): 55–81.

Quan, J., J. Monteiro, and P. Mole. 2013. "The Experience of Mozambique's Community Land Initiative (iTC) in Securing Land Rights and Improving Community Land Use: Practice, Policy and Governance Implications." Paper presented at the 2013 Annual Bank Conference on Land and Poverty, World Bank, Washington, DC.

Raleigh, C., A. Linke, H. Hegre, and J. Karlsen. 2010. "Introducing ACLED: An Armed Conflict Location and Event Dataset: Special Data Feature." *Journal of Peace Research* 47 (5): 651–60.

Ramírez-Álvarez, A. A. 2019. "Land Titling and Its Effect on the Allocation of Public Goods: Evidence from Mexico." *World Development* 124: 104660.

Restuccia, D. 2021. "From Micro to Macro: Land Institutions, Agricultural Productivity, and Structural Transformation." Background paper for this report. World Bank, Washington, DC.

Rosenthal, S. S., W. C. Strange, and J. A. Urrego. 2022. "JUE Insight: Are City Centers Losing Their Appeal? Commercial Real Estate, Urban Spatial Structure, and COVID-19." *Journal of Urban Economics* 127: 103381.

Rozelle, S., and J. F. M. Swinnen. 2004. "Success and Failure of Reform: Insights from the Transition of Agriculture." *Journal of Economic Literature* 42 (2): 404–56.

Sagashya, D. G. G., and E. Tembo. 2022. "Zambia: Private Sector Investment in Security of Land Tenure: From Piloting Using Technology to National Rollout." *African Journal on Land Policy and Geospatial Sciences* 5 (1). doi:10.48346/IMIST.PRSM/ajlp-gs.v5i1.30440.

Santos, F., D. Fletschner, and G. Daconto. 2014. "Enhancing Inclusiveness of Rwanda's Land Tenure Regularization Program: Insights from Early Stages of Its Implementation." *World Development* 62: 30–41.

Schafer, H.-B., and R. Singh. 2018. "Takings of Land by Self-Interested Governments: Economic Analysis of Eminent Domain." *Journal of Law and Economics* 61 (3): 427–59.

Schmalz, M. C., D. A. Sraer, and D. Thesmar. 2017. "Housing Collateral and Entrepreneurship." *Journal of Finance* 72 (1): 99–132.

Seifert, S., C. Kahle, and S. Hüttel. 2021. "Price Dispersion in Farmland Markets: What Is the Role of Asymmetric Information?" *American Journal of Agricultural Economics* 103 (4): 1545–68.

Severen, C., and A. J. Plantinga. 2018. "Land-Use Regulations, Property Values, and Rents: Decomposing the Effects of the California Coastal Act." *Journal of Urban Economics* 107: 65–78.

Sha, W. 2022. "The Political Impacts of Land Expropriation in China." *Journal of Development Economics* 160: 102985.

Shivji, I. 1998. *Not Yet Democracy: Reforming Land Tenure in Tanzania*. London: International Institute for Environment and Development.

Singh, R. 2019. "Seismic Risk and House Prices: Evidence from Earthquake Fault Zoning." *Regional Science and Urban Economics* 75: 187–209.

Sitko, N. J., and T. S. Jayne. 2014. "Structural Transformation or Elite Land Capture? The Growth of 'Emergent' Farmers in Zambia." *Food Policy* 48: 194–202.

Sjaastad, E., and D. Bromley. 2000. "The Prejudices of Property Rights: On Individualism, Specificity, and Security in Property Regimes." *Development Policy Review* 18 (4): 365–89.

Sodini, P., S. V. Nieuwerburgh, R. Vestman, and U. von Lilienfeld-Toal. 2016. "Identifying the Benefits from Home Ownership: A Swedish Experiment." NBER Working Paper 22882, National Bureau of Economic Research, Cambridge, MA.

Sodini, P., S. V. Nieuwerburgh, R. Vestman, and U. von Lilienfeld-Toal. 2023. "Identifying the Benefits from Homeownership: A Swedish Experiment." *American Economic Review* 113 (12): 3173–212.

Stein, H., F. P. Maganga, R. Odgaard, K. Askew, and S. Cunningham. 2016. "The Formal Divide: Customary Rights and the Allocation of Credit to Agriculture in Tanzania." *Journal of Development Studies* 52 (9): 1306–19.

Stiglitz, J. E., and A. Weiss. 1981. "Credit Rationing in Markets with Imperfect Information." *American Economic Review* 71 (3): 393.

Sundet, G. 2004. "The Politics of Land in Tanzania." Working paper, Oxford University Research Archive, Oxford, UK.

Tang, C. K. 2021. "The Cost of Traffic: Evidence from the London Congestion Charge." *Journal of Urban Economics* 121: 103302.

Tchatchoua-Djomo, R., M. van Leeuwen, and G. van der Haar. 2020. "Defusing Land Disputes? The Politics of Land Certification and Dispute Resolution in Burundi." *Development and Change* 51 (6): 1454–80.

Teklu, T., and A. Lemi. 2004. "Factors Affecting Entry and Intensity in Informal Rental Land Markets in Southern Ethiopian Highlands." *Agricultural Economics* 30 (2): 117–28.

Titman, S., and G. Twite. 2013. "Urban Density, Law and the Duration of Real Estate Leases." *Journal of Urban Economics* 74: 99–112.

Tourek, G., P. Balan, A. Bergeron, and J. Weigel. 2020. "Local Elites as State Capacity: How City Chiefs Use Local Information to Increase Tax Compliance in the D.R. Congo." Working paper, Harvard University, Cambridge, MA.

Valsecchi, M. 2014. "Land Property Rights and International Migration: Evidence from Mexico." *Journal of Development Economics* 110: 276–90.

van der Windt, P., M. Humphreys, L. Medina, J. Timmons, and M. Voors. 2018. "Citizen Attitudes toward Traditional and State Authorities: Substitutes or Complements?" *Comparative Political Studies* 52 (12): 1810–40.

Vechbanyongratana, J., and K. Niwatananun. 2020. "Historical Origins of Land Rights Insecurity and Implications for Conflict in Thailand." *Economics of Peace and Security Journal* 15 (2): 5–18.

Vélez, M. A., J. Robalino, J. C. Cardenas, A. Paz, and E. Pacay. 2020. "Is Collective Titling Enough to Protect Forests? Evidence from Afro-Descendant Communities in the Colombian Pacific Region." *World Development* 128: 104837.

Vogl, T. S. 2007. "Urban Land Rights and Child Nutritional Status in Peru, 2004." *Economics and Human Biology* 5 (2): 302–21.

Wang, S.-Y. 2012. "Credit Constraints, Job Mobility, and Entrepreneurship: Evidence from a Property Reform in China." *Review of Economics and Statistics* 94 (2): 532–51.

Wang, S.-Y. 2014. "Property Rights and Intra-Household Bargaining." *Journal of Development Economics* 107: 192–201.

Wineman, A., and L. S. O. Liverpool-Tasie. 2017. "Land Markets and Land Access among Female-Headed Households in Northwestern Tanzania." *World Development* 100: 108–22.

Winters, M. S., and J. Conroy-Krutz. 2021. "Preferences for Traditional and Formal Sector Justice Institutions to Address Land Disputes in Rural Mali." *World Development* 142: 105452.

Woods, D. 2003. "The Tragedy of the Cocoa Pod: Rent-Seeking, Land and Ethnic Conflict in Ivory Coast." *Journal of Modern African Studies* 41 (4): 641–55.

Wren-Lewis, L., L. Becerra-Valbuena, and K. Houngbedji. 2020. "Formalizing Land Rights Can Reduce Forest Loss: Experimental Evidence from Benin." *Science Advances* 6 (26): eabb6914.

Zakharenko, R. 2021. "Optimal Compulsion for Private Assembly of Property." *Regional Science and Urban Economics* 88: 103574.

Zein, T. 2021. "Fit-for-Purpose Land Administration in Ethiopia: Ten Years of Success." Paper presented at the FIG e-Working Week, June 21–25, 2021, International Federation of Surveyors, Copenhagen.

Zevelev, A. A. 2021. "Does Collateral Value Affect Asset Prices? Evidence from a Natural Experiment in Texas." *Review of Financial Studies* 34 (9): 4373–411.

Zhang, L., W. Cheng, E. Cheng, and B. Wu. 2020. "Does Land Titling Improve Credit Access? Quasi-Experimental Evidence from Rural China." *Applied Economics* 52 (2): 227–41.

Zhao, X. 2020. "Land and Labor Allocation under Communal Tenure: Theory and Evidence from China." *Journal of Development Economics* 147: 102526.

2. Land rights for sustainable urbanization

Africa has one of the fastest rates of urbanization globally, characterized by urban population growth of more than 1 percent a year and with some of the most densely populated cities on the globe (Henderson and Turner 2020). If current trends continue (Jedwab, Christiaensen, and Gindelsky 2017), Africa's urban population is expected to triple to more than 1 billion by 2050 (Collier 2017). For them to contribute to joint prosperity rather than add to urban cost, new arrivals to cities will need to be able to access affordable housing, decent services, and productive jobs.

Africa's rapid urbanization has given rise to concerns about cities' growth being driven by resource rents that will drive up urban costs and be subject to the booms and busts of global commodity cycles, especially if urban employment is concentrated in nontradable sectors. To ensure that rapid rates of future urbanization help cities move into tradable goods and services with a much larger market and greater opportunities for higher productivity, a key policy challenge is to reduce urban costs by providing public services effectively, using public land to foster mobility and increase the size of effective labor markets, and supporting both horizontal and vertical urban expansion to facilitate construction of affordable floorspace.

Access to housing, services, and jobs will be easier to provide by private agents or the public sector if land and property rights are registered and land institutions provide sufficient levels of tenure security, allow operation of competitive land markets, and facilitate use of land as collateral for credit. This would enable private owners to make long-term investments in tall structures and allow local governments to capitalize on increasing land values as a result of public investment to finance provision of basic services and mobility.

However, instead of incentivizing operation of land and credit markets to support private construction of affordable housing and public provision of infrastructure and amenities, planning rules that often changed little since colonial times—and often still reflect its mind-set, foster informality, and promote slum growth—increase urban costs through sprawl and, by posing direct and indirect impediments to enterprise growth and job creation, limit cities' dynamism and productivity. Global experience, including from developed countries, suggests that inappropriate zoning rules can give rise to enormous welfare losses. Using new data sources and methods of data collection to audit and adjust such regulations with a view toward eliminating red tape and focusing planning on rules that deal with true externalities and capitalize on market forces and fiscal incentives to encourage compliance could be more effective.

Although slum redevelopment and regularization can improve inhabitants' welfare in the short term, they will yield maximum benefits in the long term if combined with steps to prevent future slum growth and ensure that the land rights received by slumdwellers are transferable and recipients are aware of their value. Policies that focus on mixed-use zoning and incentivize private efforts at redevelopment that ensure current occupants' rights will not be neglected, protect public spaces, and support mobility can help in this respect.

Given the rates of urban population growth expected in African cities, vertical growth will need to be complemented by horizontal expansion. Tendencies toward uncontrolled slum growth with negative implications for social mobility and wealth accumulation can be reduced if expansion plans are backed by visible investment in transport infrastructure—which can be financed at least in part by well-established instruments for land value capture, land markets are active, and land prices public. If a land registry provides land ownership and price information, expropriation proceedings that hold up infrastructure construction in many countries can be either avoided entirely—by using fiscal instruments or land pooling instead—or made more effective and less confrontational and socially damaging.

Opportunities and challenges of city growth in Africa

Traditionally, high levels of urban growth gave rise to concerns about "urbanization without growth" (Fay and Opal 1999), especially as African income levels are well below those that had been attained by today's developed countries during their peak rates of urbanization (Jedwab and Vollrath 2015). Such fears are reinforced by two factors. First, in many African countries, urbanization seems to be driven by mineral exports and resource rents (Gollin, Jedwab, and Vollrath 2016), giving rise to cities focused on consumption of nontradables rather than the production of tradables. Second, in global comparison, African cities achieve density via crowding in slums rather than by investment in height (Esch et al. 2024), reducing economic potential and threatening to increase spatial segregation, widen inequality, and increase carbon footprints.[1]

Although city growth historically depended on proximity to transport routes such as rivers (Bosker and Buringh 2017) and rail (Jedwab, Kerby, and Moradi 2017) or support from a productive agricultural hinterland (Nagy 2020), global trade cut the link between city growth and the hinterland, allowing city growth based on skill-based human capital externalities that foster productive jobs based on input sharing, labor market pooling, and knowledge exchange (Rosenthal and Strange 2020). Cities' competitiveness will thus increasingly depend on their ability to attract productive firms and skilled workers and to adapt to new developments and challenges (Duranton 2015).

In Organisation for Economic Co-operation and Development (OECD) countries, agglomeration effects are increasingly found in high-skill, nonroutine interactive tasks that are difficult to automate, as evidenced in the United States (Michaels, Rauch, and Redding 2019), Japan (Dekle and Eaton 1999), Germany (Ahlfeldt et al. 2015), the Netherlands (Koster and Ozgen 2021), and China (Au and Henderson 2006). Local employment density has become more important as a factor supporting city growth (Brülhart, Desmet, and Klinke 2020). Beyond static benefits (Combes, Demurger, and Li 2017), agglomeration has dynamic effects (De La Roca and Puga 2017), implying that even temporary exposure to knowledge externalities can have a lasting impact and give rise to systems of cities where different sizes and locations specialize in different parts of the value chain and land-use intensity (Glaeser, Ponzetto, and Zou 2016).[2]

Higher levels of urban density are associated with higher wages not only in developed countries[3] but also in Brazil, China and India, (Chauvin et al. 2017). Comparing densities of built-up area between Nigeria, South Africa, and China illustrates that the access to floorspace in African cities remains low by international standards (Esch et al. 2024). Low agricultural incomes imply that Africa's urbanization is largely driven by pull rather than push forces (Henderson and Kriticos 2018), and wage gains from living in denser African cities have been comparable to or larger than those in other parts of the world (Henderson, Nigmatulina, and Kriticos 2021). Accounting for differences in the cost of living in Africa's cities may, however, reduce the nominal benefits from density estimated in this way (Grover, Lall, and Timmis 2021).

In the standard urban model, agglomeration benefits in productive cities will raise wages, in turn increasing demand for housing within a commutable distance from jobs and driving up land prices. Higher land prices will encourage the concentration of skill-intensive jobs and more intensive land use in city centers while pushing jobs that are land- rather than skill-intensive toward the urban fringe where land is cheaper. Although the average cost of floorspace in high-rise buildings exceeds that of low-rise structures (Ahlfeldt and Barr 2020), higher land prices can justify such investment and, if credit markets work, will prompt owners and developers to create additional floorspace in anticipation of demand by building high on more valuable land. Ideally, this will give rise to a virtuous circle where agglomeration benefits, skill-based increases in density, and land appreciation reinforce each other. To the extent that property taxes are levied, higher receipts from such taxes could then provide a basis for better provision of public services.

Although cities benefit from agglomeration, downsides of density, such as congestion, contagious diseases, and crime (Glaeser 2021), create "urban costs" (Duranton and Puga 2020). The size, nature, and incidence of these costs will depend on cities' ability to maintain an elastic supply of floorspace in response to demand, deliver public services including mobility, and regulate externalities from crowding, congestion, and pollution. In developed countries, the elasticities of unit land prices and total urban costs with respect to city population have been estimated at 0.72 and 0.041, respectively (Combes, Duranton, and Gobillon 2012). The elasticity of urban cost varies by city size, from 0.03 for urban areas with 100,000 inhabitants to 0.08 for cities with populations in the millions.[4]

The internal geography of cities and the interaction between cities within a country reflect the trade-off between pull forces from agglomeration economies and push forces arising from congestion (Goswami and Lall 2019). In Africa, downsides from urbanization often prevail as informality reduces credit access and the incentive to build high so that agglomeration forces may remain weak and the scope for capitalizing on rising land prices to provide public goods limited. Instead of building high, cities tend to sprawl, increasing their carbon footprint. Institutional frictions that prevent documentation of informal areas also imply that the poor are unable to afford a minimum-size dwelling with access to basic services such as water and sanitation that they could then upgrade in an incremental fashion (Marx, Stoker, and Suri 2013). On the other hand, sprawl often limits the economic viability of investment in public transport, and the number of jobs city dwellers can access is reduced (Nakamura and Avner 2021).

The challenge for urban land policies is to foster positive external effects by keeping cities attractive and affordable for newcomers, providing infrastructure and public services to allow cities to increase productivity by harnessing agglomeration economies, and reducing urban costs and negative externalities. Land markets and the price signals they generate help identify and incentivize opportunities for private investment in urban floorspace. This also allows the use of fiscal instruments, rather than more crude "command-and-control" approaches, to regulate land use in ways that reduce negative externalities and help keep land affordable without destroying incentives for wealth creation and innovation (Bertaud 2014).

Regulating land use and facilitating access to affordable floorspace

The main purpose of zoning and planning regulations is to manage externalities that may be associated with individual parties' land-use decisions. However, without data on current settlement patterns or a legal or fiscal cadaster to identify landowners or users who fail to comply with regulations, design and enforcement of meaningful and relevant plans are difficult. In many African cities, regulation remains focused on broad parameters, such as maximum floor area ratios or minimum plot sizes, that may no longer be relevant or enforceable. This can encourage corruption via discretionary enforcement, and—by increasing the cost of formal built space—can make urban land less affordable, especially for young arrivals. Regulations that cannot be enforced or are no longer appropriate do little to manage externalities, but they make provision of floorspace more expensive and thus encourage informal rather than formal city expansion. They run counter to the objective of providing a conducive environment for a productive, growing urban population and instead encourage slum growth with negative consequences.

Land-use regulation to avoid negative externalities

Recent literature on developed countries where administrative infrastructure to enforce land-use regulation and data to measure its impact are more readily available suggests that building regulations can be effective in reducing the difference between privately and socially optimal decisions arising from collective action problems, presence of externalities, or imperfect information. Stricter building codes, adopted in response to hurricanes or fire risk, resulted in less damage to homes built according to the new code requirement as well as those in the immediate neighborhood, suggesting that externalities are indeed present (Bakkensen and Blair 2022; Baylis and Boomhower 2023).

Mandates for energy efficiency or avoidance of hazardous materials can yield large social benefits. Utility billing data on properties constructed just before and after building codes mandated the use of energy-efficient materials and techniques point toward significant effects: buildings constructed after the code came into force consumed 4 and 6 percent less electricity and gas, respectively, implying average social and private payback periods of 3.5 to 6.4 years (Jacobsen and Kotchen 2013). Energy savings persisted more than a decade after the code change (Kotchen 2017). Regulation demanding lead paint remediation also had significant benefits, with each US$1 spent on lead remediation estimated to have generated US$2.60 in benefits, in addition to reducing residential turnover (Billings and Schnepel 2017).

Regulation of air quality via the 1990 Clean Air Act Amendments had long-term effects in two respects. First, it led to significant house price appreciation that was progressive, amounting to 0.3 percent of income for the lowest income quintile, more than double the appreciation for the highest quintile (Bento, Freedman, and Lang 2015). Second, it also improved socioeconomic outcomes for those affected, with individuals with a lower exposure to pollution in their year of birth having higher labor force participation and earnings at age 30 (Isen, Rossin-Slater, and Walker 2017).[5]

Although Africa is highly vulnerable to climate shocks, regulations have not kept up with new challenges or technological developments. Reports suggest that only five African countries made updates to their building regulations after 2000 (World Bank 2023). Instead, countries have planning rules that often date back to colonial times, such as minimum lot sizes that do little to improve climate resilience but limit floorspace (Lall 2017). By rationing housing supply, this reduces economic dynamism, forces households into informality (Antwi and Adams 2003), generates rents (Egbu, Olomolaiye, and Gameson 2008), increases commuting costs, and encourages sprawl and higher carbon intensity (Bertaud and Brueckner 2005).

Studies from India and the OECD highlight that regulating the amount of floorspace can have far-reaching effects. Evaluation of the impact of regulations on city compactness and transit accessibility for around 350 Indian cities in 1950 to 2010 suggests that, contrary to naive estimates, more compact cities show faster population growth.[6] City shape has little impact on service delivery quality but strongly affects wages, with households willing to pay 5 percent of their income for a one standard deviation improvement in compactness. By contrast, firms minimize the negative impacts of city shape on productivity by clustering in subcenters. Increasing the floor area ratio[7] by 1 is predicted to improve compactness by one standard deviation (Harari 2020). For a smaller sample of Indian cities, Brueckner and Sridhar (2012) come to similar conclusions, finding that even a marginal increase in permitted densities can result in significant increases in welfare.[8]

Restrictions on density have also become widespread in OECD countries. In the United Kingdom, where restrictions often take the form of urban growth boundaries, panel data for 1974–2008 from 353 local planning authorities suggest that without regulatory constraints, housing would have been much more affordable (£147,000 instead of £226,000), a result driven by large cities (Hilber and Vermeulen 2016). The same data show that more restrictive local planning rules increased vacancy rates via a labor market mismatch that arose from workers with jobs in areas with more restrictive planning rules needing to search for affordable housing elsewhere, lengthening commutes and increasing pollution and emissions while flats in desirable locations often remained empty (Cheshire, Hilber, and Koster 2018).

In the United States, high-productivity cities on both coasts adopted stringent restrictions on housing supply, with potentially far-reaching negative impacts on the dynamism of local economies. A spatial equilibrium model and data from 220 metropolitan areas suggest that from 1964 to 2009, such constraints lowered aggregate US growth by 36 percent, limiting the number of workers who could access those areas (Hsieh and Moretti 2019). A structural model shows that such planning restrictions are consistent with voting by local citizens who want to preserve high house prices, yielding quantitatively similar results (Duranton and Puga 2019).

Implications for slum formation, upgrading, and redevelopment

Regulations that require consumption of excessive amounts of land add to the monetary cost of formalizing tenure and have been shown to impose a "labor tax" that limits the productivity of individuals—often women (Field 2007)—in the labor market. If the cost of formalization is high, informality will be difficult to avoid, despite its social cost (Cai, Wang, and Zhang 2017), although it lowers poor migrants' productivity through various channels that, taken together, can result in a sizable "labor tax."

In a model of slum growth calibrated to data from Brazil, where high lot size requirements—that were increased rather than lowered during 1980–2010—contributed to informality, removing regulatory barriers and lowering the cost of formalization could have a powerful impact on reducing the extent and growth of slums (Cavalcanti, Da Mata, and Santos 2019). A general equilibrium model with high- and low-income households and serviced (formal) and unserviced (informal) housing calibrated to Brazilian conditions suggests economic growth attracts many low-income households who, with such high cost, cannot afford nonslum housing. Improving the affordability of formal housing and the scope for formalization of slums in high-wage cities could significantly increase aggregate income (Alves 2021).

If regulations that increase formalization costs or make floorspace unaffordable reduce city-level welfare and productivity, why do they remain in place? One factor may be linked to political economy considerations. US data suggest that a less elastic housing supply increases governments' ability to extract rents to benefit public-sector workers via higher wages or politicians via corruption (Diamond 2017). In China, stringent floor area ratio regulations benefited not only existing property owners by increasing land prices but also officials who could receive rents by enforcing such regulations selectively. Data from around 10,000 land auctions in 30 main Chinese cities from 2002 to 2012, matched with project data, show that floor area ratio limits were exceeded in about 20 percent of the cases. Developers with special relationships with public officials tended to make larger upward adjustments, although such loosening of constraints failed to compensate for the large welfare losses imposed by such restrictions, especially in coastal regions (Cai, Wang, and Zhang 2017).

In many settings, the governance challenges associated with enforcing land-use regulation may be heightened by conflicts of interest in public land administration as the same state institution may be responsible for public land management, acquisition, disposal (via sale or lease), land valuation, and regulatory enforcement, including the allocation of urban and industrial land to private parties. Evidence from China shows this can raise multiple governance risks and that, even after a ban on noncompetitive allocations of public land and mandatory use of auctions, it was often easy for favored bidders and local officials to enter into offline side deals that rendered the auction format ineffective (Cai, Henderson, and Zhang 2013).[9]

Data for more than a million local government land sales highlight the magnitude and pervasiveness of land-related corruption. Firms linked to members of the Politburo obtained price discounts of 55 to 60 percent compared to those lacking connections. In return, provincial party secretaries who provided these discounts were 23 percent more likely to be promoted to national leadership positions (Chen and Kung 2019). Credit card data suggest that government bureaucrats received 16 percent higher credit lines and were significantly more likely to default or receive debt forgiveness than similar nonbureaucrats. In regions providing more credit to bureaucrats, the number of bank branch openings and local government deposits was higher, an effect that disappeared after a recent crackdown on corruption (Agarwal et al. 2020).

Regulations that limit housing supply may also remain in place as keeping house prices high benefits current land and property owners at the cost of those, including young people and entrepreneurs, aiming to acquire property. The intergenerational implications of such a policy are illustrated by the case of China, where high house prices increased intergenerational coresidence and savings rates of the young relative to the middle-aged, conditional on income (Rosenzweig and Zhang 2019). The challenges of reform are highlighted by the case of São Paulo, where small increases in the maximum permitted construction density had the expected impact construction density increased density but magnitudes remained small and led to gains in consumer welfare that were outweighed by nominal house price losses, suggesting that such reforms may not be popular politically (Anagol, Ferreira, and Rexer 2021).

Unaffordable floorspace tends to push poor people into informal settlements in hazardous locations that may be established on private land (Brueckner 2013; Brueckner and Selod 2009) or public land (Shah 2014) at cities' fringes, where there is poor access to services and contagious diseases can more easily spread (Brotherhood et al. 2022). Slums are often organized by individuals with ethnic (Marx, Stoker, and Suri 2019) or political connections who may benefit from informal arrangements, even if these have negative environmental or equity effects (Tellman et al. 2021). Although slum housing and services are often of low quality, rents as a share of income are often quite high (Gulyani, Bassett, and Talukdar 2012), with tenants willing to pay a premium (about 18 percent in Nairobi) for more formal rental agreements (Talukdar 2018).

Descriptive studies point toward a pervasive role of rent-seeking squatter organizers in African cities. In Lusaka, Zambia, land invasions are reported to be organized by well-resourced groups who hire poor people to invade land that is then used to develop residential and commercial properties (Chitonge and Mfune 2015). In Nairobi, occupiers are organized along ethnic lines, with protection money paid to powerful politicians (Obala and Mattingly 2014). Challenges are more complex in conflict settings, as in Juba, South Sudan (McMichael 2016). If access to space for informal settlements is determined by powerful political players, regularizing slumdwellers' tenure without dealing with the underlying factors may not reduce, and may even increase, slum growth (Marx, Stoker, and Suri 2013).

Slum upgrading—that is, housing and infrastructure improvement—has long been recommended to improve slum households' living conditions and opportunities for economic and social advancement. Evaluation of the Kampung Improvement Program (KIP), a slum upgrading program in Jakarta, Indonesia, that affected 5 million slumdwellers in 1969–84 suggests that failure to provide transferable land rights may limit the long-term benefits from such programs. Thirty years after the program had ended, KIP areas where land demand was high were more informal and denser, had 50 percent fewer high-rises and more fragmented landholdings, with land values 12 percent lower than in nontreated neighboring areas (Harari and Wong 2019). The fact that the land rights awarded to beneficiaries from the upgrading program were not marketable is a potential reason for such an outcome as in addition to making it impossible for beneficiaries in central locations where land demand increased rapidly to sell and relocate to a location of their choice, it may also have prevented the use of land as collateral for investment in property development.

The notion that without providing real property rights, slum upgrading programs may fall short of their full potential is supported by experimental evidence from Latin America. In El Salvador, Mexico, and Uruguay, very poor population groups were provided basic prefabricated houses to improve their living conditions. Although treated households were happier, improvements in children's health or perceived security were found in only one country, with no noticeable effects on durable good ownership or labor market outcomes (Galiani et al. 2017). The aspirations of neighboring nontreated households to upgrade their housing increased sharply immediately after the intervention, but the effect disappeared completely after two years, without having led to higher housing investment (Galiani, Gertler, and Undurraga 2021). Long-term benefits of slum upgrading may thus be compromised by lack of attention to land tenure, particularly the ability to transfer land that, in a changing environment, makes it difficult to respond to emerging opportunities.

An alternative to slum upgrading is the redevelopment of entire areas. Evidence suggests that this can generate large economic benefits but that gentrification is an issue, and existing slumdwellers may lose access to jobs. Measures such as a requirement of mixed-income development or housing vouchers that presumably could be financed from the increments in land values caused by redevelopment will be important to allow affected slumdwellers to maintain their livelihoods and access opportunities for advancement.

In growing cities, the (formal and informal) building stock will periodically be replaced by higher structures via redevelopment. The role and high welfare cost of formalization frictions in Africa are highlighted in a model where development can be either high and formal, financed by formal credit, or informal. Informal development in slums—that is, low-rise dwellings built with non-loadbearing material—may be the first step toward development at the urban fringe but would be redeveloped and converted to formal tenure as the city expands. Institutional frictions that limit the operation of land markets may preclude this because land that is not formalized cannot be mortgaged, and informal tenure is not secure enough to incentivize construction of tall buildings, leading to crowding in informal settlements that would otherwise be converted and significant welfare losses. A model that incorporates these features calibrated to Nairobi suggests that for slums in old areas near the center, even after buying out slumlords, overcoming institutional frictions would yield gains of more than US$1 billion overall or about US$18,000 per slum household—30 times the typical annual slum rent payments (Henderson, Regan, and Venables 2021). Figure 2.1 illustrates the locations and relative heights of slums in Nairobi.

The level of redevelopment may also be below the social optimum if reconstruction is associated with spillovers that landowners fail to internalize. Historical evidence on land values before and after the 1872 Boston fire, which created an opportunity for large-scale, simultaneous reconstruction, suggests that such effects may have been present in this case. Land values increased among burned plots and nearby unburned plots, capitalizing economic gains comparable to the prior value of the burned buildings. This suggests that while the city had grown rapidly before, negative spillovers from outdated durable buildings constrained city growth by dampening reconstruction incentives (Hornbeck and Keniston 2017). Large redevelopment programs conducted in the United States from the 1960s (Collins and Shester 2013; Hartley et al. 2021) also point to potential gains and distributional effects from redevelopment.

FIGURE 2.1 Three-dimensional display of building heights in Nairobi, including slums

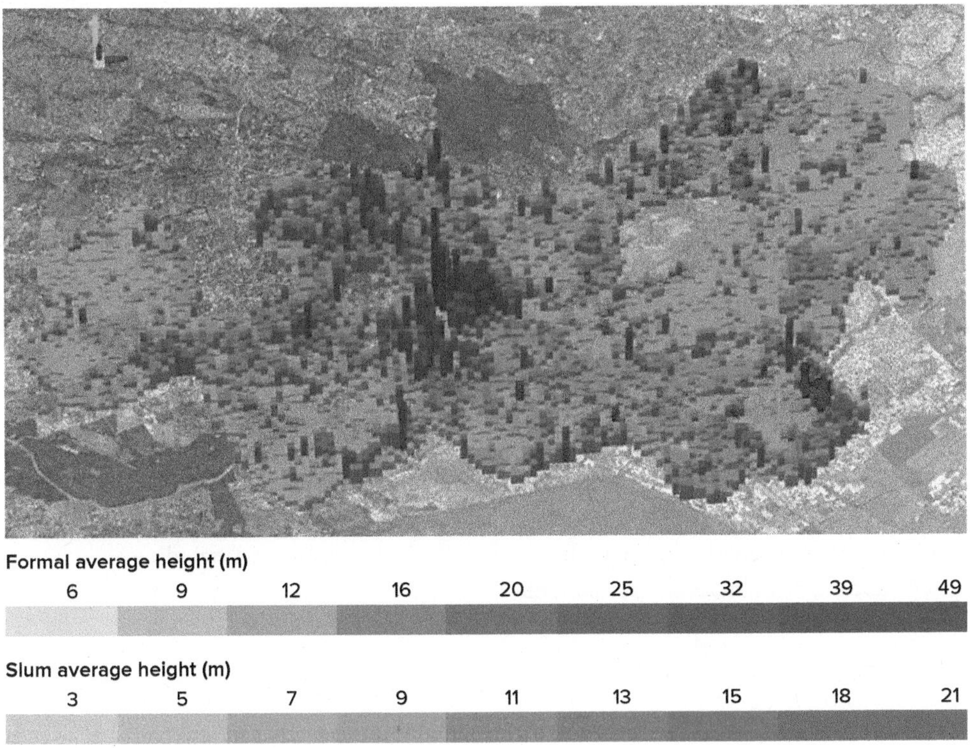

Formal average height (m)

| 6 | 9 | 12 | 16 | 20 | 25 | 32 | 39 | 49 |

Slum average height (m)

| 3 | 5 | 7 | 9 | 11 | 13 | 15 | 18 | 21 |

Source: Henderson et al. 2016, © American Association for the Advancement of Science (AAAS). Reproduced with permission from AAAS; further permission required for reuse.

Developing country evidence on the impact of redeveloping informal areas comes from Mumbai, where slums occupying some 15 percent of the city's area were transformed into upscale housing in 2006–10. Gains were large but unevenly distributed: large spillovers on surrounding locations in terms of higher formal house prices and reduced slum cover, as well as increased population density and a higher share of high-skilled residents, were combined with a reduction in the density of informal employment that was not matched by increases in formal-sector jobs (Gechter and Tsivanidis 2020).

Options to help those losing access due to redevelopment to maintain their living standards include a requirement to build mixed-income housing as part of redevelopment programs, as effectively practiced to distribute gains more equitably in the United Kingdom (Blanco and Neri 2022); transferable housing vouchers (Kumar 2021); and instruments such as land pooling (Lozano-Gracia et al. 2013). In rural Ethiopian settings, giving cash only has been shown to disadvantage those without prior nonfarm job experience (Mezgebo and Porter 2020). In China, those with migration experience were better able to deal with expropriation, and resentment generated by this intervention was lower if the projects it supported yielded public benefits and local governance was transparent (Sha 2022).

Increasing urban mobility and reducing informal city expansion

Beyond adding height, growing cities will also need to expand horizontally. Because transport infrastructure is generally highly persistent, a cost-effective and equitable strategy for urban expansion includes constructing arterial roads or rails to guide private development, providing services cost-effectively ahead rather than after development, and making a mixture of residential and commercial sites along such transport routes available to individuals, for gradual development—a strategy first applied in the 1970s under the label of "sites and services." To the extent that well-planned investment in better mobility can generate economic benefits and form the basis for land value capture to finance such investments, combining it with mixed-income development (including public housing) can increase such benefits.

Benefits from urban mobility and scope for land value capture

The importance of secure private land rights should not detract from the fact that 30 to 50 percent of a city's surface is used for public spaces, including roads, and that the way in which such spaces are used will affect not only amenities but also cities' competitiveness and land values via the number of jobs to which an individual has access. Mapping historical and contemporary road networks in 318 African cities (Baruah, Henderson, and Peng 2021) provides several insights (see figure 2.2).

First, in line with what has been found in developing countries beyond Africa (Brooks and Denoeux 2021), city layouts are persistent over time. Land use patterns established during colonial rule were thus not only maintained in historical centers but also replicated in new developments (1990–2015), resulting in a significant expansion of cities' footprints.

Second, there are marked differences between anglophone and francophone cities. The latter are characterized by more compact development, with colonial layouts often resembling a grid pattern with higher densities near the city center.

Third, the estimated impacts of such planning patterns are large. Anglophone cities cover 29 percent more area and have 54 percent more leapfrog patches and 17 percent more openness, as defined by Burchfield et al. (2006), than otherwise similar francophone cities. Arterial infrastructure is thus an important

FIGURE 2.2   Historical and current transport infrastructure in select African cities

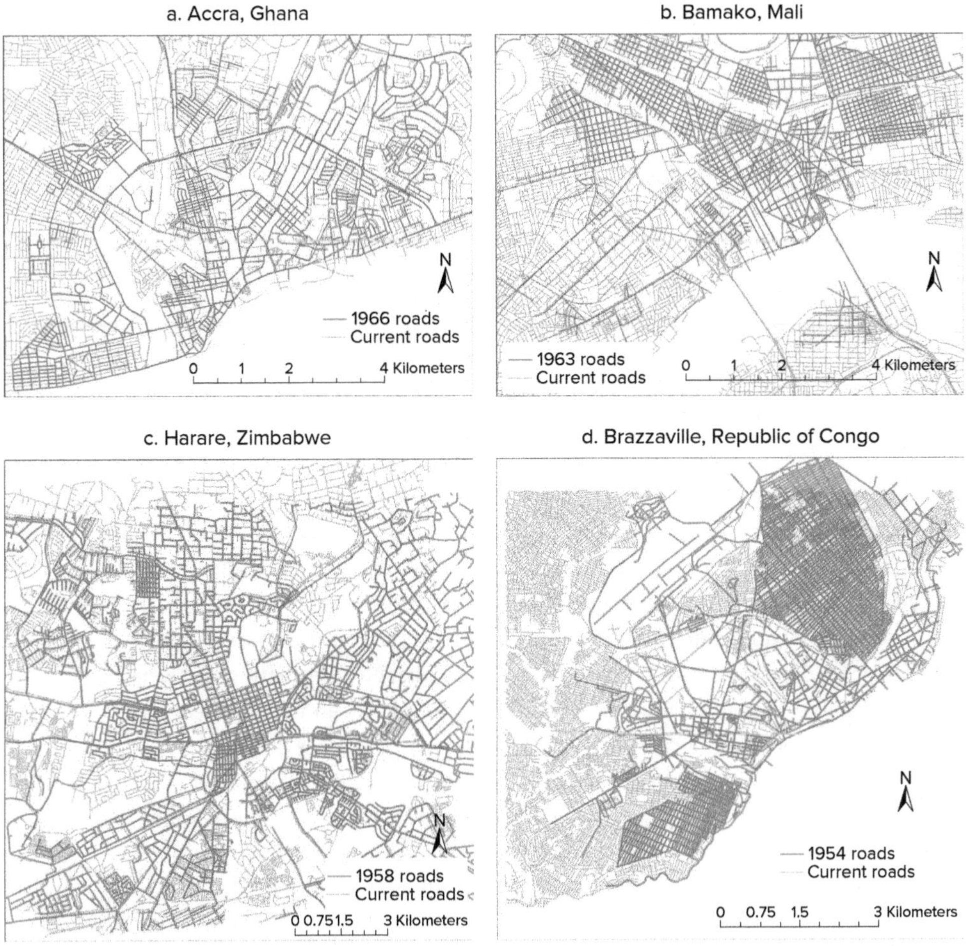

Source: Baruah, Henderson, and Peng 2021. © Oxford University Press. Reproduced with permission from Oxford University Press; further permission required for reuse.

instrument, and used judiciously it can facilitate denser development, reduce commuting costs and carbon footprints, and facilitate higher urban productivity. The findings hold for more restricted samples along borders between francophone and anglophone countries only.[10]

A link between infrastructure density and growth is supported for a sample of some 1,800 cities and towns in Africa where the density of within-city road layouts is linked to economic and city population growth. Cities with greater road density and evenness in the center grew faster, with a 1-kilometer increase in central road density predicted to increase annual population growth by half a percentage point (Brandily and Rauch 2020). The link between local mobility patterns and innovation is documented in more detail for the United States by combining data on patent origin by census block with information on street infrastructure, population, and workforce characteristics for all US census blocks. The results suggest that, via its impact on the ease of local idea exchange for highly knowledge-intensive activities, the density of the street network in a city's physical layout affects the level of innovation, explaining regional innovation differentials beyond traditional location externalities (Roche 2020).

Access to mobility beyond the local level also affects exposure to new ideas and opportunities. In England and Wales, linking individuals across censuses over 60 years (1851, 1881, and 1911) suggests that sons who grew up about 5 kilometers closer to a train station were 11 percentage points more likely to work in a different occupation than their father and 5 percentage points more likely to be upwardly mobile, with most of the effects driven by increased labor market opportunities (Costas-Fernandez, Guerra, and Mohnen 2022). In Indonesia, better roads helped manufacturers create new jobs, increased wages, and allowed workers to shift out of informal employment, in addition to having reduced perishable food prices and raised housing prices, pointing to high returns from road maintenance (Gertler et al. 2022).[11]

Building on Ahlfeldt et al. (2015), who use exogenous changes introduced by the division and unification of Berlin to identify substantial but highly localized production and residential externalities, changes in transportation options will affect land values not only directly but also indirectly by shifting patterns of land use and employment. The underlying processes can be modeled and resulting changes in land prices and commuting patterns under different counterfactual scenarios understood by extending the standard urban model with a setting where a city comprises a discrete number of locations where land is transformed into floorspace by a competitive construction sector; travel time between locations is determined by an existing transport network; competitive firms whose productivity varies across locations use floorspace, labor, and capital to produce final goods; and homogeneous workers who consume housing and a tradable final good decide where to live and work based on locations' amenities and real wages (net of commuting cost).

City models along these lines have been used to analyze historical phenomena such as the changes brought about by the introduction of the steam railway in London between 1801 and 1921, where removal of the rail network would have reduced the population by up to 51.5 percent and the value of land and buildings by 53.3 percent (Heblich, Redding, and Sturm 2020). A model calibrated on Danish registry data to predict the effects of increasing the supply of residential housing on house prices, job mobility, residential sorting, the level of commuting, and welfare shows that telecommuting benefits highly educated workers, who gain and increase their labor supply, while less educated ones benefit little from lower housing prices in urban areas caused by outmigration (Carstensen et al. 2022).

In the past, application of such models to developing country cities has often been constrained by data availability.[12] New data sources, especially satellite imagery and anonymized cell phone records that provide granular evidence on individuals' movements and commuting patterns, offer a basis to apply such models to developed countries more systematically. Registry or administrative data complemented by radar satellite imagery have been used to estimate floor-space, rather than just built area, at national (Arribas-Bel, Garcia-López, and Viladecans-Marsal 2021) or global scale (Esch et al. 2024). Commuting flows based on cell phone data have been used to infer the spatial distribution of income at the workplace and residential levels and by skill group (Kreindler and Miyauchi 2021). Combining such data with information on travel times allows estimation of the key structural parameters of the urban model for developing country cities. It allows the estimation of land prices and floorspace at a high level of granularity but also counterfactual analysis of the impacts of increased floorspace supply or the construction of new roads, thus assessing ex ante the impacts of policies that affect commuting times or residential density (Sturm, Takeda, and Venables 2022).

City-level general equilibrium models along these lines have been used increasingly to analyze the impacts of transport investment in developing countries overall and for specific groups. The bus rapid transit (BRT) system in Dar es Salaam, Tanzania, resulted in welfare gains of 3.0 percent for incumbent low-income residents and 2.5 percent for high-income residents near the BRT line. The overall gains were 2.4 percent for the poor and 2.3 percent for the rich, suggesting that the BRT was pro-poor (Balboni et al. 2021).

Distinguishing formal and informal sectors in a model for Mexico City shows that in areas near newly established subway stations, informality was reduced by 7 percent as the transit improvement allowed workers to shift from the informal to the formal sector, a shift that increased welfare gains from this investment by 20 to 25 percent (Zárate 2022). By comparison, implementation of one of the world's largest BRT systems in Jakarta in 2002–10 did not increase commuter flows but exacerbated congestion along service corridors because of weak implementation, including the quality of expansion corridors (Gaduh, Gračner, and Rothenberg 2022).[13]

In Mumbai, India, extension of the metro led to a robust and significant reduction in the level of pollution (Cropper and Suri 2022), with significant benefits accruing in particular to women, educated workers, and high-income households (Suri 2022). Evidence from India also points toward important gender differences in mobility patterns that reflect differences in the division of labor within the household (Alam et al. 2021). Rental housing transaction records and dynamic bilateral subway travel times in 2010–15 for Beijing, China, allow to assess how subway expansion affected accessibility to business clusters and low-cost rental housing. The results suggest that the formation of firms, especially in skill-intensive sectors, is responsive to better accessibility, with an elasticity of 0.44 for improved access to business clusters and 0.74 for better access to low-cost rental housing (Du and Zheng 2020).[14]

If the benefits from infrastructure investment are capitalized in land values, failure to put cost recovery schemes in place when undertaking large investments would allow landowners rather than the public to reap benefits from such investment. Modeling the BRT in Bogotá, Colombia, suggests that incorporating general equilibrium and reallocation effects increases the estimated welfare gains by 20 to 40 percent beyond what is suggested by static models and that a land value capture scheme could have further increased welfare gains by around 20 percent and provided government revenue of up to 40 percent of construction costs (Tsivanidis 2021).

Extension of transit infrastructure increased land prices in New York by 8 percent, creating US$5.5 billion in new property value, yet less than one-third of the private value created was captured via higher property tax revenue. This suggests that targeted property tax increases can help governments capture a greater share of the added value from infrastructure investment and fund future works (Gupta, Van Nieuwerburgh, and Kontokosta 2022). Having a land registry or fiscal cadaster to provide information on land prices will thus expand the ability to use land value capture for infrastructure construction in a way that, in growing cities, may translate into a permanent advantage.

Combining infrastructure expansion with mixed-income housing development

Beyond facilitating mobility and potentially increasing house prices, public transport infrastructure plays an important role to anchor and coordinate expectations and facilitate private investment in housing and densification along major infrastructure arteries. In doing so, it allows basic services such as water, drainage, and electricity to be provided ahead of development rather than after informal structures have been put up, as in many of today's developing countries. Such advance work allows realizing major cost savings: Smolka and Biderman (2012) estimate that it costs only around a third of the alternative.

A desire to capitalize on early public infrastructure investment to incentivize incremental improvements in housing quality by the poor in anticipation of urban expansion was at the core of the sites-and-services approach supported by the World Bank in the 1970s and 1980s. Key elements of this approach were (a) selecting sites strategically to ensure good connectivity to transport links that would allow residents to access jobs; (b) incorporating a range of plot sizes to reach different income groups, increase density, and avoid segregation by income; (c) developing a hierarchy of road and open space layouts; and (d) ensuring walkability and access to services by fostering mixed use and allocating space for commerce and social services.

Evaluation of the impact of this approach in seven Tanzanian cities with remotely sensed information (on building size, density, and roof quality), using a discontinuity design and household surveys, suggests that by the 2010s, treated areas had a higher share of built area (10 percent larger than a control mean of 0.16), larger buildings, and higher house values than the control. This suggests that public provision of basic infrastructure leveraged private investment in housing quality. The outcomes in newly developed areas were better than those in slums that had been upgraded at a much higher expense, and the estimated project-induced gains in land values are a multiple of the project cost (Michaels et al. 2021).

Long-term changes in Indian cities where sites-and-services projects were implemented along the same lines echo these findings. The main objective of this approach was to create neighborhoods by combining economic factors (access to mobility and jobs) with mixed-income zoning and ex ante planning to provide secure land parcels. The goal of allowing urban expansion in a way that is livable and inclusive was largely achieved (Owens, Gulyani, and Rizvi 2018), including preventing segregation in access to public facilities that otherwise adds to disadvantages faced by marginalized groups in India's urban neighborhoods (Adukia et al. 2022).

As it provided beneficiaries the tenure security needed to expand in a gradual way, the sites and services approach was also more cost-effective than alternatives (Buckley and Kalarickal 2005), in line with global experience of the benefits from mixed-use zoning, which has been shown to increase property values in Europe (Koster and Rouwendal 2012) and the United States (Nakamura, Peiser, and Torto 2018).[15] A recent review suggests that the sites-and-services approach will have to be adapted to changed circumstances in terms of, for example, higher densities, to be in line with land values. However, the approach of providing secure tenure and basic inputs to allow gradual upgrading in line with beneficiaries' means has potential to help provide affordable housing and an opportunity to climb the urban ladder gradually to individuals who otherwise would end up in informality (World Bank 2022).

Urban land and property taxes

Property taxation can strengthen the social contract and allow cities to capitalize on land value appreciation, complement regulatory instruments in encouraging efficient land use, and lay the foundation for further increases in land values by providing public services that will be capitalized into land values in the future. Yet, in most African countries, property tax is paid only for around 10 to 20 percent of urban parcels, and the revenue from such taxes remains low. Changing this will require establishment of a complete tax map, automated mass valuation based on market prices, minimal exemptions, and credible enforcement.

Desirable attributes of property taxes

Urban land values in Africa and beyond have shown dramatic increases recently: in Kampala, Uganda; Cotonou, Benin; and Addis Ababa, Ethiopia, average land prices are reported to have increased by more than 5 percent annually over the past decade. This mirrors global trends: real land and house prices in 14 industrialized economies more than tripled between 1950 and 2015, equivalent to real annual growth of 2 percent. Land price increases account for 80 percent of this rise (Knoll, Schularick, and Steger 2017).[16] Between 2003 and 2014, real Chinese housing prices rose by over 10 percent annually (Glaeser et al. 2017), with similarly large increases in values of commercial and industrial land (Qin, Zhu, and Zhu 2016). As land accounts for more than 80 percent of urban wealth in both China and India (Wang 2014), such increases will affect inequality and access to opportunity for citizens more broadly.

Although such large increases in land prices create enormous potential for land value capture, collection of property taxes in Africa remains low and static. Data for 157 countries show that in the developing world, collection of taxes from land and real estate is well below that in developed countries (table 2.1): instead of 2 percent of gross domestic product (GDP) in Western Europe and North America

TABLE 2.1 Levels of land and real estate taxation in African and world regions
share of GDP (%)

Region	Total 1990–2020	Time period 1990–95	Time period 2015–20	Number of countries
Africa, Central	0.09	0.09	0.10	10
Africa, East	0.08	0.10	0.04	4
Africa, North	0.30	0.05	0.71	3
Africa, South	0.21	0.06	0.26	9
Africa, West	0.22	0.31	0.29	12
EAP	0.39	0.60	0.44	16
ECA	0.52	0.21	0.65	21
LAC	0.52	0.46	0.71	29
ME	0.22	0.14	0.42	11
SAS	0.11	0.19	0.04	8
WENA	1.81	1.79	2.03	34
World	**0.75**	**0.71**	**0.87**	**157**

Source: Based on data from International Monetary Fund Government Finance Statistics 1990–2020.
Note: EAP = East Asia and Pacific; ECA = Eastern Europe and Central Asia; LAC = Latin America and the Caribbean; ME = Middle East; SAS = South Asia; WENA = Western Europe and North America.

and even more in the United Kingdom, the United States, Singapore, and Hong Kong SAR, China, countries in Sub-Saharan Africa collected between 0.04 and 0.29 percent of GDP in property taxes from 2015 to 2020. Raising Sub-Saharan Africa's collection levels to those of Western Europe and North America would generate incremental annual revenue of US$60 billion. Taxes on land and property have thus been identified as one of the largest sources of untapped revenue in Africa (Collier et al. 2017).

Several conceptual arguments favor reliance on property tax. Public goods are generally capitalized in land prices. Experimental evidence from Mexico suggests that infrastructure improvements, such as asphalting of residential streets, resulted in appreciation of local land values by an amount approximately equal to construction costs (Gonzalez-Navarro and Quintana-Domeque 2016). In mid-nineteenth-century Chicago, public provision of water and sewer access doubled property values, generating a total benefit about 60 times construction costs (Coury et al. 2021). In the United States, locally produced and consumed municipal services, such as trash collection, are also capitalized in property values (Gárate and Pennington-Cross 2023). This means that better provision of public services often can be financed from associated increases in property values.

In the developing world, inadequate provision of basic services disproportionately affects welfare and opportunities for the poor, who are unable to invest in private substitutes such as generators or septic tanks. In Zambia, poor water service delivery is associated with a higher incidence of sickness; girls spending more time on chores, possibly at the expense of schoolwork; and a reduction in financial transactions (Ashraf et al. 2021).[17] In the United States, where education is funded from property taxes, changes that made schools more accessible led to significant increases in house prices, including in disadvantaged neighborhoods (Bonilla-Mejia, Lopez, and McMillen 2020). Households that randomly lost access to good schools have been shown to incur moving costs and pay a housing price premium of considerable magnitude to be able to enjoy better schools (Bibler and Billings 2020).

Land taxes are not only an effective way to finance local public goods but, as land is less mobile than labor or capital, also one of the least distortive ways of raising public revenue as land rents are a true scarcity rent (Schwerhoff, Edenhofer, and Fleurbaey 2020).[18] In the standard urban model, a recurring local tax on land can finance the optimum amount of local public goods (Arnott and Stiglitz 1981). Property taxes can reduce wealth inequality without requiring distortive taxes on capital (Bonnet et al. 2021). If labor productivity in manufacturing is greater than that in agriculture, and agricultural and manufactured goods are substitutes (or the economy is open to world trade), land taxes increase aggregate economic output (Kalkuhl and Edenhofer 2017).

Fiscal cadasters have long been a key element of state capacity,[19] and land and property taxation provides a basis for the social contract between taxpayers and the state (Besley and Persson 2014). Even in fragile, low-income settings such as the Democratic Republic of Congo, increased property tax collection triggered a large "participation dividend" by raising citizens' political participation and improving their perception of government responsiveness to their concerns (Weigel 2020). Provision of public goods increased property tax payments even by nonaffected neighbors in Argentina (Carrillo, Castro, and Scartascini 2017), and in Brazil, willingness to pay property taxes is enhanced by better service delivery (Kresch et al. 2023).

Urban property taxes also increase incentives to use land effectively (Oates and Schwab 1997) and discourage land speculation (Norregaard 2013), offering scope to reduce sprawl (Ermini and Santolini 2017; Song and Zenou 2006) and vacancy rates (Segú 2020).[20] Although the fact that property taxes are levied on an illiquid asset may require some adjustments (for example, a scope for deferment by some groups of homeowners),[21] revenue from land taxes is less volatile than revenue from income or business taxes that vary with the business cycle, making projected public revenue from land taxes ideal for financing long-term local investment, as recognized by the fact that municipal bonds are often backed by property tax revenues.

Even accounting for low rates, in most African cities, at most 10 to 20 percent of properties pay tax, due to outdated tax maps and high cost of collection. In the past, this could be attributed to the high fixed cost of property tax collection that led most African countries to levy high transfer taxes (stamp duties), possibly complemented by a regressive flat or area-based recurrent property tax with ample exemptions. This drives transfers into informality, fosters petty corruption, undermines the signaling value of reported market prices, and imposes very large deadweight losses. Putting in place the regulatory and institutional framework for greater urban property tax collection can thus not only provide fiscal benefits but also generate the data needed for planning and establishing property registries. Moreover, because it will allow a reduction in transfer taxes, possibly offset by a revenue-neutral expansion of a recurrent property tax, it will also make it much easier to establish and sustain an urban land registry.

Instead of a recurrent property tax, most African countries levy transaction taxes of, on average, almost 7 percent of the property value. One reason for reliance on transfer taxes despite their disadvantages is historical: with only manual technology, the fixed cost of maintaining the apparatus for property tax collection, including land records, a tax roll, and property valuation, is high. In such a setting, transfer taxes (stamp duties) can be collected with little effort from customers who come to register their transfers. In a digital environment, the cost of establishing the infrastructure for property tax collection is much lower and the benefits from having the infrastructure needed for property taxation in place much higher, making transfer taxes less desirable.

In fact, several studies show that the modest contribution of transfer taxes to public revenue comes at a high cost in terms of governance risks and economic distortions through three channels. First, transfer taxes push property transactions into informality, undermining the registry's quality and currency. Second, they encourage corruption via underreporting of prices, often in return for a side payment to officials, who turn a blind eye. This will undermine the informational content of price data from the registry. Finally, the deadweight loss of raising revenue from transfer taxes is large, even in developed countries where such taxes are applied at levels much lower than the 5 to 7 percent of property value customary in African countries.

In the United Kingdom, transaction taxes caused large distortions to volume, timing, and price of property transactions (Best and Kleven 2018), negatively affecting land markets and labor mobility (Eerola et al. 2021; Hilber and Lyytikainen 2017). A 1.1 percent land transfer tax in Toronto, Canada, led to significant welfare losses (Dachis, Duranton, and Turner 2012), and if decisions on whether to own or rent are accounted for, it was estimated to incur a deadweight loss of 79 percent of revenue (Han, Ngai, and Sheedy 2022). Replacing transfer taxes with an equivalent recurrent land tax on a much larger base is easy technically and can increase revenue, welfare, efficiency, and transparency. If combined with the abolition of transfer taxes, establishment of a recurrent property tax could thus be attractive politically and yield large welfare gains.

Key issues to be addressed to facilitate the use of property taxes

Monitoring land and property prices is important for several reasons, including as a macroeconomic indicator of economic activity, for use in monetary policy and inflation targeting, to measure the stability and risk exposure of the financial sector, and to feed into individual decision-making as well as national accounts and consumer price indices (European Commission 2013). Accurate property valuation also creates potential to harness the potential from property taxes based on market values, especially in settings where, as a result of a large informal sector, the formal tax base is narrow.

The scope for modern technology to implement often dramatic increases in coverage and collection of property tax from a very low base is increasingly recognized (Dzansi et al. 2022). However, instead of ad hoc digitization that only marginally improves performance and fails to address major inefficiencies and inequities, a broader perspective is warranted. Five factors are particularly important: (a) completeness of the tax base, (b) realistic valuation based on market values, (c) limiting exemptions to ensure equity and fairness, (d) enforcement mechanisms to ensure credibility rather than indefinite accumulation of unpaid arrears, and (e) responsibility for administration and benefit sharing.

Tax map completeness. As basic legal provisions and administrative structures for property tax collection are in place (Franzsen and McCluskey 2017),[22] lack of a complete cadastral map is the most fundamental impediment to effective revenue generation from property tax in many African countries. Historically, creating the fiscal cadaster needed to underpin land taxation required manual mapping and data collection, a process that took developed countries years or decades to complete (D'Arcy and Nistotskaya 2018).[23] Building footprints are now available freely or can be generated from high-resolution satellite imagery or, at city scale, drones (Gevaert et al. 2020) at minimal cost.[24] Using footprints for digital field enumeration of land parcel, structure, and owner characteristics for the universe of properties to update legacy data and correct errors, ideally via a web-based public correction process (Wanjiru, Maina, and Onsomu 2019), requires only a modest investment. It will allow establishing a base layer of cadastral data to strengthen state capacity well beyond tax collection, including for planning to improve the quality of local service delivery.

Data on building volumes and footprints that can be generated routinely based on satellite imagery and as two-dimensional footprints are often freely available, as illustrated in figure 2.3. In Italy, the use of such imagery to update property tax rolls and improve fairness of taxation by minimizing tax evasion led to large increases in the collection of local property taxes. Beyond providing economic benefits, this also pushed up rates of incumbent reelection. Political returns were higher where public goods were provided efficiently and where tolerance for tax evasion had been lower at the start (Casaburi and Troiano 2016). Since 2004, Bogotá has been a pioneer in introducing policies of land taxation and land value capture, to very positive effect (Garza and Gonzalez 2021).

Automated valuation based on market prices. Once the universe of taxable properties is identified, a transparent and fair process for determining each property's tax liability needs to be established, ideally distinguishing land and buildings. As they lack the infrastructure to do so fairly, many countries, including Burkina Faso, the Comoros, Ethiopia, and Mozambique, apply rates that are flat or based on land area or building volume, possibly differentiated by zone (Monkam and Moore 2015). Especially in a setting where urban property values increase rapidly, this forgoes large amounts of revenue and is generally highly regressive.

Automated computer-assisted mass valuation (CAMA) involves regressing price data on property characteristics and using the coefficients thus obtained to generate property-specific predicted values. CAMA can overcome the disadvantage of flat rates and is thus a preferred option (Hill 2013). Beyond data on property characteristics and coordinates (Diewert and Shimizu 2022), it requires price data that are ideally obtained from registry records or, if these are not available or distorted due to high transaction taxes, sample enumeration that can be checked against other data sources, such as listings of

FIGURE 2.3 Examples of two-dimensional and three-dimensional imagery of building footprints or volumes based on satellite imagery

a. Building volumes for the center of Kigali, Rwanda

b. Building footprints for the center of Benin City, Nigeria

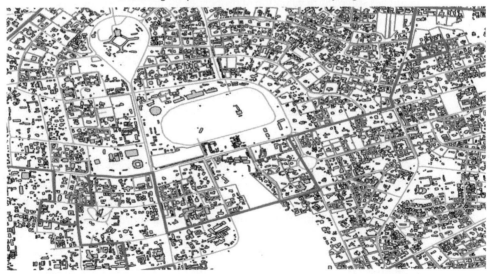

Source: Ecopia AI.

high-end properties.[25] The potential of CAMA is illustrated by the mass valuation of properties in Rwanda, which suggests that a 1 percent ad valorem tax could increase revenue up to tenfold and be more equitable than the system currently in place (Ali, Deininger, and Wild 2020).

Since the 1990s, institutional mechanisms to allow low-cost implementation of CAMA models have been gradually adopted (Gouriéroux and Laferrère 2009). They are now routinely used in most developed countries, with positive impacts on revenue and the perceived fairness and transparency of property taxation (Diewert et al. 2020). In the Netherlands, valuations of some 8 million properties via CAMA are conducted annually, yielding 2.8 percent of GDP in revenue from real estate taxes. Assessed property values are publicly available, improving market functioning and preventing fraud (for example, related to mortgages). Owners can update their data online, and interoperability provides additional benefits (Kuiiper and Kaathman 2015).[26] With repeated cross sections of geocoded microdata, transaction prices can generate adjusted house price indices at virtually any level of spatial disaggregation, as illustrated for Germany by Ahlfeldt, Heblich, and Seidel (2023). In Lithuania, assessed property values more than quadrupled as a result of adopting and gradually refining computerized mass valuation (Almy 2015) that is now at the core of a private sector–driven registry system that provides many ancillary benefits (Grover et al. 2017).

Rather than using mass valuation based on market prices, many African countries still require valuation of properties for tax purposes by a licensed valuer, property by property (Franzsen and McCluskey 2017), a process that is both costly and more prone to discretion. Using CAMA for residential properties and focusing scarce valuation capacity on commercial property have proven to be a more viable way to ensure buoyancy of tax revenue by allowing frequent revaluation. Largely for pedagogical reasons, practitioners have suggested that properties be valued by assigning "points" that are loosely derived from CAMA-type regressions to specific parcel or structure characteristics (Fish 2018). Evidence from Sierra Leone suggests that such systems can result in progressive assessments.[27] Although it will be interesting to see if such systems can increase actual collection levels, the scope for ensuring progressivity and buoyancy of tax revenue, as well as the ability to deal with appeals, may be more limited in such systems than in settings that rely on mass valuation approaches consistent with global valuation standards.

Minimal exemptions. Tax codes in many African countries contain ample exemptions (Franzsen and McCluskey 2017) that may significantly reduce the potential tax yield, as in Rwanda (Ali, Deininger, and Wild 2020). The most important exemptions are related to properties occupied by their owners, possessed by pensioners, or not having title. Although exempting these groups would seem to be politically expedient, it is difficult to justify from an economic perspective (Englund 2003) because all properties consume local services that are supplied using the proceeds from property taxes. From a social perspective, exempting owner-occupied properties forces renters to subsidize most owners, which is regressive.[28] Moreover, governance, efficiency of land use, and perceived fairness of the system may be negatively affected if exemptions are very broad or can be obtained easily.

The above factors imply that in many African countries, only few land users pay property tax. For example, in Senegal, less than 20 percent of properties are on the tax roll, and less than a quarter of those pay anything (Knebelman 2021). Similar or even lower levels of coverage are reported for Zambia (Ali and Deininger 2021), Uganda (Kopanyi and Franzsen 2018), Tanzania (Fjeldstad, Ali, and Katera 2019), Sierra Leone (Jibao and Prichard 2015), Ghana (Dzansi et al. 2022), and the Democratic Republic of Congo (Balan et al. 2020). Although a large literature finds that public disclosure of tax information or social recognition increases compliance (Slemrod, Ur Rehman, and Waseem 2022), public disclosure of property tax payment in Uganda reduced compliance, consistent with the notion that individuals overestimate compliance levels and, once they learn the truth, stop complying so they are not taken advantage of (Regan and Manwaring 2023).[29]

Credible enforcement. If issues of coverage, valuation, and exemptions that contribute to low tax morale are addressed, reducing compliance costs—for example, via electronic billing and mobile payment options (McCluskey et al. 2018)—can help further increase levels of property tax collection.[30] A low-cost but feasible option to improve enforcement would be treating property tax arrears as a high priority lien on the property or requiring tax clearance before any transfer, mortgage, or other encumbrance can be registered on a property. Implicitly deferring tax payment until the asset is liquidated can also address concerns about negative liquidity effects of property taxes, especially on seniors, who, if they are unwilling to move, might have to reduce consumption to pay increasing property taxes levied on the assessed value of their home (Brockmeyer et al. 2020).[31]

Revenue assignment, competition, and capacity building. Efforts to make property taxation more transparent and increase revenue may encounter opposition from politicians if time horizons are short and accountability weak. In Brazil, local politicians failed to take advantage of a free national program to update the cadaster and increase property tax revenue by some 10 percent on average if they feared that doing so would jeopardize their chances of reelection (Christensen and Garfias 2020). Because high-income earners can lower their tax liability by undermining fiscal capacity or by bribing local officials, revenue from property taxes is particularly low in municipalities with high levels of inequality (Hollenbach and Silva 2019). In Colombia, property is similarly systematically undervalued in municipalities that are controlled by large landlords, reducing local governments' ability to provide public goods and jeopardizing future economic development, as evidenced by much lower growth rates decades later (Sanchez-Talanquer 2020).

As it aims to finance local public goods, property tax is best administered locally.[32] Local governments, especially small ones, may, however, lack the capacity to manage all the technical requirements for transparent and fair collection. In line with evidence that improved tax administration can greatly improve tax collection (Basri et al. 2019), capacity building and technical support, possibly via subcontracting of certain functions, can have high returns. In France, cooperation between local governments increased collection by 35 percent, especially when revenue was shared (Breuillé, Duran-Vigneron, and Samson 2018). The ability to learn from neighbors to fill capacity gaps has also been identified as a key determinant of the extent to which Canadian First Nations actually use the property taxation powers granted to them (Feir, Jones, and Scoones 2023). Traditional leaders who enjoy high levels of trust or have private information on local residents may be able to play an important role in helping to increase collections (Tourek et al. 2020).

Programs that provide technical support to increase subnational governments' tax administration capacity on a competitive basis have been effective by generating competitive pressure to neutralize political resistance that higher property taxation may face. In India, a large program (JNNURM) increased urban property taxation (Awasthi, Nagarajan, and Deininger 2020). In Mexico, a competitive national program to regularize urban land rights (CORETT) was similarly successful, despite being opposed by local leaders whose opportunities for patronage it reduced (Larreguy, Marshall, and Trucco 2018).[33] In Nigeria, as detailed in spotlight 2.1, more than 30 states enumerated most of their urban properties using satellite imagery with World Bank support. This activity, completed in slightly more than a year, serves as a launchpad to improve services and lower the cost of acquiring documented land rights (Deininger, Awasthi, and McCluskey 2020), highlighting that establishment of a fiscal cadaster may provide a stepping stone for expanding coverage with documented land rights.

Beyond improving the scope for local revenue collection, generation of a comprehensive tax map with property characteristics and land valuation could have political benefits by (a) providing the basis for a reduction of transaction taxes that would remove a key obstacle to keeping property registries up to date; (b) allowing for a more realistic land-use plan and increasing the effectiveness with which public services will be provided (including by improving the informational basis for subcontracting and monitoring private-sector delivery); (c) reducing the transaction cost in land markets by publishing valuations and using them as an objective benchmark for payment of compensation in case of compulsory land acquisition, for example, for infrastructure construction;

and (d) using the information generated by tax maps and evidence of property tax payment to open up a low-cost path toward recognition of landownership rights.[34]

Implications for policy

Use cadastral data as a foundational layer for land-use planning. Clear land rights and information on land use are a basis not only for operation of land markets and access to long-term finance but also for governments to be able to regulate land use and invest in mobility in a way that maximizes beneficial agglomeration effects and reduces negative externalities and urban costs. Because zoning regulations and building codes in most African cities may not be in line with the objective of managing externalities and incentivizing desirable behavior, data from property registries can be used to audit land use and zoning regulations.

Ensure publicity of land-use restrictions. This can be a first step toward assessing the extent to which residents have access to public services and closing any gaps. It can also help eliminate regulations that, by reducing supply, increase the cost of urban floorspace and drive new arrivals into informality and replace them with rules that increase economic activity (mixed-income developments), strengthen resilience, and contribute to good governance. Ensuring publicity of zoning maps, land-use plans, and an inventory of public land, including its current use and monitoring of encroachment, will be important for private actors to take into account in their decision-making.

Make information on land values widely available. Land registries also provide price data that can help evaluate potential benefits from new infrastructure ex ante and identify ways for financing such works. City-level models can help assess potential benefits and plan arterial infrastructure development, including mechanisms for cost recovery; use land pooling rather than expropriation for cash to acquire land to maximize benefits; and promote private basic mixed housing/commercial development along arteries to avoid segmentation and gentrification and instead provide paths out of informality and toward fully transferable property rights for slumdwellers.

Use land value capture instruments to finance public infrastructure and services. As positive agglomeration effects will in turn be capitalized in land values, at least some of the associated benefits can be recouped via property taxes, and future tax revenue can be used to issue bonds that will help finance investment (for example, in infrastructure) to underpin future growth. Strengthening property taxation will require (a) establishing an up-to-date tax roll drawing on base maps from satellite or drone imagery; (b) relying on current market value, determined objectively via a computerized mass valuation model, to assess tax liability and make valuations public; (c) minimizing exemptions and ensuring that owner-occupied, untitled, and empty properties are charged property taxes; (d) enforcing property tax arrears through appropriate means, for example, requiring a tax clearance certificate for subsequent registrations; (e) assigning most of the revenue to local governments to increase collection incentives; (f) actively promoting the use of capital gains taxes and betterment levies to finance public infrastructure investment; and (g) respecting the social contract by informing the public on the use of property tax revenue.

SPOTLIGHT

Spotlight 2.1: Urban land taxation in Nigeria

In Nigeria's federal system, taxes on land and property are the responsibility of states and municipalities. As part of a broad overhaul of governance and taxation in the early 2000s, Lagos State introduced reforms that increased tax revenue more than tenfold, with associated improvements in public services (Cheeseman and De Gramont 2017). The 2001 Land Use Charge (LUC) Act simplified land and property tax in three ways. (a) Ground rent, tenement rates, and neighborhood improvement charges that had previously been assessed and collected separately were consolidated into a single charge, based on a formula.[35] (b) The tax base was broadened by requiring all properties to pay the LUC,[36] not just those that were formally registered. To make this viable politically, the rates were very modest by global standards (0.0375 percent for owner-occupied and 0.375 percent for commercial and leased properties), although it was intended that they be raised over time (Goodfellow and Owen 2018). (c) Administration was simplified by making the state government responsible for assessment and collection, with a formula-based redistribution of revenues to local councils.[37]

Translating these regulatory changes into actual revenues required expanding the coverage of the valuation roll and setting up a collection system. In Lagos, a contractor was tasked with identifying properties and, based on satellite imagery from 2007–10, identified 750,000 properties, for which three-dimensional vector data were created. Billing and collection were contracted out to service providers, who received a share of the proceeds to cover their cost. To increase payment incentives, in 2012, Lagos opened 18 zonal offices. An electronic billing system was created, and in 2016, consent fees for property registration and transfer were reduced from 15 to 3 percent of the property value (Goodfellow and Owen 2018). Reinforced by authorities placing markers or plaques on liable properties, LUC payment was widely perceived as conferring de facto recognition, a factor that, based on anecdotal evidence, was a major motivation for tax payment (Goodfellow and Owen 2020).

Although these measures resulted in remarkable one-time increases in revenue, ensuring a fair and buoyant tax will need to build on these advances in three respects:

(a) Although the state government estimates that Lagos has by now more than 2 million structures, coverage has barely increased beyond the 750,000 covered by the original exercise, no new imagery has been acquired, and even for properties already on the valuation roll, updates are ad hoc and at the initiative of owners or occupants. A systematic process for updating that is fully interoperable and integrated with the administrative databases of public agencies (for example, building permits or property transfers) or private entities (for example, water and electricity companies) can help improve the currency and usefulness of valuations. This can be combined with periodic updating of imagery to capture new developments and ensure fairness.

(b) Data suggest that, although the rates are quite low, less than 30 percent of properties pay their dues. Weak enforcement may undermine perceived fairness and payment morale. It may be necessary to find innovative ways to increase compliance, for example, by linking to other services or enforcing penalties.

(c) A process for adjusting the market values used in the valuation formula is needed to prevent erosion of real tax receipts and eliminate the need for large hikes in rates to maintain real revenue that are difficult politically. In 2018, efforts to modify the LUC Act to increase rates and penalties for non-payment backfired and had to be rescinded in 2020.[38]

The positive impact of property tax reform in Lagos prompted 13 other states to adopt LUC Acts that copy most of the Lagos provisions.[39] Several states learned from the Lagos experience and increased their capacity by establishing dedicated geographic information system agencies to maintain interoperable spatial data for use by all public bodies to (a) digitize legacy data (deeds and survey plans) to eliminate overlaps and ensure that records are current; (b) establish web portals so that documents can be submitted and property taxes paid online,[40] ensuring transparent workflows; and (c) pilot expansion of coverage by using satellite imagery to identify properties and tablets for in-person collection of property and owner details.[41]

To encourage use of the potential for collecting higher urban land-use charges, the World Bank supported the State Fiscal Transparency Accountability and Sustainability Program for Results, which envisages lump-sum transfers of US$2.5 million to states that generate or update property records for at least 50 percent of urban structures with electricity connections, link these to the collection of land-use charges, and create a system for monitoring progress. Of the 36 Nigerian states, 34 met the readiness criteria[42] qualifying them for technical assistance that includes (a) up-to-date, high-resolution imagery and three-dimensional vector data for all urban structures and two-dimensional vector data for all rural structures; (b) software and training for tablet-based field data collection; and (c) technical support and regular peer learning on how to share data across agencies and use them for automated electronic tax collection. The fact that some states are already moving beyond the initial target of covering all their urban structures suggests that this could make a significant contribution to creating local revenue from the estimated 12.5 million urban structures in Nigeria, increasing tenure security and the functioning of land markets, and improving land management, planning, and service provision.

Interestingly, the changes were achieved independently of the country's land administration system, which is one of the weakest globally, ranking 183 of the 186 countries for which data are reported in the "Registering Property" section of the World Bank's Doing Business indicators.[43] In 2009, efforts to establish a Presidential Technical Committee on Land Reform that was expected to mature into a National Land Commission (Mabogunje 2009) had little impact on land administration, which, at a cost per parcel of about US$500 (Deininger, Gao, and Xia 2020), is unaffordable for all but a narrow minority.

Notes

1 | Engineering studies that account for cities' total life-cycle greenhouse gas emissions suggest that buildings with 7 to 27 floors are optimal (Resch et al. 2016), although high-density low-rises may be preferable for stable populations (Pomponi et al. 2021). Buildings in African cities have fewer than two floors on average.

2 | Modeling a system of cities, their internal urban structures in the United States suggests that larger cities will be skill abundant and specialize in skill-intensive activities, a notion supported by the data (Davis and Dingel 2020).

3 | The spatial scale of such effects, as well as the resulting ability of private or public actors to internalize them, depends on the underlying mechanism: physical inputs can be shared over long distances via truck transport, labor market pooling is limited to commuting areas, and knowledge spillovers, although possibly embedded in larger organizations, are often highly localized.

4 | In this context, a doubling of urban density is associated with higher wage premiums (by 4 percent), patent activity (19 percent), consumption variety (12 percent), green spaces (23 percent), and use of noncar transport (7 percent), as well as reductions in vehicle mileage (–8.5 percent), energy consumption (–7 percent), pollution (–8 percent), crime (–8.5 percent), and unit costs of providing local public services (–14.4 percent), suggesting that if institutions are in place, cities can be more innovative, green, efficient, and resilient to exogenous shocks, including climate-related ones, than rural areas (Ahlfeldt and Pietrostefani 2019).

5 | Regulation to reduce sulfur pollution reduced exposure and triggered incremental reductions in mortality and ill health that added up to large gains in productivity for the working-age population (Barreca, Neidell, and Sanders 2021).

6 | A one standard deviation improvement in compactness (equivalent to a reduction in the average within-city distance of 400 meters) is estimated to be associated with a 3 percent population increase.

7 | The floor area ratio, which is often fixed by regulations, is the ratio of a building's floorspace to the size of its lot. It ranges from about 1 in São Paulo and 1.33 in Mumbai and Delhi to 20 or more in Tokyo and Singapore, with intermediate values for Shanghai (8), San Francisco and Vancouver (9), and New York (15) (Brueckner and Sridhar 2012).

8 | In New York, a lower maximum floor area ratio correlates with lower land values, earlier demolition, and less dense new construction (Moon and Ahn 2022).

9 | Hsu et al. (2017) show that the volume of land sales by prefectural leaders is closely linked to their length of tenure and presumably also linked to their prospects for promotion.

10 | In a similar setting in New York, O'Grady (2014) finds that in areas north of Lower Manhattan, where, based on an 1811 plan, expansion was guided by a grid layout, real estate values in 2013 were 30 percent higher than where this was not the case. Brooks and Lutz (2016) find that to-be-assembled land in Los Angeles trades at a 15 to 40 percent premium; apparently, land assembly there is affected by frictions.

11 | The elasticity of household welfare with respect to road quality is 0.16, and the benefit/cost ratio for road maintenance investments is 2.8.

12 | In many of these countries, definitions of urban areas based on administrative boundaries often yield estimates that are imprecise or misleading (Dijkstra et al. 2021). Spatial data on built space, complemented by night lights data as needed (Bluhm and Krause 2022), have also been used to develop new methods of defining built area (De Bellefon et al. 2021).

13 | Time savings from the opening of a new subway line in Shanghai resulted in an average house price appreciation of 3.75 percent, with the most distant residential zone enjoying the largest appreciation (Zhou et al. 2021).

14 | Severen (2018) uses a panel of bilateral commuting flows to assess how rail expansions in Los Angeles affected the spatial distribution of people and land prices, looking at the interaction of tract-specific labor demand shocks with the city's spatial configuration to identify structural parameters. The study estimates that expansion caused an increase of 7 to 13 percent in commuting between pairs of connected tracts. Although this amounts to large annual benefits (US$246 million), it covers only around one-third of the annualized construction costs.

15 | In Germany, life satisfaction is positively affected by lower average degrees of soil sealing, larger shares of vegetation, and more heterogeneous configurations of medium- and low-density urban fabric, especially in areas with higher population density (Bertram et al. 2022).

16 | Farmland prices increased at about the same rate as urban property prices.

17 | Between 1916 and 1924, higher school funding (by more than 70 percent) in the United States pushed up educational attainment and wages later in life, particularly for the children of unskilled workers. Increases in spending can explain around 50 percent of the sizable increase in educational attainment of cohorts born between 1895 and 1915 (Schmick and Shertzer 2019).

18 | US evidence also shows that if housing supply is inelastic, land and property taxes are capitalized in land (Lutz 2015) or property values (Livy 2018) so that future owners are not affected (Hoj, Rahbek Jorgensen, and Schou 2018)—a finding supported for high-value properties in Sweden (Elinder and Persson 2017).

19 | In Europe, increased capacity for tax collection was historically a key determinant of long-run economic growth (Dincecco and Katz 2016).

20 | In developed countries, the visibility and salience of property taxes (Cabral and Hoxby 2012), while increasing accountability (Presbitero, Sacchi, and Zazzaro 2014), often make getting political support for them challenging (Bahl and Wallace 2008). Fiscal policy and land-use regulation interact strongly, and governments must align those policies carefully if they are to achieve their land-use objectives (Blochliger et al. 2017).

21 | With imperfect credit markets and limited liquidity of the underlying asset, rising property values will result in higher property tax bills without increasing incomes, reducing owners' liquidity, an issue that can be addressed through deferment of tax liability, which is more pronounced in rural areas (Hoff 1991). The wealth effects generated by house price movement affect labor market participation (Liu and Yang 2020), consumption, mortgage defaults, and attitudes toward property taxation (Wong 2020). Although deferment of bills by putting a lien on the property is a response widely practiced by developed economies (Slack and Bird 2014), provision of liquidity to constrained taxpayers has been raised as an alternative policy instrument (Brockmeyer et al. 2020).

22 | As per Franzsen and McCluskey (2017), the legal basis for assessing urban property tax is in place in most of Africa: of 49 Sub-Saharan African countries, 29 have all urban areas liable for land and property taxes, 18 apply such taxes in some areas (for example, the capital), and 2 have no urban property tax.

23 | The Swedish cadaster, launched in 1530, achieved complete national coverage in 1628. Greece still lacks a functioning national cadaster. This variation is associated with vast differences in tax discipline and trust. Even a decade ago, establishing tax maps for individual cities in World Bank–supported projects took years, as the example of Tanzania shows.

24 | Satellite imagery can eliminate the need for costly and complex aerial photography (Carolini, Gelaye, and Khan 2020), but regulation of the use of drones can have large benefits (Stöcker et al. 2017) well beyond facilitating collection of property taxes.

25 | Registry records can be used if land markets are sufficiently representative and liquid and if transfer taxes do not discourage truthful land value declaration. Ben-Shahar, Golan, and Sulganik (2020) propose a method to identify transactions suspected of underreporting. They apply this to all transactions in Israel over 1998–2015 and conclude that some 8 percent of transactions are underreported, with an average price that is 30 percent below the projected true price.

26 | In Europe, owners' estimated property values are around 9 percent above assessed values, ranging between 3.2 percent in Germany and 22 percent in Italy, a discrepancy that can partly be explained by household characteristics, particularly the level of indebtedness (Le Roux and Roma 2019).

27 | Taxes to be paid decreased from US$14.30 to US$4.30 for properties in the lowest quintile and increased from US$41.60 to US$142.30 for the highest quintile. See https://africanarguments .org/2020/05/freetown-just-implemented-a-new-tax-system-that-could-quintuple-revenue/.

28 | In the United States, various housing tax benefits incentivize owners to consume too much housing. Simulations suggest that a policy eliminating most tax benefits associated with housing and indexing taxes to local wage levels would increase efficiency (Albouy and Hanson 2014). Even exempting a threshold is regressive because the tax is levied on assessed rather than market values (McMillen and Singh 2020).

29 | Reminders to pay taxes were effective if they were credible (Castro and Scartascini 2015) or described the effects of nonpayment (Chirico et al. 2017). Beliefs about the ability of the authorities to penalize defaulters also affected truthful declaration of other taxes (Lopez-Luzuriaga and Scartascini 2019). Appeals to civic duty had a limited effect (Del Carpio 2022), even if they included information about neighbors' compliance levels, and making delinquency more visible increased compliance only for small debts (Perez-Truglia and Troiano 2018).

30 | In a randomized experiment in Zambia, text message reminders significantly increased payment, especially for those on a network that allowed mobile payment. Effects were particularly large for payers outside the capital (Ali and Deininger 2021).

31 | As housing wealth is illiquid, changes in wealth (for example, via housing booms or property tax liabilities) can trigger large wealth effects and, through these, affect consumption or economic activity. In Italy, tax increases on the main dwelling led to large expenditure cuts among mortgagors who held low liquid wealth despite owning sizable illiquid assets (Surico and Trezzi 2019). In the United States, property tax limits reduced female labor force participation by 0.7 to 1.4 percentage points during the 2005–06 housing boom (Liu and Yang 2020).

32 | Because property tax is a local tax, assigning proceeds to local governments will maximize accountability. Franzsen and McCluskey (2017) show that property tax revenues are assigned exclusively to local governments in 32 countries, to the central and local levels jointly in 6, and exclusively to the center in 4.

33 | JNNRUM is the Jawaharlal Nehru National Urban Renewal Mission; CORETT is the Comisión para la Regularización de la Tenencia de la Tierra (Commission for the Regularization of Land Tenure).

34 | For example, in Peru, expected land value increments from titling even informal slum land, if adopted jointly with land taxation, are argued to allow implementation of a titling program that would be fully self-financing (Hawley, Miranda, and Sawyer 2018).

35 | The rate is computed as $LUC = M * [(LA * LV) + (BA * BV * PCR)]$, where M is the tax rate; LA, LV, BA, and BV are land and building area and value (based on lists of registered assessment values for different neighborhoods maintained by the state government); and PCR is a property code rate to account for building quality.

36 | Ground rent was a fee, pegged to the market value of land, to be paid by holders of formal title (certificate of occupancy) to the state government; tenement rates were a neighborhood-specific flat fee to be paid by occupants to the local council for access to services; and neighborhood improvement charges were payable to the state government in areas that had received specific investments. By requiring LUC to be paid by all properties, the reform eliminated the de facto exemption of untitled properties from paying ground rent, which significantly increased the tax base.

37 | Revenues are split 70/30 between state and local governments after deductions to cover charges for the private tax collection firm (10 percent), the appeals tribunal (5 percent), and a management fee (0.5 percent) for the trustee.

38 | A clause in the amendments that mandates valuations by a licensed valuer on a property-by-property basis was retained. It seems to be a step backward that will be difficult to implement, gives an excuse for nonpayment by property owners, and largely benefits licensed valuers.

39 | Beyond Lagos, LUC including ground rent was legislated in Borno, Edo, Ondo, and Osun; LUC excluding ground rent was adopted in Abia, Adamawa, Ebonyi, Enugu, Gombe, Jigawa, Kaduna, Plateau, and Sokoto.

40 | In Gombe, revenue collection increased from N8.3 million in 2011 to N136 million in 2019.

41 | Properties are digitized from satellite imagery, legacy data are preloaded on enumerators' tablets, a heavy awareness program is conducted, and properties with absent owners are geotagged for revisit with a flyer of absenteeism pasted at the front of the property and before acceptance quality assurance/quality control is done on all captured data sets submitted in real time.

42 | Eligibility criteria are to (a) constitute a steering committee headed by the governor or commissioner of finance to oversee the process and bring stakeholders together, (b) hire a state program coordinator to elaborate a workplan to meet the target within the project time frame, (c) allocate the necessary budgets to implement the workplan, and (d) agree to share depersonalized data for analytical purposes with the World Bank.

43 | With a mean Land Administration Quality Index of 5.3 (and a value below 10 for all states except the Federal Capital Territory), the subnational Doing Business assessment makes clear the low quality of land administration infrastructure overall. The differences are somewhat larger in the overall Registering Property score (which ranges from 45.7 for Kaduna, to 16 for Rivers, Cross Rivers, and Kebbi).

References

Adukia, A., S. Asher, K. Jha, P. Novosad, and B. Tan. 2022. "Residential Segregation and Unequal Access to Local Public Services: Evidence from 1.5m Neighborhoods in India." Harvard University, Cambridge, MA.

Agarwal, S., W. Qian, A. Seru, and J. Zhang. 2020. "Disguised Corruption: Evidence from Consumer Credit in China." *Journal of Financial Economics* 137 (2): 430–50.

Ahlfeldt, G., and J. Barr. 2020. "The Economics of Skyscrapers: A Synthesis." CEPR Discussion Paper 14987, Centre for Economic Policy Research, London.

Ahlfeldt, G. M., S. Heblich, and T. Seidel. 2023. "Micro-geographic Property Price and Rent Indices." *Regional Science and Urban Economics* 98: 103836.

Ahlfeldt, G. M., and E. Pietrostefani. 2019. "The Economic Effects of Density: A Synthesis." *Journal of Urban Economics* 111: 93–107.

Ahlfeldt, G. M., S. J. Redding, D. M. Sturm, and N. Wolf. 2015. "The Economics of Density: Evidence from the Berlin Wall." *Econometrica* 83 (6): 2127–89.

Alam, M. M., M. L. Cropper, M. Herrera Dappe, and P. Suri. 2021. "Closing the Gap: Gender, Transport, and Employment in Mumbai." Policy Research Working Paper 9569, World Bank, Washington, DC.

Albouy, D., and A. Hanson. 2014. "Are Houses Too Big or in the Wrong Place? Tax Benefits to Housing and Inefficiencies in Location and Consumption." *Tax Policy and the Economy* 28 (1): 63–96.

Ali, D., and K. Deininger. 2024. "Can Mobile Reminders and Electronic Payment Options Increase Africa's Property Tax Collection? Evidence from a Randomized Experiment in Zambia." Policy note, World Bank, Washington, DC.

Ali, D. A., K. Deininger, and M. Wild. 2020. "Using Satellite Imagery to Create Tax Maps and Enhance Local Revenue Collection." *Applied Economics* 52 (4): 415–29.

Almy, R. 2015. "Property Valuation and Taxation in Lithuania." *Land Tenure Journal* 15 (2): 29–48.

Alves, G. 2021. "Slum Growth in Brazilian Cities." *Journal of Urban Economics* 122: 103327.

Anagol, S., F. Ferreira, and J. Rexer. 2021. "Estimating the Economic Value of Zoning Reform." NBER Working Paper 29440, National Bureau of Economic Research, Cambridge, MA.

Antwi, A., and J. Adams. 2003. "Economic Rationality and Informal Urban Land Transactions in Accra, Ghana." *Journal of Property Research* 20 (1): 67–90.

Arnott, R. J., and J. E. Stiglitz. 1981. "Aggregate Land Rents and Aggregate Transport Costs." *Economic Journal* 91 (362): 331–47.

Arribas-Bel, D., M. À. Garcia-López, and E. Viladecans-Marsal. 2021. "Building(s and) Cities: Delineating Urban Areas with a Machine Learning Algorithm." *Journal of Urban Economics* 125: 103217.

Ashraf, N., E. Glaeser, A. Holland, and B. M. Steinberg. 2021. "Water, Health and Wealth: The Impact of Piped Water Outages on Disease Prevalence and Financial Transactions in Zambia." *Economica* 88 (351): 755–81.

Au, C.-C., and J. V. Henderson. 2006. "Are Chinese Cities Too Small?" *Review of Economic Studies* 73 (3): 549–76.

Awasthi, R., M. Nagarajan, and K. W. Deininger. 2020. "Property Taxation in India: Issues Impacting Revenue Performance and Suggestions for Reform." *Land Use Policy* 110: 104539.

Bahl, R., and S. Wallace. 2008. "Reforming the Property Tax in Developing Countries: A New Approach." International Studies Program Working Paper 08-19, Andrew Young School of Policy Studies, Georgia State University, Atlanta.

Bakkensen, L., and L. Blair. 2022. "Wind Code Effectiveness and Externalities: Evidence from Hurricane Michael." University of Arizona, Tucson.

Balan, P., A. Bergeron, G. Tourek, and J. Weigel. 2020. "Land Formalization in Weak States: Experimental Evidence from Urban Property Titling in the D.R. Congo." Working paper, Harvard University, Cambridge, MA.

Balboni, C., G. Bryan, M. Morten, and B. Siddiqi. 2021. "Could Gentrification Stop the Poor from Benefiting from Urban Improvements?" *AEA Papers and Proceedings* 111: 532–7.

Barreca, A. I., M. Neidell, and N. J. Sanders. 2021. "Long-Run Pollution Exposure and Mortality: Evidence from the Acid Rain Program." *Journal of Public Economics* 200: 104440.

Baruah, N. G., J. V. Henderson, and C. Peng. 2021. "Colonial Legacies: Shaping African Cities." *Journal of Economic Geography* 21 (1): 29–65.

Basri, M. C., M. Felix, R. Hanna, and B. A. Olken. 2019. "Tax Administration vs. Tax Rates: Evidence from Corporate Taxation in Indonesia." NBER Working Paper 26150, National Bureau of Economic Research, Cambridge, MA.

Baylis, P., and J. Boomhower. 2023. "The Economic Incidence of Wildfire Suppression in the United States." *American Economic Journal: Applied Economics* 15 (1): 442–73.

Ben-Shahar, D., R. Golan, and E. Sulganik. 2020. "Tax Evasion in the Housing Market: Identification and Exploration." *Journal of Real Estate Research* 42 (3): 315–40.

Bento, A., M. Freedman, and C. Lang. 2015. "Who Benefits from Environmental Regulation? Evidence from the Clean Air Act Amendments." *Review of Economics and Statistics* 97 (3): 610–22.

Bertaud, A. 2014. "Converting Land into Affordable Housing Floor Space." Policy Research Working Paper 6870, World Bank, Washington, DC.

Bertaud, A., and J. K. Brueckner. 2005. "Analyzing Building-Height Restrictions: Predicted Impacts and Welfare Costs." *Regional Science and Urban Economics* 35 (2): 109–25.

Bertram, C., J. Goebel, C. Krekel, and K. Rehdanz. 2022. "Urban Land Use Fragmentation and Human Well-Being." *Land Economics* 98 (2): 399–420.

Besley, T., and T. Persson. 2014. "Why Do Developing Countries Tax So Little?" *Journal of Economic Perspectives* 28 (4): 99–120.

Best, M. C., and H. J. Kleven. 2018. "Housing Market Responses to Transaction Taxes: Evidence from Notches and Stimulus in the U.K." *Review of Economic Studies* 85 (1): 157–93.

Bibler, A., and S. B. Billings. 2020. "Win or Lose: Residential Sorting after a School Choice Lottery." *Review of Economics and Statistics* 102 (3): 457–72.

Billings, S. B., and K. T. Schnepel. 2017. "The Value of a Healthy Home: Lead Paint Remediation and Housing Values." *Journal of Public Economics* 153: 69–81.

Blanco, H., and L. Neri. 2022. "Knocking It Down and Mixing It Up: Spillover Effects of Public Housing Regenerations." Working paper, New York University, New York.

Blochliger, H., C. Hilber, O. Schoni, and M. Von Ehrlich. 2017. "Local Taxation, Land Use Regulation, and Land Use: A Survey of the Evidence." OECD Economics Department Working Paper 1375, OECD Publishing, Organisation for Economic Co-operation and Development, Paris.

Bluhm, R., and M. Krause. 2022. "Top Lights: Bright Cities and Their Contribution to Economic Development." *Journal of Development Economics* 157: 102880.

Bonilla-Mejia, L., E. Lopez, and D. McMillen. 2020. "House Prices and School Choice: Evidence from Chicago's Magnet Schools' Proximity Lottery." *Journal of Regional Science* 60 (1): 33–55.

Bonnet, O., G. Chapelle, A. Trannoy, and E. Wasmer. 2021. "Land Is Back, It Should Be Taxed, It Can Be Taxed." *European Economic Review* 134: 103696.

Bosker, M., and E. Buringh. 2017. "City Seeds: Geography and the Origins of the European City System." *Journal of Urban Economics* 98: 139–57.

Brandily, P., and F. Rauch. 2020. "Within-City Roads and Urban Growth." Working paper, London School of Economics, London.

Breuillé, M.-L., P. Duran-Vigneron, and A.-L. Samson. 2018. "Inter-municipal Cooperation and Local Taxation." *Journal of Urban Economics* 107: 47–64.

Brockmeyer, A., A. Estefan, K. Ramirez Arras, and J. C. Suarez Serrato. 2020. *Taxing Property in Developing Countries: Theory and Evidence from Mexico*. Washington, DC: World Bank.

Brooks, L., and G. Denoeux. 2021. "What If You Build It and They Don't Come? How the Ghost of Transit Past Haunts Transit Present." *Regional Science and Urban Economics* 94: 103671.

Brooks, L., and B. Lutz. 2016. "From Today's City to Tomorrow's City: An Empirical Investigation of Urban Land Assembly." *American Economic Journal: Economic Policy* 8 (3): 69–105.

Brotherhood, L., T. Cavalcanti, D. Da Mata, and C. Santos. 2022. "Slums and Pandemics." *Journal of Development Economics* 157: 102882.

Brueckner, J. K. 2013. "Urban Squatting with Rent-Seeking Organizers." *Regional Science and Urban Economics* 43 (4): 561–9.

Brueckner, J. K., and H. Selod. 2009. "A Theory of Urban Squatting and Land-Tenure Formalization in Developing Countries." *American Economic Journal: Economic Policy* 1 (1): 28–51.

Brueckner, J. K., and K. S. Sridhar. 2012. "Measuring Welfare Gains from Relaxation of Land-Use Restrictions: The Case of India's Building-Height Limits." *Regional Science and Urban Economics* 42 (6): 1061–7.

Brülhart, M., K. Desmet, and G.-P. Klinke. 2020. "The Shrinking Advantage of Market Potential." *Journal of Development Economics* 147: 102529.

Buckley, R. M., and J. Kalarickal. 2005. "Housing Policy in Developing Countries: Conjectures and Refutations." *World Bank Research Observer* 20 (2): 233–57.

Burchfield, M., H. G. Overman, D. Puga, and M. A. Turner. 2006. "Causes of Sprawl: A Portrait from Space." *Quarterly Journal of Economics* 121 (2): 587–633.

Cabral, M., and C. Hoxby. 2012. "The Hated Property Tax: Salience, Tax Rates, and Tax Revolts." NBER Working Paper 18514, National Bureau of Economic Research, Cambridge, MA.

Cai, H., J. V. Henderson, and Q. Zhang. 2013. "China's Land Market Auctions: Evidence of Corruption?" *RAND Journal of Economics* 44 (3): 488–521.

Cai, H., Z. Wang, and Q. Zhang. 2017. "To Build above the Limit? Implementation of Land Use Regulations in Urban China." *Journal of Urban Economics* 98: 223–33.

Carolini, G. Y., F. Gelaye, and K. Khan. 2020. "Modelling Improvements to Property Tax Collection: The Case of Addis Ababa." ICTD Working Paper 103, International Centre for Tax and Development, Brighton, UK.

Carrillo, P. E., E. Castro, and C. Scartascini. 2017. "Do Rewards Work? Evidence from the Randomization of Public Works." IDB Working Paper IDB-WP-794, Inter-American Development Bank, Washington, DC.

Carstensen, C. L., M. J. Hansen, F. Iskhakov, J. Rust, and B. Schjerning. 2022. "A Dynamic Equilibrium Model of Commuting, Residential and Work Location Choices." University of Copenhagen, Copenhagen.

Casaburi, L., and U. Troiano. 2016. "Ghost-House Busters: The Electoral Response to a Large Anti-tax Evasion Program." *Quarterly Journal of Economics* 131 (1): 273–314.

Castro, L., and C. Scartascini. 2015. "Tax Compliance and Enforcement in the Pampas: Evidence from a Field Experiment." *Journal of Economic Behavior and Organization* 116: 65–82.

Cavalcanti, T., D. Da Mata, and M. Santos. 2019. "On the Determinants of Slum Formation." *Economic Journal* 129 (621): 1971–91.

Chauvin, J. P., E. Glaeser, Y. Ma, and K. Tobio. 2017. "What Is Different about Urbanization in Rich and Poor Countries? Cities in Brazil, China, India and the United States." *Journal of Urban Economics* 98: 17–49.

Cheeseman, N., and D. De Gramont. 2017. "Managing a Mega-City: Learning the Lessons from Lagos." *Oxford Review of Economic Policy* 33 (3): 457–77.

Chen, T., and J. K.-S. Kung. 2019. "Busting the 'Princelings': The Campaign against Corruption in China's Primary Land Market." *Quarterly Journal of Economics* 134 (1): 185–226.

Cheshire, P., C. A. L. Hilber, and H. R. A. Koster. 2018. "Empty Homes, Longer Commutes: The Unintended Consequences of More Restrictive Local Planning." *Journal of Public Economics* 158: 126–51.

Chirico, M., R. Inman, C. Loeffler, J. MacDonald, and H. Sieg. 2017. "Procrastination and Property Tax Compliance: Evidence from a Field Experiment." NBER Working Paper 23243, National Bureau of Economic Research, Cambridge, MA.

Chitonge, H., and O. Mfune. 2015. "The Urban Land Question in Africa: The Case of Urban Land Conflicts in the City of Lusaka, 100 Years after Its Founding." *Habitat International* 48: 209–18.

Christensen, D., and F. Garfias. 2020. "The Politics of Property Taxation: Fiscal Infrastructure and Electoral Incentives in Brazil." *Journal of Politics* 83 (4): 1399–1416.

Collier, P. 2017. "African Urbanization: An Analytic Policy Guide." *Oxford Review of Economic Policy* 33 (3): 405–37.

Collier, P., E. Glaeser, A. J. Venables, P. Manwaring, and M. Blake. 2017. "Land and Property Taxes for Municipal Finance." International Growth Centre, London.

Collins, W. J., and K. L. Shester. 2013. "Slum Clearance and Urban Renewal in the United States." *American Economic Journal: Applied Economics* 5 (1): 239–73.

Combes, P.-P., S. Demurger, and S. Li. 2017. "Productivity Gains from Agglomeration and Migration in the People's Republic of China between 2002 and 2013." *Asian Development Review* 34 (2): 184–200.

Combes, P.-P., G. Duranton, and L. Gobillon. 2012. "The Costs of Agglomeration: Land Prices in French Cities." CEPR Discussion Paper 9240, Centre for Economic Policy Research, London.

Costas-Fernandez, J., J.-A. Guerra, and M. Mohnen. 2022. "Train to Opportunity: The Effect of Infrastructure on Intergenerational Mobility." Working paper, University College London, London.

Coury, M., T. Kitagawa, A. Shertzer, and M. Turner. 2021. "The Value of Piped Water and Sewers: Evidence from 19th Century Chicago." NBER Working Paper 29718, National Bureau of Economic Research, Cambridge, MA.

Cropper, M. L., and P. Suri. 2022. "Air Quality Impacts of Metro Rail in Mumbai." Working paper, University of Maryland, College Park.

D'Arcy, M., and M. Nistotskaya. 2018. "The Early Modern Origins of Contemporary European Tax Outcomes." *European Journal of Political Research* 57 (1): 47–67.

Dachis, B., G. Duranton, and M. A. Turner. 2012. "The Effects of Land Transfer Taxes on Real Estate Markets: Evidence from a Natural Experiment in Toronto." *Journal of Economic Geography* 12 (2): 327–54.

Davis, D. R., and J. I. Dingel. 2020. "The Comparative Advantage of Cities." *Journal of International Economics* 123: 103291.

De Bellefon, M.-P., P.-P. Combes, G. Duranton, L. Gobillon, and C. Gorin. 2021. "Delineating Urban Areas Using Building Density." *Journal of Urban Economics* 125: 103226.

Deininger, K., R. Awasthi, and W. McCluskey. 2020. "Property Taxation for Own-Source Revenue Generation: Potential for New Technology and an Application to Nigeria." Background paper for this report. World Bank, Washington, DC.

Deininger, K., X. Gao, and F. Xia. 2020. "Assessing the Impact of Access to Land Title in Nigeria." Policy note, World Bank, Washington, DC.

Dekle, R., and J. Eaton. 1999. "Agglomeration and Land Rents: Evidence from the Prefectures." *Journal of Urban Economics* 46 (2): 200–14.

De La Roca, J., and D. Puga. 2017. "Learning by Working in Big Cities." *Review of Economic Studies* 84 (1): 106–42.

Del Carpio, L. 2022. "Are the Neighbors Cheating? Evidence from a Social Norm Experiment on Property Taxes in Peru." Research paper, Institut Européen d'Administration des Affaires (INSEAD), Fontainbleau, France.

Diamond, R. 2017. "Housing Supply Elasticity and Rent Extraction by State and Local Governments." *American Economic Journal: Economic Policy* 9 (1): 74–111.

Diewert, W. E., and C. Shimizu. 2022. "Residential Property Price Indexes: Spatial Coordinates versus Neighborhood Dummy Variables." *Review of Income and Wealth* 68 (3): 770–96.

Diewert, W. E., C. Shimizu, T. Watanabe, and K. G. Nishimura. 2020. *Property Price Index: Theory and Practice.* Tokyo: Springer.

Dijkstra, L., A. J. Florczyk, S. Freire, T. Kemper, M. Melchiorri, M. Pesaresi, and M. Schiavina. 2021. "Applying the Degree of Urbanisation to the Globe: A New Harmonised Definition Reveals a Different Picture of Global Urbanisation." *Journal of Urban Economics* 125: 103312.

Dincecco, M., and G. Katz. 2016. "State Capacity and Long-Run Economic Performance." *Economic Journal* 126 (590): 189–218.

Du, R., and S. Zheng. 2020. "Agglomeration, Housing Affordability, and New Firm Formation: The Role of Subway Network." *Journal of Housing Economics* 48: 101668.

Duranton, G. 2015. "Growing through Cities in Developing Countries." *World Bank Research Observer* 30 (1): 39–73.

Duranton, G., and D. Puga. 2019. "Urban Growth and Its Aggregate Implications." CEPR Discussion Paper 14215, Centre for Economic Policy Research, London.

Duranton, G., and D. Puga. 2020. "The Economics of Urban Density." *Journal of Economic Perspectives* 34 (3): 3–26.

Dzansi, J., A. Jensen, D. Lagakos, and H. Telli. 2022. "Technology and Local State Capacity: Evidence from Ghana." NBER Working Papers 29923, National Bureau of Economic Research, Cambridge, MA.

Eerola, E., O. Harjunen, T. Lyytikainen, and T. Saarimaa. 2021. "Revisiting the Effects of Housing Transfer Taxes." *Journal of Urban Economics* 124: 103367.

Egbu, A. U., P. Olomolaiye, and R. Gameson. 2008. "A Neo-institutional Economic Critique of the System for Allocating Urban Land and Development Rights in Nigeria." *Habitat International* 32 (1): 121–35.

Elinder, M., and L. Persson. 2017. "House Price Responses to a National Property Tax Reform." *Journal of Economic Behavior and Organization* 144: 18–39.

Englund, P. 2003. "Taxing Residential Housing Capital." *Urban Studies* 40 (5–6): 937–52.

Ermini, B., and R. Santolini. 2017. "Urban Sprawl and Property Tax of a City's Core and Suburbs: Evidence from Italy." *Regional Studies* 51 (9): 1374–86.

Esch, T., K. Deininger, R. Jedwab, and D. Palacios-Lopez. 2024. *Outward and Upward Construction: A 3D Analysis of the Global Building Stock.* Washington, DC: World Bank.

European Commission. 2013. *Handbook on Residential Property Price Indices.* Luxembourg: Publications Office of the European Union.

Fay, M., and C. Opal. 1999. "Urbanization without Growth: A Not-So-Uncommon Phenomenon." Policy Research Working Paper 2412, World Bank, Washington, DC.

Feir, D. L., M. E. C. Jones, and D. Scoones. 2023. "When Do Nations Tax? The Adoption of Property Tax Codes by First Nations in Canada." *Public Choice.* https://doi.org/10.1007/s11127-022-01039-4.

Field, E. 2007. "Entitled to Work: Urban Property Rights and Labor Supply in Peru." *Quarterly Journal of Economics* 122 (4): 1561–602.

Fish, P. 2018. "Practical Guidance Note: Training Manual for Implementing Property Tax Reform with a Points-Based Valuation." ICTD African Tax Administration Paper 2, International Centre for Tax and Development, Brighton, UK.

Fjeldstad, O.-H., M. Ali, and L. Katera. 2019. "Policy Implementation under Stress: Central-Local Government Relations in Property Tax Administration in Tanzania." *Journal of Financial Management of Property and Construction* 24 (2): 129–47.

Franzsen, R., and W. McCluskey, eds. 2017. *Property Tax in Africa: Status, Challenges, and Prospects.* Cambridge, MA: Lincoln Institute of Land Policy.

Gaduh, A., T. Gračner, and A. D. Rothenberg. 2022. "Life in the Slow Lane: Unintended Consequences of Public Transit in Jakarta." *Journal of Urban Economics* 128: 103411.

Galiani, S., P. J. Gertler, and R. Undurraga. 2021. "Aspiration Adaptation in Resource-Constrained Environments." *Journal of Urban Economics* 123: 103326.

Galiani, S., P. J. Gertler, R. Undurraga, R. Cooper, S. Martínez, and A. Ross. 2017. "Shelter from the Storm: Upgrading Housing Infrastructure in Latin American Slums." *Journal of Urban Economics* 98: 187–213.

Gárate, S., and A. Pennington-Cross. 2023. "Heterogeneity in Property Tax Capitalization: Evidence from Municipalities in Wisconsin." *Real Estate Economics* 51 (5): 1285–1314.

Garza, N., and I. Gonzalez. 2021. "An Urban System Assessment of Land Value Capture: The Colombian Case." *Land Use Policy* 109: 105598.

Gechter, M., and N. Tsivanidis. 2020. "Spatial Spillovers from Urban Renewal: Evidence from the Mumbai Mills Redevelopment." Research paper, University of California, Berkeley.

Gertler, P. J., M. Gonzalez-Navarro, T. Gracner, and A. D. Rothenberg. 2022. "Road Maintenance and Local Economic Development: Evidence from Indonesia's Highways." Research paper, University of California, Berkeley.

Gevaert, C. M., C. Persello, R. Sliuzas, and G. Vosselman. 2020. "Monitoring Household Upgrading in Unplanned Settlements with Unmanned Aerial Vehicles." *International Journal of Applied Earth Observation and Geoinformation* 90: 102117.

Glaeser, E., W. Huang, Y. Ma, and A. Shleifer. 2017. "A Real Estate Boom with Chinese Characteristics." *Journal of Economic Perspectives* 31 (1): 93–116.

Glaeser, E. L. 2021. "What Can Developing Cities Today Learn from the Urban Past?" NBER Working Paper 28814, National Bureau of Economic Research, Cambridge, MA.

Glaeser, E. L., G. A. M. Ponzetto, and Y. Zou. 2016. "Urban Networks: Connecting Markets, People, and Ideas." *Papers in Regional Science* 95 (1): 17–59.

Gollin, D., R. Jedwab, and D. Vollrath. 2016. "Urbanization with and without Industrialization." *Journal of Economic Growth* 21 (1): 35–70.

Gonzalez-Navarro, M., and C. Quintana-Domeque. 2016. "Paving Streets for the Poor: Experimental Analysis of Infrastructure Effects." *Review of Economics and Statistics* 98 (2): 254–67.

Goodfellow, T., and O. Owen. 2018. "Taxation, Property Rights and the Social Contract in Lagos." ICTD Working Paper 73, International Center for Tax and Development, Brighton, UK.

Goodfellow, T., and O. Owen. 2020. "Thick Claims and Thin Rights: Taxation and the Construction of Analogue Property Rights in Lagos." *Economy and Society* 49 (3): 406–32.

Goswami, A. G., and S. V. Lall. 2019. "Jobs and Land Use within Cities: A Survey of Theory, Evidence, and Policy." *World Bank Research Observer* 34 (2): 198–238.

Gouriéroux, C., and A. Laferrère. 2009. "Managing Hedonic Housing Price Indexes: The French Experience." *Journal of Housing Economics* 18 (3): 206–13.

Grover, A. G., S. V. Lall, and J. D. Timmis. 2021. "Agglomeration Economies in Developing Countries: A Meta-Analysis." Policy Research Working Paper 9730, World Bank, Washington, DC.

Grover, R., M.-P. Torhonen, P. Munro-Faure, and A. Anand. 2017. "Achieving Successful Implementation of Value-Based Property Tax Reforms in Emerging European Economies." *Journal of European Real Estate Research* 10 (1): 91–106.

Gulyani, S., E. M. Bassett, and D. Talukdar. 2012. "Living Conditions, Rents, and Their Determinants in the Slums of Nairobi and Dakar." *Land Economics* 88 (2): 251–74.

Gupta, A., S. Van Nieuwerburgh, and C. Kontokosta. 2022. "Take the Q Train: Value Capture of Public Infrastructure Projects." *Journal of Urban Economics* 129: 103422.

Han, L., R. Ngai, and K. Sheedy. 2022. "To Own or to Rent? The Effects of Transaction Taxes on Housing Markets." London School of Economics, London.

Harari, M. 2020. "Cities in Bad Shape: Urban Geometry in India." *American Economic Review* 110 (8): 2377–421.

Harari, M., and M. Wong. 2019. "Slum Upgrading and Long-Run Urban Development: Evidence from Indonesia." University of Pennsylvania, Philadelphia.

Hartley, D., B. Mazumder, A. Rajan, and Y. Shi. 2021. "The Effects of the Great Migration on Urban Renewal." Working Paper WP-2021-04, Federal Reserve Bank of Chicago, Chicago.

Hawley, Z., J. J. Miranda, and W. C. Sawyer. 2018. "Land Values, Property Rights, and Home Ownership: Implications for Property Taxation in Peru." *Regional Science and Urban Economics* 69: 38–47.

Heblich, S., S. J. Redding, and D. M. Sturm. 2020. "The Making of the Modern Metropolis: Evidence from London." *Quarterly Journal of Economics* 135 (4): 2059–133.

Henderson, J. V., and S. Kriticos. 2018. "The Development of the African System of Cities." *Annual Review of Economics* 10 (1): 287–314.

Henderson, J. V., D. Nigmatulina, and S. Kriticos. 2021. "Measuring Urban Economic Density." *Journal of Urban Economics* 125: 103188.

Henderson, J. V., T. Regan, and A. J. Venables. 2021. "Building the City: From Slums to a Modern Metropolis." *Review of Economic Studies* 88 (3): 1157–92.

Henderson, J. V., and M. A. Turner. 2020. "Urbanization in the Developing World: Too Early or Too Slow?" *Journal of Economic Perspectives* 34 (3): 150–73.

Henderson, J. V., A. J. Venables, T. Regan, and I. Samsonov. 2016. "Building Functional Cities." *Science* 352 (6288): 946–47.

Hilber, C. A. L., and T. Lyytikäinen. 2017. "Transfer Taxes and Household Mobility: Distortion on the Housing or Labor Market?" *Journal of Urban Economics* 101: 57–73.

Hilber, C. A. L., and W. Vermeulen. 2016. "The Impact of Supply Constraints on House Prices in England." *Economic Journal* 126 (591): 358–405.

Hill, R. J. 2013. "Hedonic Price Indexes for Residential Housing: A Survey, Evaluation and Taxonomy." *Journal of Economic Surveys* 27 (5): 879–914.

Hoff, K. 1991. "Land Taxes, Output Taxes, and Sharecropping: Was Henry George Right?" *World Bank Economic Review* 5 (1): 93–111.

Hoj, A. K., M. Rahbek Jorgensen, and P. Schou. 2018. "Land Tax Changes and Full Capitalisation." *Fiscal Studies* 39 (2): 365–80.

Hollenbach, F. M., and T. N. Silva. 2019. "Fiscal Capacity and Inequality: Evidence from Brazilian Municipalities." *Journal of Politics* 81 (4): 1434–45.

Hornbeck, R., and D. Keniston. 2017. "Creative Destruction: Barriers to Urban Growth and the Great Boston Fire of 1872." *American Economic Review* 107 (6): 1365–98.

Hsieh, C.-T., and E. Moretti. 2019. "Housing Constraints and Spatial Misallocation." *American Economic Journal: Macroeconomics* 11 (2): 1–39.

Hsu, W.-T., X. Li, Y. Tang, and J. Wu. 2017. "Determinants of Urban Land Supply in the People's Republic of China: How Do Political Factors Matter?" *Asian Development Review* 34 (2): 152–83.

Isen, A., M. Rossin-Slater, and W. R. Walker. 2017. "Every Breath You Take—Every Dollar You'll Make: The Long-Term Consequences of the Clean Air Act of 1970." *Journal of Political Economy* 125 (3): 848–902.

Jacobsen, G. D., and M. J. Kotchen. 2013. "Are Building Codes Effective at Saving Energy? Evidence from Residential Billing Data in Florida." *Review of Economics and Statistics* 95 (1): 34–49.

Jedwab, R., L. Christiaensen, and M. Gindelsky. 2017. "Demography, Urbanization and Development: Rural Push, Urban Pull and ... Urban Push?" *Journal of Urban Economics* 98: 6–16.

Jedwab, R., E. Kerby, and A. Moradi. 2017. "History, Path Dependence and Development: Evidence from Colonial Railways, Settlers and Cities in Kenya." *Economic Journal* 127 (603): 1467–94.

Jedwab, R., and D. Vollrath. 2015. "Urbanization without Growth in Historical Perspective." *Explorations in Economic History* 58: 1–21.

Jibao, S. S., and W. Prichard. 2015. "The Political Economy of Property Tax in Africa: Explaining Reform Outcomes in Sierra Leone." *African Affairs* 114 (456): 404–31.

Kalkuhl, M., and O. Edenhofer. 2017. "Ramsey Meets Thunen: The Impact of Land Taxes on Economic Development and Land Conservation." *International Tax and Public Finance* 24 (2): 350–80.

Knebelman, J. 2021. "The (Un)Hidden Wealth of the City: Property Taxation under Weak Enforcement in Senegal." PhD diss., Paris School of Economics.

Knoll, K., M. Schularick, and T. Steger. 2017. "No Price Like Home: Global House Prices, 1870–2012." *American Economic Review* 107 (2): 331–53.

Kopanyi, M., and R. Franzsen. 2018. "Property Taxation in Kampala, Uganda: An Analytic Case Study on a Successful Reform." Working paper, African Tax Institute, Pretoria.

Koster, H. R. A., and C. Ozgen. 2021. "Cities and Tasks." *Journal of Urban Economics* 126: 103386.

Koster, H. R. A., and J. Rouwendal. 2012. "The Impact of Mixed Land Use on Residential Property Values." *Journal of Regional Science* 52 (5): 733–61.

Kotchen, M. J. 2017. "Longer-Run Evidence on Whether Building Energy Codes Reduce Residential Energy Consumption." *Journal of the Association of Environmental and Resource Economists* 4 (1): 135–53.

Kreindler, G., and Y. Miyauchi. 2021. "Measuring Commuting and Economic Activity inside Cities with Cell Phone Records." *Review of Economics and Statistics* 105 (4): 899–909.

Kresch, E. P., M. Walker, M. C. Best, F. Gerard, and J. Naritomi. 2023. "Sanitation and Property Tax Compliance: Analyzing the Social Contract in Brazil." *Journal of Development Economics* 160: 102954.

Kuiiper, M., and R. Kaathman. 2015. "Property Valuation and Taxation in the Netherlands." *Land Tenure Journal* 15 (2): 47–62.

Kumar, T. 2021. "The Housing Quality, Income, and Human Capital Effects of Subsidized Homes in Urban India." *Journal of Development Economics* 153: 102738.

Lall, S. V. 2017. "Renewing Expectations about Africa's Cities." *Oxford Review of Economic Policy* 33 (3): 521–39.

Larreguy, H., J. Marshall, and L. Trucco. 2018. "Breaking Clientelism or Rewarding Incumbents? Evidence from an Urban Titling Program in Mexico." Harvard University, Cambridge, MA.

Le Roux, J., and M. Roma. 2019. "Accuracy and Determinants of Self-Assessed Euro Area House Prices." Working Paper 2328, European Central Bank, Frankfurt.

Liu, S., and X. Yang. 2020. "Property Tax Limits and Female Labor Supply: Evidence from the Housing Boom and Bust." *Journal of Housing Economics* 50: 101714.

Livy, M. R. 2018. "Intra-school District Capitalization of Property Tax Rates." *Journal of Housing Economics* 41: 227–36.

Lopez-Luzuriaga, A., and C. Scartascini. 2019. "Compliance Spillovers across Taxes: The Role of Penalties and Detection." *Journal of Economic Behavior and Organization* 164: 518–34.

Lozano-Gracia, N., C. Young, S. V. Lall, and T. Vishwanath. 2013. "Leveraging Land to Enable Urban Transformation: Lessons from Global Experience." Policy Research Working Paper 6312, World Bank, Washington, DC.

Lutz, B. 2015. "Quasi-Experimental Evidence on the Connection between Property Taxes and Residential Capital Investment." *American Economic Journal: Economic Policy* 7 (1): 300–30.

Mabogunje, A. L. 2009. "New Land Reform in Nigeria." *Science* 325 (5942): 793.

Marx, B., T. Stoker, and T. Suri. 2013. "The Economics of Slums in the Developing World." *Journal of Economic Perspectives* 27 (4): 187–210.

Marx, B., T. M. Stoker, and T. Suri. 2019. "There Is No Free House: Ethnic Patronage in a Kenyan Slum." *American Economic Journal: Applied Economics* 11 (4): 36–70.

McCluskey, W., R. Franzsen, M. Kabinga, and C. Kasese. 2018. "The Role of Information Communication Technology to Enhance Property Tax Revenue in Africa: A Tale of Four Cities in Three Countries." ICTD Working Paper 88, International Centre for Tax and Development, Brighton, UK.

McMichael, G. 2016. "Land Conflict and Informal Settlements in Juba, South Sudan." *Urban Studies* 53 (13): 2721–37.

McMillen, D., and R. Singh. 2020. "Assessment Regressivity and Property Taxation." *Journal of Real Estate Finance and Economics* 60 (1–2): 155–69.

Mezgebo, T. G., and C. Porter. 2020. "From Rural to Urban, but Not through Migration: Household Livelihood Responses to Urban Reclassification in Northern Ethiopia." *Journal of African Economies* 29 (2): 173–91.

Michaels, G., D. Nigmatulina, F. Rauch, T. Regan, N. Baruah, and A. Dahlstrand. 2021. "Planning Ahead for Better Neighborhoods: Long-Run Evidence from Tanzania." *Journal of Political Economy* 129 (7): 2112–56.

Michaels, G., F. Rauch, and S. J. Redding. 2019. "Task Specialization in U.S. Cities from 1880 to 2000." *Journal of the European Economic Association* 17 (3): 754–98.

Monkam, N., and M. Moore. 2015. "How Property Tax Would Benefit Africa." Africa Research Institute, London. https://www.africaresearchinstitute.org/publications/property-tax-benefit-africa/.

Moon, B., and S. Ahn. 2022. "The Effects of a Far Regulation in a Model of Durable Building with Redevelopment: The Case of New York City." *Regional Science and Urban Economics* 95: 103775.

Nagy, D. K. 2020. "Hinterlands, City Formation and Growth: Evidence from the U.S. Westward Expansion." Economics Working Papers, Department of Economics and Business, Universitat Pompeu Fabra, Barcelona.

Nakamura, S., and P. Avner. 2021. "Spatial Distributions of Job Accessibility, Housing Rents, and Poverty: The Case of Nairobi." *Journal of Housing Economics* 51: 101743.

Nakamura, S., R. Peiser, and R. Torto. 2018. "Are There Investment Premiums for Mixed-Use Properties?" *Journal of Real Estate Research* 40 (1): 1–39.

Norregaard, J. 2013. "Taxing Immovable Property: Revenue Potential and Implementation Challenges." IMF Working Paper 13/129, International Monetary Fund, Washington, DC.

O'Grady, T. 2014. "Spatial Institutions in Urban Economies: How City Grids Affect Density and Development." Harvard University, Cambridge, MA.

Oates, W. E., and R. M. Schwab. 1997. "The Impact of Urban Land Taxation: The Pittsburgh Experience." *National Tax Journal* 50 (1): 1–21.

Obala, L. M., and M. Mattingly. 2014. "Ethnicity, Corruption and Violence in Urban Land Conflict in Kenya." *Urban Studies* 51 (13): 2735–51.

Owens, K. E., S. Gulyani, and A. Rizvi. 2018. "Success When We Deemed It Failure? Revisiting Sites and Services Projects in Mumbai and Chennai 20 Years Later." *World Development* 106: 260–72.

Perez-Truglia, R., and U. Troiano. 2018. "Shaming Tax Delinquents." *Journal of Public Economics* 167: 120–37.

Pomponi, F., R. Saint, J. H. Arehart, N. Gharavi, and B. D'Amico. 2021. "Decoupling Density from Tallness in Analysing the Life Cycle Greenhouse Gas Emissions of Cities." *npj Urban Sustainability* 1 (1): 33.

Presbitero, A. F., A. Sacchi, and A. Zazzaro. 2014. "Property Tax and Fiscal Discipline in OECD Countries." *Economics Letters* 124 (3): 428–33.

Qin, Y., H. Zhu, and R. Zhu. 2016. "Changes in the Distribution of Land Prices in Urban China During 2007–2012." *Regional Science and Urban Economics* 57: 77–90.

Regan, T., and P. Manwaring. 2023. "Public Disclosure and Tax Compliance: Evidence from Uganda." IIEP Working Paper 2023-04, Institute for International Economic Policy, George Washington University, Washington, DC.

Resch, E., R. A. Bohne, T. Kvamsdal, and J. Lohne. 2016. "Impact of Urban Density and Building Height on Energy Use in Cities." *Energy Procedia* 96: 800–14.

Roche, M. P. 2020. "Taking Innovation to the Streets: Microgeography, Physical Structure, and Innovation." *Review of Economics and Statistics* 102 (5): 912–28.

Rosenthal, S. S., and W. C. Strange. 2020. "How Close Is Close? The Spatial Reach of Agglomeration Economies." *Journal of Economic Perspectives* 34 (3): 27–49.

Rosenzweig, M., and J. Zhang. 2019. "Housing Prices, Inter-generational Co-residence, and 'Excess' Savings by the Young: Evidence Using Chinese Data." NBER Working Paper 26209, National Bureau of Economic Research, Cambridge, MA.

Sanchez-Talanquer, M. 2020. "One-Eyed State: The Politics of Legibility and Property Taxation." *Latin American Politics and Society* 62 (3): 65–93.

Schmick, E. J., and A. Shertzer. 2019. "The Impact of Early Investments in Urban School Systems in the United States." NBER Working Paper 25663, National Bureau of Economic Research, Cambridge, MA.

Schwerhoff, G., O. Edenhofer, and M. Fleurbaey. 2020. "Taxation of Economic Rents." *Journal of Economic Surveys* 34 (2): 398–423.

Segú, M. 2020. "The Impact of Taxing Vacancy on Housing Markets: Evidence from France." *Journal of Public Economics* 185: 104079.

Severen, C. 2018. "Commuting, Labor, and Housing Market Effects of Mass Transportation: Welfare and Identification." Working Paper 18-14, Federal Reserve Bank of Philadelphia, Philadelphia.

Sha, W. 2022. "The Political Impacts of Land Expropriation in China." *Journal of Development Economics* 160: 102985.

Shah, N. 2014. "Squatting on Government Land." *Journal of Regional Science* 54 (1): 114–36.

Slack, E., and R. Bird. 2014. "The Political Economy of Property Tax Reform." OECD Working Papers on Fiscal Federalism, No. 18, Organisation for Economic Co-operation and Development, Paris.

Slemrod, J., O. Ur Rehman, and M. Waseem. 2022. "How Do Taxpayers Respond to Public Disclosure and Social Recognition Programs? Evidence from Pakistan." *Review of Economics and Statistics* 104 (1): 116–32.

Smolka, M., and C. Biderman. 2012. "Housing Informality: An Economist's Perspective on Urban Planning." In *The Oxford Handbook on Urban Economics and Planning*, edited by N. Brooks, K. Donaghy, and G.-J. Knapp, 814–33. Oxford, UK: Oxford University Press.

Song, Y., and Y. Zenou. 2006. "Property Tax and Urban Sprawl: Theory and Implications for US Cities." *Journal of Urban Economics* 60 (3): 519–34.

Stöcker, C., R. Bennett, F. Nex, M. Gerke, and J. Zevenbergen. 2017. "Review of the Current State of UAV Regulations." *Remote Sensing* 9 (5): 459.

Sturm, D. M., K. Takeda, and A. J. Venables. 2022. "How Useful Are Quantitative Urban Models for Cities in Developing Countries? Evidence from Dhaka." London School of Economics, London.

Suri, P. 2022. "Public Transit Infrastructure and Employment Accessibility: The Benefits of the Mumbai Metro." Working paper, University of Maryland, College Park.

Surico, P., and R. Trezzi. 2019. "Consumer Spending and Property Taxes." *Journal of the European Economic Association* 17 (2): 606–49.

Talukdar, D. 2018. "Cost of Being a Slum Dweller in Nairobi: Living under Dismal Conditions but Still Paying a Housing Rent Premium." *World Development* 109: 42–56.

Tellman, B., H. Eakin, M. Janssen, F. de Alba, and B. L. Turner II. 2021. "The Role of Institutional Entrepreneurs and Informal Land Transactions in Mexico City's Urban Expansion." *World Development* 140 (3): 105374.

Tourek, G., P. Balan, A. Bergeron, and J. Weigel. 2020. "Local Elites as State Capacity: How City Chiefs Use Local Information to Increase Tax Compliance in the D.R. Congo." Working paper, Harvard University, Cambridge, MA.

Tsivanidis, N. 2021. "Evaluating the Impact of Urban Transit Infrastructure: Evidence from Bogotá's Transmilenio." University of California, Berkeley.

Wang, S.-Y. 2014. "Property Rights and Intra-household Bargaining." *Journal of Development Economics* 107: 192–201.

Wanjiru, R., A. W. Maina, and E. Onsomu. 2019. "Local Government Property Tax Administration and Collaboration with Central Government: Case Studies of Kiambu, Laikipia and Machakos Counties, Kenya." ICTD Working Paper 95, International Centre for Tax and Development, Brighton, UK.

Weigel, J. L. 2020. "The Participation Dividend of Taxation: How Citizens in Congo Engage More with the State When It Tries to Tax Them." *Quarterly Journal of Economics* 135 (4): 1849–903.

Wong, F. 2020. "Mad as Hell: Property Taxes and Financial Distress." National Bureau of Economic Research, Cambridge, MA.

World Bank. 2022. *Reconsidering Sites and Services: A Global Review*. Washington, DC: World Bank.

World Bank. 2023. *Building Regulations in Sub-Saharan Africa: A Status Review of the Building Regulatory Environment*. Washington, DC: World Bank, Global Facility for Disaster Reduction and Recovery.

Zárate, R. D. 2022. "Spatial Misallocation, Informality, and Transit Improvements: Evidence from Mexico City." University of California, Berkeley.

Zhou, Z., H. Chen, L. Han, and A. Zhang. 2021. "The Effect of a Subway on House Prices: Evidence from Shanghai." *Real Estate Economics* 49 (Suppl.): 199–234.

3. Land rights for rural structural transformation

Secure land rights will increase not only owners' investment incentives but also allocative efficiency by making it easier to transfer land to those best able to make use of it in ways that benefit everybody. Because farmers have to deal with high levels of risk and multiple factor market imperfections, efforts to improve clarity and transferability of land rights will be most effective in increasing productivity if they help to improve the functioning of other factor markets and farmers' ability to insure against risk as well. Comprehensive digital and geo-referenced documentation of use rights in a way that can be integrated with farmer registries and accessed (with farmers' permission) by banks, traders, input suppliers, or providers of crop insurance may reduce frictions in land as well as other factor markets and contribute more to this objective than isolated issuance of titles.

Farms will be able to expand the cultivated area to mechanize and increase the incomes of their owners or operators only if there is a net movement of individuals out of agriculture. Recent studies suggest that although measurement error and unobservable skills account for much of the wage gap, workers can realize an income gain of 20 to 30 percent by moving out of agriculture. However, it has long been puzzling that despite an often very large gap between agricultural wages and wages in other sectors, such movement has still been limited. Experimental and observational studies support the notion that land market frictions increase the cost of labor moving out of agriculture and that reform to reduce these costs—through regulatory change, registration of rights, or measures to standardize or otherwise encourage long-term lease transactions—and improve land market functioning can contribute to structural transformation and wealth gains by making it easier for individuals to move away from agriculture.

Rural factor market operation

While land rights have historically evolved in response to local factor endowments and political factors (see spotlight 3.1), one benefit of secure, well-defined land rights is that they allow individuals who are not good at farming to take up nonagricultural pursuits and lease out land to better operators, increasing their own welfare and productivity overall. Governments can take actions to reduce informational or contractual frictions, risk, or imperfections in the operation of other markets that may reduce the rental volume or the efficiency with which rented land is used. As capital becomes a more important input to production, longer-term rental contracts encourage investment by tenants and structural transformation. Beyond documented rights, measures to encourage such contracts, such as dissemination of standardized forms and support to dispute resolution, can help improve the productivity of land use.

Agricultural land rental markets

Local markets for short-term rental of agricultural land work well in most countries without formally registered rights. Because leasing does not involve changing ownership, landowners, even if they give up self-cultivation, will not have to forsake benefits from owning land—for example, the ability to use land as collateral for loans to start nonagricultural enterprises (Deininger and Feder 2001). Leasing provides a regular income stream via rents (Deininger 2003) and, if land is transferred to more productive producers and markets are competitive, combines productivity benefits with increased welfare as income from leasing will be higher than what owners could obtain from self-cultivation (Deininger et al. 2017).

Frictions that can be informational (finding contracting partners) or related to the cost of enforcing contracts add to the transaction costs of renting that may reduce the size of the welfare and productivity benefits from rental markets or make achieving them less likely. Supply- and demand-side wedges have been shown to reduce the volume of rental market transactions well below the optimum in Ethiopia (Deininger and Jin 2006). A randomized experiment confirmed the presence of rental market frictions in Kenya, where subsidies to short-term rentals transferred land to younger, more entrepreneurial, and land-poor farmers, which resulted in higher output and value added on rented plots via more intensive application of nonlabor inputs (Acampora, Casaburi, and Willis 2022).

Rental markets can also be impeded if property rights, especially to leased-out land, are insecure. This has been reported from Brazil, where landlords' fear of losing rights to land that is leased out, often to land invasions organized by the landless, has been shown to be a major barrier to rental market activity. Owners prefer to leave their land unused rather than renting it out and risking losing it, despite a large number of landless people (Alston and Mueller 2018), suggesting this is an inferior arrangement. In Tanzania, rental is important for land market participation by women or the young, who often face higher transaction costs (Ricker-Gilbert and Chamberlin 2018) or, as in Malawi, must overcome entry barriers to land rental markets (Tione and Holden 2022).

Reducing transaction costs in land rental markets can increase farmers' efficiency and welfare (Daymard 2022). In Tanzania, efforts to reduce transaction rental costs and facilitate longer-term contracts aim to give young farmers the security to make longer-term investments and reduce the rents they pay (Ricker-Gilbert and Chamberlin 2018). Constraints on owners' ability to enforce rental contracts and get their land back at the end of the lease term imply that contracts will be for short-term periods or between close kin (Gebru, Holden, and Tilahun 2019), possibly reducing efficiency by limiting the range of potential partners (Sadoulet, de Janvry, and Fukui 1997).

Investment by tenants to promote structural change will require longer-term, more formalized contracts as tenants who lease in land under short-term contracts will not be able to make long-term investments (Ricker-Gilbert, Chamberlin, and Kanyamuka 2022). In Taiwan, China, a statewide tenancy reform in 1922 extended contract length from one to five years, replaced oral with written contracts, and established a public dispute settlement mechanism. This encouraged tenants to invest in irrigation and drainage, leading to significant efficiency gains (Fan and Yeh 2019). Schemes to incentivize long-term contracts and encourage older farmers to exit agriculture through pensions have long been used in Europe. They are also experimented within China, where receipt of a pension is estimated to significantly increase the likelihood that a senior household rents out land (Zhu et al. 2021).

Although better access to information and an expanded set of options (including migration and leasing out land for renewable energy production) tend to make land markets more competitive, restrictions on land market operation remain in place in many jurisdictions. In Ethiopia's Tigray region, landowners are not allowed to rent out more than 50 percent of their land (Holden and Ghebru 2016).[1] Laws outlawing land rental also remain in force in several Indian states; ending prohibitions on land rental by all states could double the number of producers, with significant productivity benefits (Deininger, Jin, and Nagarajan 2008). Differences in the severity of land rental market restrictions across states have been shown to explain close to 25 percent of cross-state differences in agricultural productivity overall and up to 50 percent in states with highly restricted rental markets (Bolhuis, Rachapalli, and Restuccia 2021). Land-use restrictions are another source of misallocation in Viet Nam, where elimination of rice cultivation requirements on almost half of farmers' land could increase real gross domestic product (GDP) by about 8 percent (Le 2020).

Even if they appear to have few negative effects in the short term, rental restrictions will affect landowners' decisions, drive transactions underground, reduce contract length, and thus slow structural transformation in the medium to long term. In Mexico, restrictions on land leasing and inheritance had severely restricted welfare. Policy reform to eliminate such restrictions, together with a systematic program to document land rights at the community level (spotlight 1.5 in chapter 1), helped activate long-term land rental markets, occupational shifts out of agriculture, and migration, unlocking large benefits (de Janvry et al. 2015). The benefits were especially pronounced for households with weak initial rights (Valsecchi 2014).

Not all rental market frictions are policy induced. For example, an analysis from Guatemala using agricultural census microdata suggests that land market imperfections associated with factors such as education, road access, and ethnicity reduce output—with estimated reductions between 19 and 31 percent and areas with higher levels of imperfections also characterized by greater land price dispersion and less active rental markets (Britos et al. 2022). In many rural settings, sharecropping is adopted as a second-best contract form to share risk in the presence of liquidity constraints (Otsuka, Chuma, and Hayami 1992).[2] The sharing of output reduces tenants' incentive to supply effort compared to a fixed rental contract, giving rise to "Marshallian inefficiency." In Pakistan, these efficiency losses have been estimated to amount to around 16 percent (Shaban 1987).[3] Sharecropping played an important role historically in the United States by allowing capable farmers to accumulate experience and capital and progress from pure wage workers to share tenants and then to pure cash tenants (Alston and Ferrie 2005).

Data from six African countries suggest that sharecropping continues to serve as an insurance substitute in high-risk settings (Kalkuhl, Schwerhoff, and Waha 2020). Studies from Ethiopia (Gebregziabher and Holden 2011) and Malawi (Ricker-Gilbert et al. 2019) also identify liquidity constraints and high levels of risk as motivations for tenants to choose share contracts. Evidence from Uganda highlights the efficiency cost of this arrangement; randomly varying the terms for tenants who already had contracts prompted tenants with higher output shares to use more inputs and cultivate riskier crops, with a 60 percent output gain compared to the control (Burchardi et al. 2019), reinforcing the notion of sharecropping as a second-best arrangement.

Although in the past, governments have used this efficiency loss as an argument to ban sharecropping, this amounts to addressing the symptoms rather than the underlying causes and generally reduced welfare even further by pushing transactions into informality. Reducing the risk that gives rise to this contractual form in the first place may be a more effective option. In a randomized experiment in Bangladesh, better credit access and lower risk exposure increased tenants' propensity to choose fixed rent rather than share contracts (Das, de Janvry, and Sadoulet 2019).[4] In Zambia, lowering the cost of borrowing in the lean season lowered net labor supply, driving up wages and triggering reallocation of labor from less to more capital-constrained farms, increasing output and reducing differences in the marginal product of labor and inequality of income and consumption (Fink, Jack, and Masiye 2020).

Establishment of digital georeferenced farmer registries in much of the developing world in partnership with the private sector could offer ways not only to recognize local use rights (see chapter 1) but also to reduce the risk that leads to sharecropping in the first place, for example, by bundling cash rental contracts with insurance similar to Bulte et al. (2020). The importance of contracts that bundled access to technology, finance, inputs, and markets was also instrumental for the expansion of soybean cultivation, which increased productivity up to tenfold in the Brazilian savanna (DePaula 2023).

In environments where sharecropping was widespread, land reform that would give permanent rights to tenants was often seen as an attractive option to eliminate the associated inefficiency, leading to positive effects in the short term (Banerjee, Gertler, and Ghatak 2002). However, regulations that made tenancy permanent but left owners in place created overlapping rights, undermining investment and market participation. This happened in the Indian state of West Bengal, where profits on parcels with tenancy rights were at least 20 percent lower than on parcels owned by the same household, making a scheme to buy out one party's interest economically viable (Deininger, Jin, and Yadav 2013).

In Uganda, the fact that both owners and tenants on *mailo*[5] land have rights to the same piece of land has been shown to have far-reaching effects not only in rural settings but also in urban settings. For rural land, giving occupants full rights to the land could more than double the investment in soil conservation and quintuple it for trees (Deininger and Ali 2008). Willingness by many tenants to buy out their landlords' residual interest suggests such inefficiencies can be eliminated (Musinguzi et al. 2021). In urban areas, mailo tenure impedes transfers of land from informal housing to business and commercial activities. A model suggests that transferability of mailo land would increase wages, especially for low-skilled workers, and raise real urban incomes by 2 to 6.7 percent, more than enough to compensate mailo tenants for losses in terms of amenities or rent caps (Bird and Venables 2020).

Governments are often concerned about land fragmentation, often as a result of egalitarian inheritance rules that seem to be surprisingly resilient in practice

(Gáfaro and Mantilla 2020), reducing efficiency by forcing farmers to spend large amounts of time moving between plots or by making it impossible to use machinery. In Rwanda, fragmented holdings impose costs because it takes time for cultivators to move between parcels. However, these costs are close to being outweighed by risk diversification benefits. Public action to reduce fragmentation would thus have little impact at this point (Ali, Deininger, and Ronchi 2019). In Ethiopia, land fragmentation has been shown to reduce food insecurity. Households with a larger number of more diverse parcels grow a greater variety of crop types, which mitigates the adverse effects of low rainfall on food security (Knippenberg, Jolliffe, and Hoddinott 2020). Fragmented landholdings also have reduced crop yield variability in Uganda (Veljanoska 2018).[6]

Multicropping on more fragmented parcels may partly explain these outcomes. Plot-level data from Uganda suggest that a 10 percent increase in crop diversity is associated with a 3 percent increase in revenues (Noack and Quaas 2021a). Multicropping on a parcel increases output per input unit by 14 percent, suggesting that crop diversity not only is used to insure against risk but also enhances productivity (Noack and Quaas 2021b). In Malawi, intercropped parcels achieve higher levels of productivity. In India, areas with higher crop diversity are more drought resistant, affecting farmer welfare via yield and price effects (Auffhammer and Carleton 2018).

Small plot sizes will become an obstacle if they do not allow the use of mechanical equipment (Foster and Rosenzweig 2010). In India, inheritance-related subdivision seems to have reduced parcel size below the threshold where machine use becomes viable (Deininger et al. 2017). However, regulations mandating minimum parcel sizes tend to be difficult to enforce and increase the scope for arbitrary bureaucratic enforcement and tenure insecurity or informality. In Rwanda, such restrictions led owners to register parcels below the minimum size as joint property, increasing the cost of decision-making (Ali et al. 2021). Limiting subdivision may reduce the cost of urban land assembly at higher income levels, as suggested by the experience of Taiwan, China, where a minimum lot size program increased farmland value by 15 to 18 percent, driven by periurban areas (Chang and Lin 2016).

Determinants of farm size structure

Rural markets for land and other factors of production, including credit and insurance, suffer from multiple frictions. Imperfect observability of effort caused by seasonality and spatial dispersion of agricultural activities imply that farms operated by owners with a residual claim on profit provide them with an advantage over farms operated by wage labor (Binswanger, Deininger, and Feder 1995).[7] In addition, owner-operators have higher incentives to exert effort (Frisvold 1994) and a greater familiarity with the local soil and climate, with this information often being passed down over generations (Rosenzweig and

Wolpin 1985). Except for capital-intensive "factory farming" or plantations, agricultural production is thus on owner-operated farms (Allen and Lueck 1998).[8]

If other factor markets work well, a household's labor use will not depend on its labor endowment. Imperfections in labor and land markets, however, can lead to a negative relationship between farm size and productivity (Feder 1985), a regularity that has been confirmed empirically in many settings globally (Eastwood, Lipton, and Newell 2010). However, beyond potential measurement issues (Aragón, Restuccia, and Rud 2022b), using such an observational outcome as a basis for policy advice may be inappropriate. Labor market frictions may lead small farmers to apply labor to the point where its marginal revenue product is below the opportunity wage rate (Jacoby 1993). Although this allows them to obtain higher yields than large farmers, being able to work off-farm for the market wage would allow them to earn more.

The widely documented empirical regularity of an inverse relationship between farm size and productivity was often misinterpreted as a causal relationship and used as a basis for policy recommendations. Analyses suggest that much of this relationship can be attributed to imperfections in the functioning of markets for labor and land, implying that as frictions in the operation of these markets are reduced, the relationship will weaken.

In Africa, labor market frictions that prompt farmers to work on their farm even at returns below the market wage are at the root of the well-established inverse relationship between farm size and productivity in Rwanda (Ali and Deininger 2015), as well as in Malawi, Tanzania, and Uganda (Julien, Bravo-Ureta, and Rada 2019). A test for rural labor market imperfections also indicated the presence of excess labor, especially during the lean season, with variations by gender and agroecological zone (Dillon, Brummund, and Mwabu 2019).

Cross-sectional data from Indonesia also reject separability and point toward the presence of market imperfections implying that on-farm labor demand depends on households' labor endowment (Benjamin 1995). Longitudinal data support this finding (LaFave and Thomas 2016), whereas an alternative test using consumption data suggests that imperfections affect small farmers (resulting in separation being rejected) but not larger ones (LaFave, Peet, and Thomas 2020). In India, small farmers but not larger ones allocate more than the optimum amount of labor to agricultural production (Merfeld 2020), with the shadow value of family labor estimated to be 20 percent below nonagricultural wages (Caunedo and Kala 2021).

Through better functioning of rural labor markets and substitution of lumpy capital for labor, economic development is expected to lead to a weakening and eventual disappearance or reversal of the negative relationship between farm size and productivity found in a large literature. Indian farm panel data spanning 1982–2008 indeed point in this direction by showing that the negative relationship weakened over time because of better labor market functioning. In 2008, separability of household labor supply was rejected only for villages where, because of low demand for nonagricultural labor, labor market imperfections persisted (Deininger et al. 2018). Using panel data for Bangladesh, joint estimation of a production frontier and a technical inefficiency function reveals a negative relationship between farm size and productivity that diminished over time as larger farms closed the gap with smaller ones through faster adoption of technical change (Gautam and Ahmed 2019).

Attenuation of the inverse relationship between farm size and yield is also observed in Viet Nam for 1992–2016, when rising real wages triggered mechanization and the uptake of labor-saving pesticides (Liu et al. 2020). In northern China, an inverse relationship was observed in 1995 as land and labor market constraints required households to work more for low additional returns (Benjamin and Brandt 2002). Dramatic increases in real agricultural wages and rapid development of land rental markets in response to legal changes in 2003 triggered the substitution of capital for labor (Wang, Yamauchi, and Huang 2016), for example, through the emergence of machine rental services (Wang et al. 2016). For maize producers in northern China, farm-level panel data for 2003–13 point toward a U-shaped size/productivity relationship (Sheng, Ding, and Huang 2019).

The inverse relationship has also been eroding in Latin America. Census data from farms in Brazil show a weakening of the inverse relationship between farm size and land productivity between 1985 and 2006, and by 2006, the relationship between total factor productivity (TFP) and farm size had become U-shaped (Helfand and Taylor 2021). Investments in public education support productivity growth irrespective of farm size, but impacts from technical assistance and credit are confined to larger farms (Rada, Helfand, and Magalhães 2019). By contrast, in Mexico, panel data from 2003–06 suggest that larger farms produce less output value per hectare (ha) and are less efficient than small farms (Kagin, Taylor, and Yúnez-Naude 2016).

For mechanized grain farms, a more robust positive relationship between farm size and TFP emerges. In the US Corn Belt, it appears from census data for 1982–2012 that crop farm TFP increased at a similar rate for farms of all sizes except the smallest farms, which are characterized by much higher unit costs. Farm consolidation contributed to productivity growth, with the share of output from farms cultivating more than 400 ha increasing from 17 to 59 percent over the period (Key 2019). In Australia, farm data for grain producers from 1989 to 2004 show a positive relationship between farm size and TFP caused by size-dependent capital access for farms, although the emergence of machine rental services may have diminished this advantage (Sheng and Chancellor 2019).

Although most studies from Africa point to a negative relationship between farm size and productivity, the household survey data used to arrive at this conclusion may not always be representative of the universe of farms. Adding larger farms to smallholder samples has been shown to lead to the disappearance of this relationship or its conversion into a U-shaped one in Kenya (Muyanga and Jayne 2019), Nigeria (Omotilewa et al. 2021), and Ethiopia

(Ali and Deininger 2021). In Uganda, larger farms allow farmers to earn higher and more stable incomes, although the variability of local food supply may increase (Noack and Larsen 2019). Similarly, for panel data from Tanzania, an inverse relationship between farm size and productivity if labor is valued at shadow wages disappears if market prices are used, suggesting that this relationship will weaken or reverse with better operation of factor markets (Wineman and Jayne 2021).

Once higher wages make it economically rational to use capital more intensively, the lumpy nature of certain inputs (for example, machinery, draft animals, and management) or size-dependent advantages in accessing credit, crop insurance, or upstream value chains may counter or outweigh the labor supervision advantages of small farmers and lead to a positive relationship between farm size and productivity (Eswaran and Kotwal 1986).[9] Innovations in crop breeding, tillage, and information technology also make it easier to supervise labor by tending to attenuate or eliminate the disadvantages of large operations and may alter the traditional farm size–productivity relationship.[10]

With economic development, capital substitutes for labor. Differences in capital intensity are much larger in agriculture than in other sectors. This is formalized in a model in which productive farmers pay a fixed cost to use capital-intensive technology, while less productive farmers still operate the labor-intensive technology. The model has been calibrated to data on the mechanization of US agriculture since the 1940s. It predicts substantial differences in agricultural capital intensity between rich and poor countries and has significant explanatory power for cross-country differences in agricultural productivity (Chen 2020).[11] Across countries, adjusting for quality differences in agricultural capital increases the importance of capital as a source of cross-country differences in agricultural labor productivity of 21 to 37 percent (Caunedo and Keller 2021). In such a setting, ill-functioning land markets can become a binding constraint. For example, in India, many parcels are too small for mechanization. Eliminating all land market frictions is estimated to allow increasing income per agricultural worker by 68 percent and reducing the number of farms by 82 percent (Foster and Rosenzweig 2021). However, although evidence suggests machine use could raise productivity (Bryan et al. 2022), achieving land consolidation via private exchanges raises complex market mechanism design issues (Bryan et al. 2017).[12]

Harnessing land markets for intersectoral mobility and structural transformation

With economic development, the share of individuals employed in agriculture decreases; farm size, labor productivity, and wages increase; and capital tends to substitute for labor. Figure 3.1 illustrates this for a sample of countries,

FIGURE 3.1 Changes in the share of agricultural employment and labor productivity in select countries

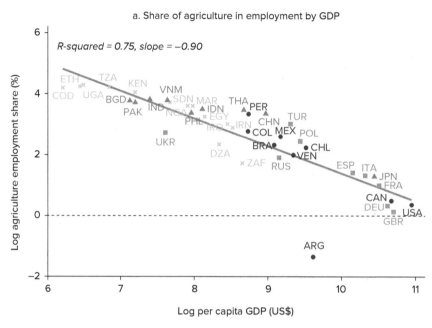

a. Share of agriculture in employment by GDP

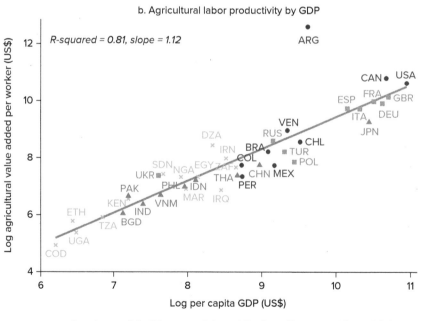

b. Agricultural labor productivity by GDP

● Americas and Caribbean ▲ Asia and Pacfic ■ Europe and Central Asia
✕ Middle East and Africa ─── Fitted values

Source: Deininger, Jin, and Ma 2022.
Note: GDP = gross domestic product. See https://www.iso.org/obp/ui/#search for country codes.

pointing to a tight negative relationship between levels of per capita GDP and the employment share in agriculture, as well as a positive relationship between GDP and agricultural labor productivity. This is mirrored by the fact that, within developing countries, value added per worker, a proxy for income, is lower in agriculture than in nonagriculture, suggesting that eliminating barriers to occupational mobility can increase overall welfare. Beyond increasing security and transferability of rural land in the longer term, policies that can support structural transformation along these lines will include improving the rural population's skills and relaxing restrictions on rural–urban labor mobility and migrants' ability to acquire urban land.

Evidence of the agricultural wage gap

In most developing countries, the share of the labor force employed in agriculture exceeds the sector's value added, so that value added per person, which with competitive labor markets would equal wages, is higher in sectors other than agriculture. Across all countries for which data are available, nonagricultural wages were 3.5 times higher than those in agriculture (Gollin 2021). Although the measurement error in hours worked is large (Arthi et al. 2018), a sizable gap even with better measurement (Gollin, Lagakos, and Waugh 2014) raises the question of whether facilitating people's movement out of agriculture can improve welfare or productivity.

Survey data on birthplace, current residence, and migration for 65 countries point toward sorting as an important factor: workers with more unobservable skills that are positively correlated with education may self-select into sectors other than agriculture (Young 2013). Panel data from the United States for 30 years also suggest that unobserved skill differences explain a large part of the wage gap. After controlling for individual fixed effects, wage gaps are close to zero for those who switched from agriculture to industry and rather small (17 percent) for those who switched to skilled services (Herrendorf and Schoellman 2018). Administrative data for all formal workers in Brazil from 1996 to 2013 also suggest that individual fixed effects explain most of that wage gap, as wage growth for individuals who switched from agriculture to other sectors was close to zero (Alvarez 2020).[13]

Data from Indonesia and Kenya for 1988–2015 suggest that (a) individual fixed effects account for 67 to 92 percent of the gap in productivity between agriculture and nonagriculture; (b) more educated workers move away from agriculture, and less educated ones move in; and (c) measures of cognitive ability that are often not covered by standard surveys are important determinants of sectoral productivity differences (Hamory et al. 2021). Individual panel data from six developing countries in Africa and Asia show that for movers, returns to migration are in the range of 20 to 30 percent. Policies that affect migration costs could thus have substantial impacts on structural transformation

(Lagakos et al. 2020). In Indonesia, removing barriers to mobility could lead one-third of workers to relocate and increase aggregate output by as much as 21 percent (Pulido and Swiecki 2019).

In Organisation for Economic Co-operation and Development countries, changes in human capital have been a key driver of structural transformation in the agriculture sector. Between-cohort effects, driven by the higher human capital endowments of new cohorts compared with their parents, accounted for 71 percent of transformation between 1870 and 1910 in the United States (Porzio, Rossi, and Santangelo 2020) and 66 percent of reallocation in 59 other countries (Hobijn, Schoellman, and Vindas 2018). Microdata for more than 60 countries show that increases in schooling having triggered a steep reduction in the agricultural labor supply by equipping younger cohorts with skills that are more valued in nonagriculture sectors.

Another driver can be land policy reform. In Asia, land reforms have been a key driver of structural transformation by providing former tenants secure and transferable land rights (Iscan 2018). Building on earlier changes in inheritance rules that had already reduced agricultural employment and boosted capital accumulation (Hayashi and Prescott 2008), land reform in Japan after World War II fostered mechanization and outmigration of labor (Kitamura 2022), and similar processes were observed in the Republic of Korea (Jeon and Kim 2000). As spotlight 3.3 details, most of the large number of land reforms that have been enacted globally over time (Bhattacharya, Mitra, and Ulubaşoğlu 2019) pursued political (Caprettini, Casaburi, and Venturini 2021) as well as economic objectives and often imposed restrictions on transferability of land or access to public goods to achieve political goals (Fergusson, Larreguy, and Riaño 2022).

Land reforms in Zimbabwe (Deininger, Hoogeveen, and Kinsey 2004), Ethiopia (Deininger and Jin 2006), Kenya and Colombia (Albertus 2019), Peru and Mexico (Albertus et al. 2016), and the Philippines imposed size limits or other restrictions on the transferability of land received by beneficiaries. As a result, their impacts on economic growth and beneficiary welfare were often negative. In the Philippines, reform-related land ceilings reduced farm size by 34 percent and agricultural productivity by 17 percent (Adamopoulos and Restuccia 2020). In Peru, failure to provide beneficiaries secure and transferable land rights caused the land reform to worsen poverty and stunt human development (Albertus and Popescu 2020).[14]

In South Africa, land reform was a central element of the African National Congress platform in 1994, with an ambitious target of redistributing 30 percent of the area under large farms within 10 years under a "willing seller–willing buyer" approach to avoid the insecurity of property rights that would be unavoidable if expropriation was used (Deininger 1999). Although there is some evidence of positive impacts on beneficiaries with the required skills and tenacity (Keswell and Carter 2014), progress fell far short of expectations, leading to repeated calls for using expropriation instead. An approach using financial incentives (for example, a time-limited land reform surcharge on agricultural property taxes), more careful identification of potential land, and a focus on fostering rural entrepreneurship may be more appropriate.

Operation of agricultural land sales markets

Although the credit market benefits from registered land rights in developed countries are well documented, in rural settings with high levels of uninsured risk, distress sales of land have historically been a major source of debt accumulation and land inequality (Kranton and Swamy 1999). Higher levels of education, better access to information, and access to safety nets appear to have significantly reduced the scope for such distress sales, especially where the distribution of landownership is not too skewed. In Uganda, active land sale markets helped to equalize the land distribution (Baland et al. 2007) and allowed farmers to reduce their exposure to climate risk (Mertens and Vranken 2018).

In Viet Nam, land rental and sale transactions transferred land from those who joined the nonfarm economy to more productive but land-poor producers, with rental markets complemented by sales and policy reforms that play a major role in improving the security of land (Deininger and Jin 2008). A 20-year panel from India suggests that markets for the sale of agricultural land have improved productivity and helped purchasers, many of them formerly landless, to accumulate assets and enhance their welfare (Deininger, Jin, and Nagarajan 2009a).

Governments often restrict the transferability of land. This directly limits owners' ability and incentive to invest in the land for the long term, reduces the value of land for consumption smoothing and as collateral in credit markets, and may impede optimum land use. It also has more far-reaching and possibly gender-biased indirect effects, as illustrated by the case of Sri Lanka. Restrictions on land market operation in the country reduced opportunities for migration and off-farm labor for women, instead forcing them to remain in agriculture; slowed structural transformation (Emran and Shilpi 2017); and permeated preexisting patterns of gender inequality (Emran and Shilpi 2020).

The longer-term impacts of restrictions on land sales are illustrated by some 90 million acres of land allotted to American Indians who received land under trust between 1887 and 1934 and, because of an unexpected legal change, failed to receive full ownership rights.[15] For agricultural land, fee simple and trust lands are similar in terms of attributes and equally likely to be irrigated. However, conditional on being irrigated, tribal trust land is 32 percentage points less likely to use capital-intensive sprinkler irrigation and up to 10 percentage points less likely to be under high-value crops, a difference attributed to the bureaucratic process for leasing and the inability to use land as collateral for loans (Ge, Edwards, and Akhundjanov 2020).

In the long term, restrictions on transferability reduce the intensity of land use, including the scope for urban conversion. Pixel-level analysis for the entire United States suggests that land under restrictions was less likely to be used for agriculture in 1974 or to be converted to urban use between 1975 and 2015, with sizable impacts on land values (Dippel, Frye, and Leonard 2020). The impact of restrictions was even more dramatic for urban land. In 1960, properties that had been converted before 1934 were five times more valuable than neighboring properties that were still under trust ownership, mainly because the former could be used as collateral for credit (Akee 2009). After 1959, when transferability restrictions on this type of urban trust land were eliminated, property values equalized across the two types, supporting the notion that restrictions on transferability had been at the root of the divergence of prices (Akee 2009).[16]

Governments may impose restrictions on the ability of nonresidents or foreigners to buy land or impose special fees on them. If these restrictions are enforced, they reduce prices, thereby benefiting renters at the cost of landowners. In Saskatchewan, farmland ownership by non-Saskatchewan residents or corporations was prohibited from 1974 to 2003.[17] Parcel-level farmland transaction data from Saskatchewan and a neighboring province suggest that the 2003 amendment led to an increase in farmland values by 1.9 to 3.1 percent per year (Lawley 2018).

Reducing misallocation by reducing land and labor market frictions

By reducing the scope for achieving an allocation of land that maximizes productivity and welfare, land market frictions have long been shown to be one of several sources that contribute to resource misallocation (Restuccia and Rogerson 2017). Measured levels of misallocation are much larger in agriculture than in nonagriculture (Adamopoulos and Restuccia 2014). Part of this can be attributed to measurement error that is particularly pervasive in agriculture (Maue, Burke, and Emerick 2020) and can inflate the extent of measured misallocation (Gollin and Udry 2020).[18] At the same time, the persistence of large wage gaps between agricultural and nonagricultural employment, even after careful adjustments (Lagakos et al. 2020), suggests that there is considerable scope for fostering structural transformation through improved rural land and factor market functioning. This would allow those with few agricultural skills to take up nonagricultural occupations.

Studies suggest that the potential for such shifts in Africa is large. In Ethiopia, where land cannot be sold and some regions restrict the share of land that can be leased out or the length of rental contracts, full marketability of agricultural land is estimated to have the potential to increase GDP by 9 percent and decrease agricultural employment by 20 percent (Gottlieb and Grobovsek 2019). Ex ante analysis shows that such reform would be pro-poor

(Restuccia 2021) and would significantly increase agricultural productivity (Chen, Restuccia, and Santaeulalia-Llopis 2017).[19] Better functioning of land and financial markets in Tanzania would also expand opportunities for the poor (Manysheva 2022). In Malawi, the gains from removing misallocation are estimated to be large overall and especially high for households not participating in land markets (Restuccia and Santaeulalia-Llopis 2017).

Reforms that improved the transferability of land rights, even if they fell short of titling, improved land market functioning as well. Ex post analysis in Ethiopia suggests that the national certification program (spotlight 1.3 in chapter 1) realized about a quarter of these benefits (Chen, Restuccia, and Santaeulàlia-Llopis 2022). Tenure regularization in Rwanda significantly lowered transaction costs, reduced the number of individuals in autarky, and increased the volume of land market transactions, with associated equity and productivity benefits (Ali, Deininger, and Goldstein 2014).

Evidence from Pakistan shows that computerization of rural land records, which did not change the nature of property rights but made it easier to access information and transfer rights, increased land market activity and allocative efficiency. Having a computerized record made it more likely for landowners to rent out land and work in nonagriculture, allowing those remaining in agriculture to increase their farm size and cultivate more land. A reduction in the dispersion of marginal returns to land within districts suggests that computerization reduced misallocation but that frictions in agricultural land markets still constrain structural change (Beg 2022).

The relevance of land market frictions and the scope for policy to reduce them in the long term is illustrated by the case of China, where reforms that were implemented in a stepwise fashion over the past decades had enormous impact (Adamopoulos et al. 2022). This case also shows the interaction between different types of policies with changes in the legal basis for land rental through the 2003 Rural Land Contracting Law and the stringency with which migration was restricted by residence permits (hukou) as key drivers. Because farmers with higher levels of human capital are more likely to migrate out, productivity may not increase and may even decline (Liu et al. 2023).

Liberalization of land rental in 2003 allowed more educated and affluent households with little comparative advantage in agriculture to rent out their land and take nonagricultural jobs (Deininger and Jin 2009), supporting the use of productive land that might otherwise have been left idle (Jin and Deininger 2009).[20] By stimulating rural land rental activity and transfers of land to more-productive farmers, the reform increased output by 8 percent and aggregate productivity by 10 percent (Chari et al. 2021). Reducing the scope for periodic land reallocation that had reduced migration incentives (Giles and Mu 2018) increased off-farm labor supply and rural incomes (Zhao 2020). In addition, better factor market functioning allowed adjustments to offset some of the negative impacts of climate change (Chen and Gong 2021).

Formal land certificates increased migration (Deininger et al. 2014) and property rights reforms, including complete land registration, measures to ease transferability, and elimination of the labor market restrictions adopted in 2008 in China's Chengdu prefecture, and almost doubled the likelihood of nonfarm enterprise start-ups (Deininger et al. 2019). Nationwide, liberalization of hukou restrictions between 2000 and 2015 reduced the cost of internal migration by as much as 45 percent and played a central role in supporting structural change, regional income convergence, and capital accumulation (Hao et al. 2020), an effect supported by better safety nets providing implicit insurance.[21] Making migration policy more egalitarian or land policy more uniform would promote urbanization (Garriga et al. 2020).

Use of a proxy for city-level land and housing supply shows that more migrants went to cities with elastic housing supply where informal housing attracted low-skilled migrants and formal housing appealed to high-skilled migrants, translating into higher GDP growth and lower wage increases in cities with a more elastic housing supply (Niu, Sun, and Zheng 2021). Relying on the fact that migrants with rural hukou have less access to mortgage finance and low-cost housing than those with urban hukou allows estimation of instrumental variable regressions with the mother's hukou status as an instrument. The results suggest that household heads with rural hukou are 20 percentage points less likely to own housing in cities and have much lower housing wealth than household heads with urban hukou (Liao and Zhang 2021).

Large-scale land-based investment

Increased demand for land in the wake of the 2007–08 spike in food and commodity prices (Deininger and Byerlee 2011) was widely expected to provide relatively land-abundant African countries an opportunity to attract investment (Collier and Venables 2012). Similar to foreign direct investment in other sectors, this would not only bring capital but also, through knowhow, market access, and competition, generate spillovers to local industries (Monge-Naranjo 2019). This was reinforced by the realization that the historical pattern of increasing output in Africa via area expansion without capital has become increasingly unsustainable.

Hopes for outside investment to help transform rural Africa were enhanced by experience from Asia, where, despite high environmental (Li and Semedi 2021) and social (Cisneros, Hellmundt, and Kis-Katos 2022) costs,[22] large agro-investment had supported structural transformation. Oil palm establishment in Indonesia after 2000 is estimated to have increased the productivity of manufacturing firms well beyond the oil palm value chain (Kraus, Heilmayr, and Koch 2021), lifted more than one-fourth of the country's rural individuals out of poverty (Edwards 2019a), and improved access to employment, infrastructure

(Edwards 2019b), nutrition, better living standards, and human capital formation (Chrisendo, Siregar, and Qaim 2022).

Such positive effects mirror the impact of large plantation investments in settings where labor markets were competitive, as in Costa Rica (Mendez and van Patten 2022) or Taiwan, China, where, in addition to generating employment opportunities for women, plantations' human capital demand helped eliminate century-old gender norms that had restricted women's advancement (Cheng, Fan, and Wu 2022).[23] These positive experiences contrast markedly with Africa's colonial history (spotlight 3.2), in which landlords aimed to reduce labor mobility through restrictions on the ability to access land and discourage human capital accumulation by potential workers, thereby stunting long-term development (Nugent and Robinson 2010).

Although not all of these increases can be attributed to large-scale land-based investment (LSLBI), analysis of satellite imagery suggests that cultivated area increased significantly. Table 3.1 shows that between 2003 and 2019, cultivated area in Sub-Saharan Africa expanded by 46.7 million ha, more than in Latin America (38 million ha), East Asia (18 million ha), or South Asia (20.7 million ha). Compared with an expansion of 6.4 million ha from 2003 to 2007, cultivated area in the region expanded by around 9.3 million ha from 2007 to 2011, 15.2 million ha from 2011

TABLE 3.1 Extent of cropland cultivation and expansion in Africa and globally, 2003–19
(hectares, millions)

Region	Total area cultivated					Net expansion, 2003–19	Number of countries
	2003	2007	2011	2015	2019		
Africa, Central	8.800	9.527	10.761	13.730	17.322	8.521	10
Africa, East	32.752	34.197	37.169	41.515	45.305	12.553	6
Africa, North	35.251	36.719	38.068	39.636	41.300	6.049	6
Africa, South	20.578	21.277	22.671	25.752	29.225	8.647	10
Africa, West	52.875	55.682	58.571	62.012	65.647	12.772	15
SSA	130.082	136.504	145.790	161.005	176.809	46.727	42
Total Africa	**150.257**	**157.402**	**167.242**	**182.645**	**198.799**	**48.543**	**47**
EAP	261.351	264.823	267.642	274.086	279.528	18.177	25
ECA	337.186	329.893	331.170	335.859	337.960	0.775	34
LAC	100.636	112.226	121.512	132.167	138.701	38.065	35
ME	29.255	29.205	29.158	31.033	33.742	4.487	15
SAS	165.060	172.590	177.074	182.039	185.833	20.773	7
WENA	354.677	352.039	352.342	358.085	361.463	6.786	20
World	**1,378.247**	**1,397.279**	**1,424.689**	**1,474.273**	**1,514.037**	**135.790**	**178**

Source: Calculations are based on the global cropland expansion map of the University of Maryland, Global Land Analysis and Discovery.
Note: EAP = East Asia and Pacific; ECA = Eastern Europe and Central Asia; LAC = Latin America and the Caribbean; ME = Middle East; SAS = South Asia; SSA = Sub-Saharan Africa; WENA = Western Europe and North America.

to 2015, and 15.8 million ha from 2015 to 2019. The 10 countries where cultivated area expanded the most are Tanzania (6.08 million ha), Nigeria (4.69 million ha), Sudan (4.23 million ha), Chad (2.67 million ha), Uganda (2.50 million ha), Zambia (2.32 million ha), the Democratic Republic of Congo (2.30 million ha), Mozambique (2.26 million ha), Angola (1.93 million ha), and Ethiopia (1.92 million ha).

Despite this large increase in cultivated area, even relative to other regions, studies point to limited direct or indirect benefits, in contrast to what has been observed for other types of foreign direct investment in Africa (Abebe, McMillan, and Serafinelli 2022) or the extractives sector (Cust and Harding 2020). Although reputable investors with strong credentials are reported to have preferred countries with strong executive constraints (Besley and Mueller 2017), LSLBI often attracted nontraditional investors who tended to focus on countries with weak land governance (Arezki, Deininger, and Selod 2015). Centralized, noncompetitive ways to identify investors or transfer land often prioritized political (Bélair 2021) or territorial (Lavers 2016) over economic objectives.[24] Land centrally assigned to investors was then often found to be occupied ("encroached"), mired in conflict, or less suitable than expected.

For Africa overall, large agricultural investments, especially by domestic investors, are reported to have increased the likelihood of organized violence (Balestri and Maggioni 2021), possibly caused by power imbalances (De Maria, Robinson, and Zanello 2023), with land deals for mixed or food crop use reported to have increased malnutrition and had a limited positive impact on livelihoods (Kinda et al. 2022). Country-level analysis based on farm and household surveys suggests that the establishment of large farms in Ethiopia did not create jobs and had little effect on smallholders' access to technology or input and insurance markets (Ali, Deininger, and Harris 2019). In Mozambique, use of improved practices and inputs by smallholders adjacent to newly established large farms increased, but yields and market participation did not rise (Deininger and Xia 2016), and large farms may have put downward pressure on wages (Glover and Jones 2019). In Zambia, spillovers from large farm establishments were at best limited and increased competition for land (Lay, Nolte, and Sipangule 2020).[25]

Centralized, noncompetitive mechanisms to transfer land to investors, combined with a need for multiple approvals from overlapping authorities that encouraged opportunistic action, have been reported to have reduced predictability and ultimately led to cancellation of investments in Tanzania (Engström and Hajdu 2018). In Madagascar, highly centralized decision-making deepened preexisting cleavages and ended up reducing tenure security for investors as well as locals (Burnod, Gingembre, and Andrianirina Ratsialonana 2013). Respect for existing rights (Maganga et al. 2016), safeguards (Nolte and Voget-Kleschin 2014), or disclosure (Cotula 2014) and job creation or skill transfer (Nanhthavong et al. 2022) often suffered.

Although some investors withdrew, those who proceeded were often unable to address environmental issues (Shete et al. 2016) or conflict (Sulle 2020) or improve productivity. Use of nonmarket mechanisms to transfer land tended to compromise the economic viability of ventures and often weakened safeguards (Nolte and Voget-Kleschin 2014), contract disclosure, and independent third-party monitoring (Cotula 2014). In Ghana, it allowed chiefs to strengthen or reestablish authority over land (Boamah 2014), channel resources to close kin (Boamah and Overa 2016), and reduce predictability for investors by opportunistically reneging on prior commitments (Lanz, Gerber, and Haller 2018).

Investments in irrigation or technology, which would be an important benefit from bringing in outsiders (Schuenemann, Thurlow, and Zeller 2017), rarely materialized. Instead, the main advantage was employment (Nolte and Ostermeier 2017), which often benefited those with better skills (Herrmann 2017), men (Tsikata and Yaro 2014), or those with connections to chiefs (Bottazzi et al. 2018). Local concerns, including environmental risks such as forest conversion (Shete et al. 2016), pesticide contamination (Zaehringer et al. 2018), and health effects (Xia and Deininger 2019), were often ignored. This may have enhanced the potential for collective action and trust in affected communities as a defensive action (Khadjavi, Sipangule, and Thiele 2021). Projects often failed (Schoneveld 2014) or pushed into neighboring land with higher fertility, triggering conflict with smallholders (Kunda-Wamuwi, Babalola, and Chirwa 2017).

Investors' expected contributions to national budgets often also failed to materialize. In Malawi, where 1.35 million ha, 25 percent of the country's arable area, had been leased to "estates" in the late 1980s, even nominal ground rent claims were not enforced, making it impossible to identify and extinguish leases that were no longer used so that affected land could be reassigned to local producers or investors, preferably in a competitive process. The implied revenue loss is large: if estates paid only half the market rental rate for land, some US$35 million (5 percent of total public spending) could be collected annually. Resistance to digital rent collection may imply that a large part of these resources is captured as rents.

Given smallholders' advantage in labor-intensive products with high value added (Rogers et al. 2021), new investment is likely to offer greater benefits for smallholders if it is focused on upstream activity (Dubbert 2019) that has been shown to generate larger income or poverty gains than investment focused on land only (Van den Broeck, Swinnen, and Maertens 2017). Outgrower arrangements offer benefits to growers by addressing price risk, which a randomized evaluation has shown to be the most important issue for smallholders in Benin (Arouna, Michler, and Lokossou 2021) and Madagascar (Bellemare, Lee, and Novak 2021). Involving small farmers as outgrowers also increases the potential for knowledge transfer (Hall, Scoones, and Tsikata 2017), including for women (Adams, Gerber, and Amacker 2019). Beyond its advantages for small farmers, a more integrated investment approach (Schoneveld 2022) that focuses on contract and outgrower arrangements helps investors by allowing capital that would otherwise be tied up in land to be used more flexibly for other purposes.

The rather disappointing results of large foreign investment in agriculture overall triggered a shift toward medium-scale "emergent" domestic farmers who are expanding rapidly Africa-wide (Jayne et al. 2019), especially in Ghana (Hausermann et al. 2018), Zambia (Jayne et al. 2014), and Tanzania (Pedersen and Kweka 2017). It is essential to provide incentives for effective land use and lay the foundation for competitive markets to ensure greater success than under LSLBI. The example of Zambia (spotlight 3.4), where titled large farms participated less rather than more in markets for land or credit and failed to achieve higher productivity than informal small ones (Ali and Deininger 2022), suggests that formal titles will not automatically lead to credit access, investment, or job creation. Instead, titles that cannot be maintained locally may be associated with speculative land acquisition that may reduce rather than improve the functioning of rural factor markets. Although land taxation can potentially deal with this issue, regulating how locally issued use rights can be administered may be more conducive to rural factor market operation in many settings.

Three actions can help to increase the likelihood that expansion of medium-scale farms, which is widespread in many African countries (Jayne et al. 2019), increases productivity and local welfare: (a) enforcing realistic land tax or ground rent payments by such enterprises, sharing the proceeds with local authorities, and allowing nonpayment to be used as a reason to initiate proceedings for revoking rights to cleanse the registry; (b) equipping local (and central) authorities with the tools and data for better planning, including by identifying opportunities for farmers to integrate into value chains with higher value added, and monitoring of land use independently; and (c) exploring the scope for using digital and georeferenced records of land-use rights, together with those created by farmer registries, to improve market access by small farmers, including by linking them to markets for inputs, outputs, savings, credit, and insurance in a way that allows reduction of transaction costs via digital interaction and their ability to use parcels' cultivation history to establish reputation and access trade finance (Villalba, Venus, and Sauer 2023).

Policy implications

Provide avenues to obtain transferable use rights. Evidence from several African countries shows that participatory and transparent documentation of land-use rights at the local level, even if such rights were not fully transferable, had benefits in terms of empowering (female) landowners and resulting in greater risk taking, investment, and land market participation. In fact, in Ethiopia, where land sales remain prohibited, such reforms are estimated to have removed around 25 percent of total misallocation, suggesting considerable potential. Thus, use rights should not be viewed as inferior rights that, if at all, can be recognized only for a limited time span to make the transition toward full title. Instead, with appropriate regulations, such rights, especially if they are linked to a digital marketplace, can go a long way toward improving the functioning of local factor markets. Use rights can be transformed into full title if and when the advantages of full transferability outweigh the cost and can lead to significant improvements in rural competitiveness.

Maximize value of use rights by linking them to digital farmer registries. Digital farmer registries that include georeferenced parcel boundaries offer many advantages, especially if combined with land-use monitoring based on remote sensing. Digital registries of use rights that unambiguously identify farmers and their land can help (a) increase the competitiveness of local output and input markets by digitally linking farmers to private suppliers, (b) decrease information frictions in land rental markets via wider dissemination of land supply and demand, and (c) increase farmers' productivity and reduce their risk exposure by bundling land rentals with insurance to eliminate the need to use sharecropping or by using georeferenced parcel boundaries to tailor parametric insurance products to specific conditions.

Provide investors with transferable land at market prices through a transparent and competitive process. LSLBI was viewed by many as an opportunity to leverage private capital and knowhow to help modernize Africa's small-farm sector through spillover benefits. Evidence suggests these expectations were not fulfilled: in stark contrast to rural transformations brought about by large investments in Indonesia and Brazil, most ventures in Africa struggled to get off the ground, generating few if any spillover benefits for neighboring smallholder farmers and, in some cases, led to land grabs. A key reason for limited success seems to have been an overreliance on centralized and noncompetitive mechanisms for land allocation that lent itself to political influence. It also implied a failure to provide investors marketable land rights, which made it difficult for them to access credit and invest or for struggling ones to transfer their land to more successful entrepreneurs.

Attract investment through public goods that benefit everybody. Although outside investment can provide much-needed access to technology, markets, and capital, LSLBI's rather disappointing record suggests that the focus on highly capital- and land-intensive farming was not in line with most African countries' endowments and that centralized land allocation creates little competition and may lack local information and be open to abuse and manipulation. In locations where smallholder farms are active, aiming to attract investors higher up in the value chain to supply regional markets or in contract farming may be more in line with most African countries' capacity and factor endowments. It could also transfer skills and help local farmers to build on their comparative advantage and link to broader markets. For new investment in locations where smallholder farms are active, contract farming focused on higher-value crops and regional markets may be more in line with most countries' local capacity and factor endowments, transfer skills to local populations, and help link local farmers to outside markets and value chains.

Reduce speculative landholding through a tax on holdings above a certain size. For land that has already been transferred to investors or "emergent farmers," collection of ground rent or land taxes could generate revenue and increase incentives for productive land use, and in the case of nonpayment, land rights could be revisited and possibly canceled to allow allocation in more transparent and competitive ways with local participation. A land tax on commercial farms above a certain size could encourage productive land use and reduce incentives for speculation, create a basis to properly cancel unused land rights, and, by creating evidence of land use, increase current occupants' security.

SPOTLIGHTS

Spotlight 3.1: Emergence and nature of property rights to land

Historically, property rights to land emerged with the transition from shifting cultivation, where location is not fixed and fallow periods are used to restore soil fertility, to sedentary agriculture, in which rights to specific parcels give individual land users an incentive to invest in keeping the soil fertile (Boserup 1965). Thus, the idea of ownership emerged with the transition to sedentary agriculture (Apicella et al. 2014). Even in hunter-gatherer societies, land for individual cultivation and common property coexist, with the extent of land-ownership and territoriality varying with resource density and often changing with it (Baker 2003).

Historical patterns of land access and use continue to affect social relationships in the present. Reliance on irrigation allowed landed elites in arid areas to monopolize water and arable land, resulting in more centralized states. Irrigation dependence is a strong predictor of land inequality in current countries and premodern societies; even today, countries with irrigated agriculture are far less democratic than those where agriculture is rainfed (Bentzen, Kaarsen, and Wingender 2017).[26] Unequal access to resources has also been linked to hereditary inequality and economic stratification (Dow and Reed 2013), especially in locations where mobility was constrained by natural barriers such as deserts. High agricultural productivity and restricted mobility are identified and empirically confirmed as key predictors of state formation as a precursor to city development (Schönholzer 2021).

In rainfed agriculture, cereals are easier to appropriate but need to be stored to provide food during the planting and growing seasons, whereas roots and tubers grow continuously but are bulky, making trade and transport difficult. The suitability of land for cereal cultivation has been linked to differences in the size of the state, the distribution of power within it, and the nature of property rights to land (Mayshar, Moav, and Pascali 2021), with effects that persist in modern times (Mayshar, Moav, and Neeman 2017). The suitability of land for wheat production has been argued to be a key factor in explaining variation in the strength of family ties across societies and countries (Ang and Fredriksson 2017).

Reliance on fishing instead of arable agriculture, as proxied by reef density, predicts the global prevalence of matrilineal inheritance patterns (BenYishay, Grosjean, and Vecci 2017). Women's comparative advantage in animal husbandry rather than crop cultivation would suggest that large shifts that made crop agriculture less attractive, such as the increase in land availability after the Black Death in the fourteenth century or after the English enclosures in the seventeenth century, would increase women's options outside marriage. This hypothesis is confirmed in the data since in both cases, women's age at marriage increased (Voigtlander and Voth 2013).[27]

Social norms and property institutions evolved together. Alesina, Giuliano, and Nunn (2011) show that a region's suitability for plow agriculture affected historical norms and preferences about fertility that still affect gender norms and the type of property rights adopted. Descendants of societies (across countries, districts within countries, and ethnicities within districts) that traditionally practiced plow agriculture have less equal gender norms and female participation in the labor force, as well as entrepreneurial and political activity, and this result holds even for children of immigrants in Europe and the United States (Alesina, Giuliano, and Nunn 2013). In India, exogenous variations in soil texture that affect the type of tillage affect female empowerment (Carranza 2014). In Viet Nam, the suitability of land for the plow has influenced traditional postmarital residence rules and current under-five sex ratios (Grogan 2018), a relationship that weakened only recently.[28]

Spotlight 3.2: Long-term effects of unequal land distribution

Exogenous interventions have long shaped land and labor relations in Africa. Nunn (2008) documents a robust negative relationship between the number of slaves exported from a country and its current economic performance. In addition, contemporary levels of trust by individuals whose ancestors were heavily raided during the slave trade are significantly below those among ethnic groups that were not, a relationship that is argued to be causal and run through cultural norms and values (Nunn and Wantchekon 2011). This is consistent with more recent evidence that cross-country and ethnic group differences in the intensity of exposure to enslavement between 1400 and 1900 are negatively associated with current access to mobile financial services, credit, and trust in financial institutions (Levine, Lin, and Xie 2020).

The nature of colonial interventions related to land differed between relatively densely populated and land-abundant countries. In densely populated areas such as India, colonial dominance could rely on indirect rule through local authorities. Banerjee and Iyer (2005) show that differences in how the British recognized property rights and collected land tax revenue still affect economic outcomes. In areas where large landlords were responsible for collecting land revenue, agricultural investments and productivity are lower than in areas where individual cultivators paid directly. In the early 1990s, landlord-dominated regions still had less access to public goods such as health and education (Banerjee, Iyer, and Somanathan 2005). In Java, areas close to sugar factories established in the mid-nineteenth century by the Dutch are richer, more industrialized, better educated, and better endowed with infrastructure today than nearby, equally suitable areas (Dell and Olken 2020).

If land is abundant, getting locals to work in mines or colonial ventures requires coercion, and the institutions to do so often have long-term impacts (Deininger and Binswanger 1995). For example, the *mita*, an extensive forced labor system practiced by the Spanish in Latin America from 1573 to 1812 that forced locals to supply labor for silver mining, continues to affect outcomes today (Dell 2010): where the system was practiced, current consumption is lower and the prevalence of stunting is higher, with land tenure and public goods provision as channels. Similar findings are reported for Caribbean (Dippel, Greif, and Trefler 2020) and Puerto Rican (Bobonis and Morrow 2014) sugar plantations.[29]

Along the same lines, practices to obtain labor in the colonization of Africa in the late nineteenth and early twentieth centuries included (a) imposing head or hut taxes to force locals into the cash economy; (b) limiting the areas where locals could acquire land rights to reserves, a practice adopted all over eastern and southern Africa and most egregiously used in South Africa's 1913 Natives Land Act; and (c) licensing requirements or other output and input market distortions such as monopoly marketing boards (Binswanger, Deininger, and Feder 1995).

Landownership inequality may adversely affect the emergence of public schooling as a key institution for promoting human capital and thus the pace and nature of the transition from agriculture to industry (Galor, Moav, and Vollrath 2009). A negative effect of landownership concentration on education expenditure was found for the United States at the beginning of the twentieth century. Among rural counties in the United States in 1890, Vollrath (2013) finds that land inequality was negatively related to local property tax revenues used for schooling. For counties in nineteenth-century Prussia, a negative link between landownership concentration and school enrollment emerges in the cross section (Cinnirella and Hornung 2016b). Land reforms that gradually abolished serfdom were key to increase demand for education[30]; as agriculture became more intensive in human capital, landlords' incentives may have shifted to promoting workers' access to human capital (Ashraf et al. 2018).

Across the world, early land inequality reduced math and science skills even a century later. Studies show that numerical cognitive skills and human capital effects are highly persistent, so that overcoming severe inequality and investing quickly in numerical education may have been preconditions for entering human capital–intensive industries (Baten and Juif 2014). Across Europe, inequality in land distribution is negatively correlated with human capital formation as landowners had no incentives to promote educational institutions or were unwilling to pay the taxes necessary to fund them, explaining much of the differences in development between rural European regions historically (Baten and Hippe 2018).

Local finance. Across countries, and controlling for a wide range of other variables, initial land inequality is a reliable predictor of financial development (Erickson and Vollrath 2007). Evidence from the United States in the early twentieth century also indicates that counties with disproportionately large landholdings had fewer banks per capita, higher cost of credit, and less access to credit, suggesting that even in settings with well-developed political institutions, elites may have instruments to restrict financial development (Rajan and Ramcharan 2011). Land inequality can also impede the development of microfinance institutions independent of any public intervention. Suesse and Wolf (2020) explore the determinants of the expansion of credit cooperatives between 1852 and 1913 in 236 Prussian counties. They find that while structural transformation (declining staple prices) was a major factor in the emergence of such cooperatives, which facilitated the diversification of farm output, land inequality in some regions inhibited their spread.

Land use. Current property tax valuations for about 380,000 square miles of land in the United States, together with the quasi-random variation from checkerboard allocation, have been used to show that historical land concentration has had persistent effects, lowering investment by 23 percent, overall property value by 4.5 percent, and population by 3 to 8 percent. Investment gaps were higher historically and can be linked to large landlords using land for ranching rather than crop farming and to the investment disincentives of share tenancy, an inefficiency that persisted because of land market frictions (Smith 2021). Baland and Robinson (2008) similarly show that rents conceded by landlords through share tenancy give them a comparative advantage in controlling the political activities of their workers, increasing incentives for land concentration that were eliminated by the introduction of the secret ballot in Chile in 1958. Landlords' ability to make transfers to share tenants to gain electoral support and control politics is also observed in Pakistan, where technical change made tenancy less profitable, improved electoral competition, reduced the likelihood of landlords being elected, and changed the composition of public goods in landlord-dominated areas (Beg 2017).

Politics. Landlords unable to compete may resort to political lobbying. Adamopoulos (2008) develops a model in which, if landownership is sufficiently concentrated, landed elites who are unable to compete on productivity may successfully lobby to protect their rents through restrictions on international trade that will also affect the timing and speed of industrialization. Calibrating the model to Canada and Argentina in the early twentieth century replicates differences in equilibrium tariffs that are similar to those observed until 1950, although as land becomes less important as a factor of production, the role of land inequality diminishes.

Spotlight 3.3: Redistributive land reform

Historically, redistributive land reforms have been important. Bhattacharya, Mitra, and Ulubaşoğlu (2019) identify 372 land reform episodes that took place from 1900 to 2010 in 165 countries, with many of the episodes coinciding with political transitions. Implementing such reforms will require decisions on the selection of land and beneficiaries, the transferability of rights received by beneficiaries, and the obligations they would have to assume (for example, payment) for land transferred to them (Lipton 2009). Although economic objectives are maximized by short and minimalist reforms that provide secure rights, the political goal of keeping an incumbent regime in power was often better served by keeping property rights insecure—or putting in place a complex administrative apparatus to exercise control—so the threat of withdrawing rights could be used to ensure political support from beneficiaries (Fergusson 2013).

Selection of land and beneficiaries was easy for tenancy reforms providing ownership to sitting tenants. The success of such reforms largely depended on the opportunities (and incentives) for investment they provided to the beneficiaries. In the United States, the Cherokee Nation provided free land for its former slaves after the Civil War. Linked data that follow these individuals point toward lower racial inequality, with land and the associated increase in incomes facilitating investment in physical and human capital (Miller 2020).

Swiftly implemented reforms provided secure and transferable land rights, as at the end of World War II in Japan, Korea, and Taiwan, China. At the time, incomes in Korea and Taiwan, China, were far below those of many countries in Africa. The reforms distributed 30 to 40 percent of the cultivated area in the three countries, affecting about two-thirds of rural households (Jeon and Kim 2000).[31] Property rights were secure, allowing productivity-enhancing investment and access to credit markets (often stimulated by land reform bonds) to act as a catalyst for rural nonfarm development. In each of these cases, the reforms were responsible for at least half of the actual reallocation of labor away from agriculture (Iscan 2018).[32]

India's tenancy reform was less successful because of political constraints. Delays in the announcement and implementation of the reform triggered anticipatory tenant evictions and the resumption of self-cultivation by landlords (Appu 1997). To counter these, landownership ceilings were imposed and share tenancy was abolished, despite the potentially adverse effects of such measures.[33] In West Bengal, shortly after 1978, an aggressive locally driven program to register tenants and provide them with heritable use rights covered some 4 million households. The reform is estimated to have led to short-term gains of 51 to 63 percent (Banerjee, Gertler, and Ghatak 2002). Restrictions on beneficiaries' ability to sublease land and a failure to liquidate landlords' rights reduced the benefits, however, by essentially freezing investment.

Using tenants-cum-owners, Deininger, Jin, and Yadav (2013) estimate that this arrangement was associated with static efficiency losses of 25 percent.

Beyond affecting productivity, awarding nontransferable land-use rights also affects gender relations. Because land rights lose their value if there is no male heir, a higher intensity of program implementation affected the chances of survival for male and female children (Bhalotra et al. 2019). This mirrors evidence from China, where awarding land-use rights during the 1978–84 reforms affected sex ratios, especially for second births after a firstborn girl, leading to as many as 1 million "missing girls" (Almond et al. 2007). Tenancy reform in the Philippines benefited around half a million households and, aided by Green Revolution technology, improved household welfare (Balisacan and Fuwa 2004; Otsuka 1991), increasing investment and human capital accumulation (Deininger, Maertens, and Olinto 2001).

Distributing large estates was less successful, however. To make the program legally feasible, a ceiling of 5 ha was imposed on ownership, including by banks and on operational holdings, constraining farm size growth. Cost was reduced by giving land under collective titles that are not suitable as collateral and difficult to split. Adamopoulos and Restuccia (2020) estimate that the reform reduced average farm size by 34 percent and agricultural productivity by 17 percent.

In Italy, redistribution of large estate land gave rise to a long-lasting clientelist system characterized by political patronage that provided persistent electoral benefits to the Christian Democratic Party (Caprettini, Casaburi, and Venturini 2021) but is argued to have slowed structural transformation (Albertus 2022). Political imperatives were also pervasive in Latin America. In Mexico, the intensity of land distribution increased during election years and when the threat of rural unrest was greater (Albertus et al. 2016). Communities were more likely to challenge the dominance of the ruling party (the Institutional Revolutionary Party) when they were given land in more remote locations where service delivery was more difficult, thus increasing their dependence on the party's clientelist network (Fergusson, Larreguy, and Riaño 2022).[34]

Reforms in Kenya and Zimbabwe show that equity, social justice, and productivity aspects of land reform may be compromised if beneficiary selection becomes politicized. In Kenya, demand-driven efforts by small farmers, who had organized land-buying associations, with public support, to acquire and then subdivide large farms, were abandoned to allow greater political influence in beneficiary selection (Scott, MacArthur, and Newbery 1976). Yet, as rights were secure and transferable, this affected equity but not productivity.

Zimbabwe initially followed a similar and quite successful model (Deininger, Hoogeveen, and Kinsey 2004). Property rights were kept insecure to shore up political support for the ruling party, undermining beneficiaries' ability to invest or leave agriculture. Fast-track reforms that, from the 2000s, expropriated large white-owned farms generated minimal economic benefits and offered beneficiaries few options for economic advancement (Scoones, Mavedzenge, and Murimbarimba 2019) while inflicting high cost. Continued debates on the legitimacy of a settlement to compensate white farmers (Moyo 2021; Sixpence and Chigora 2020), which, as part of reforms to regain access to global financial markets, was approved by a referendum, highlight the continued relevance of political considerations.

South Africa's reliance on discriminatory legislation for almost a century and the importance of land access for welfare (Lovo 2014) made land reform a key element of postapartheid debates. A target was set to redistribute 30 percent of the area under large farms within a decade, and a "willing seller–willing buyer" approach was chosen to avoid the insecurity of property rights associated with expropriation (Deininger 1999).[35] Analysis using a pipeline design suggests that although beneficiary living standards dropped initially and attrition was large, spending had risen 50 percent above its pretransfer level three to four years after the reform, suggesting that beneficiaries with skills and tenacity can benefit from land access (Keswell and Carter 2014).[36]

However, after failing to reach the initial target for redistribution, there was a perception that land reform created more jobs in the consulting business than in agriculture. Course corrections in the national program were frequent (Hall and Kepe 2017; Rusenga 2020), with many studies documenting unsuccessful projects (Kirsten et al. 2016; O'Laughlin et al. 2013), and calls for expropriation have increased. A 2018 panel report, while including some new ideas (Zantsi and Greyling 2021), did not give a clear direction (Gran 2021; Makombe 2018). A more rigorous quantification of demand might be more promising, including demand from young entrepreneurs who want to make a living in farming, and an approach that, on this basis, commits to and publicly monitors progress toward quantitative targets, offers potential beneficiaries without agricultural vocation an alternative asset, and works to increase supply through financial incentives (for example, a time-limited land reform surcharge on agricultural property taxes).

Spotlight 3.4: An ill-functioning registry reduces large- and medium-size farm performance in Zambia

In Zambia, agricultural productivity is relatively low, and much of the country's 74 million ha of land area, of which 58 percent has a high or medium level of suitability for agriculture, is not used. The belief that large farms are essential for agricultural growth has long been a central tenet of the country's agricultural strategy. Long before the 2007–08 commodity price boom, settlement schemes and "farm blocks" were established as clusters where, in addition to land, infrastructure and market access would be easily available to stimulate commercial agriculture and boost food security (Middelberg, van der Zwan, and Oberholster 2020).

The success of this strategy is debatable, partly because as a form of political patronage, land was often given to retired or retrenched civil servants whose agricultural qualifications and ambitions were limited (Roth 1995). Zambia's policy stance in favor of large farms is also evident from its adoption of one of Africa's most dualistic land policies, which maintains a clear dichotomy between customary and statutory land rights inherited from colonial times. The only way to have land rights formally documented is to convert customary land to "state land." Effecting this conversion is complex and costly, with considerable administrative discretion and few safeguards. It is resisted by chiefs and difficult to implement, especially as the Ministry of Lands is highly centralized.

Ali and Deininger (2022) explore whether titling helps medium-scale farmers access credit or expand their operations. To overcome the lack of data on this group of farmers, a full mapping of all large- and medium-size farms was added to the mapping exercise for the 2020 census in Zambia's Eastern Province. Maps generated in this way were overlaid with administrative records (deed and sketch plans) to assess the accuracy of cadastral records—which was found to be quite low. Farm census data were then used as a frame for a detailed survey of large farms that, by providing data on performance, allows for inferences on the impact of land titles on investment, productivity, and land prices. From the results, it appears that land cultivated by large farms is perceived to be no more transferable than that by smallholders, defeating the purpose of formalizing rights and making rights supposedly associated with titles difficult or impossible to exercise.

Instrumental variable regressions indicate that land titles have only limited impact on investment, reduce participation in land rental markets, and have no effect on credit access or productivity. If anything, titling large farms in Zambia has less impact—in terms of investment, land market activity, credit access, and productivity—than what the literature reports for impacts on small farms. This suggests that institutional constraints may prevent even large farms from realizing the benefits from titles, despite being better positioned to do so or to defray the fixed cost of getting or using titles. Instead, supply-side rationing leads to speculative land acquisition rather than higher market activity and structural transformation.

If Zambia—and, to the extent that these results generalize, other countries where large-scale, land-based investment is suitable—is to benefit from establishing large farms or from future commodity price booms, it will be important to eliminate the regulatory and institutional barriers to widespread coverage and use of land titles as a basis for competitive land and credit markets. Experience suggests that this is likely to require adoption of fully digital documents and workflows to enhance transparency and reduce the scope for fraud, establishment of clear service standards, and fee reductions based on gains in the efficiency of service delivery. Digital records would make it possible to impose a land tax that would augment farmers' incentives to use land effectively and—if the proceeds were to be shared with traditional authorities and local governments—keep records in good shape and remove obstacles to farm growth for local benefit. Given their agricultural potential and access to other infrastructure, farm blocks are obvious candidates for introducing such changes, possibly first on a pilot basis. Efforts to design the necessary information technology infrastructure and evaluate the economic, social, and environmental benefits of rolling them out could provide relevant lessons well beyond Zambia.

Notes

1 | In developed countries' capital-intensive agriculture, tenants may have more market power than landlords. Indeed, Kirwan (2009) uses parcel-level data on land rental prices in the United States to show that, contrary to theory, tenants capture 75 percent of public subsidies, suggesting that there is imperfect competition in local markets for farmland rental. Providing information may be better suited to overcome market power and lack of information even in developed countries (Seifert, Kahle, and Hüttel 2021).

2 | In the United States, sharecropping using simple rules is often adopted to deal with moral hazard and measurement costs (Allen and Lueck 2009).

3 | Landlord monitoring has been shown to have the potential to reduce some of the static inefficiency of sharecropping in Ethiopia (Deininger, Ali, and Alemu 2008) and Pakistan (Jacoby and Mansuri 2008), although it comes at a cost.

4 | In the United States, technical change that made monitoring easier and reduced the scope for tenants to mine the soil triggered a large shift from sharecropping to fixed rental contracts (Allen and Borchers 2016).

5 | The *mailo* system originates in the 1900 Uganda agreement that, in central and western Uganda, provided the local king (*kabaka*) and his notables with de facto freehold rights to close to 9,000 square miles, thus automatically converting any occupants on such land into tenants (West 1965). Efforts to clarify tenants' obligations, protect them or their heirs against eviction, and document their rights are still ongoing.

6 | A natural experiment along the former inner German border suggests that increased farm size at the border reduces the overall richness of bird species by 10 or 20 percent for cropland or all species, respectively, mainly via landscape simplification, implying that negative biodiversity impacts from increasing farm size and land-use intensification can be mitigated through land-use complexity (Noack and Quaas 2021a).

7 | A desire to reduce the potentially adverse effects of price fluctuations caused by imperfect insurance markets can have the same effect (Barrett 1996).

8 | Family farms are the most common form of farming globally (Lowder, Skoet, and Raney 2016), although their size differs widely, depending on the extent to which capital can be used to substitute for labor (Lowder, Sánchez, and Bertini 2021).

9 | In India, the Green Revolution increased the importance of knowledge and capital, weakening the size–productivity relationship: large farms dominated in districts suited to new technology, while small farms continued to dominate and be most efficient where traditional methods prevailed (Deolalikar 1981).

10 | Pest-resistant or herbicide-tolerant varieties allow the use of zero tillage, reducing labor requirements. Remote guidance of machinery via the Global Positioning System renders supervision of labor less relevant, and a history of remotely sensed imagery can substitute for cultivators' intimate knowledge of field conditions (Deininger and Byerlee 2012).

11 | By affecting labor demand, substitution of purchased inputs for labor will have distributional implications, depending on who supplies the labor being displaced. For example, in Malawi, herbicide adoption improved weed control, saved labor, and reduced land degradation. However, it hurt the poorest, who relied disproportionately on weeding labor and had few alternative opportunities (Bouwman, Andersson, and Giller 2021).

12 | Although land consolidation in France was a long-term exercise that lasted from 1945 to 2008, increases in mechanization facilitated by the program led to long-term growth in population (+9.5 percent), employment (+15 percent), and income (+0.5 percent) but also increased populism, as indicated by the far-right vote share (+6.1 percent) that can plausibly be explained by the program's top-down nature and the fact that mechanization led to significant immigration and changes in social organization (Loumeau 2022).

13 | During the period, the raw wage gap narrowed from 2.6 to 1.8, and the share of employment in agriculture dropped from 24 to 14 percent, driven by productivity growth, compression of skill differences, and skill-biased technical changes.

14 | In Colombia, reform improved intergenerational mobility and acquisition of human capital, but the need to finance the resulting large and often highly politicized bureaucracy (Faguet, Sánchez, and Villaveces 2020) implied that the economic costs exceeded the benefits by a wide margin (Galan 2020).

15 | From 1887, Indians had received land under trust, a form of ownership that restricted transferability and mandated equal division of inheritance. While the intention was to convert all such land to fully transferable fee simple, such conversions were stopped abruptly via the 1934 Indian Reorganization Act, which placed all remaining tribally and individually held American Indian lands into trust status. With the express purpose to protect against land loss, leases were restricted to a maximum of five years, any sale required government approval, and land could not be seized by banks, states, or local governments and could not be willed to a single heir.

16 | A negative effect of homesteading on modern land use that cannot be explained by legal rights, land quality, title characteristics, or unobserved settler characteristics (Allen and Leonard 2021) suggests that the way in which land is acquired may have persistent effects.

17 | The 2003 amendment opened the market to Canadian residents and corporations but maintained the restriction on foreign ownership of farmland.

18 | Aragón, Restuccia, and Rud (2022b) argue that use of parcel rather than farm-level information introduces significant measurement error.

19 | Globally, it is estimated that a hypothetical shift to unrestricted transferability of land (via "titling") would potentially increase output by as much as 82.5 percent (Chen 2017).

20 | Off-farm employment, older educated operators, large farms, and old-age pensions increase the likelihood of leasing out farmland (Zou, Mishra, and Luo 2020).

21 | Eggleston, Sun, and Zhan (2018) find that in China, rural adults whose parents were eligible for a pension were more likely to migrate and work in a nonfarm sector than those with parents who were just below the pension eligibility age. The pension effect is larger for those with parents in poor health.

22 | A moratorium on new clearing was imposed to reverse decades-long tropical forest loss (Chen, Kennedy, and Xu 2019).

23 | This is in line with the fact that in the US South, a shock in the early twentieth century that disrupted cotton cultivation reduced violence and racism by triggering large-scale outmigration of African Americans (Feigenbaum, Mazumder, and Smith 2020).

24 | Case studies show that political objectives may change quickly (Widengard 2019) or not be shared by local officials (Dieterle 2022).

25 | Beyond Africa, similar results are reported from Cambodia (Anti 2021) and the Lao People's Democratic Republic (Nanhthavong et al. 2020).

26 | Descendants of irrigation societies innovate less today and are more likely to work in routine-intensive occupations, even when they live outside their ancestral homelands (Buggle 2020).

27 | Eder and Halla (2020) argue that in the preindustrial period, regions focusing on animal husbandry rather than crop farming had higher illegitimacy ratios in the past, with female descendants today still more likely to approve of illegitimacy and give birth outside marriage. This has been tested with an instrumental variable approach for local agricultural suitability in Austria.

28 | Hansen, Jensen, and Skovsgaard (2015) find that in cereal agriculture, women spend more time processing cereals than in the field, have higher fertility rates, and spend less time outside the home. They argue that this should translate into a negative relationship between the length of time a society has spent in sedentary agriculture and female empowerment. This hypothesis is tested with and receives support from samples, including all countries in the world, European regions, and immigrants and children of immigrants in the United States, and is robust to a wide range of controls.

29 | Fredriksson and Gupta (2022) argue that inherent land productivity was a positive determinant of colonization as well as its duration, possibly because of the need for immediate and continued food self-sufficiency and the potential to export to a food- and resource-scarce Europe.

30 | The same data also suggest a robust negative association between average formal education and the share of married women, in line with studies of the role of gender-specific human capital in the demographic transition (Cinnirella and Hornung 2016a).

31 | Transferring land rights from collectives to individuals set off spurts of investment and productivity growth in China (Lin 1992) and Viet Nam (Pingali and Xuan 1992). Market-oriented reforms in many of the states of the Russian Federation, while initially leading to a significant drop in output (Rozelle and Swinnen 2004), later led to the development of land markets (Swinnen, Van Herck, and Vranken 2016), and many have joined the European Union.

32 | Reforms in Ireland from 1870 to 1919 (Guinnane and Miller 1997) and in Spain in 1932 (Carmona, Roses, and Simpson 2019) were also tenancy reforms that contributed to and were facilitated by structural transformation and rising wages.

33 | As it was combined with abolition of intermediaries (*zamindars*), land reform still had a positive overall effect (Besley and Burgess 2000). Yet, equity benefits were modest compared to possible alternative reform designs. Besley et al. (2016) use state borders to show that 30 years after they were implemented, tenancy reforms had allowed relatively richer middle castes to accumulate land but reduced access to land for poorer low-caste tenants. This finding is consistent with the notion that prohibiting leasing hurts small, land-poor producers the most (Deininger, Jin, and Nagarajan 2009b). Deininger, Jin, and Nagarajan (2008) estimate that abolishing restrictions on leasing could give 15 million more farmers access to land.

34 | In El Salvador, reform cooperatives are less likely to produce cash crops and more likely to produce staple crops, are more productive in producing staple crops, and have more equitable worker incomes than outside-owned haciendas (Montero 2021).

35 | Market-supported land transfer was also supported by a World Bank–funded project in Malawi that included resources for a formal impact evaluation, yet it never produced any results beyond the finding that resettled households achieved greater long-term food security because having more land was coupled with a more diversified crop portfolio, and formalizing property rights improved land security for male and female household heads, but resettlement jeopardized the land security of women in male-headed households (Mueller et al. 2014).

36 | In Brazil, after four years of ownership, market-assisted land reform had increased production by 74 percent and income by 37 percent (Helfand, Sielawa, and Singhania 2019).

References

Abebe, G., M. McMillan, and M. Serafinelli. 2022. "Foreign Direct Investment and Knowledge Diffusion in Poor Locations." *Journal of Development Economics* 158: 102926.

Acampora, M., L. Casaburi, and J. Willis. 2022. "Land Rental Markets: Experimental Evidence from Kenya." NBER Working Paper 30495, National Bureau of Economic Research, Cambridge, MA.

Adamopoulos, T. 2008. "Land Inequality and the Transition to Modern Growth." *Review of Economic Dynamics* 11 (2): 257–82.

Adamopoulos, T., L. Brandt, C. Chen, D. Restuccia, and X. Wei. 2022. "Land Security and Mobility Frictions." NBER Working Paper 29666, National Bureau of Economic Research, Cambridge, MA.

Adamopoulos, T., and D. Restuccia. 2014. "The Size Distribution of Farms and International Productivity Differences." *American Economic Review* 104 (6): 1667–97.

Adamopoulos, T., and D. Restuccia. 2020. "Land Reform and Productivity: A Quantitative Analysis with Micro Data." *American Economic Journal: Macroeconomics* 12 (3): 1–39.

Adams, T., J.-D. Gerber, and M. Amacker. 2019. "Constraints and Opportunities in Gender Relations: Sugarcane Outgrower Schemes in Malawi." *World Development* 122: 282–94.

Akee, R. 2009. "Checkerboards and Coase: The Effect of Property Institutions on Efficiency in Housing Markets." *Journal of Law and Economics* 52 (2): 395–410.

Albertus, M. 2019. "The Effect of Commodity Price Shocks on Public Lands Distribution: Evidence from Colombia." *World Development* 113: 294–308.

Albertus, M. 2022. "The Persistence of Rural Underdevelopment: Evidence from Land Reform in Italy." *Comparative Political Studies.* https://doi.org/10.1177/00104140221089653.

Albertus, M., A. Diaz-Cayeros, B. Magaloni, and B. R. Weingast. 2016. "Authoritarian Survival and Poverty Traps: Land Reform in Mexico." *World Development* 77: 154–70.

Albertus, M., and B. G. Popescu. 2020. "Does Equalizing Assets Spur Development? Evidence from Large-Scale Land Reform in Peru." *Quarterly Journal of Political Science* 15 (2): 255–95.

Alesina, A., P. Giuliano, and N. Nunn. 2011. "Fertility and the Plough." *American Economic Review* 101 (3): 499–503.

Alesina, A., P. Giuliano, and N. Nunn. 2013. "On the Origins of Gender Roles: Women and the Plough." *Quarterly Journal of Economics* 128 (2): 469–530.

Ali, D. A., and K. Deininger. 2015. "Is There a Farm Size-Productivity Relationship in African Agriculture? Evidence from Rwanda." *Land Economics* 91 (2): 317–43.

Ali, D. A., and K. Deininger. 2021. "Does Mechanization Reverse the Inverse Farm Size-Productivity Relationship? Evidence from Ethiopia." Policy research working paper, World Bank, Washington, DC.

Ali, D. A., and K. Deininger. 2022. "Institutional Determinants of Large Land-Based Investments' Performance in Zambia: Does Title Enhance Productivity and Structural Transformation?" *World Development* 157: 105932.

Ali, D. A., K. Deininger, and M. Goldstein. 2014. "Environmental and Gender Impacts of Land Tenure Regularization in Africa: Pilot Evidence from Rwanda." *Journal of Development Economics* 110: 262–75.

Ali, D. A., K. Deininger, and A. Harris. 2019. "Does Large Farm Establishment Create Benefits for Neighboring Smallholders? Evidence from Ethiopia." *Land Economics* 95 (1): 71–90.

Ali, D. A., K. Deininger, G. Mahofa, and R. Nyakulama. 2021. "Sustaining Land Registration Benefits by Addressing the Challenges of Reversion to Informality in Rwanda." *Land Use Policy* 110: 104317.

Ali, D. A., K. Deininger, and L. Ronchi. 2019. "Costs and Benefits of Land Fragmentation: Evidence from Rwanda." *World Bank Economic Review* 33 (3): 750–71.

Allen, D. W., and A. Borchers. 2016. "Conservation Practices and the Growth of US Cash Rent Leases." *Journal of Agricultural Economics* 67 (2): 491–509.

Allen, D. W., and B. Leonard. 2021. "Property Right Acquisition and Path Dependence: Nineteenth-Century Land Policy and Modern Economic Outcomes." *Economic Journal* 131 (640): 3073–102.

Allen, D. W., and D. Lueck. 1998. "The Nature of the Farm." *Journal of Law and Economics* 41 (2): 343–86.

Allen, D. W., and D. Lueck. 2009. "Customs and Incentives in Contracts." *American Journal of Agricultural Economics* 91 (4): 880–94.

Almond, D., L. Edlund, H. Li, and J. Zhang. 2007. "Long-Term Effects of the 1959–1961 China Famine: Mainland China and Hong Kong." NBER Working Paper 13384, National Bureau of Economic Research, Cambridge, MA.

Alston, L. J., and J. P. Ferrie. 2005. "Time on the Ladder: Career Mobility in Agriculture, 1890–1938." NBER Working Paper 11231, National Bureau of Economic Research, Cambridge, MA.

Alston, L. J., and B. Mueller. 2018. "Priests, Conflicts and Property Rights: The Impacts on Tenancy and Land Use in Brazil." *Man and the Economy* 5 (1): 20180003. https://doi.org/10.1515/me-2018-0003.

Alvarez, J. A. 2020. "The Agricultural Wage Gap: Evidence from Brazilian Micro-Data." *American Economic Journal: Macroeconomics* 12 (1): 153–73.

Ang, J. B., and P. G. Fredriksson. 2017. "Wheat Agriculture and Family Ties." *European Economic Review* 100: 236–56.

Anti, S. 2021. "Land Grabs and Labor in Cambodia." *Journal of Development Economics* 149: 102616.

Apicella, C. L., E. M. Azevedo, N. A. Christakis, and J. H. Fowler. 2014. "Evolutionary Origins of the Endowment Effect: Evidence from Hunter-Gatherers." *American Economic Review* 104 (6): 1793–805.

Appu, P. S. 1997. *Land Reforms in India: A Survey of Policy, Legislation and Implementation.* New Delhi: Vikas Publishing House.

Aragón, F. M., D. Restuccia, and J. P. Rud. 2022a. "Are Small Farms Really More Productive than Large Farms?" *Food Policy* 106: 102168.

Aragón, F. M., D. Restuccia, and J. P. Rud. 2022b. "Assessing Misallocation in Agriculture: Plots versus Farms." NBER Working Paper 29749, National Bureau of Economic Research, Cambridge, MA.

Arezki, R., K. Deininger, and H. Selod. 2015. "What Drives the Global 'Land Rush'?" *World Bank Economic Review* 29 (2): 207–33.

Arouna, A., J. D. Michler, and J. C. Lokossou. 2021. "Contract Farming and Rural Transformation: Evidence from a Field Experiment in Benin." *Journal of Development Economics* 151: 102626.

Arthi, V., K. Beegle, J. De Weerdt, and A. Palacios-Lopez. 2018. "Not Your Average Job: Measuring Farm Labor in Tanzania." *Journal of Development Economics* 130: 160–72.

Ashraf, Q., F. Cinnirella, O. Galor, B. Gershman, and E. Hornung. 2018. "Capital-Skill Complementarity and the Emergence of Labor Emancipation." CEPR Discussion Paper 12822, Centre for Economic Policy Research, London.

Auffhammer, M., and T. A. Carleton. 2018. "Regional Crop Diversity and Weather Shocks in India." *Asian Development Review* 35 (2): 113–30.

Baker, M. J. 2003. "An Equilibrium Conflict Model of Land Tenure in Hunter-Gatherer Societies." *Journal of Political Economy* 111 (1): 124–73.

Baland, J.-M., F. Gaspart, J. P. Platteau, and F. Place. 2007. "The Distributive Impact of Land Markets in Uganda." *Economic Development and Cultural Change* 55 (2): 283–311.

Baland, J. M., and J. A. Robinson. 2008. "Land and Power: Theory and Evidence from Chile." *American Economic Review* 98 (5): 1737–65.

Balestri, S., and M. A. Maggioni. 2021. "This Land Is My Land! Large-Scale Land Acquisitions and Conflict Events in Sub-Saharan Africa." *Defence and Peace Economics* 32 (4): 427–50.

Balisacan, A. M., and N. Fuwa. 2004. "Going beyond Crosscountry Averages: Growth, Inequality and Poverty Reduction in the Philippines." *World Development* 32 (11): 1891–907.

Banerjee, A., and L. Iyer. 2005. "History, Institutions, and Economic Performance: The Legacy of Colonial Land Tenure Systems in India." *American Economic Review* 95 (4): 1190–213.

Banerjee, A., L. Iyer, and R. Somanathan. 2005. "History, Social Divisions, and Public Goods in Rural India." *Journal of the European Economic Association* 3 (2–3): 639–47.

Banerjee, A. V., P. J. Gertler, and M. Ghatak. 2002. "Empowerment and Efficiency: Tenancy Reform in West Bengal." *Journal of Political Economy* 110 (2): 239–80.

Barrett, C. B. 1996. "On Price Risk and the Inverse Farm Size-Productivity Relationship." *Journal of Development Economics* 51 (2): 193–215.

Baten, J., and R. Hippe. 2018. "Geography, Land Inequality and Regional Numeracy in Europe in Historical Perspective." *Journal of Economic Growth* 23 (1): 79–109.

Baten, J., and D. Juif. 2014. "A Story of Large Landowners and Math Skills: Inequality and Human Capital Formation in Long-Run Development, 1820–2000." *Journal of Comparative Economics* 42 (2): 375–401.

Beg, S. 2017. "Traditional Elites: Political Economy of Agricultural Technology and Tenancy." Working Paper 17-03, Department of Economics, University of Delaware, Newark.

Beg, S. 2022. "Digitization and Development: Property Rights Security, and Land and Labor Markets." *Journal of the European Economic Association* 20 (1): 395–429.

Bélair, J. 2021. "Farmland Investments in Tanzania: The Impact of Protected Domestic Markets and Patronage Relations." *World Development* 139: 105298.

Bellemare, M. F., Y. N. Lee, and L. Novak. 2021. "Contract Farming as Partial Insurance." *World Development* 140: 105274.

Benjamin, D. 1995. "Can Unobserved Land Quality Explain the Inverse Productivity Relationship?" *Journal of Development Economics* 46 (1): 51–84.

Benjamin, D., and L. Brandt. 2002. "Property Rights, Labour Markets, and Efficiency in a Transition Economy: The Case of Rural China." *Canadian Journal of Economics* 35 (4): 689–716.

Bentzen, J. S., N. Kaarsen, and A. M. Wingender. 2017. "Irrigation and Autocracy." *Journal of the European Economic Association* 15 (1): 1–53.

BenYishay, A., P. Grosjean, and J. Vecci. 2017. "The Fish Is the Friend of Matriliny: Reef Density and Matrilineal Inheritance." *Journal of Development Economics* 127: 234–49.

Besley, T., and R. Burgess. 2000. "Land Reform, Poverty Reduction, and Growth: Evidence from India." *Quarterly Journal of Economics* 115 (2): 389–430.

Besley, T., J. Leight, R. Pande, and V. Rao. 2016. "Long-Run Impacts of Land Regulation: Evidence from Tenancy Reform in India." *Journal of Development Economics* 118: 72–87.

Besley, T., and H. Mueller. 2017. "Institutions, Volatility, and Investment." *Journal of the European Economic Association* 16 (3): 604–49.

Bhalotra, S., A. Chakravarty, D. Mookherjee, and F. J. Pino. 2019. "Property Rights and Gender Bias: Evidence from Land Reform in West Bengal." *American Economic Journal: Applied Economics* 11 (2): 205–37.

Bhattacharya, P. S., D. Mitra, and M. A. Ulubaşoğlu. 2019. "The Political Economy of Land Reform Enactments: New Cross-National Evidence (1900–2010)." *Journal of Development Economics* 139: 50–68.

Binswanger, H. P., K. Deininger, and G. Feder. 1995. "Power, Distortions, Revolt and Reform in Agricultural Land Relations." *Handbook of Development Economics* 3B: 2659–772.

Bird, J., and A. J. Venables. 2020. "Land Tenure and Land-Use in a Developing City: A Quantitative Spatial Model Applied to Kampala, Uganda." *Journal of Urban Economics* 119: 103268.

Boamah, F. 2014. "How and Why Chiefs Formalise Land Use in Recent Times: The Politics of Land Dispossession through Biofuels Investments in Ghana." *Review of African Political Economy* 41 (141): 406–23.

Boamah, F., and R. Overa. 2016. "Rethinking Livelihood Impacts of Biofuel Land Deals in Ghana." *Development and Change* 47 (1): 98–129.

Bobonis, G. J., and P. M. Morrow. 2014. "Labor Coercion and the Accumulation of Human Capital." *Journal of Development Economics* 108: 32–53.

Bolhuis, M., S. Rachapalli, and D. Restuccia. 2021. "Misallocation in Indian Agriculture." NBER Working Paper 29363, National Bureau of Economic Research, Cambridge, MA.

Boserup, E. 1965. *Conditions of Agricultural Growth: The Economics of Agrarian Change under Population Pressure.* New York: Aldine Publishing.

Bottazzi, P., D. Crespo, L. O. Bangura, and S. Rist. 2018. "Evaluating the Livelihood Impacts of a Large-Scale Agricultural Investment: Lessons from the Case of a Biofuel Production Company in Northern Sierra Leone." *Land Use Policy* 73: 128–37.

Bouwman, T. I., J. A. Andersson, and K. E. Giller. 2021. "Herbicide Induced Hunger? Conservation Agriculture, Ganyu Labour and Rural Poverty in Central Malawi." *Journal of Development Studies* 57 (2): 244–63.

Britos, B., M. A. Hernandez, M. Robles, and D. R. Trupkin. 2022. "Land Market Distortions and Aggregate Agricultural Productivity: Evidence from Guatemala." *Journal of Development Economics* 155: 102787.

Bryan, G., J. de Quidt, M. Silva-Vargas, T. Wilkening, and N. Yadav. 2022. "Market Design for Land Trade: Evidence from Uganda and Kenya." London School of Economics, London.

Bryan, G., J. de Quidt, T. Wilkening, and N. Yadav. 2017. "Land Trade and Development: A Market Design Approach." CESifo Working Paper 6557, CESifo Group, Munich.

Buggle, J. C. 2020. "Growing Collectivism: Irrigation, Group Conformity and Technological Divergence." *Journal of Economic Growth* 25 (2): 147–93.

Bulte, E., F. Cecchi, R. Lensink, A. Marr, and M. van Asseldonk. 2020. "Does Bundling Crop Insurance with Certified Seeds Crowd-In Investments? Experimental Evidence from Kenya." *Journal of Economic Behavior and Organization* 180: 744–57.

Burchardi, K. B., S. Gulesci, B. Lerva, and M. Sulaiman. 2019. "Moral Hazard: Experimental Evidence from Tenancy Contracts." *Quarterly Journal of Economics* 134 (1): 281–347.

Burnod, P., M. Gingembre, and R. Andrianirina Ratsialonana. 2013. "Competition over Authority and Access: International Land Deals in Madagascar." *Development and Change* 44 (2): 357–79.

Caprettini, B., L. Casaburi, and M. Venturini. 2021. "Redistribution, Voting, and Clientelism: Evidence from the Italian Land Reform." CEPR Discussion Paper 15679, Centre for Economic Policy Research, London.

Carmona, J., J. R. Roses, and J. Simpson. 2019. "The Question of Land Access and the Spanish Land Reform of 1932." *Economic History Review* 72 (2): 669–90.

Carranza, E. 2014. "Soil Endowments, Female Labor Force Participation, and the Demographic Deficit of Women in India." *American Economic Journal: Applied Economics* 6 (4): 197–225.

Caunedo, J., and N. Kala. 2021. "Mechanizing Agriculture." MIT Working Paper, Massachusetts Institute of Technology, Cambridge, MA.

Caunedo, J., and E. Keller. 2021. "Capital Obsolescence and Agricultural Productivity." *Quarterly Journal of Economics* 136 (1): 505–61.

Chang, H.-H., and T.-C. Lin. 2016. "Does the Minimum Lot Size Program Affect Farmland Values? Empirical Evidence Using Administrative Data and Regression Discontinuity Design in Taiwan." *American Journal of Agricultural Economics* 98 (3): 785–801.

Chari, A., E. M. Liu, S.-Y. Wang, and Y. Wang. 2021. "Property Rights, Land Misallocation, and Agricultural Efficiency in China." *Review of Economic Studies* 88 (4): 1831–62.

Chen, B., C. M. Kennedy, and B. Xu. 2019. "Effective Moratoria on Land Acquisitions Reduce Tropical Deforestation: Evidence from Indonesia." *Environmental Research Letters* 14 (4): 044009.

Chen, C. 2017. "Untitled Land, Occupational Choice, and Agricultural Productivity." *American Economic Journal: Macroeconomics* 9 (4): 91–121.

Chen, C. 2020. "Technology Adoption, Capital Deepening, and International Productivity Differences." *Journal of Development Economics* 143: 102388.

Chen, C., D. Restuccia, and R. Santaeulalia-Llopis. 2017. "The Effects of Land Markets on Resource Allocation and Agricultural Productivity." NBER Working Paper 24034, National Bureau of Economic Research, Cambridge, MA.

Chen, C., D. Restuccia, and R. Santaeulàlia-Llopis. 2022. "The Effects of Land Markets on Resource Allocation and Agricultural Productivity." *Review of Economic Dynamics* 45: 41–54.

Chen, S., and B. Gong. 2021. "Response and Adaptation of Agriculture to Climate Change: Evidence from China." *Journal of Development Economics* 148: 102557.

Cheng, N., E. Fan, and T.-M. Wu. 2022. "Sweet Unbinding: Sugarcane Cultivation and the Demise of Foot-Binding." *Journal of Development Economics* 157: 102876.

Chrisendo, D., H. Siregar, and M. Qaim. 2022. "Oil Palm Cultivation Improves Living Standards and Human Capital Formation in Smallholder Farm Households." *World Development* 159: 106034.

Cinnirella, F., and E. Hornung. 2016a. "Land Inequality, Education, and Marriage: Empirical Evidence from Nineteenth-Century Prussia." CEPR Discussion Paper 11486, Centre for Economic Policy Research, London.

Cinnirella, F., and E. Hornung. 2016b. "Landownership Concentration and the Expansion of Education." *Journal of Development Economics* 121: 135–52.

Cisneros, E., T. Hellmundt, and K. Kis-Katos. 2022. "Conflicts of Rural Transformation: The Effects of Oil Palm Expansion in Indonesia." University of Göttingen, Göttingen, Germany.

Collier, P., and A. J. Venables. 2012. "Land Deals in Africa: Pioneers and Speculators." *Journal of Globalization and Development* 3 (1). https://doi.org/10.1515/1948-1837.1228.

Cotula, L. 2014. "Testing Claims about Large Land Deals in Africa: Findings from a Multi-country Study." *Journal of Development Studies* 50 (7): 903–25.

Cust, J., and T. Harding. 2020. "Institutions and the Location of Oil Exploration." *Journal of the European Economic Association* 18 (3): 1321–50.

Das, N., A. de Janvry, and E. Sadoulet. 2019. "Credit and Land Contracting: A Test of the Theory of Sharecropping." *American Journal of Agricultural Economics* 101 (4): 1098–114.

Daymard, A. 2022. "Land Rental Market Reforms: Can They Increase Outmigration from Agriculture? Evidence from a Quantitative Model." *World Development* 154: 105865.

de Janvry, A., K. Emerick, M. Gonzalez-Navarro, and E. Sadoulet. 2015. "Delinking Land Rights from Land Use: Certification and Migration in Mexico." *American Economic Review* 105 (10): 3125–49.

De Maria, M., E. J. Z. Robinson, and G. Zanello. 2023. "Fair Compensation in Large-Scale Land Acquisitions: Fair or Fail?" *World Development* 170: 106338.

Deininger, K. 1999. "Making Negotiated Land Reform Work: Initial Experience from Colombia, Brazil and South Africa." *World Development* 27 (4): 651–72.

Deininger, K. 2003. *Land Policies for Growth and Poverty Reduction.* World Bank Policy Research Report Series. Washington, DC: World Bank.

Deininger, K., and D. A. Ali. 2008. "Do Overlapping Property Rights Reduce Agricultural Investment? Evidence from Uganda." *American Journal of Agricultural Economics* 90 (4): 869–82.

Deininger, K., D. A. Ali, and T. Alemu. 2008. "Assessing the Functioning of Land Rental Markets in Ethiopia." *Economic Development and Cultural Change* 57 (1): 67–100.

Deininger, K., and H. P. Binswanger. 1995. "Rent Seeking and the Development of Large-Scale Agriculture in Kenya, South Africa, and Zimbabwe." *Economic Development and Cultural Change* 43 (3): 493.

Deininger, K., and D. Byerlee. 2011. *Rising Global Interest in Farmland: Can It Yield Sustainable and Equitable Benefits?* Washington, DC: World Bank.

Deininger, K., and D. Byerlee. 2012. "The Rise of Large Farms in Land Abundant Countries: Do They Have a Future?" *World Development* 40 (4): 701–14.

Deininger, K., and G. Feder. 2001. "Land Institutions and Land Markets." In *Handbook of Agricultural Economics*, edited by B. Gardner and G. Rausser, 287–331. Amsterdam: Elsevier, North Holland.

Deininger, K., H. Hoogeveen, and B. H. Kinsey. 2004. "Economic Benefits and Costs of Land Redistribution in Zimbabwe in the Early 1980s." *World Development* 32 (10): 1697–709.

Deininger, K., and S. Jin. 2006. "Tenure Security and Land-Related Investment: Evidence from Ethiopia." *European Economic Review* 50 (5): 1245–77.

Deininger, K., and S. Jin. 2008. "Land Sales and Rental Markets in Transition: Evidence from Rural Vietnam." *Oxford Bulletin of Economics and Statistics* 70 (1): 67–101.

Deininger, K., and S. Jin. 2009. "Securing Property Rights in Transition: Lessons from Implementation of China's Rural Land Contracting Law." *Journal of Economic Behavior and Organization* 70 (1–2): 22–38.

Deininger, K., S. Jin, S. Liu, T. Shao, and F. Xia. 2019. "Property Rights Reform to Support China's Rural–Urban Integration: Village-Level Evidence from the Chengdu Experiment." *Oxford Bulletin of Economics and Statistics* 81 (6): 1214–51.

Deininger, K., S. Jin, Y. Liu, and S. K. Singh. 2018. "Can Labor-Market Imperfections Explain Changes in the Inverse Farm Size-Productivity Relationship? Longitudinal Evidence from Rural India." *Land Economics* 94 (2): 239–58.

Deininger, K., S. Jin, and M. Ma. 2022. "Structural Transformation of the Agricultural Sector in Low- and Middle-Income Economies." *Annual Review of Resource Economics* 14 (1): 221–41.

Deininger, K., S. Jin, and H. K. Nagarajan. 2008. "Efficiency and Equity Impacts of Rural Land Market Restrictions: Evidence from India." *European Economic Review* 52 (5): 892–918.

Deininger, K., S. Jin, and H. K. Nagarajan. 2009a. "Determinants and Consequences of Land Sales Market Participation: Panel Evidence from India." *World Development* 37 (2): 410–21.

Deininger, K., S. Jin, and H. K. Nagarajan. 2009b. "Land Reforms, Poverty Reduction, and Economic Growth: Evidence from India." *Journal of Development Studies* 45 (4): 496–521.

Deininger, K., S. Jin, F. Xia, and J. Huang. 2014. "Moving Off the Farm: Land Institutions to Facilitate Structural Transformation and Agricultural Productivity Growth in China." *World Development* 59: 505–20.

Deininger, K., S. Jin, and V. Yadav. 2013. "Does Sharecropping Affect Long-Term Investment? Evidence from West Bengal's Tenancy Reforms." *American Journal of Agricultural Economics* 95 (3): 772–90.

Deininger, K., D. Monchuk, H. K. Nagarajan, and S. K. Singh. 2017. "Does Land Fragmentation Increase the Cost of Cultivation? Evidence from India." *Journal of Development Studies* 53 (1): 82–98.

Deininger, K., M. Maertens, and P. Olinto. 2001. "Redistribution, Investment, and Human Capital Accumulation: The Case of Agrarian Reform in the Philippines." Working paper, World Bank, Washington, DC.

Deininger, K., and F. Xia. 2016. "Quantifying Spillover Effects from Large Land-Based Investment: The Case of Mozambique." *World Development* 87: 227–41.

Dell, M. 2010. "The Persistent Effects of Peru's Mining Mita." *Econometrica* 78 (6): 1863–903.

Dell, M., and B. A. Olken. 2020. "The Development Effects of the Extractive Colonial Economy: The Dutch Cultivation System in Java." *Review of Economic Studies* 87 (1): 164–203.

Deolalikar, A. B. 1981. "The Inverse Relationship between Productivity and Farm Size: A Test Using Regional Data from India." *American Journal of Agricultural Economics* 63 (2): 275–9.

DePaula, G. 2023. "Bundled Contracts and Technological Diffusion: Evidence from the Brazilian Soybean Boom." *Journal of Development Economics* 165: 103163.

Dieterle, C. 2022. "Global Governance Meets Local Land Tenure: International Codes of Conduct for Responsible Land Investments in Uganda." *Journal of Development Studies* 58 (3): 582–98.

Dillon, B., P. Brummund, and G. Mwabu. 2019. "Asymmetric Non-separation and Rural Labor Markets." *Journal of Development Economics* 139: 78–96.

Dippel, C., D. Frye, and B. Leonard. 2020. "Property Rights without Transfer Rights: A Study of Indian Land Allotment." NBER Working Paper 27479, National Bureau of Economic Research, Cambridge, MA.

Dippel, C., A. Greif, and D. Trefler. 2020. "Outside Options, Coercion, and Wages: Removing the Sugar Coating." *Economic Journal* 130 (630): 1678–714.

Dow, G. K., and C. G. Reed. 2013. "The Origins of Inequality: Insiders, Outsiders, Elites, and Commoners." *Journal of Political Economy* 121 (3): 609–41.

Dubbert, C. 2019. "Participation in Contract Farming and Farm Performance: Insights from Cashew Farmers in Ghana." *Agricultural Economics* 50 (6): 749–63.

Eastwood, R., M. Lipton, and A. Newell. 2010. "Farm Size." In *Handbook of Agricultural Economics*, edited by P. L. Pingali and R. E. Evenson, 3323–97. Amsterdam: Elsevier, North Holland.

Eder, C., and M. Halla. 2020. "Economic Origins of Cultural Norms: The Case of Animal Husbandry and Bastardy." *European Economic Review* 125: 103421.

Edwards, R. B. 2019a. "Export Agriculture and Rural Poverty: Evidence from Indonesian Palm Oil." Working paper, Dartmouth College, Hanover, NH.

Edwards, R. B. 2019b. "Spillovers from Agricultural Processing." Working paper, Dartmouth College, Hanover, NH.

Eggleston, K., A. Sun, and Z. Zhan. 2018. "The Impact of Rural Pensions in China on Labor Migration." *World Bank Economic Review* 32 (1): 64–84.

Emran, M. S., and F. Shilpi. 2017. "Land Market Restrictions, Women's Labour Force Participation and Wages in a Rural Economy." *Oxford Bulletin of Economics and Statistics* 79 (5): 747–68.

Emran, M. S., and F. Shilpi. 2020. "Do Land Market Restrictions Hinder Structural Change in a Rural Economy? Evidence from Sri Lanka." *Bangladesh Development Studies* 43 (3/4): 1–35.

Engström, L., and F. Hajdu. 2018. "Conjuring 'Win-World'–Resilient Development Narratives in a Large-Scale Agro-Investment in Tanzania." *Journal of Development Studies* 55: 1–20.

Erickson, L., and D. Vollrath. 2007. "Land Distribution and Financial System Development." IMF Working Paper 07/83, International Monetary Fund, Washington, DC.

Eswaran, M., and A. Kotwal. 1986. "Access to Capital and Agrarian Production Organization." *Economic Journal* 96: 482–98.

Faguet, J.-P., F. Sánchez, and M.-J. Villaveces. 2020. "The Perversion of Public Land Distribution by Landed Elites: Power, Inequality and Development in Colombia." *World Development* 136: 105036.

Fan, E., and S. J. Yeh. 2019. "Tenure Security and Long-Term Investment on Tenanted Land: Evidence from Colonial Taiwan." *Pacific Economic Review* 24 (4): 570–87.

Feder, G. 1985. "The Relation between Farm Size and Farm Productivity: The Role of Family Labor, Supervision and Credit Constraints." *Journal of Development Economics* 18 (2–3): 297–313.

Feigenbaum, J. J., S. Mazumder, and C. B. Smith. 2020. "When Coercive Economies Fail: The Political Economy of the US South after the Boll Weevil." NBER Working Paper 27161, National Bureau of Economic Research, Cambridge, MA.

Fergusson, L. 2013. "The Political Economy of Rural Property Rights and the Persistence of the Dual Economy." *Journal of Development Economics* 103: 167–81.

Fergusson, L., H. Larreguy, and J. F. Riaño. 2022. "Political Competition and State Capacity: Evidence from a Land Allocation Program in Mexico." *Economic Journal* 132 (648): 2815–34.

Fink, G., B. K. Jack, and F. Masiye. 2020. "Seasonal Liquidity, Rural Labor Markets, and Agricultural Production." *American Economic Review* 110 (11): 3351–92.

Foster, A. D., and M. R. Rosenzweig. 2010. "Is There Surplus Labor in Rural India?" Working paper, Department of Economics, Yale University, New Haven, CT.

Foster, A. D., and M. R. Rosenzweig. 2021. "Are There Too Many Farms in the World? Labor Market Transaction Costs, Machine Capacities, and Optimal Farm Size." *Journal of Political Economy* 130 (3): 636–80.

Fredriksson, P. G., and S. K. Gupta. 2022. "Land Productivity and Colonization." *Economic Modelling* 113: 105890.

Frisvold, G. B. 1994. "Does Supervision Matter? Some Hypothesis Tests Using Indian Farm-Level Data." *Journal of Development Economics* 43 (2): 217–38.

Gáfaro, M., and C. Mantilla. 2020. "Land Division: A Lab-in-the-Field Bargaining Experiment." *Journal of Development Economics* 146: 102525.

Galan, J. S. 2020. *Tied to the Land? Intergenerational Mobility and Agrarian Reform in Colombia.* Bogota: Universidad de los Andes.

Galor, O., O. Moav, and D. Vollrath. 2009. "Inequality in Landownership, the Emergence of Human-Capital Promoting Institutions, and the Great Divergence." *Review of Economic Studies* 76 (1): 143–79.

Garriga, C., A. Hedlund, Y. Tang, and P. Wang. 2020. "Rural-Urban Migration and House Prices in China." *Regional Science and Urban Economics* 91: 103613.

Gautam, M., and M. Ahmed. 2019. "Too Small to Be Beautiful? The Farm Size and Productivity Relationship in Bangladesh." *Food Policy* 84: 165–75.

Ge, M., E. C. Edwards, and S. B. Akhundjanov. 2020. "Irrigation Investment on an American Indian Reservation." *American Journal of Agricultural Economics* 102 (4): 1083–104.

Gebregziabher, G., and S. T. Holden. 2011. "Distress Rentals and the Land Rental Market as a Safety Net: Contract Choice Evidence from Tigray, Ethiopia." *Agricultural Economics* 42: 45–60.

Gebru, M., S. T. Holden, and M. Tilahun. 2019. "Tenants' Land Access in the Rental Market: Evidence from Northern Ethiopia." *Agricultural Economics* 50 (3): 291–302.

Giles, J., and R. Mu. 2018. "Village Political Economy, Land Tenure Insecurity, and the Rural to Urban Migration Decision: Evidence from China." *American Journal of Agricultural Economics* 100 (2): 521–44.

Glover, S., and S. Jones. 2019. "Can Commercial Farming Promote Rural Dynamism in Sub-Saharan Africa? Evidence from Mozambique." *World Development* 114: 110–21.

Gollin, D. 2021. "Agricultural Productivity and Structural Transformation: Evidence and Questions for African Development." CEPR Research Program on Structural Transformation and Economic Growth, Centre for Economic Policy Research, London.

Gollin, D., D. Lagakos, and M. E. Waugh. 2014. "The Agricultural Productivity Gap." *Quarterly Journal of Economics* 129 (2): 939–93.

Gollin, D., and C. Udry. 2020. "Heterogeneity, Measurement Error, and Misallocation: Evidence from African Agriculture." *Journal of Political Economy* 129 (1): 1–80.

Gottlieb, C., and J. Grobovsek. 2019. "Communal Land and Agricultural Productivity." *Journal of Development Economics* 138: 135–52.

Gran, T. 2021. "Comment: How a Government Panel on Land Reform in South Africa Is Stuck in Old Ways." *Agrekon* 60 (1): 80–4.

Grogan, L. 2018. "Labor Market Conditions and Cultural Change: Evidence from Vietnam." *Journal of Human Capital* 12 (1): 99–124.

Guinnane, T. W., and R. I. Miller. 1997. "The Limits to Land Reform: The Land Acts in Ireland, 1870–1909." *Economic Development and Cultural Change* 45 (3): 591–612.

Hall, R., and T. Kepe. 2017. "Elite Capture and State Neglect: New Evidence on South Africa's Land Reform." *Review of African Political Economy* 44 (151): 122–30.

Hall, R., I. Scoones, and D. Tsikata. 2017. "Plantations, Outgrowers and Commercial Farming in Africa: Agricultural Commercialisation and Implications for Agrarian Change." *Journal of Peasant Studies* 44 (3): 515–37.

Hamory, J., M. Kleemans, N. Y. Li, and E. Miguel. 2021. "Reevaluating Agricultural Productivity Gaps with Longitudinal Microdata." *Journal of the European Economic Association* 19 (3): 1522–55.

Hansen, C. W., P. S. Jensen, and C. V. Skovsgaard. 2015. "Modern Gender Roles and Agricultural History: The Neolithic Inheritance." *Journal of Economic Growth* 20 (4): 365–404.

Hao, T., R. Sun, T. Tombe, and X. Zhu. 2020. "The Effect of Migration Policy on Growth, Structural Change, and Regional Inequality in China." *Journal of Monetary Economics* 113: 112–34.

Hausermann, H., D. Ferring, B. Atosona, G. Mentz, R. Amankwah, A. Chang, K. Hartfield, E. Effah, et al. 2018. "Land-Grabbing, Land-Use Transformation and Social Differentiation: Deconstructing 'Small-Scale' in Ghana's Recent Gold Rush." *World Development* 108: 103–14.

Hayashi, F., and E. C. Prescott. 2008. "The Depressing Effect of Agricultural Institutions on the Prewar Japanese Economy." *Journal of Political Economy* 116 (4): 573–632.

Helfand, S. M., V. H. Sielawa, and D. Singhania. 2019. "A Matter of Time: An Impact Evaluation of the Brazilian National Land Credit Program." *Journal of Development Economics* 141: 102361.

Helfand, S. M., and M. P. H. Taylor. 2021. "The Inverse Relationship between Farm Size and Productivity: Refocusing the Debate." *Food Policy* 99: 101977.

Herrendorf, B., and T. Schoellman. 2018. "Wages, Human Capital, and Barriers to Structural Transformation." *American Economic Journal: Macroeconomics* 10 (2): 1–23.

Herrmann, R. T. 2017. "Large-Scale Agricultural Investments and Smallholder Welfare: A Comparison of Wage Labor and Outgrower Channels in Tanzania." *World Development* 90: 294–310.

Hobijn, B., T. Schoellman, and A. Vindas. 2018. "Structural Transformation by Cohort." Working paper, Arizona State University, Tempe.

Holden, S. T., and H. Ghebru. 2016. "Land Rental Market Legal Restrictions in Northern Ethiopia." *Land Use Policy* 55: 212–21.

Iscan, T. B. 2018. "Redistributive Land Reform and Structural Change in Japan, South Korea, and Taiwan." *American Journal of Agricultural Economics* 100 (3): 732–61.

Jacoby, H. G. 1993. "Shadow Wages and Peasant Family Labour Supply: An Econometric Application to the Peruvian Sierra." *Review of Economic Studies* 60 (4): 903–21.

Jacoby, H. G., and G. Mansuri. 2008. "Land Tenancy and Non-contractible Investment in Rural Pakistan." *Review of Economic Studies* 75 (3): 763–88.

Jayne, T. S., A. Chapoto, N. Sitko, C. Nkonde, M. Muyanga, and J. Chamberlin. 2014. "Is the Scramble for Land in Africa Foreclosing a Smallholder Agricultural Expansion Strategy?" *Journal of International Affairs* 67 (2): 35–53.

Jayne, T. S., M. Muyanga, A. Wineman, H. Ghebru, C. Stevens, M. Stickler, A. Chapoto, W. Anseeuw, D. van der Westhuizen, and D. Nyange. 2019. "Are Medium-Scale Farms Driving Agricultural Transformation in Sub-Saharan Africa?" *Agricultural Economics* 50: 75–95.

Jeon, Y. D., and Y. Y. Kim. 2000. "Land Reform, Income Redistribution, and Agricultural Production in Korea." *Economic Development and Cultural Change* 48 (2): 253–68.

Jin, S. Q., and K. Deininger. 2009. "Land Rental Markets in the Process of Rural Structural Transformation: Productivity and Equity Impacts from China." *Journal of Comparative Economics* 37 (4): 629–46.

Julien, J. C., B. E. Bravo-Ureta, and N. E. Rada. 2019. "Assessing Farm Performance by Size in Malawi, Tanzania, and Uganda." *Food Policy* 84: 153–64.

Kagin, J., J. E. Taylor, and A. Yúnez-Naude. 2016. "Inverse Productivity or Inverse Efficiency? Evidence from Mexico." *Journal of Development Studies* 52 (3): 396–411.

Kalkuhl, M., G. Schwerhoff, and K. Waha. 2020. "Land Tenure, Climate and Risk Management." *Ecological Economics* 171: 106573.

Keswell, M., and M. R. Carter. 2014. "Poverty and Land Redistribution." *Journal of Development Economics* 110: 250–61.

Key, N. 2019. "Farm Size and Productivity Growth in the United States Corn Belt." *Food Policy* 84: 186–95.

Khadjavi, M., K. Sipangule, and R. Thiele. 2021. "Social Capital and Large-Scale Agricultural Investments: An Experimental Investigation." *Economic Journal* 131 (633): 420–49.

Kinda, S. R., N. E. Kere, T. U. Yogo, and M. A. Simpasa. 2022. "Do Land Rushes Really Improve Food Security in Sub-Saharan Africa?" *Food Policy* 113: 102285.

Kirsten, J., C. Machethe, T. Ndlovu, and P. Lubambo. 2016. "Performance of Land Reform Projects in the North West Province of South Africa: Changes over Time and Possible Causes." *Development Southern Africa* 33 (4): 442–58.

Kirwan, B. E. 2009. "The Incidence of U.S. Agricultural Subsidies on Farmland Rental Rates." *Journal of Political Economy* 117 (1): 138–64.

Kitamura, S. 2022. "Tillers of Prosperity: Land Ownership, Reallocation, and Structural Transformation." Research paper, Osaka University.

Knippenberg, E., D. Jolliffe, and J. Hoddinott. 2020. "Land Fragmentation and Food Insecurity in Ethiopia." *American Journal of Agricultural Economics* 102 (5): 1557–77.

Kranton, R. E., and A. V. Swamy. 1999. "The Hazards of Piecemeal Reform: British Civil Courts and the Credit Market in Colonial India." *Journal of Development Economics* 58 (1): 1–24.

Kraus, S., R. Heilmayr, and N. Koch. 2021. *Spillovers to Manufacturing Plants from Multi-Million Dollar Plantations: Evidence from the Indonesian Palm Oil Boom.* Berlin: Mercator Research Institute on Global Commons and Climate Change.

Kunda-Wamuwi, C. F., F. D. Babalola, and P. W. Chirwa. 2017. "Investigating Factors Responsible for Farmers' Abandonment of *Jatropha Curcas* L. as Bioenergy Crop under Smallholder Out-Grower Schemes in Chibombo District, Zambia." *Energy Policy* 110: 62–68.

LaFave, D., and D. Thomas. 2016. "Farms, Families, and Markets: New Evidence on Completeness of Markets in Agricultural Settings." *Econometrica* 84 (5): 1917–60.

LaFave, D. R., E. D. Peet, and D. Thomas. 2020. "Farm Profits, Prices and Household Behavior." NBER Working Paper 26636, National Bureau of Economic Research, Cambridge, MA.

Lagakos, D., S. Marshall, A. M. Mobarak, C. Vernot, and M. E. Waugh. 2020. "Migration Costs and Observational Returns to Migration in the Developing World." *Journal of Monetary Economics* 113: 138–54.

Lanz, K., J.-D. Gerber, and T. Haller. 2018. "Land Grabbing, the State and Chiefs: The Politics of Extending Commercial Agriculture in Ghana." *Development and Change* 49 (6): 1526–52.

Lavers, T. 2016. "Agricultural Investment in Ethiopia: Undermining National Sovereignty or Tool for State Building?" *Development and Change* 47 (5): 1078–101.

Lawley, C. 2018. "Ownership Restrictions and Farmland Values: Evidence from the 2003 Saskatchewan Farm Security Act Amendment." *American Journal of Agricultural Economics* 100 (1): 311–37.

Lay, J., K. Nolte, and K. Sipangule. 2020. "Large-Scale Farms in Zambia: Locational Patterns and Spillovers to Smallholder Agriculture." *World Development* 140: 105277.

Le, K. 2020. "Land Use Restrictions, Misallocation in Agriculture, and Aggregate Productivity in Vietnam." *Journal of Development Economics* 145: 102465.

Levine, R., C. Lin, and W. Xie. 2020. "The African Slave Trade and Modern Household Finance." *Economic Journal* 130 (630): 1817–41.

Li, T. M., and P. Semedi. 2021. *Plantation Life: Corporate Occupation in Indonesia's Oil Palm Zone.* Durham, NC: Duke University Press.

Liao, Y., and J. Zhang. 2021. "Hukou Status, Housing Tenure Choice and Wealth Accumulation in Urban China." *China Economic Review* 68: 101638.

Lin, J. Y. 1992. "Rural Reforms and Agricultural Growth in China." *American Economic Review* 82 (1): 34–51.

Lipton, M. 2009. *Land Reform in Developing Countries: Property Rights and Property Wrongs.* London: Taylor and Francis.

Liu, S., S. Ma, L. Yin, and J. Zhu. 2023. "Land Titling, Human Capital Misallocation, and Agricultural Productivity in China." *Journal of Development Economics* 165: 103165.

Liu, Y., C. B. Barrett, T. Pham, and W. Violette. 2020. "The Intertemporal Evolution of Agriculture and Labor over a Rapid Structural Transformation: Lessons from Vietnam." *Food Policy* 94: 101913.

Loumeau, G. 2022. "Land Consolidation Reforms: A Natural Experiment on the Economic and Political Effects of Agricultural Mechanization." Working Paper 22/376, Center of Economic Research at ETH Zurich, Zurich.

Lovo, S. 2014. "Analyzing the Welfare-Improving Potential of Land in the Former Homelands of South Africa." *Agricultural Economics* 45 (6): 679–92.

Lowder, S. K., M. V. Sánchez, and R. Bertini. 2021. "Which Farms Feed the World and Has Farmland Become More Concentrated?" *World Development* 142: 105455.

Lowder, S. K., J. Skoet, and T. Raney. 2016. "The Number, Size, and Distribution of Farms, Smallholder Farms, and Family Farms Worldwide." *World Development* 87: 16–29.

Maganga, F. P., K. Askew, R. Odgaard, and H. Stein. 2016. "Dispossession through Formalization: Tanzania and the G8 Land Agenda in Africa." *Asian Journal of African Studies* 40 (4): 3–49.

Makombe, G. 2018. "Land Reform in South Africa: The Conversation that Never Took Place." *Qualitative Report* 23 (6): 1401–21.

Manysheva, K. 2022. *Land Property Rights, Financial Frictions, and Resource Allocation in Developing Countries.* Evanston, IL: Northwestern University.

Maue, C. C., M. Burke, and K. J. Emerick. 2020. "Productivity Dispersion and Persistence among the World's Most Numerous Firms." NBER Working Paper 26924, National Bureau of Economic Research, Cambridge, MA.

Mayshar, J., O. Moav, and Z. Neeman. 2017. "Geography, Transparency, and Institutions." *American Political Science Review* 111 (3): 622–36.

Mayshar, J., O. Moav, and L. Pascali. 2021. "The Origin of the State: Land Productivity or Appropriability?" *Journal of Political Economy* 130 (4): 1091–144.

Méndez, E., and D. Van Patten. 2022. "Multinationals, Monopsony, and Local Development: Evidence from the United Fruit Company." *Econometrica* 90 (6): 2685–2721.

Merfeld, J. 2020. "Labor Elasticities, Market Failures, and Misallocation: Evidence from Indian Agriculture." IZA Discussion Paper 13682, Bonn.

Mertens, K., and L. Vranken. 2018. "Investing in Land to Change Your Risk Exposure? Land Transactions and Inequality in a Landslide Prone Region." *World Development* 110: 437–52.

Middelberg, S. L., P. van der Zwan, and C. Oberholster. 2020. "Zambian Farm Blocks: A Vehicle for Increased Private Sector Investments." *Open Agriculture* 5 (1): 817–25.

Miller, M. C. 2020. " 'The Righteous and Reasonable Ambition to Become a Landholder': Land and Racial Inequality in the Postbellum South." *Review of Economics and Statistics* 102 (2): 381–94.

Monge-Naranjo, A. 2019. "Markets, Externalities, and the Dynamic Gains of Openness." *International Economic Review* 60 (3): 1131–70.

Montero, E. 2021. "Cooperative Property Rights and Development: Evidence from Land Reform in El Salvador." *Journal of Political Economy* 130 (1): 48–93.

Moyo, P. 2021. "Contested Compensation: The Politics, Economics and Legal Nuances of Compensating White Former Commercial Farmers in Zimbabwe." *Review of African Political Economy* 48 (170): 630–45.

Mueller, V., A. Quisumbing, H. L. Lee, and K. Droppelmann. 2014. "Resettlement for Food Security's Sake: Insights from a Malawi Land Reform Project." *Land Economics* 90 (2): 222–36.

Musinguzi, M., T. Huber, D. Kirumira, and P. Drate. 2021. "Assessment of the Land Inventory Approach for Securing Tenure of Lawful and Bona Fide Occupants on Private Mailo Land in Uganda." *Land Use Policy* 110: 104562.

Muyanga, M., and T. S. Jayne. 2019. "Revisiting the Farm Size-Productivity Relationship Based on a Relatively Wide Range of Farm Sizes: Evidence from Kenya." *American Journal of Agricultural Economics* 101 (4): 1140–63.

Nanhthavong, V., S. Bieri, A.-T. Nguyen, C. Hett, and M. Epprecht. 2022. "Proletarianization and Gateways to Precarization in the Context of Land-Based Investments for Agricultural Commercialization in Lao PDR." *World Development* 155: 105885.

Nanhthavong, V., M. Epprecht, C. Hett, J. G. Zaehringer, and P. Messerli. 2020. "Poverty Trends in Villages Affected by Land-Based Investments in Rural Laos." *Applied Geography* 124: 102298.

Niu, D., W. Sun, and S. Zheng. 2021. "The Role of Informal Housing in Lowering China's Urbanization Costs." *Regional Science and Urban Economics* 91: 103638.

Noack, F., and A. Larsen. 2019. "The Contrasting Effects of Farm Size on Farm Incomes and Food Production." *Environmental Research Letters* 14 (8): 084024.

Noack, F., and M. Quaas. 2021a. "Ecology of Scope and the Productivity of Small-Scale Farming." Working paper, University of British Columbia, Vancouver, BC.

Noack, F., and M. Quaas. 2021b. "Economies of Scale and Ecology of Scope." Working paper, University of British Columbia, Vancouver, BC.

Nolte, K., and M. Ostermeier. 2017. "Labour Market Effects of Large-Scale Agricultural Investment: Conceptual Considerations and Estimated Employment Effects." *World Development* 98: 430–46.

Nolte, K., and L. Voget-Kleschin. 2014. "Consultation in Large-Scale Land Acquisitions: An Evaluation of Three Cases in Mali." *World Development* 64: 654–68.

Nugent, J. B., and J. A. Robinson. 2010. "Are Factor Endowments Fate?" *Revista de Historia Economica* 28 (1): 45–82.

Nunn, N. 2008. "The Long-Term Effects of Africa's Slave Trades." *Quarterly Journal of Economics* 123 (1): 139–76.

Nunn, N., and L. Wantchekon. 2011. "The Slave Trade and the Origins of Mistrust in Africa." *American Economic Review* 101 (7): 3221–52.

O'Laughlin, B., H. Bernstein, B. Cousins, and P. E. Peters. 2013. "Introduction: Agrarian Change, Rural Poverty and Land Reform in South Africa since 1994." *Journal of Agrarian Change* 13 (1): 1–15.

Omotilewa, O. J., T. S. Jayne, M. Muyanga, A. B. Aromolaran, L. S. O. Liverpool-Tasie, and T. Awokuse. 2021. "A Revisit of Farm Size and Productivity: Empirical Evidence from a Wide Range of Farm Sizes in Nigeria." *World Development* 146: 105592.

Otsuka, K. 1991. "Determinants and Consequences of Land Reform Implementation in the Philippines." *Journal of Development Economics* 35 (2): 339–55.

Otsuka, K., H. Chuma, and Y. Hayami. 1992. "Land and Labor Contracts in Agrarian Economies: Theories and Facts." *Journal of Economic Literature* 30 (4): 1965–2018.

Pedersen, R. H., and O. Kweka. 2017. "The Political Economy of Petroleum Investments and Land Acquisition Standards in Africa: The Case of Tanzania." *Resources Policy* 52: 217–25.

Pingali, P. L., and V. T. Xuan. 1992. "Vietnam: Decollectivization and Rice Productivity Growth." *Economic Development and Cultural Change* 40 (4): 697–718.

Porzio, T., F. Rossi, and G. Santangelo. 2020. "The Human Side of Structural Transformation." The Warwick Economics Research Paper Series (TWERPS), Department of Economics, University of Warwick, Warwick.

Pulido, J., and T. Swiecki. 2019. "Barriers to Mobility or Sorting? Sources and Aggregate Implications of Income Gaps across Sectors and Locations in Indonesia." Working paper, University of British Columbia.

Rada, N., S. Helfand, and M. Magalhães. 2019. "Agricultural Productivity Growth in Brazil: Large and Small Farms Excel." *Food Policy* 84: 176–85.

Rajan, R., and R. Ramcharan. 2011. "Land and Credit: A Study of the Political Economy of Banking in the United States in the Early 20th Century." *Journal of Finance* 66 (6): 1895–931.

Restuccia, D. 2021. "From Micro to Macro: Land Institutions, Agricultural Productivity, and Structural Transformation." Working paper, World Bank, Washington, DC.

Restuccia, D., and R. Rogerson. 2017. "The Causes and Costs of Misallocation." *Journal of Economic Perspectives* 31 (3): 151–74.

Restuccia, D., and R. Santaeulalia-Llopis. 2017. "Land Misallocation and Productivity." NBER Working Paper 23128, National Bureau of Economic Research, Cambridge, MA.

Ricker-Gilbert, J., and J. Chamberlin. 2018. "Transaction Costs, Land Rental Markets, and Their Impact on Youth Access to Agriculture in Tanzania." *Land Economics* 94 (4): 541–55.

Ricker-Gilbert, J., J. Chamberlin, and J. Kanyamuka. 2022. "Soil Investments on Rented versus Owned Plots: Evidence from a Matched Tenant-Landlord Sample in Malawi." *Land Economics* 98 (1): 165–86.

Ricker-Gilbert, J., J. Chamberlin, J. Kanyamuka, C. B. L. Jumbe, R. Lunduka, and S. Kaiyatsa. 2019. "How Do Informal Farmland Rental Markets Affect Smallholders' Well-Being? Evidence from a Matched Tenant-Landlord Survey in Malawi." *Agricultural Economics* 50 (5): 595–613.

Rogers, S., B. Wilmsen, X. Han, Z. J. Wang, Y. Duan, J. He, J. Li, W. Lin, and C. Wong. 2021. "Scaling Up Agriculture? The Dynamics of Land Transfer in Inland China." *World Development* 146: 105563.

Rosenzweig, M. R., and K. I. Wolpin. 1985. "Specific Experience, Household Structure, and Intergenerational Transfers: Farm Family Land and Labor Arrangements in Developing Countries." *Quarterly Journal of Economics* 100 (5): 961–87.

Roth, M. 1995. "Land Tenure, Land Markets, and Institutional Transformation in Zambia." LTC Research Paper 124, Land Tenure Center, University of Wisconsin, Madison.

Rozelle, S., and J. F. M. Swinnen. 2004. "Success and Failure of Reform: Insights from the Transition of Agriculture." *Journal of Economic Literature* 42 (2): 404–56.

Rusenga, C. 2020. "Setting Them Up to Fail: Enforcement of the Agribusiness Model on Land Reform Projects in South Africa." *Les lancer vers l'échec: application du modèle agro-industriel aux projets de réforme agraire en Afrique du Sud* 47 (165): 382–98.

Sadoulet, E., A. de Janvry, and S. Fukui. 1997. "The Meaning of Kinship in Sharecropping Contracts." *American Journal of Agricultural Economics* 79 (2): 394–406.

Schoneveld, G. C. 2014. "The Geographic and Sectoral Patterns of Large-Scale Farmland Investments in Sub-Saharan Africa." *Food Policy* 48: 34–50.

Schoneveld, G. C. 2022. "Transforming Food Systems through Inclusive Agribusiness." *World Development* 158: 105970.

Schönholzer, D. 2021. "The Origin of the Incentive Compatible State: Environmental Circumscription." Working paper, Stockholm University, Stockholm.

Schuenemann, F., J. Thurlow, and M. Zeller. 2017. "Leveling the Field for Biofuels: Comparing the Economic and Environmental Impacts of Biofuel and Other Export Crops in Malawi." *Agricultural Economics* 48 (3): 301–15.

Scoones, I., B. Mavedzenge, and F. Murimbarimba. 2019. "Young People and Land in Zimbabwe: Livelihood Challenges after Land Reform." *Les jeunes et les terres agricoles au Zimbabwe: défis de subsistance après la réforme agraire* 46 (159): 117–34.

Scott, M. F. G., J. D. MacArthur, and D. M. G. Newbery. 1976. *Project Appraisal in Practice: The Little-Mirrlees Method Applied in Kenya.* London: Heineman Educational Books.

Seifert, S., C. Kahle, and S. Hüttel. 2021. "Price Dispersion in Farmland Markets: What Is the Role of Asymmetric Information?" *American Journal of Agricultural Economics* 103 (4): 1545–68.

Shaban, R. A. 1987. "Testing between Competing Models of Sharecropping." *Journal of Political Economy* 95 (5): 893–920.

Sheng, Y., and W. Chancellor. 2019. "Exploring the Relationship between Farm Size and Productivity: Evidence from the Australian Grains Industry." *Food Policy* 84: 196–204.

Sheng, Y., J. Ding, and J. Huang. 2019. "The Relationship between Farm Size and Productivity in Agriculture: Evidence from Maize Production in Northern China." *American Journal of Agricultural Economics* 101 (3): 790–806.

Shete, M., M. Rutten, G. C. Schoneveld, and E. Zewude. 2016. "Land-Use Changes by Large-Scale Plantations and Their Effects on Soil Organic Carbon, Micronutrients and Bulk Density: Empirical Evidence from Ethiopia." *Agriculture and Human Values* 33 (3): 689–704.

Sixpence, P., and P. Chigora. 2020. "Land Compensation and Land Conflict Resolution in Zimbabwe: Challenges and Prospects for the Second Republic's Relations with the West." *Journal of Public Administration and Development Alternatives (JPADA)* 5 (1.1): 82–96.

Smith, C. 2021. "Land Concentration and Long-Run Development in the Frontier United States." Working paper, Massachusetts Institute of Technology, Cambridge, MA.

Suesse, M., and N. Wolf. 2020. "Rural Transformation, Inequality, and the Origins of Microfinance." *Journal of Development Economics* 143: 102429.

Sulle, E. 2020. "Bureaucrats, Investors and Smallholders: Contesting Land Rights and Agro-Commercialisation in the Southern Agricultural Growth Corridor of Tanzania." *Journal of Eastern African Studies* 14 (2): 332–53.

Swinnen, J., K. Van Herck, and L. Vranken. 2016. "The Diversity of Land Markets and Regulations in Europe, and (Some of) Its Causes." *Journal of Development Studies* 52 (2): 186–205.

Tione, S. E., and S. T. Holden. 2022. "Nonconvex Transaction Costs and Land Rental Market Participation in Malawi." *Land Economics* 98 (1): 150–64.

Tsikata, D., and J. A. Yaro. 2014. "When a Good Business Model Is Not Enough: Land Transactions and Gendered Livelihood Prospects in Rural Ghana." *Feminist Economics* 20 (1): 202–26.

Valsecchi, M. 2014. "Land Property Rights and International Migration: Evidence from Mexico." *Journal of Development Economics* 110: 276–90.

Van den Broeck, G., J. Swinnen, and M. Maertens. 2017. "Global Value Chains, Large-Scale Farming, and Poverty: Long-Term Effects in Senegal." *Food Policy* 66: 97–107.

Veljanoska, S. 2018. "Can Land Fragmentation Reduce the Exposure of Rural Households to Weather Variability?" *Ecological Economics* 154: 42–51.

Villalba, R., T. E. Venus, and J. Sauer. 2023. "The Ecosystem Approach to Agricultural Value Chain Finance: A Framework for Rural Credit." *World Development* 164: 106177.

Voigtlander, N., and H.-J. Voth. 2013. "How the West 'Invented' Fertility Restriction." *American Economic Review* 103 (6): 2227–64.

Vollrath, D. 2013. "Inequality and School Funding in the Rural United States, 1890." *Explorations in Economic History* 50 (2): 267–84.

Wang, X., F. Yamauchi, and J. Huang. 2016. "Rising Wages, Mechanization, and the Substitution between Capital and Labor: Evidence from Small Scale Farm System in China." *Agricultural Economics* 47 (3): 309–17.

Wang, X., F. Yamauchi, K. Otsuka, and J. Huang. 2016. "Wage Growth, Landholding, and Mechanization in Chinese Agriculture." *World Development* 86: 30–45.

West, H. W. 1965. *The Mailo System in Buganda: A Preliminary Case Study in African Land Tenure.* Entebbe, Uganda: Government Printer.

Widengard, M. 2019. "Land Deals, and How Not All States React the Same: Zambia and the Chinese Request." *Review of African Political Economy* 46 (162): 615–31.

Wineman, A., and T. S. Jayne. 2021. "Factor Market Activity and the Inverse Farm Size-Productivity Relationship in Tanzania." *Journal of Development Studies* 57 (3): 443–64.

Xia, F., and K. Deininger. 2019. "Spillover Effects of Tobacco Farms on the Labor Supply, Education, and Health of Children: Evidence from Malawi." *American Journal of Agricultural Economics* 101 (4): 1181–202.

Young, A. 2013. "Inequality, the Urban-Rural Gap, and Migration." *Quarterly Journal of Economics* 128 (4): 1727–85.

Zaehringer, J. G., G. Wambugu, B. Kiteme, and S. Eckert. 2018. "How Do Large-Scale Agricultural Investments Affect Land Use and the Environment on the Western Slopes of Mount Kenya? Empirical Evidence Based on Small-Scale Farmers' Perceptions and Remote Sensing." *Journal of Environmental Management* 213: 79–89.

Zantsi, S., and J. C. Greyling. 2021. "Land Redistribution in South Africa's Land Reform Policy: A Better Way to Select Beneficiaries." *Agrekon* 60 (2): 108–27.

Zhao, X. 2020. "Land and Labor Allocation under Communal Tenure: Theory and Evidence from China." *Journal of Development Economics* 147: 102526.

Zhu, J., S. Jin, Z. Tang, and T. Awokuse. 2021. "The Effect of Pension Income on Land Transfers: Evidence from Rural China." *Economic Development and Cultural Change* 71 (1): 333–71.

Zou, B., A. K. Mishra, and B. Luo. 2020. "Do Chinese Farmers Benefit from Farmland Leasing Choices? Evidence from a Nationwide Survey." *Australian Journal of Agricultural and Resource Economics* 64 (2): 322–46.

4. Land rights for climate resilience

Through a greater frequency of droughts and extreme weather events, climate change already has made its mark on rural areas in Africa, contributing to an increase in the number and severity of land-related conflicts, especially at the agropastoral frontier. To adapt to warming temperatures that, based on global models, will reduce Africa's comparative advantage in agriculture, there is need for (a) strengthening of local forums for conflict resolution, resource governance, and improved insurance against risks to prevent temporary shocks from triggering permanent loss of productive assets; (b) better management of natural resources such as land and water and adjustment of technology; (c) integration into regional and global markets, ideally helped by public investments to improve market access and reduce transport cost; and (d) diversification of income sources beyond agriculture.

The impacts of climate change are less directly visible in urban areas, but they are no less far-reaching as higher temperatures reduce productivity and increase conflict. Moreover, cities are often located on coasts, on floodplains, or in river valleys, exposing them to increased risk from floods, storms, and sea-level rise. Disproportionate expansion of building activity in areas prone to risk of flooding or sea-level rise, partly driven by policies that may have unwittingly encouraged moral hazard, often increased such risks. Better information on potential local impacts of climate change, land prices, and land rights will be important to identify and communicate risks, evaluate their magnitude, evaluate different adaptation options, and put in place appropriate fiscal instruments to align incentives for public and private adaptation.

Climate change mitigation through aboveground carbon storage and avoided deforestation

Deforestation has been a major contributor to carbon emissions and loss of biodiversity globally, especially in developing countries, where pressure for land-use change remains strong and property rights protection is often weak (Balboni et al., forthcoming). Because preventing loss of carbon- and species-rich primary forest offers larger ecological and economic benefits than regeneration, mitigation can help reduce forest and biodiversity loss by (a) securing property rights, often first for groups rather than individuals, to reduce contestability of resource claims and provide incentives for long-term investment; (b) putting in place regulation, backed by credible public and private enforcement to reduce forest and biodiversity loss; and (c) using tax or subsidy schemes to reduce the gap between social and private benefits of sustainable resource management, ideally by tapping climate finance instruments availed by the global community.

Prevention of deforestation via definition of property rights

Property rights are a necessary condition for mitigation via greater conservation of forests or ecosystems that provide environmental services and public goods. Although reforestation and landscape restoration programs are widely debated, preventing forest loss in the first place is often more effective. For example, a well-known reforestation program in Chile that subsidized afforestation from 1986 to 2011 appears to have realized neither environmental nor economic benefits: increases in tree cover were based on exotic species, decreasing the area under native forests, biodiversity, and carbon stored in aboveground biomass (Heilmayr, Echeverría, and Lambin 2020). Economically, the program was associated with declines in rural population and increased unemployment (Jordán and Heilmayr 2022).

A key factor that often increases deforestation is that rights can be claimed by occupation and agricultural use (that is, cutting of trees), making them highly contestable. This is well documented for the Brazilian Amazon, where land-related violence at the municipal level can be attributed to insecure land rights, and better property rights protection is associated with an increase in forest cover (Fetzer and Marden 2017). Since 1985, pastures and croplands in Brazil have replaced nearly 650 million hectares (ha) of forests and savannas (Stabile et al. 2020). This took place largely via land acquisition at the frontier (Tatum 2013), often for cattle expansion (Bowman et al. 2012) that was driven by poverty and inequality in the interior (Sant'Anna 2017), accompanied by conflict (Fearnside 2001; Sauer 2018). Recent legal changes have made such occupation easier, and implementing them as planned would be associated with large losses of public revenue and increased emissions, creating negative global externalities (Brito et al. 2019).

Official data suggest that of Brazil's 850 million ha, 307 million ha are public land (55 million ha not yet designated), 375 million ha are private, and 138 million ha are unregistered or with unknown tenure (Sparovek et al. 2019). Deforestation occurs mainly on land directly or indirectly under state responsibility and where property rights are not clearly established (Reydon, Fernandes, and Telles 2020). To reduce deforestation and land speculation, it will be essential to assign responsibility for the 55 million ha of undesignated public land and register them, together with the 138 million ha of unregistered land. Once rights are established in this way, it will be possible to define parameters of land use and use such land to create local benefits (Stabile et al. 2020).[1]

Securing rights to indigenous land has been one way to reduce deforestation significantly in this context. Starting in 1995, Brazil legalized the rights of hundreds of indigenous communities to more than 40 million ha in the Amazon. Satellite data since the 1980s, together with the timing of recognition that was driven by factors independent of those affecting deforestation, allow analysis of this intervention. Deforestation in indigenous territories whose boundaries had been recognized via presidential decree was significantly lower (Baragwanath and Bayi 2020) than just across the border. By contrast, mere demarcation (that is, the step preceding formal declaration that is less valuable for enforcement in court) had no effect (BenYishay et al. 2017), even if communities received support for local surveillance and enforcement of their rights.[2]

Beyond Brazil, recognizing indigenous lands reduced deforestation in Peru (Blackman et al. 2017) and Colombia, where community organizations restricted resource access by outsiders (Vélez et al. 2020), community titling improved welfare (Peña et al. 2017),[3] and positive spillovers to neighboring communities materialized (Romero and Saavedra 2021). Estimation of deforestation and degradation rates from 2010 to 2018 on large tracts of indigenous lands, protected areas, and protected indigenous areas relative to matched nonprotected areas globally suggests that documented indigenous lands have achieved levels of deforestation and degradation similar to those of protected areas at a lower cost (Sze et al. 2022). In the Congo basin, the requirement of having forest management plans in all logging concessions was associated with a 74 percent reduction in the incidence of deforestation because it allowed timber companies to adhere to appropriate harvesting cycles rather than overexploiting the resource (Tritsch et al. 2020).

Individual land certification or titling in Brazil had a more ambiguous effect than community titling, largely because titling increased access to (subsidized) credit in a setting where private landowners perceived deforestation to be more profitable than intensification. To implement the environmental restrictions mandated by the 2012 Forest Code, which requires landowners to conserve a share of their property (80 percent in the Amazon and 20–35 percent in the Cerrado) with native vegetation, Brazil's government established the rural environmental cadaster (Cadastro Ambiental Rural or CAR) as a tool for voluntary self-registration of rural properties on 400 million ha of private land.[4]

Registering rights in the CAR requires landowners to georeference property boundaries and remaining forest using satellite imagery at their own expense, possibly with nongovernmental organization support (Azevedo et al. 2017). Municipal-level analysis for 284 municipalities in Mato Grosso and Para, two states that together account for around 120 million ha of eligible area, shows that the net effect of registration was to increase deforestation as registration facilitated access to subsidized credit, especially for small farms that then used such credit to replace natural vegetation with pasture (Jung et al. 2022).

Brazil's Terra Legal program was established in 2009 to reduce tenure insecurity arising from a multiplicity of possibly overlapping legacy documents that, over centuries, had been issued by different agencies on some 60 million ha of land that is formally public but has long been occupied by private parties.[5] The program issues preliminary titles sporadically, that is, at the request of private parties who are responsible for the preparatory activities. Documents are expected to mature into full title after 10 years if deforestation restrictions are adhered to and no competing claims surface. An early evaluation that used within-farm variation for program applicants, some of whom had their land titled in the first phase while others did not,[6] found a program-induced reduction of deforestation of around 10 percent in the short term (Assunção, Gonzalez-Navarro, and Szerman 2019).

Two other studies analyzing the same program find that small farmers used provisional titles to access credit and deforest. Farm-level panel data for 10,647 properties titled by the program from 2011 to 2016 point toward a drop in deforestation just before titling. However, that drop was outweighed by small- and medium-size farmers increasing deforestation shortly after the program in response to higher crop and cattle prices and access to subsidized credit (Probst et al. 2020). Use of county-level forest cover data for 2007–12 (before and after program launch) finds increased deforestation by small farms in counties with high levels of Terra Legal registration (Lipscomb and Prabakaran 2020). Both suggest that issuance of land titles to enhance effective resource management should account for potential credit effects, which may differ by farm size and access to markets and technology.

Whether availability of credit will result in intensification or expansion of area through deforestation will depend on the relative private profitability of both activities. The benefits from exogenous interventions to facilitate intensification are illustrated by a study of the impact of electrification in Brazil between 1970 and 2000. Access to electricity improved crop yields and led farmers to intensify by shifting from land-intensive cattle grazing to cropping. Deforestation reductions persist 25 years after program completion—in the absence of higher productivity, deforestation would have been almost double the actual rate (Szerman et al. 2022). In a setting with large yield gaps and ready access to technology to bridge such gaps in Brazil's Amazon, a 10-year farm panel also highlights this trade-off by showing that reductions in deforestation go together with higher cattle productivity, consistent with a model in which policy-induced reductions in the benefits from clearing new land cause credit-constrained farmers to shift investments to capital-intensive farming (Koch et al. 2019). Panel data from rural Mexico also suggest that better farmers rely less on common property resources, implying that interventions that raise agricultural productivity help resource conservation (Manning and Taylor 2015).

Improved scope for intensification also increased the potential for resource conservation in Africa. For Malawi, Abman et al. (2020) use a discontinuity in eligibility for agricultural extension to show that, via crop rotation and manure use, access to extension advice fostered intensification and reduced deforestation by an estimated 13 percent. By contrast, unconditional payments not associated with access to better technology increased land clearance (Wilebore et al. 2019) in Sierra Leone and Liberia, and a nationwide development program in The Gambia had few effects on household wealth and livestock holdings but significantly increased forest loss, an effect driven by villages with little market access whose intensification options were most limited (Heß, Jaimovich, and Schündeln 2021).

In Ethiopia, weather shocks led poor households to reduce tree cover and expand cultivated area as an alternative to migration and off-farm employment (He and Chen 2022). In Cameroon, introduction of new cocoa varieties reduced deforestation if combined with high tenure security but increased it if tenure security was low, highlighting that tenure security is an important determinant of intensification (Vorlaufer et al. 2017). In Malawi, forest resources provided a key safety net as forest product collection helped smooth consumption and protected against asset depletion in the wake of covariate shocks (Mulungu and Kilimani 2023).

Deforestation, largely by fire, is also a major source of environmental degradation in Indonesia, where air pollution caused by forest fires was estimated to cause annual damages of US$16 billion (Qaim et al. 2020).[7] Villages likely to burn tend to be remoter, poorer, and less developed, and they historically used fire for agriculture, suggesting that better market access and technology in the course of economic development might create opportunities to reverse the trend (Edwards et al. 2020). By allowing farmers to increase input intensity and productivity on already cultivated land, property rights to land could help reduce deforestation. In Sumatra, panel data show that plots with titles were cultivated more intensively and had higher productivity than untitled plots, a finding that has been interpreted as implying that restrictions on title issuance at forest margins may make area expansion and forest loss more likely by reducing the scope for intensification (Krishna et al. 2017).[8]

Contrary to the deforestation-reducing effect of indigenous titling in Brazil, a recent study finds that the issuance of land-use rights certificates that would allow communities in and around state forests to log selectively, use nontimber forest products, and practice agroforestry had no effect in Indonesia (Kraus et al. 2021). This could be caused by the limited nature of the use rights awarded or the fact that benefits from sustainable use are low if compared to those from deforesting.

The Democratic Republic of Congo, which contains the world's second-largest rainforest and can absorb two-thirds of all of Africa's carbon emissions, is a key player to prevent deforestation and loss of biodiversity, which are driven by concessions or smallholder expansion (Nackoney et al. 2022) and further exacerbated by conflict (Nackoney et al. 2014). Although the 2012 Forest Code includes many best-practice elements, including recognition of customary ownership and use rights, public competitive bidding for forest concession allocation, and publicity as well as third-party monitoring of concessions, the effectiveness of such provisions will depend on implementing regulations. If the challenges that prevented implementation of such provisions in the past can be overcome, they could provide the country an opportunity to derive major benefits from climate finance.

Regulation to encourage resource conservation

Recent improvements in the ability to monitor land-use change, pollution, and carbon balances have greatly enhanced the scope not only for regulation but also for financial mechanisms to reduce deforestation and improve carbon sequestration. Free availability of decades of remote sensing data (since the late 1970s) from the Landsat archive and, more recently, the Copernicus Sentinel constellation (Tassa 2020) on the Google Earth Engine cloud computing platform (Gorelick et al. 2017) has greatly reduced the barriers that traditionally made monitoring of land use at scale prohibitively expensive.[9]

Such imagery allows for consistent analysis at any level of disaggregation (Burke et al. 2020) and, if ground-truth data of reliable quality are available, use of machine learning approaches to classify land cover or predict yields (Lobell et al. 2020). Georeferenced parcel-level data that are increasingly available from the Living Standards Measurement Surveys provide a reliable source of ground-truth data for several African countries (Burke and Lobell 2017).

Beyond information on land use, a wide range of environmental outcomes, including forest cover and carbon balances, can be monitored, independently verified, and publicized using satellite imagery (Csillik et al. 2019; Harris et al. 2021), creating opportunities to establish benchmarks for effective land use that can be used as a basis for contracting outcomes in climate finance.

An example that demonstrates the potential of using such information at different levels is the successful linking of eligibility for credit to maintaining a certain level of forest cover. Since 2008, Brazil's DETER system, which monitors deforestation daily and triggers enforcement or further ground-based investigation in high-risk cases (Doblas et al. 2022), has allowed objective compliance monitoring. Using this system at the farm level as a precondition for accessing subsidized public credit has proved to be highly effective in reducing deforestation (Assunção et al. 2020). Beyond monitoring deforestation at the farm level (Bragança and Dahis 2022), information from DETER was used at the municipality level to target a randomly selected "priority list" of municipalities with more specific environmental monitoring and enforcement, an intervention estimated to have reduced deforestation by 40 percent and cut emissions by 39.5 million tons (Assunção et al. 2019).[10] Municipalities with high deforestation were then "blacklisted," a measure that significantly reduced deforestation (Assunção and Rocha 2019).[11]

The effectiveness of public efforts to prevent forest loss was enhanced by the ability to leverage commodity traders' reputations. The Responsible Soy Project, adopted following the opening of a new soybean export facility in Brazil's Amazon, significantly decreased deforestation rates on enrolled properties, especially smaller properties, more credit-constrained ones, and those initially not in compliance with the Forest Code (Jung and Polasky 2018). Use of the blacklist by private traders helped to reduce deforestation and pasture expansion and redirect soy expansion instead toward existing pastures and cropland (Damm, Cisneros, and Börner 2022).

The potentially far-reaching impact of effective enforcement is also highlighted by 15 years of daily satellite data on fire hot spots in Indonesia. The data show that although firms overuse fire compared to a situation where the risk of the spread of fire is internalized, they reduce burning on days when winds are particularly strong or in the direction of protected forests or settled areas, indicating their sensitivity to the risk of punishment. Better enforcement could thus increase the effectiveness of regulations aiming to limit forest loss from burning: if firms treated all forested land in the same way as land near protected forest or populated areas, fires would be reduced by 80 percent (Balboni, Burgess, and Olken 2020).

One drawback of "command-and-control" systems compared with financial incentives to ensure compliance with environmental regulations is that the effectiveness of monitoring may vary with political cycles. Changes in deforestation on both sides of Brazil's Amazonian border highlight this; from

2001 to 2005, fields on the Brazilian side of the border were three times more likely to be deforested than those outside the border. Policies adopted from 2006 to 2014 led to a temporary disappearance of this difference, but indicators reverted to near prereform levels after 2014, when support for environmental regulation and enforcement waned in Brazil (Burgess, Costa, and Olken 2019). Policies enacted after 2014 also included an amnesty for illegal deforestation that is estimated to have resulted in the loss of nearly 1 million ha of forest by 2017 (Albuquerque Sant'Anna and Costa 2021) and may have permanently undermined policy credibility.

Politically motivated actions are not limited to the national level. Data from 2002 to 2012 for a panel of municipalities show that deforestation increased by 8 to 10 percent in election years if an incumbent mayor ran for reelection, pointing to the use of forest resources to support political campaigns (Pailler 2018). The scope for local discretion in implementing national policies and the responsiveness of politicians to local interest groups are illustrated by the fact that municipalities led by farmer mayors had more land-related conflicts and higher deforestation rates and carbon dioxide (CO_2) emissions than those led by nonfarmers before central monitoring was introduced. Differences disappeared when an objective benchmark for central monitoring was adopted (Bragança and Dahis 2022). The central government also systematically focused on designating federal protected areas in municipalities controlled by opposition mayors rather than ones from the ruling party (Kopas, Mangonnet, and Uprelainen 2018).

The influence of political considerations on deforestation is also evident in Indonesia, where, in the absence of effective monitoring or economic incentives for forest conservation, decentralization led to higher levels of deforestation and lower timber prices (Burgess et al. 2012). District panel data from 2001 to 2016 show how economic and political incentives reinforce each other in driving forest loss and conversion of land to oil palm, with potentially large social and environmental impacts. Deforestation levels increased by around 7 percent for a 1–standard deviation increase in local oil palm prices and by 19 percent if an election was on the horizon (Cisneros, Kis-Katos, and Nuryartono 2021). Oil palm expansion was associated with local conflicts that were exacerbated by negative economic shocks, implying a need for clear property rights and mechanisms to resolve conflicts (Cisneros, Hellmundt, and Kis-Katos 2022) and for regulation to minimize environmental damage (Naylor et al. 2019).

Objective information on deforestation outcomes can also support industry standards or pledges for "zero deforestation," in which companies commit to eliminating deforestation from supply chains as a possible complement to public regulation (Moffette, Skidmore, and Gibbs 2021). Evidence on soy from Brazil and oil palm from Indonesia suggests that such initiatives can be effective if they can rely on public monitoring. The Amazon Soy Moratorium, an agreement by grain traders not to purchase soy grown on recently deforested land, reduced deforestation in suitable locations in the Amazon by 0.66 percentage points, preventing around 18,000 km² of deforestation from 2006 to 2016. The agreement's success depended on the ability to draw on public property registries and deforestation monitoring (Heilmayr et al. 2020). Moreover, private-sector players may focus on areas with low deforestation risk. Extensive data that link traders to international markets show that commodity agreements in Brazil's soy sector focused on areas with low deforestation risk to start (zu Ermgassen et al. 2020) and that instead, deforestation may "leak" to unregulated ecosystems (Moffette and Gibbs 2021).

In 2017, the Roundtable on Sustainable Palm Oil certified around 20 percent of global palm oil production. Data from all Indonesian oil palm plantations for 2001 to 2015 suggest that certification had no impact on forest loss in peatlands or on active fires, but it lowered deforestation by one-third, largely because of selection, as in 2015, when the certified plantations contained less than 1 percent of Indonesia's residual forest (Carlson et al. 2018). This is in line with the notion that older plantations with little remaining forest are more likely to be certified. Panel data from 11,000 villages similarly suggest that in the short run, the Roundtable on Sustainable Palm Oil reduced deforestation on flat land but not on sloped land (Lee et al. 2020), reinforcing the need for coherence and consistency between national instruments at different levels and private standards, including subnational experiments (Pacheco et al. 2020).[12]

Another potential way to protect vulnerable habitats through regulation is to declare them as protected areas. Analysis across 71 countries from 2000 to 2012 suggests that protected areas were more effective in democratic countries with less corruption and better property rights protection (Abman 2018), possibly because they allow citizens' complaints that have been shown to be effective in enhancing regulatory efficiency (Colmer, Evans, and Shimshack 2023) or because they can elicit complementary efforts at local enforcement (van der Zon, de Jong, and Arts 2023). Yet, effective enforcement is still an issue. For 292 protected areas in the Brazilian Amazon, indigenous ownership was more effective at avoiding deforestation than public protection in locations with high deforestation pressure (Nolte et al. 2013). This echoes similar evidence from India, where local effectiveness increased with length of exposure to community management (Baland et al. 2010). The link between effectiveness of enforcement and institutional capacity also emerges in Colombia, where protected areas reduced deforestation, but effectiveness varied with context. National protected areas in Colombia were effective near settlements and in municipalities with more public goods and less violence. In remote, less developed regions with little or no state presence, national protected areas did not stop coca expansion and gold mining, which were much lower on collective lands (Bonilla-Mejía and Higuera-Mendieta 2019).[13]

Financial incentives for provision of environmental services

If the returns from extensive land use are modest, as in Brazil's Amazon, taxes or subsidies could be effective in reducing deforestation. Use of variation in transport costs to recover farmers' willingness to deforest suggests that a land tax of around US$40 per ha, if enforced, would achieve the requirement of keeping 80 percent under forest at a fraction of the cost of the command-and-control approaches currently applied and improve equity via tax receipt redistribution (Souza-Rodrigues 2019). Further, taxing emissions from deforestation at the social cost of carbon (SCC) would almost stop agricultural cultivation in the Amazon.

Instead of land taxes, conditional cash transfers, or payments for ecosystem services (PES), have been widely discussed to protect biodiversity, safeguard watersheds, and mitigate climate change by reducing forest loss (Börner et al. 2017). Analysis of 18 forest conservation programs finds that such programs provided some climate benefits by reducing annual deforestation rates by between 0.14 and 0.23 percentage points (Chabe-Ferret and Voia 2021). Total benefits depend on the persistence of effects after the program ends and the SCC: for an SCC of US$31 per ton, benefits amount to 32 to 45 percent of the program costs if effects stop with the program (and programs would be viable only at an SCC of US$100 per ton) but increase to 56 to 78 percent if they decrease progressively over 10 years and 194 to 263 percent if they persist forever.

In Uganda, a two-year randomized trial in 121 villages (60 treated) that paid farmers if they kept their parcels forested reduced deforestation and forest degradation, with tree cover declining by 2 to 5 percent in treatment villages and 7 to 10 percent in control villages, with no evidence that tree cutting had shifted to nearby land. Using estimated effects at an SCC of US$39 per ton implies that the benefits in terms of delayed CO_2 emissions compare favorably to the program cost (Jayachandran et al. 2016). Enrollment costs can reduce overall take-up and affect the composition of landholders selecting into the program, providing opportunities for targeting (Jack and Jayachandran 2019). Credit-constrained farmers may decline participation even if the net present value of PES income exceeds that of their opportunity costs (Jayachandran 2013).

A key aspect in designing effective PES schemes is to ensure additionality—avoid paying for efforts that would have occurred without the intervention or crowding-out efforts—and sustainability (Howard 2020), including availability of fiscal resources (Etchart et al. 2020) and targeting (Holland et al. 2014). Analysis of Bolsa Floresta, a Brazilian program that combines direct conditional payments with investments focused on livelihoods in 15 Brazilian reserves, found conservation effects to be small because of limited additionality since the program enrolled sites with low deforestation pressure (Cisneros et al. 2022), similar to evidence from Peru (Giudice et al. 2019). A program in the Brazilian Amazon, which targeted smallholders with shifting cultivation and extensive cattle, decreased the deforestation rate by up to 50 percent (Simonet et al. 2019). Leakage was significant in China, where a PES program encouraged afforestation of productive farmland (Yan 2019).[14]

PES will increase land demand and, if property rights are not clearly defined, may result in small farmers or land users who have only tenuous rights being replaced (Kansanga and Luginaah 2019). A review of 21 initiatives in five countries shows that expectations about availability of PES schemes strengthening tenure security have often not been fulfilled (Sunderlin et al. 2018), implying that clear land tenure may in many contexts be a precondition for PES to achieve not only environmental but also equity objectives. If possible environmental gains are higher in more developed areas (Sims and Alix-Garcia 2017), PES may not necessarily be a tool for reducing poverty (Alix-Garcia et al. 2019). Sustainability of PES has also been an issue in contexts such as Uganda (Kemigisha et al. 2023).

A randomized evaluation of a 2018 program to encourage community-level reductions of fire intensity via awareness raising and training on fire prevention, a small capital grant to mobilize firefighting resources, and the promise of a large conditional cash transfer at the end of the year if no fire occurs (as per satellite imagery) made no meaningful difference in fire outcomes. Although program villages increased fire prevention efforts, a combination of collective action failure and the limited size of the payment on offer seems to explain this result (Edwards et al. 2021). A mixture of community forest management with PES to reduce free-riding has been suggested for Zambia (Ngoma et al. 2020). Reforestation poses challenges and will need careful design and safeguards if positive carbon and biodiversity outcomes are to be achieved (Heilmayr, Echeverría, and Lambin 2020).

If landowners have private information about the benefits of alternative uses of their land, auctions (in the form of a subsidy auction that pays landowners to conserve or a tax auction where landowners pay for the right to develop) designed to make truthful revelation of such private information a dominant strategy would allow a regulator to implement a landscape pattern that maximizes the present value of net benefits (Lewis and Polasky 2018). An experiment in Malawi showed not only that auctions are viable, even in a low-income setting (Ajayi, Jack, and Leimona 2012), but also that private information matters. Landholders who received tree planting contracts via auction rather than a lottery kept more trees alive over the next three years than lottery awardees did, reducing the cost per surviving tree by around 30 percent (Jack 2013).

Climate adaptation in rural areas

Global models suggest that climate change–induced future warming will reduce Africa's comparative advantage in agriculture, although with large variability across locations. Adaptation will require (a) efficient use of existing resources via arrangements to improve management of water and adjust technology and practices to warmer conditions; (b) insurance against risks to prevent temporary shocks from triggering a permanently lower growth path via loss of productive assets; (c) integration into regional and global markets and changes to higher-value crops, ideally helped by public investments to reduce transport cost and improve market access; and (d) diversification of income sources beyond agriculture via part- or full-time participation in nonagricultural labor markets.

Reducing the rural sector's vulnerability to climate change

By changing the productivity of land use, climate change has already affected and is likely to further alter relative and absolute land values. Global data show that agricultural productivity has suffered considerable reductions because of climate change; recent estimates put the magnitude of climate-induced reduction in global agricultural total factor productivity since 1961 at 21 percent, equivalent to productivity growth in the past seven years. This effect is not uniform across countries or regions; in fact, climate-induced losses have been more severe in warmer regions, including Africa (Ortiz-Bobea et al. 2021). Based on 1979–2016 data, losses from prolonged heat waves are up to an order of magnitude larger than changes in mean temperatures. Extrapolating from historical estimates implies that by the end of the twenty-first century, climate damages in agriculture may be 5 to 10 times larger than predicted by a focus on mean temperature shifts alone (Miller et al. 2021).

Studies illustrate that, without access to mitigation mechanisms such as insurance or savings, migration, or trade, farmers' requirement to meet subsistence needs may prompt them to respond to extreme weather events in ways that leave them more vulnerable to future shocks and may undermine the asset and human capital endowments that form the basis for long-term resilience. In Kenya, panel data that exploit within-season variation in temperature suggest that, as with higher temperatures, as pressure from pests, crop diseases, and weeds increases, farmers are forced to shift from productive inputs, such as fertilizer, to defensive ones, such as pesticides or weeding labor, reducing overall productivity (Jagnani et al. 2021). In Peru, small farmers similarly respond to extreme heat by increasing the area planted or selling livestock, reducing their assets and compromising their long-term resilience, to maintain consumption in the short term (Aragon, Oteiza, and Rud 2021). In Thailand, exposure to consecutive moderate droughts decreased migration, possibly pointing to a poverty trap, especially for poorer rural households (Quiñones, Liebenehm, and Sharma 2021). Conceptually, if the agricultural production function has a fixed-cost element, multiple equilibria and poverty traps can arise and an argument can be made for efforts to prevent rural households' decapitalization, for example, through insurance premium subsidies (Janzen, Carter, and Ikegami 2021).

Indian district-level data on daily weather and annual mortality from 1957 to 2000 suggest that hot days led to increased mortality in rural but not urban India, an effect driven by heat in the growing season reducing agricultural productivity and wages. The importance of ways to smooth consumption via savings, credit, and insurance is illustrated by the fact that rural bank branch expansion helped mitigate productivity effects (Burgess et al. 2017). However, by encouraging moral hazard rather than adaptation, policies such as subsidized crop insurance can exacerbate losses. In the United States, premium subsidies increased from 20 to 60 percent over 1989–2013, and analysis suggests that insured crops are much more sensitive to extreme heat than uninsured ones, plausibly because crop insurance encouraged moral hazard and prevented farmers from engaging in costly adaptation (Annan and Schlenker 2015).

For around 0.5 million commercial farms in Brazil, regressing land value on climate suggests that the effects of climate change vary widely depending on climate, farms' land quality, and access to irrigation. A 1°C warming is more detrimental to farms in warm climates with high-quality land, whereas a 100-millimeter decrease in annual rainfall hurts farms in dry climates with low-quality land. Heterogeneity in climate impacts is particularly large within the subset of farms in the warmest or driest climates, consistent with the notion that the most vulnerable farms have reached the limit for climate adaptation (DePaula 2020).

Evidence from Brazilian regions hit by repeated negative climatic shocks also points to the limits to adaptation and the scope for nonlinear responses. Although local economies were able to insure against negative weather shocks via financial integration with other regions in the short term, repeated shocks that may be taken as a signal for permanently decreased investment opportunities triggered capital outflows followed by climate-induced migration that reduced population and employment in agriculture and services. Local manufacturing was able to absorb only some of the displaced workers. Regions targeted by migrants expanded employment in agriculture and services but not in manufacturing. Social security data show that emigrants often moved to firms connected to the migrants' social networks, mostly outside manufacturing, which seems to indicate labor market frictions (Albert, Bustos, and Ponticelli 2021). Similarly, the 1930s American Dust Bowl caused massive erosion that substantially and persistently reduced agricultural land values. For decades, there was limited adjustment of farmland away from activities that became less productive, with outmigration being the main mechanism for adjustment (Hornbeck 2012).

Better access to irrigation can increase resilience to climate-induced shocks. Although the economic viability of traditional large irrigation works in Africa remains doubtful (Kikuchi et al. 2021), better water management, possibly via improved dissemination of existing technology among farmers, as in Niger, where training on water conservation technology increased adoption of such technology and output, led to spillovers on neighboring farmers (Aker and Jack 2021). Africa also has ample potential for small-scale irrigation that can be harnessed efficiently if property rights are secure, possibly complemented by arrangements to incentivize effective allocation and use of scarce water resources.

In India, informal networks invest in irrigation, reducing reliance on local informal insurance networks (Mazur 2023). Exogenous differences in the ability to access irrigation water were associated with marked differences in welfare (Boudot-Reddy and Butler 2022). District-level analysis from Indonesia also shows that, while low rainfall in the agricultural season reduced agricultural production and increased natural resource conflict, the link was weakened by irrigation but not by other infrastructure, such as large dams (Gatti, Baylis, and Crost 2021).

Irrigation also played a key role in increasing agricultural production post–World War II in the US West (Edwards and Smith 2018). In a key California aquifer, introduction of a groundwater market increased groundwater levels and generated substantial net benefits, largely from water trading, that were capitalized in land values (Ayres, Meng, and Plantinga 2021). The value of clarifying property rights and allowing trade not only for land but also for water can have dramatic effects, as in one US state (Idaho) where such reforms (a) triggered a 140 percent increase in the frequency of water right trades, (b) improved efficiency of water use, and (c) prompted farmers to use irrigation water for higher-value land uses. The present value of these changes (US$402.7 million) far outweighs the one-time cost (US$94 million) of this measure (Browne and Ji 2023).

Temporary input subsidies to adopt more drought-resilient technology can reduce informational market failures, stimulating learning about new technologies by recipients and their networks (Carter, Laajaj, and Yang 2021). Historical evidence from the 1930s suggests that in the wake of environmental crisis, agricultural technology development was strongly redirected toward relevant crops and, within these, toward biochemical and planting technologies to mitigate economic losses from environmental distress (Moscona 2022). However, patent data imply that even in the United States, such directed innovation offset only 20 percent of potential losses in agricultural land values due to adverse climate trends since 1960 and could potentially offset 13 percent of projected damage by 2100 (Moscona and Sastry 2023).

Trade is an important complement of adaptation investment since it allows access to noncovariate sources of demand. Expected increases in temperature will shift the comparative advantage toward nonagriculture and depress local demand for nontradables. Trade in nonagricultural goods is essential to make up for such shortfalls: over the past five decades, African cities with firms that sold their output in global markets have been able to absorb drought shocks and even expand, while those depending only on local markets have suffered significant declines as demand has dried up (Henderson, Storeygard, and Deichmann 2017).

Data from India suggest that the ability of nonagricultural sectors to absorb workers can play a key role in attenuating the economic consequences of agricultural productivity shocks and that without scope for labor reallocation, local economic losses from climate change could be much higher (Colmer 2021). Climate change prompts rural–urban interstate migration by those at the lower end of the income distribution (Sedova and Kalkuhl 2020) and less diversification into nonagriculture. Similar patterns are found in India, where district-level temperature increases between 1951 and 2011 were associated with a lower share of nonagricultural workers, an effect that intensified over time. A plausible explanation is that higher temperatures reduced agricultural productivity, diminishing demand for nonagricultural goods and services as well as rural–urban mobility (Liu, Shamdasani, and Taraz 2023). Panel data on Chinese manufacturing firms between 2000 and 2006 suggest that exogenous increases in rural–urban migration caused by agricultural income shocks triggered the use of more labor-intensive manufacturing processes and declining productivity via labor-oriented technological change and the adoption of labor-intensive product varieties (Imbert et al. 2022).

Trade cost–induced price wedges can prevent producers from specializing in crops in which they have a comparative advantage even within countries. In Africa, lower trade costs will reduce the cost of bulky inputs, especially fertilizer, in a way that is more efficient and less costly and prone to abuse than offering subsidies to smallholders (Porteous 2020). High transport costs will (a) increase the price of food and encourage households to remain in autarky, thus forgoing gains from specialization (Gollin and Rogerson 2014); (b) prevent places with comparative advantage in perishable high-value crops, which offer higher returns to labor, from participating in regional or global markets and instead keep them producing low-value nonperishables or remaining in autarky (Pellegrina and Gafaro 2021); and (c) increase the price and reduce the use of bulky inputs, such as fertilizer or improved seed, although these are critical for higher productivity and structural transformation (McArthur and McCord 2017).

Data from colonial India suggest that railroads decreased trade costs and interregional price gaps, increased interregional and international trade, and enlarged real income levels (Donaldson 2018). A spatial general equilibrium model for Peru suggests that road building could raise productivity by 4.9 percent and the median farmer's welfare by 2.7 percent, although around 20 percent of farmers would be worse off (Sotelo 2020). In Colombia, removing barriers to market participation for farmers could increase agricultural value added by as much as 12 percent (Pellegrina and Gafaro 2021).[15] In the United States, crop market data from some 2,600 counties from 1880 to 1997 point to substantial long-run gains from economic integration, with benefits being similar in size to that of productivity improvements over the same period (Costinot and Donaldson 2016). Improved market access caused by expansion of the railroad network from 1870 to 1890 triggered significant increases in county-level agricultural land values. A counterfactual removal of all railroads in 1890 would have decreased the total value of US agricultural land by 60 percent, with limited potential for mitigating these losses via roads or shipping (Donaldson and Hornbeck 2016).

Evidence from global and regional models

Economic models of climate change have mostly been two-sector models (agriculture and manufacturing), with costly trade, innovation, technology diffusion over space, and land values capturing amenities as well as externalities from positive human capital spillovers, and negative externalities from a stock of carbon that is generated in production and accumulated over time, increasing temperatures through a damage function (Desmet and Rossi-Hansberg 2015). Costinot, Donaldson, and Smith (2016) were the first to use data on the agronomic potential of major crops in key countries at grid cell level from the Food and Agriculture Organization and incorporated a spatially explicit technical production possibility frontier into such models, showing that trade and adjustment in production patterns are important adaptation mechanisms that can significantly reduce the negative impact of climate change.

Applying such a model globally points to potentially large welfare losses in Africa and Latin America and gains at higher latitudes that were too cold for agriculture in the past, with migration and trade as potential coping mechanisms (Alvarez and Rossi-Hansberg 2021; Desmet, Nagy, and Rossi-Hansberg 2018). With high trade costs, African countries might still be able to satisfy subsistence needs more cost-effectively from own production rather than imports, creating a possibility of higher temperatures pulling labor into a less productive agriculture sector, with potentially large welfare reductions for the poorest quartile of the world's population (Nath 2020).

Adding a transportation network and trade and migration flows to a general equilibrium model for Sub-Saharan Africa provides two insights (Conte 2022). First, it is important to consider the mean and variance of climate change effects and allow for the possibility of crop switching. Map 4.1 illustrates that with these assumptions, average effects are heterogeneous, with marked decreases in the Sahel, Central Africa, and a belt that stretches from southern Angola to South Africa and southern Mozambique. At the same time, mean suitability increases in the highlands of the rift valley and southern

MAP 4.1   Expected impacts of climate change on the average and standard deviation of crop yields in Sub-Saharan Africa, 2000 versus 2080

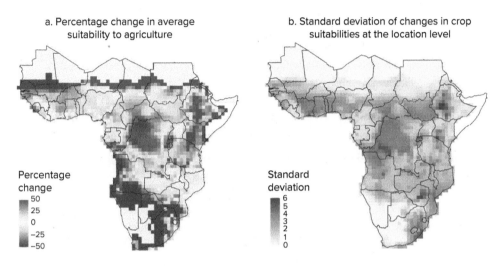

a. Percentage change in average
suitability to agriculture

b. Standard deviation of changes in crop
suitabilities at the location level

Percentage
change
50
25
0
−25
−50

Standard
deviation
6
5
4
3
2
1
0

Source: Conte 2022. © Conte. Reproduced with permission from Conte; further permission required for reuse.

Africa, with more modest increases on the Atlantic Coast of Central Africa. At the same time, variability increases almost everywhere, highlighting the importance of insurance against temporary shocks. Second, detailed results highlight the importance of trade and migration; in fact, a counterfactual where intra-African barriers to migration and trade frictions are reduced to those prevailing in the European Union eliminates aggregate climate-induced losses and may even allow Sub-Saharan Africa to benefit if climate change results in an acceleration of structural change. Of course, this would require significant adjustments in institutions and mobility.

Adaptation in urban areas

The spatial scale of the agricultural production process makes it particularly vulnerable to climate change causing crop failures or reductions in yield. Adaptation options such as air conditioning, which have significantly reduced the negative effects of heat in the United States (Barreca et al. 2016), imply that industry or services are often less affected by climate change than agriculture. However, even if such opportunities are realized, a key impact of climate change is related to increased frequency of flooding or wind damage from extreme weather events or vulnerability to sea-level rise (SLR).

Higher temperatures in urban areas have been shown to reduce worker productivity, including through increased levels of absenteeism on hot days (Somanathan et al. 2021), as well as increased mortality and violence (Burke, Hsiang, and Miguel 2015; Hsiang, Burke, and Miguel 2013). Temperature changes predicted by most climate models, together with temperature elasticities of interpersonal violence and intergroup conflict (4 and 14 percent, respectively), imply warming can cause potentially large effects (Carleton, Hsiang, and Burke 2016). Ease of adaptation may vary by wealth; for example, in the United States, temperature increased crime rates overall (which are 1.72 and 1.90 percent higher when daily maximum temperature exceeds 75°F and 90°F, respectively), but monetary losses from crime were up to five times larger for low-income compared with more affluent neighborhoods (Heilmann, Kahn, and Tang 2021).

Because many cities are in floodplains, climate change will affect urban land use and values via higher frequency of extreme weather events such as cyclones or floods, changes in amenity values caused by higher temperatures, and susceptibility to SLR in the long term. However, the settled area susceptible to such risk is expanding rather than shrinking. In the United States, the share of housing stock near the Atlantic and Gulf coasts in blocks prone to one-foot SLR rose from 12 percent in 1990 to 26 percent in 2010, creating challenges for policy makers (Lin, McDermott, and Michaels 2022). Combining gridded population data with elevation and poverty maps suggests that 19 percent of the world's population (1.47 billion people, 89 percent of whom live in low- and middle-income countries) is already exposed to a high risk of 1-in-100-year flood events (Maruyama Rentschler and Salhab 2020).[16] Moreover, the share of the housing stock affected by such risk keeps expanding: from 1985 to 2015, 36,500 km^2 of settlements were built in the world's highest-risk zones, with 82 percent in low- and middle-income countries (Rentschler et al. 2022).

Flooding already has reduced infrastructure reliability and urban economic activity in several African cities since, beyond firms' direct flood exposure, flooding of roads decreases connectivity between firms and access to essential services (Maruyama Rentschler et al. 2019). For example, regular floods in Kinshasa, Democratic Republic of Congo, translate into travel delays that are estimated to cost commuters around US$1.2 million daily and hinder labor market participation, especially by the poor (He et al. 2021).[17] In Dar es Salaam, Tanzania, which is frequently flooded, a major flood is estimated to have had indirect effects of 2 to 4 percent of city GDP, with the poor being the least likely to recover, and access to finance playing a key role in recovery (Erman et al. 2019).

Detailed inundation maps, together with remotely sensed imagery of nightlights, show that although low-elevation urban areas are flooded more often, they also have a higher density of economic activity that allows them to recover from shocks through flooding as rapidly as those at higher elevations, possibly because of higher levels of innovation and agglomeration effects (Kocornik-Mina et al. 2020). In developing country cities, growth of population in high-risk areas of cities is often driven by displacement with little planning. Data on more than 3,300 flood events, combined with city-level observations of social disorder events from 1985 to 2015, suggest that flood exposure is associated with higher intensity of social disorder, especially in public services provision, prices, and wages (Castells-Quintana, Lopez-Uribe, and McDermott 2022).

A global model suggests that under an intermediate climate scenario, permanent flooding caused by local sea-level change will reduce global real GDP by 0.19 percent in present value terms, with the main effects being indirect rather than direct damages. By 2200, 1.46 percent of the population will be displaced, with much larger effects in coastal locations. Without dynamic investment and migration responses, expected losses in real GDP will be more severe, amounting to 4.5 percent (Desmet et al. 2021). For the United States, data from 1998 to 2018 suggest that increased flood risk has already reduced firm entry, employment, and output by some 0.52 percent of GDP (Jia, Ma, and Xie 2022). Most studies on this are from developed countries, which have the damage data (due to insurance), but the same issues are highly relevant for developing countries.

Regulation to avoid negative externalities

Regulation is one instrument to facilitate adaptation to disaster risk by building more resilient structures. Administrative data on public expenditures for firefighting or wildfire protection in the western United States suggest that policy and institutions influence the costs of climate change, in this case by providing a large implicit subsidy to homeowners. The expected net present value of the subsidy can exceed 20 percent of a home's value, and its size increases with fire risk and decreases with density of development (Boomhower 2019). The same data also highlight the scope for regulation: after a deadly fire in 1991, changes in building codes were introduced to reduce the wedge between private and social benefits that can arise from owners lacking full information or external effects in the presence of free riding.

Combining administrative data on all US homes damaged by wildfire since 2007, differences in the timing of building code effectiveness across jurisdictions, and assessor data for all destroyed or surviving homes suggests that these changes were effective. Inside wildfire perimeters, homes built according to the new code requirements had much greater resilience to fire. There is also evidence of an external effect: because of reduced structure-to-structure spread, the presence of homes built to the stricter code increases the survival probability of adjacent ones. Had all homes been built to the improved standard, losses in recent wildfires would have been reduced by several billion dollars (Baylis and Boomhower 2023).

Similarly, data from realized losses as a result of floods in the United States show that regulation—in this case, building codes from 2001 that mandated more wind-resistant building technology—has been effective in reducing subsequent damages from hurricanes. High-resolution imagery after a major hurricane not only documents vintage effects coinciding with the passage of stricter building codes but also points toward external effects as buildings surrounded by homes built to code were less likely to suffer damage (Bakkensen and Blair 2022). Embedding the effects of floodplain regulation in areas at risk of flooding in Florida in a static model of residential choices with elastic housing supply shows that the policy reduces expected flood damages by 60 percent, three-fourths through compliance and one-fourth by relocation of new construction to lower-risk areas. However, regulation through command-and-control approaches is often rather crude. Fiscal instruments, and a tax on flood risk that could be levied as a surcharge on property taxes, are more flexible and could potentially achieve higher social welfare gains (Ostriker and Russo 2022).[18]

Storm victims' ability to access postdisaster aid that is highly visible politically may also give rise to moral hazard that encourages households to stay in or even move to risky areas, thus increasing aggregate risk exposure (Boustan, Kahn, and Rhode 2012). Although such ex post support is more regressive than offering insurance ex ante (Billings, Gallagher, and Ricketts 2022), its availability has been raised as one possible explanation for the fact that, despite a damage function that is an order of magnitude larger than in other developed countries, the extent of adaptation to extreme weather events in the United States is remarkably limited (Bakkensen and Mendelsohn 2016).

Better private decision-making through risk information and land prices

If markets for land and property take all available information into account, properties located in high-risk areas such as floodplains should be less valuable. Longitudinal evidence suggests that extreme weather events indeed affect land values but that the effects may be short-lived.[19] In the United States after a major flood in 1994, the prices of properties in the 100-year floodplain decreased, but the effect disappeared after four to nine years (Atreya, Ferreira, and Kriesel 2013). For English houses, property prices declined by 24.9 and 21.1 percent in inundated versus noninundated areas in inland or coastal locations, respectively, but this discount disappeared after four to five years, although it persisted somewhat longer for low-priced properties (Beltran, Maddison, and Elliott 2019). Analysis of transaction prices for some 460,000 transactions of properties within 0.25 miles of the coast from 2007 to 2016 suggests that homes exposed to SLR sell for around 7 percent less than observationally equivalent unexposed properties equidistant from the beach. The discount has grown over time and is driven by sophisticated buyers and communities worried about global warming, and the lack of a relationship between SLR exposure and rental rates supports the notion of this being a causal effect (Bernstein, Gustafson, and Lewis 2019).[20] Transaction-level data that link home transaction prices to the risk of flooding show significant heterogeneity, with steeper risk discounts in neighborhoods where residents believe in climate change than in those where it is denied (Baldauf, Garlappi, and Yannelis 2020).

Lenders and insurers have greater incentives to scrutinize information on risk exposure than individual house buyers. Municipal bond markets began pricing increased risk of SLR exposure in 2013, an effect that is larger for bonds with long maturity and not only driven by near-term flood risk. The fact that the SLR exposure premium exhibits a different trend from that of house prices and is unaffected by controlling for them suggests that it is indeed uncertainty about SLR's future impact, rather than reduced current asset values, that drives the effect on bond prices (Goldsmith-Pinkham et al. 2023).

Through the value of real estate pledged as collateral, climate change may affect the financial system (Bakkensen, Phan, and Wong 2023). Analysis of some 200,000 loans in US counties with potential SLR exposure points to an "SLR premium" for long-term (but not short-term) loans. This premium is smaller if climate change impacts are less salient or in areas with more climate change deniers, suggesting that although mortgage lenders perceive the risk of SLR, attention and beliefs are potential barriers for this risk to be priced in residential mortgage markets (Nguyen et al. 2022). Moreover, properties located in the highest-risk flood area, within 400 to 500 meters of the coastline, commanded a significant price premium (Atreya and Czajkowski 2019).

Construction permit data for 2011–16 suggest that vulnerability to SLR is associated with much-reduced construction in areas where residents believe in climate change but not in areas where residents are skeptical, suggesting that awareness or beliefs affect adaptation (Barrage and Furst 2019). This does not mean that information has no value. To the contrary, comparing homes for which the flood risk was incorrectly assessed based on outdated elevation data to correctly classified ones shows that such misclassification led owners to underestimate their flood risk, invest less in adaptation, and buy less insurance. Feeding this into a model suggests that identifying and properly pricing the estimated 6 million high-risk homes outside the floodplain would increase social welfare by US$138 billion (Mulder 2022).

By having prices reflect climate risk, markets should discourage excessive development in hazardous areas. However, regulatory floodplain maps together with two decades of sales data for all homes in the United States suggest that this is not always the case. Using only information on current risk from publicly available flood hazard maps suggests that single-family homes in US flood zones are overvalued by 2 to 8 percent of their value, or around US$44 billion. Deviations are less pronounced for commercial buyers and in markets where buyers are more aware of climate change risks, suggesting that policies to communicate risk effectively may be important to make market prices reflect risk more accurately (Hino and Burke 2021). Overvaluation is high in coastal counties without flood risk disclosure laws and high rates of climate change denial (Gourevitch et al. 2023).

The adverse impact of policies that subsidize insurance is visible in England, where a public reinsurance scheme to make protection against extreme weather events more affordable was introduced in April 2016. Data on all property transactions since 1995, together with a map of high-risk areas, suggest that introduction of a reinsurance scheme that lowers insurance premia for high-risk properties increased transaction volumes and prices of at-risk properties, fully offsetting the negative direct effects of flood risk on property prices. Although all at-risk areas benefited, high-income areas and high-end properties benefited relatively more, receiving an implicit subsidy (Garbarino, Guin, and Lee 2023). Adjustment toward a fair rate and the impact of automating publication of data on pollution on private averting behavior in China (Greenstone et al. 2022) point toward great potential.

Public investment in resilience

Evidence from the United States, Europe, Asia, and Latin America illustrates that if they are combined with maps of flood risk, property prices convey essential information to inform adaptation. Given the challenges Africa will face from climate change, both increased urban flooding and greater demand for housing from migrants, creating institutions that can provide similar information for Africa is a high priority to inform policy makers about available options and help finance adaptation measures via land value surcharges and taxes to minimize moral hazard.

Spatially detailed data on flood exposure in the Netherlands together with information on all home sales from 1999 to 2011 suggest that people's willingness to pay to avoid flood risk exceeds the level of public spending on this issue by 9 to 36 percent (Bosker et al. 2019). To prevent coastal flooding from submerging large parts of Jakarta, the Indonesian government started constructing a US$40 billion sea wall. Use of a spatial model of urban development suggests that, unless government can commit to policies ex ante, this intervention may create moral hazard and overbuilding in flood-prone areas (Hsiao 2021b) to the extent that the land value creation from flood mitigation would be sufficient to justify these investments. This finding implies that surcharges on property taxes could be used to finance such an intervention (Avner et al. 2022).

Institutional arrangements for conflict resolution

In Africa, productivity shocks affect the opportunity cost of key agricultural resources and may be mediated by customary structures. If land fertility differs, exogenous changes in input prices will affect land rents and thus the opportunity cost of fighting in proportion to soil fertility. Conflict data from 1997 to 2013 for all of Sub-Saharan Africa suggest that changes in relative land productivity are associated with higher conflict frequency, especially for cells with more heterogeneous land endowment (Berman, Couttenier, and Soubeyran 2021). Beyond this "production channel," whereby climate shocks in rural areas lower production and reduce the opportunity cost of engaging in violence, climate-induced changes in prices for key staples will also affect wages and real income, possibly making it easier to recruit fighters (McGuirk and Burke 2020). Extreme temperatures also affect the incidence of conflict (Breckner and Sunde 2019).

Shocks may have particularly pronounced effects if they interact with preexisting conditions, as in the case of Brazil, where adverse rainfall shocks led the rural poor to invade large landholdings, and the effect of shocks was twice the average in highly unequal or polarized municipalities (Hidalgo et al. 2010).[21] County panel data (2003–07) from one state show that higher insecurity, proxied by land invasions, is associated with higher shares of annual crops, reducing crop production and threatening to undermine environmental sustainability via land degradation (Orellano et al. 2015).[22]

Climate-related shocks can also increase conflict, requiring decentralized ways to govern resource access and manage conflict, including resource conflict. Weather shocks are particularly relevant for agriculture, where uninsured shocks can lead to persistent negative impacts. Gridded data on within-year variations in weather and crop-growing seasons and spatial variation in crop cover for all of Africa from 1997 to 2011 show that negative shocks in the growing season of key local crops not only affect the incidence of conflict but also have persistent impacts that spill over to neighboring areas (Harari and La Ferrara 2018).[23]

Descriptive evidence and case studies suggest that pastoralists are particularly vulnerable because their land-use rights are seasonal and depend on watering points and transit corridors that are easily disturbed. It also suggests that disputes between mobile and sedentary groups about boundaries can easily become a flashpoint for conflict (McPeak and Little 2018). Sedentary and pastoral groups have long engaged in a mutually beneficial, symbiotic relationship that ensured sustainability of the latter via access to floodplains or wetlands in the dry season.

A key feature, especially of Sahelian countries in West Africa, is the presence of transhumance, whereby pastoralists whose homelands receive sufficient water to allow cattle to graze in the wet season (map 4.2, panel a) move south to graze their animals on fields that have been harvested and are owned by sedentary farmers (map 4.2, panel b). This is beneficial to both sides because, in addition to clearing fields of crop residues, sedentary farmers receive free fertilization through animal dung.

Agricultural intensification (for example, a shift to irrigation) or climate-induced shocks that affect the timing of cropping seasons so they no longer coincide with transhumance may upset this pattern by transforming a complementary pattern of resource use into a confrontational relationship. Data on almost three decades of violent conflict in Africa suggest that droughts

MAP 4.2   Transhumant migration patterns during the wet and dry seasons and climate change in Africa

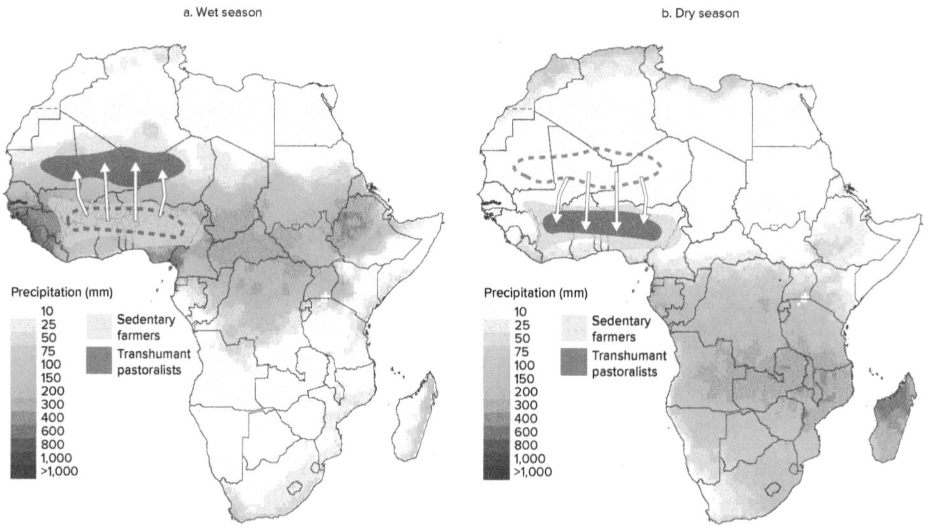

a. Wet season

b. Dry season

Precipitation (mm)
10
25
50
75
100
150
200
300
400
600
800
1,000
>1,000

Sedentary farmers

Transhumant pastoralists

Source: Based on McGuirk and Nunn 2020. © McGuirk and Nunn. Used with permission of McGuirk and Nunn; further permission required for reuse.
Note: mm = millimeters.

in pastoral areas tend to trigger agropastoral conflict in neighboring agricultural areas by exacerbating competition over scarce wetlands essential for dry season herd survival. Observed increases in the level of conflict are much larger in zones suitable for agriculture and pastoralism than in zones that are purely only agricultural or pastoral. However, political participation eliminated the increased likelihood of conflict (McGuirk and Nunn 2020).

In mixed agropastoral areas, a 1°C increase in temperature led to a 54 percent increase in the probability of conflict, compared with a 17 percent increase in areas populated by only farmers or only herders. Three facts support the notion that competition for resources is a major driver of farmer–herder violence: (a) conflict is more prevalent in areas where rangeland and farmland abut that are also particularly vulnerable to climate shocks; (b) temperature spikes in a nomadic group's homeland affect conflict far beyond that territory; and (c) the effect is particularly pronounced for land-related conflicts. Policies to enforce property rights for pastoral resources, improve land dispute resolution, foster participatory democracy, and empower local communities all have been shown to reduce such violence (Eberle, Rohner, and Thoenig 2020).

Notes

1 | A rent model shows that land speculation is an important driver of extensive ranching profitability and suggests that policies that alter the incentives to clear forest for pasture, discourage land speculation, and increase accountability for land management practices are needed if intensification of the cattle sector is to deter new deforestation (Bowman et al. 2012).

2 | Legal protection against incursion by loggers or plantation companies thus seems to be an important way to protect standing forest, in line with descriptive evidence (da Silva Medina, Pokorny, and Campbell 2022).

3 | Without a credit channel (which is implausible as rights are inalienable), effects are attributed to titling having established a longer time horizon, created a more secure natural resource base, and allowed for capitalizing on economies of scale in the protection of rights against outsider intrusion.

4 | Both the CAR and the Terra Legal program offer interesting lessons on modalities through which use rights (at the community or individual level) could be registered and combined with regulation of land use in the African context.

5 | Formally, the program targets some 1,800 *glebas federais não-destinadas*, which are blocks of land that officially belong to the federal government but are not managed by any government agency. If no federal agency claims an interest in a particular gleba, private titles can be issued to individuals who have occupied an area of at most 1,500 ha since at least 2004. Title issuance is free for parcels smaller than 100 ha and requires payment for land as well as georeferencing if the total land area is between 100 and 400 ha or greater than 400 ha, respectively, over a 20-year period with no up-front payments and a 3-year grace period (Assunção, Gonzalez-Navarro, and Szerman 2019). Titles remain provisional for 10 years, with issuance of permanent title contingent on compliance with adherence to environmental standards, particularly keeping the minimum designated area under forest.

6 | The researchers note that only around one-third of the applications had been titled by 2014, making this a valid identification strategy. At the same time, from the data reported in their study, it does not seem that the assumption of parallel trends preintervention can be maintained.

7 | The fires caused haze that affected economic activity as far away as Singapore (Agarwal, Wang, and Yang 2021) and often emitted more carbon dioxide per day than the entire US economy.

8 | Limited tradability of nontitled land implies that clearing land for sale was not a driver of deforestation (Kubitza et al. 2018).

9 | Landsat offers a 30-meter (m) pixel size and 16-day revisit frequency with a pixel size of 10 m and a 5-day revisit frequency. Standard products are increasingly made available for free, including for agricultural monitoring in Africa (Michler et al. 2022; Nakalembe et al. 2021). For example, time-series data show that between 2003 and 2019, cropped area increased by 9 percent to a total of 1,244 million ha. The annual rate of expansion almost doubled, mostly in Africa, where 49 percent of expansion replaced natural vegetation and tree cover (Potapov et al. 2022). Global soybean area more than doubled from 26.4 million ha to 55.1 million ha over the same period (Song et al. 2021).

10 | An ex post optimal list would have resulted in carbon emissions that were 7.4 percent lower than the actual list, amounting to savings of more than US$900 million and emissions that were more than 25 percent lower (on average) than a randomly selected list.

11 | A capacity-building program for municipalities did not reduce deforestation beyond the effect of the blacklist (Sills et al. 2020).

12 | If they combine coordination and commitment among importers rather than unilateral action by specific trade blocs, import tariffs can achieve a significant impact in the medium term (Hsiao 2021a). However, coordination is essential because in a setting where agribusiness has monopsony power, unilateral tariffs will imply that farmers in the poorest regions, where supply is most inelastic, bear the largest burden of such regulation through lower farmgate prices (Domínguez-Iino 2021).

13 | Overall, collective lands were more effective than national (strict-use) protected areas, and regional (multiple-use) protected areas had no impact.

14 | In Argentina's Dry Chaco, another global deforestation hot spot, powerful landholders were associated with larger illegal deforestation events; thus, more flexible subnational forest regulation and land inequality would escalate illegal deforestation (Blum et al. 2022). The area under secure tenure allowed locals to maintain high levels of forest cover from 1976 to 2016 but was associated with high levels of deforestation by extra-local agents unless effectively monitored (Faingerch et al. 2021).

15 | The importance of understanding the potential distributional implications of improving trade links is highlighted by Farrokhi and Pellegrina (2021), who use a multicountry general equilibrium model based on data on potential agricultural productivity at global scale. They find that over 1980–2015, reductions in cross-country trade costs for outputs and inputs had considerable welfare impact. Liberalizing trade in output led to efficiency gains, mainly through crop specialization, and welfare gains, especially for low-income countries that spend much of their income on food. Increased input trade favored middle-income countries that use modern technology over low-income ones, narrowing the gap between high- and middle-income countries but widening it between low- and middle-income countries.

16 | The poor are often disproportionally exposed to droughts and floods, particularly in urban areas (Winsemius et al. 2018). Across the world, 132 million individuals, of whom 55 percent are in Sub-Saharan Africa, are extremely poor (<US$1.90 per day) and live in high flood-risk areas.

17 | Assessment of some 14 million kilometers of urban roads in 2,564 settlements suggests that some 3.64 percent that affect 11.58 percent of simulated trips are affected by a one-in-five-years flood, allowing identification and prioritization measures for urban transport resilience (He et al. 2022).

18 | Embedding the effects of building regulation in areas at risk of flooding in Florida in a static model of residential choices with elastic housing supply shows that the policy reduces expected flood damages by inducing compliance and relocation of new construction to lower-risk areas.

19 | Failure to control for relevant characteristics leads to wide divergence in results from cross-sectional studies (Beltran, Maddison, and Elliott 2018).

20 | Properties that are expected to be damaged only further in the future (more than 100 years) sell for a lower discount (4 percent).

21 | Interestingly, the effects of rainfall shocks were also increased by a higher share of land being under fixed-rent contracts; share tenancy can act as an insurance substitute. Other political or socioeconomic variables, among them political competition, sharecropping, police expenditures, and social welfare spending, had no impact on the magnitude of shocks.

22 | In Colombia, higher individual ownership of land and participation in export crop production increase individuals' exposure to exogenous commodity price shocks. If they cannot be insured or hedged, such shocks can reduce the opportunity cost of participating in insurgent groups, consistent with the finding that negative price shocks increase conflict intensity in districts with more individual owners (Guardado 2018).

23 | In Somalia, a 1 standard deviation increase in drought intensity and length raises the likelihood of conflict by 62 percent via changes in livestock prices (Maystadt and Ecker 2014). Meta-analysis suggests that higher prices for lootable artisanal minerals and oil, a capital-intensive commodity, heightened conflict, whereas price increases for labor-intensive agricultural commodities reduced it by increasing the opportunity cost of fighting (Blair, Christensen, and Rudkin 2021).

References

Abman, R. 2018. "Rule of Law and Avoided Deforestation from Protected Areas." *Ecological Economics* 146: 282–89.

Abman, R., T. Garg, Y. Pan, and S. Singhal. 2020. "Agriculture and Deforestation." University of California San Diego.

Agarwal, S., L. Wang, and Y. Yang. 2021. "Impact of Transboundary Air Pollution on Service Quality and Consumer Satisfaction." *Journal of Economic Behavior and Organization* 192: 357–80.

Ajayi, O. C., B. K. Jack, and B. Leimona. 2012. "Auction Design for the Private Provision of Public Goods in Developing Countries: Lessons from Payments for Environmental Services in Malawi and Indonesia." *World Development* 40 (6): 1213–23.

Aker, J. C., and K. Jack. 2021. "Harvesting the Rain: The Adoption of Environmental Technologies in the Sahel." NBER Working Paper 29518, National Bureau of Economic Research, Cambridge, MA.

Albert, C., P. Bustos, and J. Ponticelli. 2021. "The Effects of Climate Change on Labor and Capital Reallocation." NBER Working Paper 28995, National Bureau of Economic Research, Cambridge, MA.

Albuquerque Sant'Anna, A., and L. Costa. 2021. "Environmental Regulation and Bail Outs under Weak State Capacity: Deforestation in the Brazilian Amazon." *Ecological Economics* 186: 107071.

Alix-Garcia, J. M., K. R. E. Sims, V. H. Orozco Olvera, L. Costica, J. D. F. Medina, S. Romo-Monroy, and S. Pagiola. 2019. "Can Environmental Cash Transfers Reduce Deforestation and Improve Social Outcomes? A Regression Discontinuity Analysis of Mexico's National Program (2011–2014)." Policy Research Working Paper 8707, World Bank, Washington, DC.

Alvarez, J. L. C., and E. Rossi-Hansberg. 2021. "The Economic Geography of Global Warming." NBER Working Paper 28466, National Bureau of Economic Research, Cambridge, MA.

Annan, F., and W. Schlenker. 2015. "Federal Crop Insurance and the Disincentive to Adapt to Extreme Heat." *American Economic Review* 105 (5): 262–66.

Aragon, F. M., F. Oteiza, and J. P. Rud. 2021. "Climate Change and Agriculture: Subsistence Farmers' Response to Extreme Heat." *American Economic Journal: Economic Policy* 13 (1): 1–35.

Assunção, J., C. Gandour, R. Rocha, and R. Rocha. 2020. "The Effect of Rural Credit on Deforestation: Evidence from the Brazilian Amazon." *Economic Journal* 130 (626): 290–330.

Assunção, J., M. Gonzalez-Navarro, and D. Szerman. 2019. "Property Rights and Resource Extraction: Evidence from Deforestation in the Amazon." Pontifícia Universidade Católica do Rio de Janeiro.

Assunção, J., R. McMillan, J. Murphy, and E. Souza-Rodrigues. 2019. "Optimal Environmental Targeting in the Amazon Rainforest." NBER Working Paper 25636, National Bureau of Economic Research, Cambridge, MA.

Assunção, J., and R. Rocha. 2019. "Getting Greener by Going Black: The Effect of Blacklisting Municipalities on Amazon Deforestation." *Environment and Development Economics* 24 (2): 115–37.

Atreya, A., and J. Czajkowski. 2019. "Graduated Flood Risks and Property Prices in Galveston County." *Real Estate Economics* 47 (3): 807–44.

Atreya, A., S. Ferreira, and W. Kriesel. 2013. "Forgetting the Flood? An Analysis of the Flood Risk Discount over Time." *Land Economics* 89 (4): 577–96.

Avner, P., V. Viguie, B. A. Jafino, and S. Hallegatte. 2022. "Flood Protection and Land Value Creation: Not All Resilience Investments Are Created Equal." *Economics of Disasters and Climate Change* 6 (3): 417–49.

Ayres, A. B., K. C. Meng, and A. J. Plantinga. 2021. "Do Environmental Markets Improve on Open Access? Evidence from California Groundwater Rights." *Journal of Political Economy* 129 (10): 2817–60.

Azevedo, A. A., R. Rajão, M. A. Costa, M. C. C. Stabile, M. N. Macedo, T. N. P. dos Reis, A. Alencar, B. S. Soares-Filho, and R. Pacheco. 2017. "Limits of Brazil's Forest Code as a Means to End Illegal Deforestation." *Proceedings of the National Academy of Sciences* 114 (29): 7653–58.

Bakkensen, L., and L. Blair. 2022. "Wind Code Effectiveness and Externalities: Evidence from Hurricane Michael." University of Arizona, Tucson.

Bakkensen, L., T. Phan, and R. Wong. 2023. "Leveraging the Disagreement on Climate Change: Theory and Evidence." Working Paper 23-01, Federal Reserve Bank of Richmond, Richmond, VA.

Bakkensen, L. A., and R. O. Mendelsohn. 2016. "Risk and Adaptation: Evidence from Global Hurricane Damages and Fatalities." *Journal of the Association of Environmental and Resource Economists* 3 (3): 555–87.

Baland, J.-M., P. Bardhan, S. Das, and D. Mookherjee. 2010. "Forests to the People: Decentralization and Forest Degradation in the Indian Himalayas." *World Development* 38 (11): 1642–56.

Balboni, C., A. Berman, R. Burgess, and B. A. Olken. Forthcoming. "The Economics of Tropical Deforestation." *Annual Review of Economics*.

Balboni, C., R. Burgess, and B. A. Olken. 2020. "The Origins and Control of Forest Fires in the Tropics." London School of Economics, London.

Baldauf, M., L. Garlappi, and C. Yannelis. 2020. "Does Climate Change Affect Real Estate Prices? Only If You Believe in It." *Review of Financial Studies* 33 (3): 1256–95.

Baragwanath, K., and E. Bayi. 2020. "Collective Property Rights Reduce Deforestation in the Brazilian Amazon." *Proceedings of the National Academy of Sciences* 117 (34): 20495.

Barrage, L., and J. Furst. 2019. "Housing Investment, Sea Level Rise, and Climate Change Beliefs." *Economics Letters* 177: 105–8.

Barreca, A., K. Clay, O. Deschenes, M. Greenstone, and J. S. Shapiro. 2016. "Adapting to Climate Change: The Remarkable Decline in the US Temperature-Mortality Relationship over the Twentieth Century." *Journal of Political Economy* 124 (1): 105–59.

Baylis, P., and J. Boomhower. 2023. "The Economic Incidence of Wildfire Suppression in the United States." *American Economic Journal: Applied Economics* 15 (1): 442–73.

Beltran, A., D. Maddison, and R. J. R. Elliott. 2018. "Is Flood Risk Capitalised into Property Values?" *Ecological Economics* 146: 668–85.

Beltran, A., D. Maddison, and R. J. R. Elliott. 2019. "The Impact of Flooding on Property Prices: A Repeat-Sales Approach." *Journal of Environmental Economics and Management* 95: 62–86.

BenYishay, A., S. Heuser, D. Runfola, and R. Trichler. 2017. "Indigenous Land Rights and Deforestation: Evidence from the Brazilian Amazon." *Journal of Environmental Economics and Management* 86: 29–47.

Berman, N., M. Couttenier, and R. Soubeyran. 2021. "Fertile Ground for Conflict." *Journal of the European Economic Association* 19 (1): 82–127.

Bernstein, A., M. T. Gustafson, and R. Lewis. 2019. "Disaster on the Horizon: The Price Effect of Sea Level Rise." *Journal of Financial Economics* 134 (2): 253–72.

Billings, S. B., E. A. Gallagher, and L. Ricketts. 2022. "Let the Rich Be Flooded: The Distribution of Financial Aid and Distress after Hurricane Harvey." *Journal of Financial Economics* 146 (2): 797–819.

Blackman, A., L. Corral, E. S. Lima, and G. P. Asner. 2017. "Titling Indigenous Communities Protects Forests in the Peruvian Amazon." *Proceedings of the National Academy of Sciences* 114 (16): 4123.

Blair, G., D. Christensen, and A. Rudkin. 2021. "Do Commodity Price Shocks Cause Armed Conflict? A Meta-Analysis of Natural Experiments." *American Political Science Review* 115 (2): 709–16.

Blum, D., S. Aguiar, Z. Sun, D. Müller, A. Alvarez, I. Aguirre, S. Domingo, and M. Mastrangelo. 2022. "Subnational Institutions and Power of Landholders Drive Illegal Deforestation in a Major Commodity Production Frontier." *Global Environmental Change* 74: 102511.

Bonilla-Mejía, L., and I. Higuera-Mendieta. 2019. "Protected Areas under Weak Institutions: Evidence from Colombia." *World Development* 122: 585–96.

Boomhower, J. 2019. "Drilling Like There's No Tomorrow: Bankruptcy, Insurance, and Environmental Risk." *American Economic Review* 109 (2): 391–426.

Börner, J., K. Baylis, E. Corbera, D. Ezzine-de-Blas, J. Honey-Rosés, U. M. Persson, and S. Wunder. 2017. "The Effectiveness of Payments for Environmental Services." *World Development* 96: 359–74.

Bosker, M., H. Garretsen, G. Marlet, and C. van Woerkens. 2019. "Nether Lands: Evidence on the Price and Perception of Rare Natural Disasters." *Journal of the European Economic Association* 17 (2): 413–53.

Boudot-Reddy, C., and A. Butler. 2022. "Agricultural Productivity and Local Economic Development: Evidence from Private Investment in Irrigation." University of Edinburgh, Edinburgh.

Boustan, L. P., M. E. Kahn, and P. W. Rhode. 2012. "Moving to Higher Ground: Migration Response to Natural Disasters in the Early Twentieth Century." *American Economic Review* 102 (3): 238–44.

Bowman, M. S., B. S. Soares-Filho, F. D. Merry, D. C. Nepstad, H. Rodrigues, and O. T. Almeida. 2012. "Persistence of Cattle Ranching in the Brazilian Amazon: A Spatial Analysis of the Rationale for Beef Production." *Land Use Policy* 29 (3): 558–68.

Bragança, A., and R. Dahis. 2022. "Cutting Special Interests by the Roots: Evidence from the Brazilian Amazon." *Journal of Public Economics* 215: 104753.

Breckner, M., and U. Sunde. 2019. "Temperature Extremes, Global Warming, and Armed Conflict: New Insights from High Resolution Data." *World Development* 123: 104624.

Brito, B., P. Barreto, A. Brandão, S. Baima, and P. H. Gomes. 2019. "Stimulus for Land Grabbing and Deforestation in the Brazilian Amazon." *Environmental Research Letters* 14 (6): 064018.

Browne, O. R., and X. J. Ji. 2023. "The Economic Value of Clarifying Property Rights: Evidence from Water in Idaho's Snake River Basin." *Journal of Environmental Economics and Management* 119: 102799.

Burgess, R., F. Costa, and B. A. Olken. 2019. "The Brazilian Amazon's Double Reversal of Fortune." London School of Economics, London.

Burgess, R., O. Deschenes, D. Donaldson, and M. Greenstone. 2017. "Weather, Climate Change and Death in India." London School of Economics, London.

Burgess, R., M. Hansen, B. A. Olken, P. Potapov, and S. Sieber. 2012. "The Political Economy of Deforestation in the Tropics." *Quarterly Journal of Economics* 127 (4): 1707–54.

Burke, M., A. Driscoll, D. Lobell, and S. Ermon. 2020. "Using Satellite Imagery to Understand and Promote Sustainable Development." NBER Working Paper 27879, National Bureau of Economic Research, Cambridge, MA.

Burke, M., S. M. Hsiang, and E. Miguel. 2015. "Climate and Conflict." *Annual Review of Economics* 7 (1): 577–617.

Burke, M., and D. B. Lobell. 2017. "Satellite-Based Assessment of Yield Variation and Its Determinants in Smallholder African Systems." *Proceedings of the National Academy of Sciences* 114 (9): 2189–94.

Carleton, T., S. M. Hsiang, and M. Burke. 2016. "Conflict in a Changing Climate." *European Physical Journal Special Topics* 225 (3): 489–511.

Carlson, K. M., R. Heilmayr, H. K. Gibbs, P. Noojipady, D. N. Burns, D. C. Morton, N. F. Walker, G. D. Paoli, and C. Kremen. 2018. "Effect of Oil Palm Sustainability Certification on Deforestation and Fire in Indonesia." *Proceedings of the National Academy of Sciences* 115 (1): 121.

Carter, M., R. Laajaj, and D. Yang. 2021. "Subsidies and the African Green Revolution: Direct Effects and Social Network Spillovers of Randomized Input Subsidies in Mozambique." *American Economic Journal: Applied Economics* 13 (2): 206–29.

Castells-Quintana, D., M. D. P. Lopez-Uribe, and T. K. J. McDermott. 2022. "Population Displacement and Urban Conflict: Global Evidence from More Than 3300 Flood Events." *Journal of Development Economics* 158: 102922.

Chabe-Ferret, S., and A. Voia. 2021. "Are Forest Conservation Programs a Cost-Effective Way to Fight Climate Change? A Meta-Analysis." Toulouse School of Economics, Toulouse, France.

Cisneros, E., J. Börner, S. Pagiola, and S. Wunder. 2022. "Impacts of Conservation Incentives in Protected Areas: The Case of Bolsa Floresta, Brazil." *Journal of Environmental Economics and Management* 111: 102572.

Cisneros, E., T. Hellmundt, and K. Kis-Katos. 2022. "Conflicts of Rural Transformation: The Effects of Oil Palm Expansion in Indonesia." University of Göttingen, Göttingen, Germany.

Cisneros, E., K. Kis-Katos, and N. Nuryartono. 2021. "Palm Oil and the Politics of Deforestation in Indonesia." *Journal of Environmental Economics and Management* 108: 102453.

Colmer, J. 2021. "Temperature, Labor Reallocation, and Industrial Production: Evidence from India." *American Economic Journal: Applied Economics* 13 (4): 101–24.

Colmer, J., M. F. Evans, and J. Shimshack. 2023. "Environmental Citizen Complaints." CEP Discussion Papers, Centre for Economic Performance, London School of Economics, London.

Conte, B. 2022. "Climate Change and Migration: The Case of Africa." University of Barcelona, Barcelona.

Costinot, A., and D. Donaldson. 2016. "How Large Are the Gains from Economic Integration? Theory and Evidence from U.S. Agriculture, 1880–1997." NBER Working Paper 22946, National Bureau of Economic Research, Cambridge, MA.

Costinot, A., D. Donaldson, and C. Smith. 2016. "Evolving Comparative Advantage and the Impact of Climate Change in Agricultural Markets: Evidence from 1.7 Million Fields around the World." *Journal of Political Economy* 124 (1): 205–48.

Csillik, O., P. Kumar, J. Mascaro, T. O'Shea, and G. P. Asner. 2019. "Monitoring Tropical Forest Carbon Stocks and Emissions Using Planet Satellite Data." *Scientific Reports* 9 (1): 17831.

da Silva Medina, G., B. Pokorny, and B. Campbell. 2022. "Forest Governance in the Amazon: Favoring the Emergence of Local Management Systems." *World Development* 149: 105696.

Damm, Y., E. Cisneros, and J. Börner. 2022. "Beyond Deforestation Reductions: Public Disclosure, Land-Use Change and Commodity Sourcing." University of Bonn, Bonn, Germany.

DePaula, G. 2020. "The Distributional Effect of Climate Change on Agriculture: Evidence from a Quantile Analysis of Brazilian Census Data." *Journal of Environmental Economics and Management* 104: 102378.

Desmet, K., R. E. Kopp, S. A. Kulp, D. K. Nagy, M. Oppenheimer, E. Rossi-Hansberg, and B. H. Strauss. 2021. "Evaluating the Economic Cost of Coastal Flooding." *American Economic Journal: Macroeconomics* 13 (2): 444–86.

Desmet, K., D. K. Nagy, and E. Rossi-Hansberg. 2018. "The Geography of Development." *Journal of Political Economy* 126 (3): 903–83.

Desmet, K., and E. Rossi-Hansberg. 2015. "On the Spatial Economic Impact of Global Warming." *Journal of Urban Economics* 88: 16–37.

Doblas, J., M. S. Reis, A. P. Belluzzo, C. B. Quadros, D. R. V. Moraes, C. A. Almeida, L. E. P. Maurano, A. F. A. Carvalho, S. J. S. Sant'Anna, and Y. E. Shimabukuro. 2022. "DETER-R: An Operational Near-Real Time Tropical Forest Disturbance Warning System Based on Sentinel-1 Time Series Analysis." *Remote Sensing* 14 (15): 3658.

Domínguez-Iino, T. 2021. "Efficiency and Redistribution in Environmental Policy: An Equilibrium Analysis of Agricultural Supply Chains." Working paper, University of Chicago, Chicago.

Donaldson, D. 2018. "Railroads of the Raj: Estimating the Impact of Transportation Infrastructure." *American Economic Review* 108 (4–5): 899–934.

Donaldson, D., and R. Hornbeck. 2016. "Railroads and American Economic Growth: A 'Market Access' Approach." *Quarterly Journal of Economics* 131 (2): 799–858.

Eberle, U. J., D. Rohner, and M. Thoenig. 2020. "Heat and Hate: Climate Security and Farmer-Herder Conflicts in Africa." CEPR Discussion Paper 15542, Centre for Economic Policy Research, London.

Edwards, E. C., and S. M. Smith. 2018. "The Role of Irrigation in the Development of Agriculture in the United States." *Journal of Economic History* 78 (4): 1103–41.

Edwards, R. B., W. P. Falcon, G. Hadiwidjaja, M. M. Higgins, R. L. Naylor, and S. Sumarto. 2021. "Fight Fire with Finance: A Randomized Field Experiment to Curtail Land-Clearing Fire in Indonesia." Stanford University, Palo Alto, CA.

Edwards, R. B., R. L. Naylor, M. M. Higgins, and W. P. Falcon. 2020. "Causes of Indonesia's Forest Fires." *World Development* 127: 104717.

Erman, A., M. Tariverdi, M. Obolensky, X. Chen, R. C. Vincent, S. Malgioglio, J. Rentschler, S. Hallegatte, and N. Yoshida. 2019. "Wading Out the Storm: The Role of Poverty in Exposure, Vulnerability and Resilience to Floods in Dar es Salaam." Policy Research Working Paper 8976, World Bank, Washington, DC.

Etchart, N., J. L. Freire, M. B. Holland, K. W. Jones, and L. Naughton-Treves. 2020. "What Happens When the Money Runs Out? Forest Outcomes and Equity Concerns following Ecuador's Suspension of Conservation Payments." *World Development* 136: 105124.

Faingerch, M., M. Vallejos, M. Texeira, and M. E. Mastrangelo. 2021. "Land Privatization and Deforestation in a Commodity Production Frontier." *Conservation Letters* 14 (4): e12794.

Farrokhi, F., and H. S. Pellegrina. 2021. "Trade, Technology, and Agricultural Productivity." Working paper, Purdue University, Lafayette, IN.

Fearnside, P. M. 2001. "Land-Tenure Issues as Factors in Environmental Destruction in Brazilian Amazonia: The Case of Southern Para." *World Development* 29 (8): 1361–72.

Fetzer, T., and S. Marden. 2017. "Take What You Can: Property Rights, Contestability and Conflict." *Economic Journal* 127 (601): 757–83.

Garbarino, N., B. Guin, and C.-H. Lee. 2023. "The Effects of Subsidized Flood Insurance on Real Estate Markets." Working Paper 995, Bank of England, London.

Gatti, N., K. Baylis, and B. Crost. 2021. "Can Irrigation Infrastructure Mitigate the Effect of Rainfall Shocks on Conflict? Evidence from Indonesia." *American Journal of Agricultural Economics* 103 (1): 211–31.

Giudice, R., J. Börner, S. Wunder, and E. Cisneros. 2019. "Selection Biases and Spillovers from Collective Conservation Incentives in the Peruvian Amazon." *Environmental Research Letters* 14 (4): 045004.

Goldsmith-Pinkham, P., M. T. Gustafson, R. C. Lewis, and M. Schwert. 2023. "Sea-Level Rise Exposure and Municipal Bond Yields." *Review of Financial Studies* 36 (11): 4588–635.

Gollin, D., and R. Rogerson. 2014. "Productivity, Transport Costs and Subsistence Agriculture." *Journal of Development Economics* 107: 38–48.

Gorelick, N., M. Hancher, M. Dixon, S. Ilyushchenko, D. Thau, and R. Moore. 2017. "Google Earth Engine: Planetary-Scale Geospatial Analysis for Everyone." *Remote Sensing of Environment* 202: 18–27.

Gourevitch, J. D., C. Kousky, Y. Liao, C. Nolte, A. B. Pollack, J. R. Porter, and J. A. Weill. 2023. "Unpriced Climate Risk and the Potential Consequences of Overvaluation in US Housing Markets." *Nature Climate Change* 13 (3): 250–57.

Greenstone, M., G. He, R. Jia, and T. Liu. 2022. "Can Technology Solve the Principal-Agent Problem? Evidence from China's War on Air Pollution." *American Economic Review: Insights* 4 (1): 54–70.

Guardado, J. 2018. "Land Tenure, Price Shocks, and Insurgency: Evidence from Peru and Colombia." *World Development* 111: 256–69.

Harari, M., and E. La Ferrara. 2018. "Conflict, Climate, and Cells: A Disaggregated Analysis." *Review of Economics and Statistics* 100 (4): 594–608.

Harris, N. L., D. A. Gibbs, A. Baccini, R. A. Birdsey, S. de Bruin, M. Farina, L. Fatoyinbo, et al. 2021. "Global Maps of Twenty-First Century Forest Carbon Fluxes." *Nature Climate Change* 11 (3): 234–40.

He, X., and Z. Chen. 2022. "Weather, Cropland Expansion, and Deforestation in Ethiopia." *Journal of Environmental Economics and Management* 111: 102586.

He, Y., J. Rentschler, P. Avner, J. Gao, X. Yue, and J. Radke. 2022. "Mobility and Resilience: A Global Assessment of Flood Impacts on Road Transportation Networks." Policy Research Working Paper 10049, World Bank, Washington, DC.

He, Y., S. Thies, P. Avner, and J. Rentschler. 2021. "Flood Impacts on Urban Transit and Accessibility: A Case Study of Kinshasa." *Transportation Research: Part D: Transport and Environment* 96: 102889.

Heß, S., D. Jaimovich, and M. Schündeln. 2021. "Environmental Effects of Development Programs: Experimental Evidence from West African Dryland Forests." *Journal of Development Economics* 153: 102737.

Heilmann, K., M. E. Kahn, and C. K. Tang. 2021. "The Urban Crime and Heat Gradient in High and Low Poverty Areas." *Journal of Public Economics* 197: 104408.

Heilmayr, R., C. Echeverría, and E. F. Lambin. 2020. "Impacts of Chilean Forest Subsidies on Forest Cover, Carbon and Biodiversity." *Nature Sustainability* 3 (9): 701–9.

Heilmayr, R., L. L. Rausch, J. Munger, and H. K. Gibbs. 2020. "Brazil's Amazon Soy Moratorium Reduced Deforestation." *Nature Food* 1 (12): 801–10.

Henderson, J. V., A. Storeygard, and U. Deichmann. 2017. "Has Climate Change Driven Urbanization in Africa?" *Journal of Development Economics* 124: 60–82.

Hidalgo, F. D., S. Naidu, S. Nichter, and N. Richardson. 2010. "Economic Determinants of Land Invasions." *Review of Economics and Statistics* 92 (3): 505–23.

Hino, M., and M. Burke. 2021. "The Effect of Information about Climate Risk on Property Values." *Proceedings of the National Academy of Sciences* 118 (17): e2003374118.

Holland, M. B., F. de Koning, M. Morales, L. Naughton-Treves, B. E. Robinson, and L. Suárez. 2014. "Complex Tenure and Deforestation: Implications for Conservation Incentives in the Ecuadorian Amazon." *World Development* 55: 21–36.

Hornbeck, R. 2012. "The Enduring Impact of the American Dust Bowl: Short- and Long-Run Adjustments to Environmental Catastrophe." *American Economic Review* 102 (4): 1477–507.

Howard, G. 2020. "Additionality Violations in Agricultural Payment for Service Programs: Experimental Evidence." *Land Economics* 96 (2): 244–64.

Hsiang, S. M., M. Burke, and E. Miguel. 2013. "Quantifying the Influence of Climate on Human Conflict." *Science* 341 (6151): 1235367.

Hsiao, A. 2021a. "Coordination and Commitment in International Climate Action: Evidence from Palm Oil." University of Chicago, Chicago.

Hsiao, A. 2021b. "Rising Sea Levels: Adaptation and Urban Development in Jakarta." University of Chicago, Chicago.

Imbert, C., M. Seror, Y. Zhang, and Y. Zylberberg. 2022. "Migrants and Firms: Evidence from China." *American Economic Review* 112 (6): 1885–914.

Jack, B. K. 2013. "Private Information and the Allocation of Land Use Subsidies in Malawi." *American Economic Journal: Applied Economics* 5 (3): 113–35.

Jack, B. K., and S. Jayachandran. 2019. "Self-Selection into Payments for Ecosystem Services Programs." *Proceedings of the National Academy of Sciences* 116 (12): 5326.

Jagnani, M., C. B. Barrett, Y. Liu, and L. You. 2021. "Within-Season Producer Response to Warmer Temperatures: Defensive Investments by Kenyan Farmers." *Economic Journal* 131 (633): 392–419.

Janzen, S. A., M. R. Carter, and M. Ikegami. 2021. "Can Insurance Alter Poverty Dynamics and Reduce the Cost of Social Protection in Developing Countries?" *Journal of Risk and Insurance* 88 (2): 293–324.

Jayachandran, S. 2013. "Liquidity Constraints and Deforestation: The Limitations of Payments for Ecosystem Services." *American Economic Review* 103 (3): 309–13.

Jayachandran, S., J. de Laat, E. F. Lambin, and C. Y. Stanton. 2016. "Cash for Carbon: A Randomized Controlled Trial of Payments for Ecosystem Services to Reduce Deforestation." NBER Working Paper 22378, National Bureau of Economic Research, Cambridge, MA.

Jia, R., X. Ma, and V. W. Xie. 2022. "Expecting Floods: Firm Entry, Employment, and Aggregate Implications." NBER Working Paper 30250, National Bureau of Economic Research, Cambridge, MA.

Jordán, F., and R. Heilmayr. 2022. "Forestry Plantations and the Demise of Rural Livelihoods." University of California, Santa Barbara.

Jung, S., C. Dyngeland, L. Rausch, and L. V. Rasmussen. 2022. "Brazilian Land Registry Impacts on Land Use Conversion." *American Journal of Agricultural Economics* 104 (1): 340–63.

Jung, S., and S. Polasky. 2018. "Partnerships to Prevent Deforestation in the Amazon." *Journal of Environmental Economics and Management* 92: 498–516.

Kansanga, M. M., and I. Luginaah. 2019. "Agrarian Livelihoods under Siege: Carbon Forestry, Tenure Constraints and the Rise of Capitalist Forest Enclosures in Ghana." *World Development* 113: 131–42.

Kemigisha, E., F. Babweteera, J. Mugisha, and A. Angelsen. 2023. "Payment for Environmental Services to Reduce Deforestation: Do the Positive Effects Last?" *Ecological Economics* 209: 107840.

Kikuchi, M., Y. Mano, T. N. Njagi, D. Merrey, and K. Otsuka. 2021. "Economic Viability of Large-Scale Irrigation Construction in Sub-Saharan Africa: What If Mwea Irrigation Scheme Were Constructed as a Brand-New Scheme?" *Journal of Development Studies* 57 (5): 772–89.

Koch, N., E. K. H. J. zu Ermgassen, J. Wehkamp, F. J. B. Oliveira Filho, and G. Schwerhoff. 2019. "Agricultural Productivity and Forest Conservation: Evidence from the Brazilian Amazon." *American Journal of Agricultural Economics* 101 (3): 919–40.

Kocornik-Mina, A., T. K. J. McDermott, G. Michaels, and F. Rauch. 2020. "Flooded Cities." *American Economic Journal: Applied Economics* 12 (2): 35–66.

Kopas, J., J. Mangonnet, and J. Uprelainen. 2018. "Playing Politics with Environmental Protection: The Political Economy of Designating Protected Areas." Columbia University, New York.

Kraus, S., J. Liu, N. Koch, and S. Fuss. 2021. "No Aggregate Deforestation Reductions from Rollout of Community Land Titles in Indonesia Yet." *Proceedings of the National Academy of Sciences* 118 (43): e2100741118.

Krishna, V. V., C. Kubitza, U. Pascual, and M. Qaim. 2017. "Land Markets, Property Rights, and Deforestation: Insights from Indonesia." *World Development* 99: 335–49.

Kubitza, C., V. V. Krishna, K. Urban, Z. Alamsyah, and M. Qaim. 2018. "Land Property Rights, Agricultural Intensification, and Deforestation in Indonesia." *Ecological Economics* 147: 312–21.

Lee, J. S. H., D. A. Miteva, K. M. Carlson, R. Heilmayr, and O. Saif. 2020. "Does Oil Palm Certification Create Trade-Offs between Environment and Development in Indonesia?" *Environmental Research Letters* 15 (12): 124064.

Lewis, D. J., and S. Polasky. 2018. "An Auction Mechanism for the Optimal Provision of Ecosystem Services under Climate Change." *Journal of Environmental Economics and Management* 92: 20–34.

Lin, Y., T. K. J. McDermott, and G. Michaels. 2022. "Cities and the Sea Level." London School of Economics, London.

Lipscomb, M., and N. Prabakaran. 2020. "Property Rights and Deforestation: Evidence from the Terra Legal Land Reform in the Brazilian Amazon." *World Development* 129: 104854.

Liu, M., Y. Shamdasani, and V. Taraz. 2023. "Climate Change and Labor Reallocation: Evidence from Six Decades of the Indian Census." *American Economic Journal: Economic Policy* 15 (2): 395–423.

Lobell, D. B., G. Azzari, M. Burke, S. Gourlay, Z. Jin, T. Kilic, and S. Murray. 2020. "Eyes in the Sky, Boots on the Ground: Assessing Satellite- and Ground-Based Approaches to Crop Yield Measurement and Analysis." *American Journal of Agricultural Economics* 102 (1): 202–19.

Manning, D. T., and J. E. Taylor. 2015. "Agricultural Efficiency and Labor Supply to Common Property Resource Collection: Lessons from Rural Mexico." *Journal of Agricultural and Resource Economics* 40 (3): 365–86.

Maruyama Rentschler, J. E., J. M. Braese, N. K. W. Jones, and P. Avner. 2019. "Three Feet Under: The Impact of Floods on Urban Jobs, Connectivity, and Infrastructure." Policy Research Working Paper 8898, World Bank, Washington, DC.

Maruyama Rentschler, J. E., and M. Salhab. 2020. "People in Harm's Way: Flood Exposure and Poverty in 189 Countries." Policy Research Working Paper 9447, World Bank, Washington, DC.

Maystadt, J.-F., and O. Ecker. 2014. "Extreme Weather and Civil War: Does Drought Fuel Conflict in Somalia through Livestock Price Shocks?" *American Journal of Agricultural Economics* 96 (4): 1157–82.

Mazur, K. 2023. "Sharing Risk to Avoid Tragedy: Informal Insurance and Irrigation in Village Economies." *Journal of Development Economics* 161: 103030.

McArthur, J. W., and G. C. McCord. 2017. "Fertilizing Growth: Agricultural Inputs and Their Effects in Economic Development." *Journal of Development Economics* 127: 133–52.

McGuirk, E., and M. Burke. 2020. "The Economic Origins of Conflict in Africa." *Journal of Political Economy* 128 (10): 3940–97.

McGuirk, E. F., and N. Nunn. 2020. "Nomadic Pastoralism, Climate Change, and Conflict in Africa." NBER Working Paper 28243, National Bureau of Economic Research, Cambridge, MA.

McPeak, J. G., and P. D. Little. 2018. "Mobile Peoples, Contested Borders: Land Use Conflicts and Resolution Mechanisms among Borana and Guji Communities, Southern Ethiopia." *World Development* 103: 119–32.

Michler, J. D., A. Josephson, T. Kilic, and S. Murray. 2022. "Privacy Protection, Measurement Error, and the Integration of Remote Sensing and Socioeconomic Survey Data." *Journal of Development Economics* 158: 102927.

Miller, S., K. Chua, J. Coggins, and H. Mohtadi. 2021. "Heat Waves, Climate Change, and Economic Output." *Journal of the European Economic Association* 19 (5): 2658–94.

Moffette, F., and H. K. Gibbs. 2021. "Agricultural Displacement and Deforestation Leakage in the Brazilian Legal Amazon." *Land Economics* 97 (1): 1–26.

Moffette, F., M. Skidmore, and H. K. Gibbs. 2021. "Environmental Policies That Shape Productivity: Evidence from Cattle Ranching in the Amazon." *Journal of Environmental Economics and Management* 109: 102490.

Moscona, J. 2022. "Environmental Catastrophe and the Direction of Invention: Evidence from the American Dust Bowl." Working paper, Massachusetts Institute of Technology, Cambridge, MA.

Moscona, J., and K. A. Sastry. 2023. "Does Directed Innovation Mitigate Climate Damage? Evidence from U.S. Agriculture." *Quarterly Journal of Economics* 138 (2): 637–701.

Mulder, P. 2022. "Mismeasuring Risk: The Welfare Effects of Flood Risk Information." University of Pennsylvania, Philadelphia.

Mulungu, K., and N. Kilimani. 2023. "Does Forest Access Reduce Reliance on Costly Shock-Coping Strategies? Evidence from Malawi." *Ecological Economics* 209: 107827.

Nackoney, J., G. Molinario, P. Potapov, S. Turubanova, M. C. Hansen, and T. Furuichi. 2014. "Impacts of Civil Conflict on Primary Forest Habitat in Northern Democratic Republic of the Congo, 1990–2010." *Biological Conservation* 170: 321–28.

Nackoney, J., M. Demol, H. A. Akpona, M. Bauters, P. Boeckx, J. Dupain, C. Facheux, et al. 2022. "Coupled Forest Zoning and Agricultural Intervention Yields Conflicting Outcomes for Tropical Forest Conservation in the Democratic Republic of the Congo (DRC)." *Environmental Research Letters* 17 (6): 064002.

Nakalembe, C., I. Becker-Reshef, R. Bonifacio, G. Hu, M. L. Humber, C. J. Justice, J. Keniston, et al. 2021. "A Review of Satellite-Based Global Agricultural Monitoring Systems Available for Africa." *Global Food Security* 29: 100543.

Nath, I. B. 2020. "The Food Problem and the Aggregate Productivity Consequences of Climate Change." NBER Working Paper 27297, National Bureau of Economic Research, Cambridge, MA.

Naylor, R. L., M. M. Higgins, R. B. Edwards, and W. P. Falcon. 2019. "Decentralization and the Environment: Assessing Smallholder Oil Palm Development in Indonesia." *Ambio* 48 (10): 1195–208.

Ngoma, H., A. T. Hailu, S. Kabwe, and A. Angelsen. 2020. "Pay, Talk or 'Whip' to Conserve Forests: Framed Field Experiments in Zambia." *World Development* 128: 104846.

Nguyen, D. D., S. Ongena, S. Qi, and V. Sila. 2022. "Climate Change Risk and the Cost of Mortgage Credit." *Review of Finance* 26 (6): 1509–49.

Nolte, C., A. Agrawal, K. M. Silvius, and B. S. Soares-Filho. 2013. "Governance Regime and Location Influence Avoided Deforestation Success of Protected Areas in the Brazilian Amazon." *Proceedings of the National Academy of Sciences* 110 (13): 4956.

Orellano, V., P. F. Azevedo, M. S. Saes, and V. E. Nascimento. 2015. "Land Invasions, Insecure Property Rights and Production Decisions." *Journal of Agricultural Economics* 66 (3): 660–71.

Ortiz-Bobea, A., T. R. Ault, C. M. Carrillo, R. G. Chambers, and D. B. Lobell. 2021. "Anthropogenic Climate Change Has Slowed Global Agricultural Productivity Growth." *Nature Climate Change* 11 (4): 306–12.

Ostriker, A., and A. Russo. 2022. "The Effects of Floodplain Regulation on Housing Markets." Massachusetts Institute of Technology, Cambridge, MA.

Pacheco, P., G. Schoneveld, A. Dermawan, H. Komarudin, and M. Djama. 2020. "Governing Sustainable Palm Oil Supply: Disconnects, Complementarities, and Antagonisms between State Regulations and Private Standards." *Regulation and Governance* 14 (3): 568–98.

Pailler, S. 2018. "Re-election Incentives and Deforestation Cycles in the Brazilian Amazon." *Journal of Environmental Economics and Management* 88: 345–65.

Pellegrina, H. S., and M. Gafaro. 2021. "Trade, Farmers' Heterogeneity, and Agricultural Productivity: Evidence from Colombia." New York University, New York.

Peña, X., M. A. Vélez, J. C. Cárdenas, N. Perdomo, and C. Matajira. 2017. "Collective Property Leads to Household Investments: Lessons from Land Titling in Afro-Colombian Communities." *World Development* 97: 27–48.

Porteous, O. 2020. "Trade and Agricultural Technology Adoption: Evidence from Africa." *Journal of Development Economics* 144: 102440.

Potapov, P., S. Turubanova, M. C. Hansen, A. Tyukavina, V. Zalles, A. Khan, X.-P. Song, A. Pickens, Q. Shen, and J. Cortez. 2022. "Global Maps of Cropland Extent and Change Show Accelerated Cropland Expansion in the Twenty-First Century." *Nature Food* 3 (1): 19–28.

Probst, B., A. BenYishay, A. Kontoleon, and T. N. P. dos Reis. 2020. "Impacts of a Large-Scale Titling Initiative on Deforestation in the Brazilian Amazon." *Nature Sustainability* 3 (12): 1019–26.

Qaim, M., K. T. Sibhatu, H. Siregar, and I. Grass. 2020. "Environmental, Economic, and Social Consequences of the Oil Palm Boom." *Annual Review of Resource Economics* 12 (1): 321–44.

Quiñones, E. J., S. Liebenehm, and R. Sharma. 2021. "Left Home High and Dry: Reduced Migration in Response to Repeated Droughts in Thailand and Vietnam." *Population and Environment* 42 (4): 579–621.

Rentschler, J., P. Avner, M. Marconcini, R. Su, E. Strano, L. Bernard, C. Riom, and S. Hallegatte. 2022. "Rapid Urban Growth in Flood Zones: Global Evidence since 1985." Policy Research Working Paper 10014, World Bank, Washington, DC.

Reydon, B. P., V. B. Fernandes, and T. S. Telles. 2020. "Land Governance as a Precondition for Decreasing Deforestation in the Brazilian Amazon." *Land Use Policy* 94: 104313.

Romero, M., and S. Saavedra. 2021. "Communal Property Rights and Deforestation." *Journal of Development Studies* 57 (6): 1038–52.

Sant'Anna, A. A. 2017. "Land Inequality and Deforestation in the Brazilian Amazon." *Environment and Development Economics* 22 (1): 1–25.

Sauer, S. 2018. "Soy Expansion into the Agricultural Frontiers of the Brazilian Amazon: The Agribusiness Economy and Its Social and Environmental Conflicts." *Land Use Policy* 79: 326–38.

Sedova, B., and M. Kalkuhl. 2020. "Who Are the Climate Migrants and Where Do They Go? Evidence from Rural India." *World Development* 129: 104848.

Sills, E., A. Pfaff, L. Andrade, J. Kirkpatrick, and R. Dickson. 2020. "Investing in Local Capacity to Respond to a Federal Environmental Mandate: Forest and Economic Impacts of the Green Municipality Program in the Brazilian Amazon." *World Development* 129: 104891.

Simonet, G., J. Subervie, D. Ezzine-de-Blas, M. Cromberg, and A. E. Duchelle. 2019. "Effectiveness of a REDD+ Project in Reducing Deforestation in the Brazilian Amazon." *American Journal of Agricultural Economics* 101 (1): 211–29.

Sims, K. R. E., and J. M. Alix-Garcia. 2017. "Parks versus PES: Evaluating Direct and Incentive-Based Land Conservation in Mexico." *Journal of Environmental Economics and Management* 86: 8–28.

Somanathan, E., R. Somanathan, A. Sudarshan, and M. Tewari. 2021. "The Impact of Temperature on Productivity and Labor Supply: Evidence from Indian Manufacturing." *Journal of Political Economy* 129 (6): 1797–827.

Song, X.-P., M. C. Hansen, P. Potapov, B. Adusei, J. Pickering, M. Adami, A. Lima, et al. 2021. "Massive Soybean Expansion in South America since 2000 and Implications for Conservation." *Nature Sustainability* 4 (9): 784–92.

Sotelo, S. 2020. "Domestic Trade Frictions and Agriculture." *Journal of Political Economy* 128 (7): 2690–738.

Souza-Rodrigues, E. 2019. "Deforestation in the Amazon: A Unified Framework for Estimation and Policy Analysis." *Review of Economic Studies* 86 (6): 2713–44.

Sparovek, G., B. P. Reydon, L. F. Guedes Pinto, V. Faria, F. L. M. de Freitas, C. Azevedo-Ramos, T. Gardner, et al. 2019. "Who Owns Brazilian Lands?" *Land Use Policy* 87: 104062.

Stabile, M. C. C., A. L. Guimarães, D. S. Silva, V. Ribeiro, M. N. Macedo, M. T. Coe, E. Pinto, P. Moutinho, and A. Alencar. 2020. "Solving Brazil's Land Use Puzzle: Increasing Production and Slowing Amazon Deforestation." *Land Use Policy* 91: 104362.

Sunderlin, W. D., C. de Sassi, E. O. Sills, A. E. Duchelle, A. M. Larson, I. A. P. Resosudarmo, A. Awono, D. L. Kweka, and T. B. Huynh. 2018. "Creating an Appropriate Tenure Foundation for REDD+: The Record to Date and Prospects for the Future." *World Development* 106: 376–92.

Sze, J. S., L. R. Carrasco, D. Childs, and D. P. Edwards. 2022. "Reduced Deforestation and Degradation in Indigenous Lands Pan-Tropically." *Nature Sustainability* 5: 123–30.

Szerman, D., J. Assunção, M. Lipscomb, and A. M. Mobarak. 2022. "Agricultural Productivity and Deforestation: Evidence from Brazil." Discussion Paper 1091, Yale University, New Haven, CT.

Tassa, A. 2020. "The Socio-Economic Value of Satellite Earth Observations: Huge, Yet to Be Measured." *Journal of Economic Policy Reform* 23 (1): 34–48.

Tatum, R. C. 2013. "A Hard Row to Hoe: Farming on the Economic Frontier under Incomplete Property Rights." *Environment and Development Economics* 18 (5): 576–94.

Tritsch, I., G. Le Velly, B. Mertens, P. Meyfroidt, C. Sannier, J.-S. Makak, and K. Houngbedji. 2020. "Do Forest-Management Plans and FSC Certification Help Avoid Deforestation in the Congo Basin?" *Ecological Economics* 175: 106660.

van der Zon, M., W. de Jong, and B. Arts. 2023. "Community Enforcement and Tenure Security: A Fuzzy-Set Qualitative Comparative Analysis of Twelve Community Forest Management Initiatives in the Peruvian Amazon." *World Development* 161: 106071.

Vélez, M. A., J. Robalino, J. C. Cardenas, A. Paz, and E. Pacay. 2020. "Is Collective Titling Enough to Protect Forests? Evidence from Afro-Descendant Communities in the Colombian Pacific Region." *World Development* 128: 104837.

Vorlaufer, T., T. Falk, T. Dufhues, and M. Kirk. 2017. "Payments for Ecosystem Services and Agricultural Intensification: Evidence from a Choice Experiment on Deforestation in Zambia." *Ecological Economics* 141: 95–105.

Wilebore, B., M. Voors, E. H. Bulte, D. Coomes, and A. Kontoleon. 2019. "Unconditional Transfers and Tropical Forest Conservation: Evidence from a Randomized Control Trial in Sierra Leone." *American Journal of Agricultural Economics* 101 (3): 894–918.

Winsemius, H. C., B. Jongman, T. I. E. Veldkamp, S. Hallegatte, M. Bangalore, and P. J. Ward. 2018. "Disaster Risk, Climate Change, and Poverty: Assessing the Global Exposure of Poor People to Floods and Droughts." *Environment and Development Economics* 23 (3): 328–48.

Yan, Y. 2019. "Unintended Land Use Effects of Afforestation in China's Grain for Green Program." *American Journal of Agricultural Economics* 101 (4): 1047–67.

zu Ermgassen, E. K. H. J., B. Ayre, J. Godar, M. G. Bastos Lima, S. Bauch, R. Garrett, et al.2020. "Using Supply Chain Data to Monitor Zero Deforestation Commitments: An Assessment of Progress in the Brazilian Soy Sector." *Environmental Research Letters* 15 (3): 035003.